ANTIQUES
SOURCE BOOK

THIS IS A CARLTON BOOK

Copyright © 2004 Martin Miller

This edition published by Carlton Books Limited 2005
20 Mortimer Street
London W1T 3JW

Edited and designed for Carlton Books by PAGE*One*

A CIP catalogue for this book is available from the British Library.

0 68135 573 5

ANTIQUES
SOURCE BOOK

The Definitive Guide to Retail
Prices for Antiques and Collectables

MARTIN MILLER

Contents

ACKNOWLEDGEMENTS

GENERAL EDITOR
Martin Miller

CO-ORDINATING EDITOR
Caroline Proctor

EDITORS
Clair Whiteman
Richard Bundy
Marianne Blake

PHOTOGRAPHERS
Abigail Zoe Martin
Julia Morley
James Beam Van Etten

DESIGNERS
Gill Andrews
Jessica Barr
Pauline Hoyle
Alexandra Huchet
Louise Kerby
Robert Law
Michelle Pickering
Tim Stansfield
Mark Tattham

How to Use This Book

by Martin Miller

I am thrilled to be delivering information on how to use the *Antiques Source Book*.

I started publishing antiques price guides in 1969 – and they have always been very successful – but one criticism that I have heard is from people saying, rather wistfully, "I loved the book, but what a pity that everything in it was already sold". And it was perfectly true, the books were designed more as compilations of information from auction sales which had already taken place than as immediate guides; as reference books, rather than handbooks.

The difference between the *Antiques Source Book* and other antiques guides is that here we have used retailers, rather than auction houses, as our sources of information. The *Antiques Source Book* is a retail price guide, which means that you have a reliable guide to the sort of price you should pay. We do not purport to show everything the market has to offer; we carefully select a cross-section that is truly representative of the market place.

The book is designed for maximum visual interest and appeal. It can be treated as a "thorough read" as well as a tool for dipping in and out of. The Contents and Index will tell you in which area to find anything that you are specifically seeking, but the collector, enthusiast or interior designer will profit most from reading through a section or several sections and gathering information and inspiration as they go.

The book covers every aspect of antiques collecting, from furniture through to glassware and jewellery through to porcelain. It also covers the area of "collectables" – items that are not technically old enough to qualify as antiques but which are nevertheless ardently accumulated by enthusiasts – comic books, telephones and gardening tools to name a few. There is, in fact, something for every pocket from furniture worth tens of thousands of dollars to items worth no more than ten dollars. What they have in common is that we consider them to be good buys, as examples of their genres and as financial investments.

The *Antiques Source Book* is not only useful to collectors, it is also of considerable interest to anyone who likes to be suprised to discover that unconsidered trifles they may possess are actually gathering value at a significant rate, or who might be interested to discover how hopelessly under-insured they are! Every item in the book is illustrated and all illustrations are followed by a brief description, including details of period, size, condition and a guide price. As an additional aid to the potential buyer – or valuer – we include a useful introduction to each section and "expert tip" boxes throughout, giving advice on what to buy and what to avoid, and, most particularly, what to look out for.

All in all, the book is designed to help people develop a love for antiques and give them tips on how best to hunt them out.

I have found antiques a lifetime's joy and I am delighted to pass on anything I can to spread the joy around.

Introduction

A contemporary and practical guide to antiques and collectables

The way in which antiques are viewed and valued is constantly changing. The distinction, for instance, between "antique", "collectable" and "second-hand" has become very fuzzy in recent years. Curiously, in this disposable age – or perhaps because so much is disposable – the artefacts of today are valued much more by modern collectors than their equivalents were by previous generations, who generally considered that anything owned by their parents was, by definition, not worth having.

The definition of an antique as "a work of art, piece of furniture or decorative item of more than a hundred years old" has become more flexible, as technology has speeded up and, consequently, the products of that technology have developed the invisible patina of age at a faster rate. And so in this book, which takes a completely modern look at antiques, we include such items as film posters, automobilia, kitchenalia, musical instruments, taxidermy and twentieth-century glass, ceramics, metalware, lighting and furniture, alongside some treasures of the ancient world, classical pieces of porcelain and some of the most notable items of furniture on the market at the moment.

There are, after all, guitars out there that cost a few hundred dollars thirty years ago and are now retailing at over $75,000. You could hardly call them second-hand.

It is not just the monetary value that makes a modern antique, though. There are three other factors which we come back to throughout the book; quality, rarity and personal preference. If you are looking at collecting and dealing in antiques purely from a commercial viewpoint – and this we heartily deplore – then good quality and rarity are your best hedges against failure. If you are collecting for the right reasons, for the love of the subject and the items involved, then obviously you will trust your own judgement and, if you finish up with something that may not be worth as much as you had hoped, at least its presence won't offend you.

Given the proliferation of antiques and collectables on the market, it is important to find the best way to buy and sell them. There are three traditional ways in which antiques change hands: at auction, in antiques shows and markets and through retail dealers. In addition to these, there are direct sales through the placing of advertisements and, increasingly and amid an unquenchable blaze of publicity, buying and selling directly on the Internet.

If you are seeking to combine buying and selling antiques with acquiring an adrenaline rush, then you can't beat the auction. From the big city salerooms to the smallest of provincial auction houses, there is always a buzz of excitement at the auction and, given the large throughput of lots, always the possibility, real or imagined, of uncovering a hitherto undiscovered masterpiece. The downside of the auction, from the point of view of both buyer and seller, is that it is quite expensive. Commission plus tax will be added to the hammer price if you are buying, and commission and such overheads as insurance, if you are selling. If you do decide to sell by auction, try to get more than one valuer's opinion and make sure that you agree all charges in advance.

Antiques shows and markets are great fun and a very painless way of buying antiques – although selling takes a little more time and effort. Shows vary from the large "vetted" shows, with serious dealers from across the country taking part and admission fees charged to charity shows, where only the seller

pays. The former are very like buying from a dealer, but with the convenience of having a number of dealers under the same roof. In the latter, everything tends to be fairly inexpensive, but that doesn't necessarily indicate that it is a bargain – or that it is what it purports to be.

Permanent markets also have great amusement value, and give you a real chance of picking up something of worth and collectable interest that you may not find elsewhere. These markets are good places to discover dealers who specialize in unusual types of collectables which do not warrant the acquisition of a whole shop. These items will tend to be fairly priced, because they are priced by specialists.

It is the fairness of pricing which is the great advantage of doing your buying and selling in the shop of a reputable dealer. In the *Antiques Source Book* we use retailers, rather than auction houses, as our source of guide prices. A reputable and experienced dealer's assessment of the price of an antique is at least as reliable – and usually a great deal more reasoned – than a price achieved at auction, and even though prices may vary slightly from one dealer to another, you have a reliable guide to the sort of price you should pay.

The *Antiques Source Book* is a must-have for all antiques enthusiasts.

Antiquities

Antiquities not only provide the collector with great investment opportunities, just as impressive are the stories they tell.

Antiquities give the lie to the idea that the older an artifact grows, the more valuable it becomes. Many of the ancient items within these pages sell for remarkably reasonable prices, making collecting genuinely affordable.

Often, the objects we now call antiquities – statues and works of art, as well as household goods, glass, funerary artifacts and even items discarded as rubbish, have been collected since they were mere antiques.

For example, Roman nobilityavidly collected articles from earlier civilisations.

The affordability of antiquities can be explained, perhaps, by the abundance of material available as well as by the difficulty of authenticating pieces. Age is usually established by comparison with other items. More precise scientific testing is available, but it is an expensive process. The most practical solution for collectors is to visit a dealer who offers a guarantee of authenticity.

Bronze Luristan Dagger ▶
- *circa 2400 BC*
A bronze dagger from Luristan with a green patina and foliate design on each side.
- *length 36cm*
- **Guide price $270**

Islamic Oil Lamp ◀
- **9th century AD**
Bronze Islamic oil lamp with green patina with an unusual stylised bird handle.
- *height 28cm*
- **Guide price $1,780**

Bactrian Stone Idol ▶
- *2000 BC*
Alabaster Bactrian stone idol from Afghanistan.
- *height 37cm*
- **Guide price $1,600**

Egg-shaped Tent Peg ◀
- *circa 250 BC*
Egg-shaped green-glaze stone with two holes used as a tent peg.
- *height 26cm*
- **Guide price $1,070**

Harra Pan Vase ▲
- 1800–2200 BC

Small terracotta vase of ovoid form with a deep truncated neck and geometric design applied to the body, from the Harra Pan civilisation.
- *height 9cm*
- **Guide price $450**

Terracotta Vase ▲
- 1800–2200 BC

Terracotta vase of ovoid form with a long inverted neck and a circular pattern on a black glaze.
- *height 18cm*
- **Guide price $890**

Terracotta Wine Strainer ▲
- 1800–2200 BC

Terracotta wine strainer of cylindrical form, with uniform perforations within the body.
- *height 15cm*
- **Guide price $1,070**

Alabaster Cup ▼
- 3000 BC

Alabaster cup from Afghanistan, carved from one piece of stone, with a concave body, and an extended stem, raised on a splayed foot.
- *height 24cm*
- **Guide price $2,670**

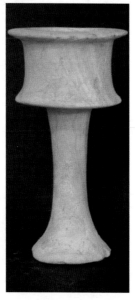

Amlash Teapot ▼
- *6–8th century*

Amlash teapot made from terracotta with two ear-shaped side handles and a large domed cover.
- *height 12cm*
- **Guide price $6,230**

Sumarian Mask ▲
- 2300–2000 BC

Sumarian mask with an expressionless composure and recesses for the eyes.
- *height 7cm*
- **Guide price $24,920**

Roman Glass ▲
- *2nd century BC*

Roman glass flask of ovoid form with fluted neck and spiral decoration with good iridescence.
- *height 10cm*
- **Guide price $13,350**

Oak Gargoyle ▼
- *Medieval*

English anthropomorphic carved oak gargoyle.
- *20cm x 18cm*
- **Guide price $1,690**

German Lock ▲
- *circa 1600 AD*

Rare and intricate steel door lock from Nuremburg.
- *18cm x 40cm*
- **Guide price $1,780**

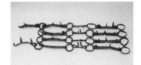

Carved Buddha ▲
- *500 BC*

A carved stone head of Buddha, Gandhara period.
- *height 18cm*
- **Guide price $710**

Merman Weather Vane ▼
- *17th century AD*

Early weather vane styled as a merman with original gilding.
- *80cm x 1m*
- **Guide price $4,450**

Medieval Comb ▼
- *15th century AD*

Medieval boxwood comb. In extremely good condition.
- *15cm x 9cm*
- **Guide price $1,690**

Steel Dog Collar ▲
- *15th century AD*

Dog collar with restraining spikes.
- *length 41cm*
- **Guide price $890**

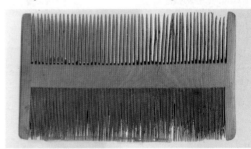

Powder Horn ▲
- *circa 1560 AD*

Ivory powder horn inset with coral and green stones and silver rosettes.
- *16cm x 8cm*
- **Guide price $1,050**

Roman Earrings ▼
- *2nd–3rd century AD*
Pair of Roman earrings with
circular garnets set in gold-roped
banding, with suspended gold
strands and beads.
- *length 3cm*
- **Guide price $3,560**

Alabaster Drinking Vessel ▼
- *circa 2000 BC*
Bactrian Afghanistan alabaster
cylindrical drinking vessel, with
engraved circular designs and
turned lip.
- *height 10.5cm*
- **Guide price $1,160**

Islamic Pendant ▲
- *circa 9–10th century AD*
Islamic gold pendant in the shape
of a bird with beautiful intricate
work.
- *height 0.5cm*
- **Guide price $5,340**

Roman Gold Earrings ▲
- *circa 1st–3rd century AD*
Pair of late roman gold earrings of
teardrop form with beaded
circular design.
- *height 3cm*
- **Guide price $3,560**

Roman Gold Pendant ▼
- *7–8th century AD*
Late Roman square gold pendant
set with one amethyst lozenge
shaped stone and flanked by two
circular turquoise stones.
- *width 1.4cm*
- **Guide price $800**

Gold Pendant ▲
- *circa 15th century AD*
Lozenge shaped green stone set
within a circular gold pendant
with a herringbone design.
- *width 1cm*
- **Guide price $360**

Bactrian Vessel ▲
- *circa 2000 BC*
Bactrian alabaster drinking vessel
of cylindrical form from
Afghanistan.
- *height 12cm*
- **Guide price $980**

Window Weight ▼

- *circa 17th century AD*
Late 17th century window weight with carved figures of William and Mary.
- *20cm x 9cm*
- **Guide price $570**

Jacob's Ladder ▶

- *Circa 15th century AD*
Fine oak carving of Jacob's Ladder.
- *48cm x 30cm*
- **Guide price $21,400**

Bronze Crewell Spur ▲

- *circa 14th century AD*
Spur with revolving stimulator.
- *length 14cm*
- **Guide price $530**

Steel Spur ▲

- *circa 14th century AD*
Early steel spur in original condition.
- *length 14cm*
- **Guide price $540**

Carved Figure ▲

- *circa 1650 AD*
Boxwood carving of a hooded monk with his arms folded, original condition.
- *17cm x 4cm*
- **Guide price $980**

Corpus Christi ▲

- *circa 1420 AD*
Rare early French gothic carving of Corpus Christi.
- *height 35cm*
- **Guide price $2,670**

Expert Tips

Always make sure you have an export license and a museum certificate that confirms the authenticity and origin of the item.

Bronze Sundial ◀

- *circa 17th century AD*
Bronze English sundial with original patina.
- *17cm x 17cm*
- **Guide price $820**

Apothecary Jar ▶
- *circa 1600 AD*
Unusual apothecary jar from
Sienna, Italy.
- *height 23cm*
- **Guide price $3,920**

Bronze Leopard ▲
- *circa 2nd century AD*
Bronze figure of a leopard with
his paw on the head of Medusa.
- *5cm x 8cm*
- **Guide price $4,180**

Bronze Eagle
with Green Patination ▲
- *circa 2nd century AD*
A small bronze eagle with original
green patination.
- *height 6cm*
- **Guide price $1,340**

Chariot Furniture ▲
- *circa 2nd century AD*
Bronze chariot fitting styled as a
figure of a man.
- *height 13cm*
- **Guide price $3,560**

Green Man ▲
- *circa 16th century AD*
Fine oak carving of the Green
Man.
- *24cm x 14cm*
- **Guide price $1,340**

Fortuna ▶
- *circa 2nd century AD*
Bronze figure of Fortuna.
- *height 18cm*
- **Guide price $3,560**

Bronze Head of Slave ▲
- *circa 1st century AD*
Small bronze head of a slave.
- *height 2cm*
- **Guide price $170**

Roman Leopard ▲

- *1st century AD*

Roman bronze leopard with raised paw and head slightly turned, standing on a circular base.
- *height 4.5cm*
- **Guide price $4,450**

Egyptian Mace Head ▲

- *late 4000 BC*

Egyptian black stone mace head.
- *height 10cm*
- **Guide price $1,780**

Bronze Cat ▲

- *635–525BC*

Bronze cat from the Saite period dynasty or late bronze dynasty .
- *height 9.5cm*
- **Guide price $10,680**

Venetian Flask ▲

- *5th century BC*

Venetian flask with a pinched lip and strap handle, raised on a pedestal base, with a yellow and green diagonal design on a black ground.
- *height 10cm*
- **Guide price $3,560**

Aubergine Glass Flask ▲

- *7th century AD*

Aubergine glass flask with a single handle, a narrow neck and a bulbous body with applied circular raised design.
- *height 9cm*
- **Guide price $1,250**

Transluscent Bowl ▼

- *1st century AD*

Roman translucent, green pillar-moulded glass bowl of shallow form with vertical ribbing, the tondo with three wheel-cut concentric circles.
- *diameter 15cm*
- **Guide price $3,560**

Pottery Candleholder ▼

- *circa 8th century*

Byzantine pottery candle holder modelled as a church, with carved arches and openings with a geometric design.
- *height 29cm*
- **Guide price $3,560**

Bronze Figure of Aphrodite ▼

- *circa 2nd century AD*

Small bronze figure of Aphrodite, goddess of love.
- *height 9cm*
- **Guide price $620**

Bronze Oil Lamp with Leaf Design ▲

- *3rd century AD*

Bronze oil lamp with stylised foliate thumb rest with original patina.
- *4cm x 16cm*
- **Guide price $360**

Gold Earrings ▼

- *4th century AD*

Gold Roman earrings with large garnet setting.
- *length 6cm*
- **Guide price $1,960**

Bronze Key Ring ▲

- *2nd century AD*

Bronze ring with key to lock.
- *diameter 2.5cm*
- **Guide price $180**

Hellenistic Earring ▶

- *2nd century BC*

Gold Hellenistic earring with a green stone.
- *length 2cm*
- **Guide price $340**

Gold Hoop Earrings with Beads ▲

- *12th century AD*

Large gold hoop earrings with beaded circular design.
- *diameter 4cm*
- **Guide price $1,960**

Medusa Ring ◀

- *4th century AD*

Gold ring with an agate cameo of Medusa.
- *diameter 1cm*
- **Guide price $2,140**

Egyptian Hand Earring ▼

- *2nd century BC*
Turquoise Egyptian gold hoop
earring styled as a hand with a
pearl clasp.
- *diameter 1.5cm*
- **Guide price $80**

Hellenistic Earring ▲

- *2nd century BC*
Gold hoop Egyptian earring with
a fine head of a bull.
- *diameter 2cm*
- **Guide price $800**

Charging Rhinoceros Figure ▼

- *1st century AD*
Rhinoceros in charging position.
Han Dynasty.
- *15cm x 38cm*
- **Guide price $890**

Roman Seal ▲

- *1st century BC*
Roman seal of Mercury in a
modern setting.
- *diameter 1cm*
- **Guide price $850**

Roman Oil Lamp ▲

- *2nd–3rd century AD*
Roman pottery oil lamp,
depicting a figure of Mercury.
- *length 10cm*
- **Guide price $270**

Terracotta Storage Jar ▼

- *1500 BC*
Painted terraccotta pot with
geometric design.
- *30cm x 30cm*
- **Guide price $750**

Terracotta Han Dynasty ◄

- *1st century AD*
T'ang Dynasty terracotta horse
with original patina.
- *18cm x 36cm*
- **Guide price $2,670**

Celtic Warrior ▶

- **100 BC**
A small figure of a bronze Celtic
Warrior found in Norfolk.
- *height 7cm*
- **Guide price $1,020**

Claudius Bronze ▲

- **1st century AD**
Small Romano British bronze
head of Claudius found in
Colchester.
- *height 2.5cm*
- **Guide price $400**

Roman Sandal ▲

- **circa 2nd century AD**
A small Romano British brooch
in the form of a sandal.
- *length 2cm*
- **Guide price $115**

Fibula Brooch ▲

- **2nd century AD**
A Romano British fibula brooch
found in Wiltshire.
- *length 2cm*
- **Guide price $80**

Votive Altar ▼

- **circa 1st–2nd century AD**
Bronze altar with blue and green
enamel decoration, with original
patina, dedicated to the god
Jupiter.
- *height 2cm*
- **Guide price $890**

Romano British Brooch ▶

- **2nd century AD**
A Romano British brooch in
the form of a wheel with
enameling. Found in Salisbury,
Wiltshire.
- *height 2cm*
- **Guide price $450**

Bronze Cherub Head Decoration ▼

- **2nd century AD**
Small bronze head of Cupid being
part of decoration for a drinking
vessel found in Dorset.
- *height 1cm*
- **Guide price $130**

Expert Tips

*Considering its age, beauty and
fragility, Roman glass is a
relatively affordable investment
for the antiquities collector, and
is a good place to start.*

Green Glass Flask ▲
- *3rd–4th century AD*
Bottle-shaped green glass flask,
with globular body and
cylindrical neck wound with clear
spiral threads, four applied
handles, flared foot and surface
encrustation.
- *height 11cm*
- **Guide price $11,570**

Aubergine Glass Jar ▼
- *7th century AD*
Small ovoid aubergine glass jar,
with moulded rim and extensive
iridescence.
- *height 7cm*
- **Guide price $1,420**

Roman Iridescent Flask ▼
- *4th century AD*
Iridescent green flask with silver
and gold decoration.
- *height 12cm*
- **Guide price $1,780**

Roman Cameo Ring ▶
- *circa 1st century AD*
Roman gold cameo ring
decorated with an outstretched
hand squeezing an ear inscribed
"Remember me and always be
mine".
- *width 2cm*
- **Guide price $8,900**

Indented Glass Flask ▲
- *4–6th century AD*
Green glass flask, with applied
handle and six-sided body, with
indented sides.
- *height 15cm*
- **Guide price $1,780**

Roman Flask ▲
- *1st century AD*
Roman blue glass flask, the body
encircled with spiral threads.
- *height 9.4cm*
- **Guide price $2,670**

Bronze Bull's Head Decoration ▼

- *2nd–3rd century AD*
Fine Romano British bronze bull's head part of decoration to a vessel found in Bath.
- *height 2cm*
- **Guide price $150**

Bronze Fibula Brooch ▲

- *2nd century AD*
Found in Southwark, London a small bronze fibula brooch.
- *length 5cm*
- **Guide price $70**

Roman Bronze Brooch ▲

- *2nd–3rd century AD*
Roman British bronze fibula brooch.
- *height 7cm*
- **Guide price $140**

Gold Cornelian Ring ▼

- *3rd century*
Ibex cornelian and gold ring, European.
- *diameter 1.6cm*
- **Guide price $1,060**

Cabuchon Garnet Ring ▲

- *1st–2nd century AD*
Romano British gold ring with a cabuchon garnet depicting a figure of a wood nymph found in Bromley, Kent.
- diameter 1.6cm
- **Guide price $1,060**

Hellenistic Ring ▲

- *4th century BC*
Gold ring with Cabuchon garnet from the Hellenistic period.
- *diameter 2cm*
- **Guide price $1,200**

Bronze Snake Ring ▶

- *1st century AD*
Bronze Romano British snake ring.
- *diameter 2cm*
- **Guide price $170**

Gold Hoop Earring ◀
- *2nd century AD*
Romano British gold hoop
earring with lozenge shape drop
holding a small Cabuchon garnet.
- *diameter 2cm*
- **Guide price $240**

Romano British Earring ▼
- *2nd century AD*
Small gold-scrolled hoop earring
found by the River Thames,
London.
- *diameter 2cm*
- **Guide price $350**

Roman Bronze Key ▲
- *2nd century AD*
Rare bronze Romano British key.
Found in the River Thames,
London.
- *length 5cm*
- **Guide price $670**

Oyster Spoon ▲
- *2nd century AD*
Romano British bronze oyster
spoon, found in York.
- *length 12cm*
- **Guide price $490**

Blue Glass Melon Beads ▲
- *1st or 2nd century AD*
Three "Blue glass melon beads"
Romano British found in
Gloucester.
- *diameter 1cm*
- **Guide price $140**

Expert Tips

*While ancient locks of iron and
wood are unlikely to survive intact,
bronze keys are sturdier and more
easily collectable today.*

Three Roman Casket Keys ▲
- *1st–2nd century AD*
Three bronze Romano British
casket keys.
- *diameter 1cm*
- **Guide price $115 each**

Leaf-shaped Bronze Lamp Base ▶
- *2nd –3rd century AD*
Bronze Romano British lamp
fitting in the form of a leaf found
in Dorset.
- *length 10cm*
- **Guide price $220**

Roman British Weight ▶
- **2nd–3rd century AD**
Romano British bronze weight in the shape of a heart.
- *length 2cm*
- **Guide price $150**

Celtic Bronze Torque ▲
- **250 BC**
Celtic bronze torque fragment found in Norfolk.
- *length 2cm*
- **Guide price $170**

Gandhara Vessel ▼
- **500 BC**
Bronze jug in the form of a cow standing on three feet. Used for wine.
- *height 20cm*
- **Guide price $106,800**

Expert Tips
Interested collectors should go and have a look at the British Museum collections of antiquities, the best in the world

Mummy Beads ◀
- **300 BC**
Cornelian beads and Mummy beads necklace.
- *length*
- **Guide price $450**

Oil Vessel ▲
- **1st–2nd century AD**
Terra nigre oil vessel with handle in good condition.
- *height 13cm*
- **Guide price $310**

Buddha Head ▲
- **100 BC**
Carved stone head of Buddha with gold patina from Hadda.
- *height 23cm*
- **Guide price $16,020**

Gandhara Relief

- **1st century AD**
Black stone carved frieze of
Buddha and figures seated on an
elephant with attendants.
  - *30cm x 30cm*
  - **Guide price $24,920**

Islamic Drinking Vessel

- **2500 BC**
Islamic terracotta drinking cup
with a geometric pattern of green
and yellow, standing on a circular
container for wine.
  - *height 28cm*
  - **Guide price $2,670**

Bronze Flower Vessel from Afghanistan

- **100 BC**
Islamic vessel from Afghanistan
for flowers made from bronze with
cartouches of chickens, rabbits,
and musicians.
  - *height 55cm*
  - **Guide price $19,580**

Terracotta Wine Vessel

- **1st century AD**
Large bulbous terracotta vessel for
holding wine with six cartouches
of birds and gazelles. Floral design
with three handles.
  - *height 32cm*
  - **Guide price $16,020**

Marble Eagle

- **500 AD**
Finely carved marble eagle with
extended wings and painted red
eyes.
  - *height 12cm*
  - **Guide price $3,560**

Egyptian Glass Bangle ▲
- **9th century AD**
Egyptian glass bangle, funerary artifact.
- *diameter 7cm*
- **Guide price $310**

Mother and Child ▲
- **2500 BC**
Mohenjo-Daro, Indus Valley figure of a mother and child from Afghanistan.
- *height 10cm*
- **Guide price $2,670**

Buddhist Temple ▲
- **500 BC**
Crystal Buddhist stupa standing on marble base, used as a portable shrine.
- *height 19cm*
- **Guide price $17,800**

Fertility Goddess ▼
- **2500 BC**
Mohenjo-Daro, Indus Valley figure of fertility goddess from Afghanistan.
- *height 10cm*
- **Guide price $2,670**

Expert Tips

To test that Roman pottery is the genuine article, wet it with your fingers and if it smells very earthy its probably the real thing. Make sure you go to a reputable dealer.

Mohenjo Daro ◄
- **2500 BC**
Terracotta sugar bowl base with fish design surmounted by drinking vessel with hexagonal design.
- *height 17cm*
- **Guide price $1,780**

Architectural & Garden Furniture

The boom in television gardening programmes has lead to an increase in demand for garden furniture and garden design.

Classic architectural and garden furniture pieces are currently a flourishing market as they can be easily incorporated into a modern home or garden to add historical elegance. Carved mantelpieces and antique glass panels are some of the common indoor pieces available while statues, foutains, steps, friezes and iron garden furniture are some of the more popular items for exterior design.

Many of the wood, stone, metal or marble pieces on the market are usually salvaged from old buildings and vary in condition. Architectural pieces can be quite large and difficult to move on your own, so check what delivery services (and charges) are offered by the dealer. A tape measure is essential if you are planning to buy an item for an existing space. The results are rewarding as historical pieces can blend in well with modern houses.

Look beyond the large cities when shopping, as dealers often have large warehouses in rural locations. Be warned, though, that prices are rising since makeover programmes have greatly increased the demand.

Five Stone Steps with Balustrades ◀

- *circa 1870*
Fine set of five stone steps flanked by sweeping scrolled balustrades.
- *90cm x 1.52m*
- **Guide price $17,800**

Cast Iron Bull ▼

- *circa 1950*
Impressive cast iron bull with left leg raised in an aggressive manner, mounted on a stylised rocky base.
- *1.55m x 2.5m*
- **Guide price $29,510**

Stone Lion's Head ▲

- *circa 1880*
A circular stone lion's head with a finely carved naturalistic expression.
- *48cm x 38cm*
- **Guide price $1,470**

Italian Water Fountain ▲
- *early 20th century*

Charming Italian Rosso Verona marble and bronze fountain by Raffaello Romanelli. The marble bowl is supported on the shoulders of a bronze satyr crouching on a marble base. A laughing cherub stands with arms raised in the centre of the bowl, while being squirted by a frog crouching on the rim.
- *height 1.7m*
- *diameter of bowl 92cm*
- **Guide price $62,300**

Stoneware Urns ▲
- *mid 19th century*

One of a pair of stoneware urns, each semi-lobed body with a frieze of stylised foliage beneath a rope twist and lobed rim, on a circular foot and square base stamped, "Pulhams Terra Cotta Boxbourne".
- *height 67cm*
- **Guide price $16,910**

One of a Pair of Urns ▼
- *1910*

Pair of cast iron urns with egg and dart moulded rim above a lobed body, raised on a fluted, splayed foot on a square base.
- *58.5cm diameter*
- **Guide price $820**

Stone Finials ▼
- *circa 1880*

One of a pair of English sandstone finials, finely carved with scrolled and leaf designs, surmounted with a stylised acorn finial.
- *height 2m*
- **Guide price $13,350**

Sir Walter Raleigh ▶
- *circa 1880*

Stone statue of Sir Walter Raleigh dressed in a tunic and breeches and holding his cloak.
- *height 1.2m*
- **Guide price $40,940**

Carved Stone Lions ▲
- *circa 1890*

One of a pair of late 19th-century stone lions in a crouching position, with tail swept onto one side and a finely carved expression.
- *44cm x 1m*
- **Guide price $24,920**

Cast Iron Fountain ▲
- *19th century*

Cast iron fountain from Ardennes, France, in the form of a young boy holding a staff in one hand and pointing with the other.
- *height 1.22m*
- **Guide price $6,050**

Stone Frieze with Goats and Cherubs ▶

- *circa 1870*

A stone frieze finely carved with goats and cherubs within a foliate design, this being one of five pairs, each pair being sold separately.
- *60cm x 1.4m*
- **Guide price $10,150**

Terracotta Garden Bricks with Rose Design ▲

- *circa 1900*

Square terracotta garden bricks with carved rose motif, one of 30 sold separately.
- *22cm x 22cm*
- **Guide price $40**

Ram's Heads ▼

- *circa 1880*

Pair of finely carved stone ram's head mounted on square bases.
- *38cm x 30cm*
- **Guide price $7,030**

Ceramic Pillars ◀

- *circa 1880*

English stone and ceramic pillars with vertical scrolling acanthus and leaf design. One of six.
- *height 1.8m*
- **Guide price $2,270**

Gothic Niches ▶

- *circa 1880*

One of a pair of Bathstone Gothic revival niches with foliate carving to the sides and surmounted by a cross with trailing foliage.
- *2.7m x 1.19m*
- **Guide price 72,090**

Bishop's Head ▲

- *circa 1890*

A finely carved stone head of a bishop.
- *height 34cm*
- **Guide price $1,200**

Expert Tips

This may seem an obvious tip but make sure you can get it home, cheaply, and it fits — no guesswork!

Stone Trough ▼

- *circa 1820*

A stone trough with attractive weathering of lichen and moss.
- *40cm x 78cm*
- **Guide price $460**

Cast Iron Garden Roller ▼

- *circa 1870*

Cast iron garden roller with turned wooden handle and cast iron medallion with maker's logo.
- *height 1.2m*
- **Guide price $400**

Georgian Columns ▼

- *circa 1730s*

Three early Georgian stone columns with reeded capital, supported by square columns with chamfered corners, raised on stepped, plinth bases.
- *height 1.95m*
- **Guide price $1,400**

Roll Top Bench ▲

- *20th century*

A two-seater roll top iron bench, with ladder back and seat, and scrolled arms and legs.
- *width 1.2m*
- **Guide price $760**

Neptune Fountain ▲

- *circa 1890*

Cast iron wall fountain showing Neptune sitting on his throne while wrestling with a carp.
- *height 1.55m*
- **Guide price $3,160**

Palladian Chimneypiece ▼

- *circa 1730*

An English Palladian statuary marble chimneypiece, after a design by William Kent. The projecting inverted breakfront shelf with moulded edge above a band of lotus moulding and a boldly carved egg and dart moulding, the frieze centred by a rectangular panel carved with a bacchante mask, the hair intertwined with berried vines, and a border of Sienna marble.
- *1.66m x 2.31m*
- **Guide price $560,700**

Stone Trough ▼

- *circa 1820*

A rectangular stone trough with good patination.
- *38cm x 89cm*
- **Guide price $450**

French Copper Bath ▼

- *circa 1880*

French double skinned bath with copper lining, raised on cast iron claw feet.
- *length 1.67m*
- **Guide price $14,150**

Brass Lantern ▼

- *1880*

Brass lantern with glass front and sides with pagoda top and small round brass finials.
- *height 45cm*
- **Guide price $200**

Chinese Garden Seat ▶

- *1880*

Chinese ceramic garden seat with a cream glaze, pierced lattice panels and lion mask decoration.
- *height 39cm*
- **Guide price $620**

Galvanised Flower Bucket ▲

- *1960*

French flower vendors galvanised display bucket with carrying handles.
- *height 48cm*
- **Guide price $40**

Galvanised Tub ▲

- *1880*

One of a pair of galvanised water butts with an inverted linear design.
- *height 54cm*
- **Guide price $170**

Ceramic Garden Seat ▶

- *1880*

Chinese ceramic garden seat, in a green glaze, with black floral designs and a repeating pattern of spots.
- *height 39cm*
- **Guide price $620**

Enamel Bucket ▼

- *1920*

French enamelled water bucket with a red rim, pale green body, hand-painted strawberries and original handle.
- *height 29cm*
- **Guide price $140**

Expert Tips

Garden furniture, unlike interior furniture, does not need to be perfect in order to create a beautiful garden, as some wear and tear can add mystery and delight to any design. All that is needed is a little imagination.

Green Stucco Pot ◀

- *1950*

Stoneware urn of ovoid form with green glazed lip and neck with rusticated finish to the body.
- *height 44cm*
- **Guide price $430**

Oak Doors with Foliate Frieze ▶

- *1860*

An impressive pair of light oak doors with carved pine fruit griffins and mermaids set in a foliate frieze.

- *3.3m x 2.44m*
- **Guide price $28,480**

Victorian Cloche ▲

- *1880*

A small Victorian cast iron vegetable cloche with original white enamel paint with handle.

- *48cm x 34cm*
- **Guide price $250**

Victorian Planter ▼

- *circa 1870*

A two-tiered wrought iron Victorian planter with the original green enamel paintwork.

- *86cm x 90cm*
- **Guide price $1,330**

Garden Trolley ◀

- *circa 1920*

A wrought iron garden trolley with a pierced floral design and original white enamel paint.

- *71cm x 48cm*
- **Guide price $400**

Circular Cast Iron Table with Scrolled Legs ▼

- *circa 1870*

A circular cast iron table base; decorative scrolled legs and feet with a circular marble top.

- *diameter 74cm*
- **Guide price $1,510**

Lead Statue of Mercury ▼

- *circa 1900*

A fine lead statue of Mercury with left hand raised on circular base.

- *height 1.1m*
- **Guide price $4,980**

Balloon Back Chairs ◀

- *circa 1920*

Two wrought iron balloon back chairs being part of a set of six with a circular wrought iron table, original paint.

- *height 83cm*
- **Guide price $4,450**

Door Lock and Steel Key ▼

- *circa 1870*
A door lock with key made of steel.
- *20cm x20cm*
- **Guide price** $700

Brass Bird-shaped Door Hinge ▶

- *circa 1900*
A brass door hinge in the form of a stylised neck of a bird.
- *20cm x 13cm*
- **Guide price** $270

Sandstone Finials ▲

- *circa 1880*
One of a pair of fine highly decorative sandstone finials, carved with shells and figures from Scotland.
- *height 1.5m*
- **Guide price** $4,450

Satyr's Head ▼

- *circa 1900*
A French stone-carved head of a satyr.
- *height 50cm*
- **Guide price** $2,850

Brass Oval Window Locks ◀

- *circa 1890*
A pair of fine oval brass window locks with a circular pierced floral design on the handles.
- *14cm x 9cm*
- **Guide price** $710

Brass Door Handles ▲

- *circa 1880*
Pair of fine brass door handles.
- *diameter 23cm*
- **Guide price** $310

Cricular Brass Bell ▲

- *1880*
Circular brass bell stand with ornate foliate and acorn design.
- *20cm x 14cm*
- **Guide price** $400

Victorian Iron Gates ▲

- *circa 1880*

Pair of Victorian iron gates, heavily constructed with ball and spike finial designs.

- *2m x 3m*
- **Guide price $9,080**

Expert Tips

Decorative fireplaces were mass-produced from the 1840s, so it is important to check the grate is complete with basket and hood, as perfect replacements are difficult to find.

Oak Bar ▲

- *circa 1920*

Circular oak bar with moulded panelled doors, consisting of a four door fridge unit, marble surround and surfaces.

- *length 6.35m*
- **Guide price $10,500**

Architectural Fireplace ▶

- *1800–1900*

Carved wooden fireplace flanked by two architectural columns surmounted by a moulded mantle, with traces of white paint.

- *height 1.28m*
- **Guide price $4,180**

Gothic Window ▼

- *circa 1800*

Carved gothic sandstone window.

- *89cm x 69cm*
- **Guide price $1,300**

Fire Dogs and Grate ▶

- *circa 1900*

Victorian serpentine-fronted cast-iron grate and fire back with a raised design of tulips, surmounted by two cherubs holding a wreath.

- *75cm x 80cm*
- **Guide price $6,400**

English Rococo Chimneypiece ▲

- *circa 1840*

An English white marble chimneypiece signed D Aí. The serpentine shaped shelf with moulded edge above an elaborately carved frieze decorated with scrolled acanthus leaves, with a central scallop carved shell above the hearth opening and a double moulded surround with relief flower heads above three small acanthus motifs terminating in scrolled leaves.

- *1.22m x 1.93m*
- **Guide price $67,640**

Bronze Angel ▼

- *circa 1900*

Fine bronze head of an angel with pursed lips used as a fountain.

- *44cm x 40cm*
- **Guide price $2,140**

Victorian Chimneypiece ▶

- *circa 1854*

Belgian black marble shelf above a frieze with fluted column jambs and oak and walnut overmantle with mirror plate. Cornice centred by a portrait of Isaac Newton in full relief.

- *3.76m x 2.44m*
- **Guide price $121,050**

Victorian Marble Chimneypiece ▲

- *late 19th century*

Chimneypiece in Gothic Revival taste having an arched aperture with foliate carvings to the spandrels and a curb fender en-suite.

- *1.44m x 1.83m*
- **Guide price $9,790**

Terracotta Urns ▼

- *circa 1870*

One of a pair of fine terracotta urns by Pulham Broxbourne.

- *height 50cm*
- **Guide price $1,960**

Expert Tips

Timber copies of marble fireplaces are very effective. Add plaster mouldings and a marble paint finish.

Marble Chimneypiece ◀

- *circa 1780*

Georgian chimneypiece with lambrequin carved breakfront shelf above a plain frieze centred by a tablet carved relief of Diana and Cupid.

- *1.56m x 1.79m*
- **Guide price $64,080**

English Brass Andirons ▲

- *circa 1880*

The wrythen standards with lobed ball finials and raised on scrolled hairy paw feet.

- *86cm x 55cm*
- **Guide price $18,510 for pair**

Iron Hob Grate ◀

- *circa 1800*

Grate in the manner of George Bullock with railed basket flanked by pilasters with brass anthemion appliques and paw feet.

- *48.5cm x 1.07m*
- **Guide price $12,100**

Stained Glass Windows ▶

- *circa 1895*

Each Victorian window depicts a female saint framed by an architectural border.

- *1.3cm x 40cm*
- **Guide price $53,400**

Florentine Entranceway ▲

- *circa 16th century*

Scalloped demi-lune overdoor with foliate surmounts above the frieze panel.

- *3.84m x 1.85m*
- **Guide price $31,150**

Stone Winged Lions ▲

- *Late 19th century*

After cast iron originals by "Societe Anonyme ... du Val d'Osne", Paris. Each sentinel beast with displaying wings raised on a rectangular plinth.

- *height 1.47m*
- **Guide price $10,150**

Panelled Room ▲

- *early 18th century*

Raised and fielded panelling with two ionic order stop-fluted pilasters, three archways of which one incorporates a door.

- *height 3.35m*
- **Guide price $39,160**

Pine Chimneypiece ▶

- *late 19th–early 20th century*

Constructed from some period elements, the moulded breakfront shelf with acanthine and egg and dart ornaments above an ogee section acanthine carved eared aperture.

- *1.33m x 1.32m*
- **Guide price $7,650**

Stone Pool Surround ▲

- *20th century*

Eight Italian cornucopia shaped planters linked by ornate kerbstones, pleasantly weathered with adjustable pool diameter.

- *height 36cm*
- **Guide price $5,790**

Terracotta Sphinxes ◀

- *Late 19th century*

Each recumbent female figure is attired in Nemes headwear and armour al antica on a rectangular plinth bearing the signature Emil Muller.

- *92cm x 1.14m*
- **Guide price $29,370 the pair**

Pottery Urn ▲
- *circa 1940*
One of a pair of pottery urns with lobed designs around the body and egg and dart motif to the splayed lip, standing on a pedestal base.
- *height 43cm*
- **Guide price $850**

French Chair ▲
- *circa 1950*
One of a set of four French wrought iron garden chairs with pierced geometric designs to back splat and seat.
- *height 87cm*
- **Guide price $1,210**

Mythical Yarli Lions ▼
- *18th century*
One of a pair of Mythical Yarli lions with elephant trunks, standing on top of human heads. Has traces of original paint remaining in excellent condition. Vellore Tamil Naou.
- *height 1.66m*
- **Guide price $13,880**

Indian Jarli Window ▼
- *17th century*
Indian Mughal Jarli window carved from red sandstone flanked by four cartouches in the form of Mirabs arches. The central Jarli of interlocking honeycomb is topped by a floral finial with a flower to left and right from Northern Rajastan.
- *83cm x 1.15m*
- **Guide price $10,320**

Wicker Chair ▶
- *circa 1920*
French provincial wicker conservatory chair painted pistachio green with a deep horseshoe back, apron front and splayed legs.
- *height 67cm*
- **Guide price $430**

Wrought Iron Chair ▲
- *circa 1950*
Set of four French wrought iron patio chairs with a heart-shaped back, scrolled arms and original white enamel paint.
- *height 87cm*
- **Guide price $1,210**

Carved Ceiling Panel ▲
- *circa 1850*
Carved rosewood ceiling panel with central flower within a stylised leaf motif, from Southern India.
- *length 56cm*
- **Guide price $550**

Brass Urns ▼
• *circa 1910*
One of a pair of brass urns from the modern movement, with unusual angular double handles, the whole on a pedestal foot resting on a square base.
• *height 48cm*
• **Guide price $1,560**

Zinc Urns ▼
• 1920
One of a pair of French urns made from zinc with unusual angular designs and a marbled finish.
• *height 31cm*
• **Guide price $1,210**

Garden Folding Stool ▲
• 1950
Folding picnic stool with a candy striped linen seat supported by four teak legs.
• *height 41cm*
• **Guide price $140**

Stone Flower Pot ▲
• 1970
Stone flower pot with a fluted body with carved designs in relief.
• *height 24cm*
• **Guide price $40**

Pink Pottery Bucket ▼
• 1910
French ceramic pail with salmon pink glaze and white interior with a raffia covered handle.
• *height 24cm*
• **Guide price $30**

Expert Tips

Unglazed period pottery of any value should be covered up and protected if left outside in the winter because ice can destroy it as it expands in the cracks.

Salt Glazed Urn ▼
• 1910
French salt glazed pottery urn with pinched lip and banding, the body centred with a flower motif in relief on a pedestal base.
• *height 41cm*
• **Guide price $210**

Watering Can ◄
• 1920
Zinc watering can with an elongated spout.
• *height 26cm*
• **Guide price $60**

Lead Cistern ▲
- *18th century*
Cistern with front panel cast in relief with strapwork centred by a relief cast figure.
- *79cm x 74cm*
- **Guide price $3,830**

Carved Pine Altar ▲
- *Late 19th century*
Victorian altar, the sides pierced with gothic tracery arcades and trefoils – some losses to the carving.
- *95cm x 1.68m*
- **Guide price $850**

Pine-front Entranceway ▼
- *Early 19th century*
Neo-classical painted pine front entranceway in the late Georgian taste with triangular pediment above six panel door and fluted pilasters.
- *282cm x 149cm*
- **Guide price $8,900**

Stained Glass Window ◄
- *19th century*
French stained glass roundel window depicting a praying saint kneeling at an altar.
- *diameter 1.03m*
- **Guide price $3,120**

Victorian Tazza Urns ▲
- *Late 19th century*
Shallow-lobed tazza bowls by the Handyside foundry of Derbyshire raised on a socle foot and stamped to the plinth.
- *49cm x 79cm*
- **Guide price $3,380 the pair**

Bronze Swan Doorstop ▼
- *circa 1890*
Victorian cast-bronze swan doorstop.
- *height 38cm*
- **Guide price $800**

Mahogany Wheelbarrow ◄
- *circa 1890*
A fine English late 19th century wheelbarrow of finely figured mahogany with brass mounts.
- *45cm x 46cm x 1.07m*
- **Guide price $32,040**

Arms & Armour

There are many avenues to choose from for the collector of militaria
including weapons, pictures, prints, postcards and medals.

There are many facets to collecting weapons and war paraphernalia. While full suits of armour are prohibitively expensive, interesting collections can be made from different suits. In particular, military headdress is a popular theme and rare specimens from the eighteenth and nineteenth century hold their value. A variety of military uniforms from the later centuries are widely available, while earlier specimens are much rarer and command a high price.

In terms of weaponry, one of the larger collecting areas is edged weapons. Bayonets and small swords from the nineteenth century can be acquired at fair prices, while the superb quality of many Indian, Persian and Arabic pieces is boosting their value.

Antique firearms must be inspected by a gunsmith before firing. The earliest specimens from the seventeenth century are rare but tend to be of high quality. Those predating the 1870s, when modern firearm design began, are greatly prized.

Colt Navy Revolver ▼
- **1853**
Colt navy revolver, most of the original cylinder has seen naval action in the Gulf of Mexico.
- *length 19cm*
- **Guide price $1,780**

Single Action Pistol ◄
- *circa 1863*
Single Action pistol, 44 calibre, with Starr original finish.
- *length 20cm*
- **Guide price $2,490**

Buffalo Bill Revolver ▼
- *circa 1970*
Percussion Revolver, 31 calibre, as used on frontier mining camps from the "Buffalo Bill" Historical Society Museum, Wyoming. Non-firing replica, with pellets and brass powder containers set in a presentation box.
- *width 30cm*
- **Guide price $1,330**

Double-Action Revolver ▼
- **1860**
Coopers double-action revolver with walnut stock 50 per cent original finish 36 calibre.
- *length 10cm*
- **Guide price $1,330**

Belgian Courtier's Sword ▼

- *circa 1860*

Belgian courtier's sword with mother-of-pearl grip and brass gilt guard, with foliate designs together with a black leather scabbard with gilt mounts. Inscribed "Docteur Lorthioir" and the maker's mark 49 Rue des Fabrique, Brussels.
- *length 85cm*
- **Guide price $360**

Fintlock Pistol ▲

- *circa 1790*

English flintlock three barrel tap action pistol made by Clarke of London. 62 Cheapside London.
- *length 21cm*
- **Guide price $3,380**

Captain's Jacket and Hat ▼

- *1855*

Scarlet tunic of a Captain in the First Royal Tower Hamlets Miliita (The King's Own Light Infantry). Collar insignia of Crown and Pip with tin case by Flight Military Tailors, Winchester, containing belts and sashes. Plus an Officer's shako (without plume) with K.O.L.I plate.
- *large*
- **Guide price $2,940**

General's Aiguilettes ▼

- *1940*

Third Reich General's aiguilettes, in good condition with only minor damage to parts of the gilt wiring.
- *length 42cm*
- **Guide price $330**

Royal Engineers Busby ▼

- *circa 1910*

Royal engineers officer's bear fur busby with the gilt flaming bomb incorporating the Regiments insignia and patent leather chinstrap.
- *height 14cm*
- **Guide price $670**

Thirty-two Calibre Percussion Revolver ◄

- *1860*

Thirty-two calibre double action Adams revolver, with hexagonal barrel, made under licence by Mass Arms. Co. U.S.A. with modern bullet mould.
- *length 21.5cm*
- **Guide price $980**

Double-Trigger Revolver ▶

- **1864**

First mould double-trigger Tranta revolver in 36 bore inscribed "Strand of London", ten per cent original finish.
- *length 20cm*
- **Guide price $1,420**

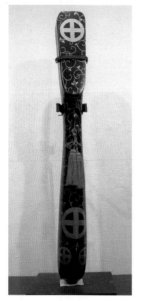

Japanese Quiver ▲

- *circa 1800*

A Japanese quiver for carrying arrows, made of wood with black lacquer and a gold floral pattern, with two small circles being the crest of the Satsuma family.
- *height 39cm*
- **Guide price $3,560**

Tsuba Sword Guard ▲

- *circa 1850*

A Japanese sword guard, or Tsuba, depicting an Oni, or demon, made of iron.
- *8cm x 6cm*
- **Guide price $1,420**

Tachi Sword ◀

- *circa 1750*

A Japanese long sword, or Tachi, used for wearing with armour. The blade is signed "Suke-Sada" the scabbardf is wood with bronze lacquer and bound in leather.
- *length 42cm*
- **Guide price $7,120**

Hoshi Kabuto ▲

- *circa 1750*

An iron plate helmet, or Hoshi Kabuto, with visor and a circular crest, for the Japanese army.
- *height 30cm*
- **Guide price $3,920**

Expert Tips

Always wear cotton gloves when handling weapons to prevent the formation of rust deposits – store in a dry and well-ventilated place

Silver Ho Ho Bird ◀

- *circa 1750*

A Japanese Tachi with a silver Ho Ho bird mounted on the hilt, with two silver hanging loops on the lacquered terracotta scabbard.
- *length 42cm*
- **Guide price $7,120**

Pith Helmet

- *circa 1915*

Turn of the century linen pith helmet for the overseas campaign in India, in fine original condition.

- *size 7*
- **Guide price $210**

Luftwaffe Belt

- *1940*

Luftwaffe other ranks late pattern standard leather belt, with some wear, but complete.

- *5cm x 3cm*
- **Guide price $80**

SS Steel Helmet

- *1940*

SS M-44 Steel helmet, a rare early double decal version complete with inner lining and chin strap, stamped "54" on lining and a maker's stamp on inside of helmet, with most of original finish still present.

- *size 8*
- **Guide price $2,130**

Japanese N.C.O. Sword

- *circa 1939*

Japanese N.C.O. Katena sword with polished folded steel blade and original paintwork to handle. No. 79275, with matching scabbard number.

- *length 59cm*
- **Guide price $520**

Officers Belt Pistol

- *circa 1840*

Officers 16 bore percussion pistol, with double back action locks, by Roper of Halifax.

- *length 30cm*
- **Guide price $1,560**

Khula–Khad Helmet

- *circa 1800*

Fine Indo Persian Khula-Khad helmet formed as a face with horns, with chiselled steel designs, gold inlays and chain mail neck guard.

- *height 30cm*
- **Guide price $5,700**

Japanese Dagger

- *circa 1870*

A Japanese Tanto dagger with cloisonne hilt and scabbard, the blade is unsigned.

- *length 35cm*
- **Guide price $3,200**

Pinfire Revolver

- *circa 1870*

Continental pinfire carbine revolver with "Fabrique de Le Page Freres a Liege, Maison a Paris 12 Rue de Eugieue" etched on barrel.

- *length 66cm*
- **Guide price $2,140**

Gentleman's Helmet ▶

- **early 17th century**
Gentleman's steel close helmet,
possibly Flemish.
- *44cm x 36cm*
- **Guide price $14,150**

Hilt Decoration ▼

- *circa 1800*
Sword furniture for the hilt or
Menuki in the form of gilt sea
shells.
- *length 2cm*
- **Guide price $270**

Sword Furniture ▼

- *circa 1800*
A Kodzuka and Kogai sword
furniture made of Shkudo with
gilt dragon.
- *length 20cm*
- **Guide price $2,670**

Dragon Sword Guard ▶

- *circa 1800*
A Tsuba, or sword guard, made of
sentoku, a mixture of bronze and
copper, depicting a dragon
- *7.2cm x 5cm*
- **Guide price $890**

Tanto Blade ▼

- *circa 1800*
A Japanese dagger or Tanto
signed "Suke Sada" with Kodzuka
and Minouki on the hilt.
- *length 22cm*
- **Guide price $3,560**

Japanese Dagger ▼

- *circa 1850*
A European style Japanese
presentation dagger for a Dutch
or Portuguese sea captain
inscribed with the maker's name
"Nabu take" with silver scabbard.
- *length 15cm*
- **Guide price $3,200**

Steel Arrowhead ▲

- *circa 1900*
A Japanese steel arrowhead with
a floral blossom crest.
- *length 20cm*
- **Guide price $270**

Trooper's Sabre ▼

- *circa 1908*

British trooper's sabre, pattern dated and inscribed WWI paint.
- *length 1.1m*
- Guide price $490

Deane Harding Percussion Pistol ▼

- *circa 1840*

Deane Harding 54 calibre officer's percussion cap and ball pistol, with hexagonal barrel and original grip and varnish. London proof marks.
- *length 30cm*
- Guide price $1,340

Luftwaffe Paratrooper Helmet ▶

- *1940*

Luftwaffe paratrooper's helmet. Rare double decal version, with both Luftwaffe eagle and national shield. The chinstrap and liner are complete showing makers mark: Baumuster: Heisler Berlin C2 Hersteller F. W. Muller JR and sizes; Koptwelte GR 61 Stahlhaube Nr. 71, all clearly readable. Helmet stamped on the inside, "ET71", paintwork and overall finish excellent.
- *size 8*
- Guide price $6,230

Schutzenschnur Silver Luftwaffe ▲

- *1940*

Pilot officer's silver braid of the Luftwaffe with an eagle and national insignia.
- *length 14cm*
- Guide price $180

Russian Dagger ▼

- *circa 1880*

Russian Kinjal dagger with ornate silver hilt and scabbard, the blade with long grooves and foliate design in mechanical watering.
- *length 51cm*
- Guide price $2,490

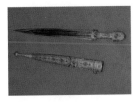

Pocket Flintlock Pistols ▼

- *circa 1720*

Pair of English Queen Anne pocket flintlock pistols, with cannon barrels and silver lion mask butt caps, signed John Segelas. Hammers fitted with dog catches.
- *length 18cm*
- Guide price $6,050

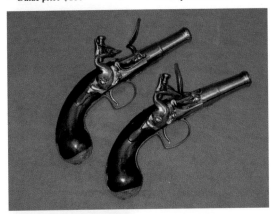

French Belt Pistol ▼

- *1813*

French cavalryman's belt pistol with flintlock action, brass mounts and walnut furniture.
- *length 21.5cm*
- Guide price $1,780

Civil War Helmet ▼

- *circa 1640*
English civil war and steel
"Lobster Tail" helmet.
- *20cm x 40cm*
- **Guide price** $4,900

Scottish Dirk ▲

- *early 18th century*
Scottish dirk with brass and
leather sheaf, intricate Celtic
carved wooden hilt, and brass
fittings.
- *length 45cm*
- **Guide price** $5,250

Pikeman's Helmet ▲

- *early 17th century*
English steel pikeman's helmet.
- *44cm x 24cm*
- **Guide price** $4,900

Fine Tinderlighter ▶

- *circa 1780*
Large brass flintlock tinderlighter
of fine quality with original stand
and candle holder, frame and
tinder container finely engraved.
- *12cm x 19cm*
- **Guide price** $4,980

Knife Pistol ▲

- *circa 1859*
Unwin & Rogers curiousa knife
pistol featuring nickel barrel with
Birmingham proof marks, horn
side panels, folding trigger, bullet
mould and tweezers.
- *length 17cm*
- **Guide price** $1,690

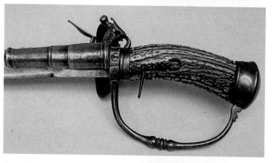

Sword Pistol ▲

- *circa 1720*
Flintlock sword-pistol with top
serrated blade, two stage cannon-
style barrel on left of hilt, all steel
hilt with the shell guard chiselled
with a lion type animal, and
staghorn grip.
- *length 70cm*
- **Guide price** $6,050

Pair of Flintlock Pistols ▶

- *circa 1880*
Pocket flintlock belt pistols by
Sharpe of London fitted with
belthooks, folding triggers,
checkered butts, and top sliding
safeties.
- *length 20cm*
- **Guide price** $3,920

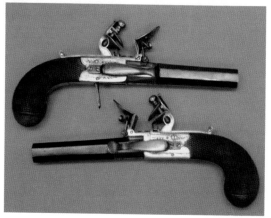

Automobilia

Motor racing and rallies are as popular today as they have ever been along with the collecting of automobile memorabilia.

Since a car is one of the most expensive purchases that people make, there is a great deal of ancillary material, from models, clocks, lights and hub caps, to commemorative badges, posters, paintings and photographs. They all have their collectors and so, they all have a price.

Most automobilia is based around clubs, racetracks and personalities. For example, any memorabilia relating to the Brooklands and Monte Carlo racetracks or the Morgan, Aston Martin and MG car clubs is highly collectable. Collectors are often prepared to pay high prices for a certain badge or mascot to add to their collection.

A huge industry has sprung up around the classic car and for avid colllectors the auto sales held around the country provide an opportunity to acquire prized items such as racing programmes, garage signs, car parts or archival photography. While a vintage car may be too expensive for most people, memorabilia is affordable.

S.A.M.T.C. Lion Badge ▶

- *circa 1960*
S.A.M.T.C. white badge with enamelled crown and badge with rampant lion.
- *14cm x 12cm*
- **Guide price $120**

Eagle Insignia Car Mascot ▼

- *circa 1960*
Square black and white Car Recovery Service Club badge with eagle insignia.
- *height 14cm*
- **Guide price $15**

Chrome Lady Car Mascot ▼

- *circa 1960*
Chrome flying lady mascot for car.
- *height 14cm*
- **Guide price $210**

R.A.C. Key ▼
- *circa 1960*
Metal key, property of the Royal
Automobile Club, London, SW1.
- *height 7cm*
- Guide price $10

Lines Bros. Car ▲
- *1930s*
Morris-type open roadster, pressed
steel with folding windscreen,
period running boards and
opening driver's door.
- *40cm x 90cm*
- Guide price $3,110

A.A. Badge ▲
- *circa 1960*
Automobile Association metal
badge with yellow ochre
background.
- *11cm x 10cm*
- Guide price $40

Horn-Playing Satyr Car Mascot ◄
- *1960s*
A rude devil cocking-a-snook car
mascot for rear mounting.
Chromed brass by Desmo.
- *length 12cm*
- Guide price $270

A.A. key ▲
- *circa 1970*
Metal A. A. key.
- *height 7cm*
- Guide price $5

Word Wildlife Fun Panda Car Mascot ►
- *circa 1960*
World Wildlife Fund badge with a
panda on a bottle green
background being held by a pair
of hands.
- *height 14cm*
- Guide price $40

Expert Tips

Rarity and condition are important in the field of automobile collection. Some knowledge is essential in establishing what is rare as well as documentation to authenticate provenance.

Bentley Mascot ▼
- *1950s*

Bentley flying winged B radiator mounted mascot, designed by Charles Sykes. This example is post World War II and is shown to be leaning forward. Cast brass, chronuim plated.
- *height 7cm*
- **Guide price $450**

Bentley Mascot ▼
- *1920s*

Bentley flying winged B radiator mounted mascot designed by Charles Sykes. This example is from the 1920s roadster sports model and is a large brass-casting used for a short period.
- *wing span 22cm*
- **Guide price $710**

Bentley Winged B ▶
- *1960–80*

Bentley winged B radiator shell badge, pressed steel, chrome-plated with enamel central black B label.
- *height 14.5cm*
- **Guide price $180**

B.A.R.C. Badge ▲
- *1930s*

Brooklands Automobile Racing Club membership badge issued during the inter-war period up until the closure of the circuit in 1939. Die struck brass, chrome plated and vitreous coloured enamels. Produced by Spencer. London. Usually with members issue No. stamped on the reverse.
- *height 14cm*
- **Guide price $710**

Brighton & Hove Motor Club Badge ▲
- *2001*

Brighton & Hove Motor Club badge of the present day, cut brass, chrome and plastic-based enamel colours.
- *diameter 6cm*
- **Guide price $35**

Bentley B ▼
- *1940s*

Bentley flying winged B radiator mounted mascot, designed by Charles Sykes. This example is shown to be leaning backward. Cast brass, chronuim-plated.
- *wing span 17cm*
- **Guide price $535**

Bentley Flying B ▼
- *1920*

Bentley flying winged B radiator mounted mascot designed by Charles Sykes.
- *height 17cm*
- **Guide price $540**

J.C.C. Badge ▼
- *1960–70*

The Junior Car Club existed to cater for light cars and motorcycles including Morgan type three wheelers. Membership badge in die struck brass, nickel or chrome-plated with vitreous enamel colours.
- *height 14cm*
- **Guide price $360**

Morgan Pedal Car ▼
- *1980s*
Morgan Roadster made by The
Morgan Model Co. in moulded
fibreglass with vinyl seat and
dropdown windscreen.
- *35cm x 95cm*
- Guide price $1,690

Brookland's Junior Racing Drivers' Club Badge ▼
- *1930s*
Brookland's Junior Car Club
badge for the Junior Racing
Drivers' Club. Multi-coloured
vitreous enamels on chromed
shield.
- *height 12cm*
- Guide price $2,670

Bugatti Racing Car ▲
- *1990s*
Bugatti type 35 Grand Prix racing
car replica produced by Elantec-
Eureka. Aluminium body,
working gearshift and handbrake
levers and authentic dashboard.
- *50cm x 125cm*
- Guide price $4,900

Brookland's Entry Pass Badges ▲
- *1912*
Brass and enamel Brookland's
annual entry pass badges for
members (large central badge)
and guests pair of brooches in
original box of issue.
- *10cm x 4cm*
- Guide price $450

Pressed Steel Pedal Car ▼
- *1960s*
A Ford style saloon, made by Tri-
Ang Toys Ltd, marketed as a
"Lightning".
- *30cm x 90cm*
- Guide price $220

Austin Pathfinder Pedal Car ▼
- *circa 1949*
Pressed steel monocoque body
with vinyl upholstered seat. Has
dummy engine under removable
bonnet and perspex windscreen.
- *40cm x 1.1m*
- Guide price $4,450

Brookland's Automobile Racing Club Badge ▼
- *1921*
Brookland's Automobile Racing
Club Badge in original box,
membership number stamped on
reverse, brass and red enamel.
- *10cm x 4cm*
- Guide price $450

Books, Maps & Atlases

The binding of a book can considerably add to its appeal and in some cases can be more fascinating than the words contained within.

Books have long been regarded as collectable items, as well as tools for education and entertainment. Although the printing press was introduced just 500 years ago, the first real books appeared shortly after the fall of the Roman empire.

In the 1600s, booksellers at St Paul's Churchyard expected clients to read the latest books unbound before they ordered a copy bound to their taste. Once bound, these books were rarely read, so pristine condition tends to be the norm for that period.

The binding leathers used on a volume give you some idea of its age. Medieval deer or sheepskin editions are very rare; calf with blocked and tooled binding predominated in the sixteenth century when vellum became popular for undecorated books; and goatskin enjoyed a brief popularity in the 1650s.

Today's collector on a budget should try to predict the next bestseller. Failing that, always buy first editions, keep them in mint condition and, if possible, secure the author's signature.

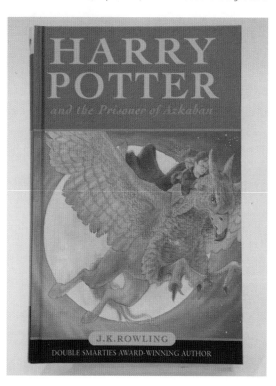

Prisoner of Azkaban ▶
- **1998**

Harry Potter and The Prisoner of Azkaban signed by the author J.K. Rowling. First issue published by Bloomsbury.
- *19cm x 13cm*
- **Guide price $13,350**

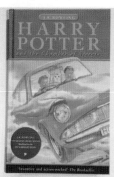

Chamber of Secrets ▲
- **1998**

Harry Potter and The Chamber of Secrets signed by the author J.K. Rowling. First published in Great Britain in 1998 by Bloomsbury, London.
- *19cm x 13cm*
- **Guide price $3,740**

Rebellion and Civil Wars ▼

● *1712*
The History of the Rebellion and Civil Wars in England, begun in the year 1641. Oxford: printed at the Theatre. A very good early edition of Clarendon. Clarendon was Chancellor to both Charles I and Charles II. Panelled calf, banded and ruled in gilt.
● Guide price $880

Dream Days ▼

● *1899*
Dream Days by Kenneth Graham, New York & London.
● Guide price $180

The Noh Plays of Japan ▼

● *1922*
The Noh Plays of Japan by Arthur Waley. New York: Alfred A. Knopf. First American edition. Translations of the most celebrated Noh plays. Eight plates of masks. Original linen-backed boards.
● Guide price $220

Complete English Traveller ▲

● *1771–1773*
The Complete English Traveller by Robert Sanders and Nathaniel Spencer. London: J. Cooke. First edition. A handsome and well illustrated folio containing sixty plates that offer a general survey of the whole of Great Britain.
● Guide price $1,690

A Treatise on Money ▲

● *1930*
A Treatise on Money by John Maynard. New York: Harcourt, Brace & Co. First edition: the American issue of the London sheets. Two volumes. Demy 8vo.
● Guide price $630

The Fortune of War ▼

● *1979*
The Fortune of War, Patrick O'Brian. London: William Collins Sons & Co. First edition. The sixth of the Jack Aubrey and Stephen Maturin novels.
● Guide price $710

Maitland's History of London ▼

● *1756*
Maitland's History of London, Vol I & II. London: for T. Osborn & J. Shipton and J. Hodges. Second edition. Originally published in one volume in 1739. Five general maps (two folding), 19 maps of wards and parishes (five folding); views of over 60 principal buildings on 42 plates (three folding), and over 80 churches.
● Guide price $5,250

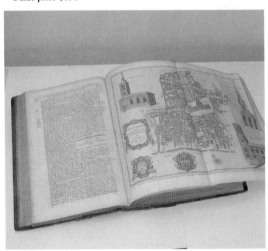

The Life of Count de Grammont ▲
● *18th century*
Memoirs of the Life of Count de Grammont, containing, in particular, the amorous intrigues of the court of England in the reign of King Charles II. Printed: London and sold by J. Round, W. Taylor and J. Brown, 1714.
● **Guide price $630**

Malay Sketches ▲
● *1896*
Malay Sketches by Sir Frank Athelstane Swettenham, the distinguished colonial administrator and linguist. London: John Lane. Second edition (i.e. impression) of the original 1895 publication.
● **Guide price $90**

Orange Fairy Book ▶
● *1906*
First edition of the *Orange Fairy Book* by Andrew Lang. Published in 1906.
● **Guide price $540**

Prehistoric Man ▼
● *1862*
Prehistoric Man by Sir Daniel Wilston. Cambridge: Macmillan & Co. First edition. Extensive researches into the origin of civilisation in the old and the new world. Colour frontispiece. Map bound without half-titles, in a handsome half roan.
● **Guide price $450**

Antiquities of Surrey ▼
● *1736*
Antiquities of Surrey by Nathanael Salmon. London: for the Author. First edition; mottled calf expertly re-backed and refurnished, banded and gilt.
● **Guide price $540**

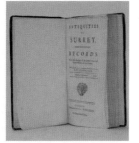

Grimm's Household Tales ▲
● *1946*
Grimm's Household Tales by Brothers Grimm (Jacob Ludwig & Wilhelm Carl). London: Eyre & Spottiswode. Bound in a later full morocco, banded and gilt; all edges gilt.
● **Guide price $450**

Shakespeare ▲
● *1925–32*
The Tragedies, Comedies and Histories of Shakespeare. London. Oxford University Press. A prettily bound set of the three separately published volumes of the Oxford India-paper edition. Edited by W. J. Craig with a full glossary.
● **Guide price $450**

The Saint ◀
- **1961**
The Saint to the Rescue by Leslie Charters, published by Hodder and Stoughton London and printed by G. Bertram.
- *19cm x 13cm*
- **Guide price $390**

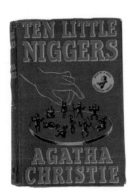

Casino Royale ▶
- **1953**
Casino Royale, author Ian Fleming published by Jonathon Cape, Bedford Square, London. First edition, second issue.
- *19cm x 13cm*
- **Guide price $5,250**

Ten Little Niggers ▲
- **1939**
Ten Little Niggers by Agatha Christie. First edition, published for the Crime Club by Collins, Pall Mall, London.
- *19cm x 13cm*
- **Guide price $11,570**

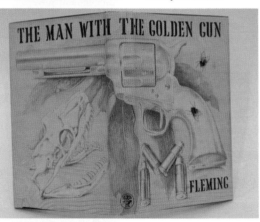

Thunderball ▲
- **1961**
Thunderball by Ian Fleming. First published by Glidrose Publications.
- *19cm x 13cm*
- **Guide price $980**

A Christmas Carol ▶
- **1915**
A Christmas Carol by Charles Dickens, illustrated by Arthur Rackam and published by William Henemahn, London.
- *19cm x 12cm*
- **Guide price $2,580**

The Man with the Golden Gun ▲
- **1965**
The Man with the Golden Gun by Ian Fleming, "The new James Bond". Printed in Great Britain by Richard Cay. The Chaucer Press, Jonathon Cape.
- *19cm x 13cm*
- **Guide price $270**

Expert Tips

With old books and maps look out for foxing, or orange stains, because these types of blemishes can be expensive to remove.

Peer Gynt

- 1920

Peer Gynt, first Rackam edition, published by George G. Harrap & Co. Ltd., illustrated by Arthur Rackam.

- *27cm x 20cm*
- **Guide price $440**

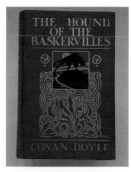

The Hound of the Baskervilles

- 1902

The Hound of the Baskervilles, a Sherlock Holmes adventure by A. Conan Doyle, published George Newnes London.

- *19cm x 14cm*
- **Guide price $4,450**

Tour of the Seine

- 1829

Picturesque Tour of the Seine by Jean Baptiste Balthazar. Illustrated with 24 highly finished and coloured engravings and drawings by A. Pugin and J. Gendall. With a map by R. Ackerman, London 1821. Fine contemporary binding of Blake straight grained Morocco gilt titles and in-filled box design to spine. Raised bands and elaborate gilt border.

- *34cm x 28cm*
- **Guide price $7,560**

Charles Dickens

- 1906

The Works, Letters, and Life of Charles Dickens with plates by illustrators Cruickshank Leech & co., London. The National Edition in 40 vol. Chapman and Hall Ltd., 1906-8 with a signed manuscript and letter addressed to Dr. Hudson in superb contemporary binding by Birsall Morocco with raised bands, gilt titles to spines top edged gilt. The Dr. Hudson to whom Dickens' letter is addressed is presumably Fredrick Hudson, surgeon of Manchester. With regard to the arrangement for the performance of *The Frozen Deep*, the play he wrote with Wilke Collins.

- *18cm x 13cm*
- **Guide price $15,130**

Marine Dictionary

- 1815

A set of five volumes of a marine dictionary explaining the technical terms and phrases with astronomy, navigation, French sea-phrases and terms. Compiled by William Falconer, this volume had been modernised by William Burney. Printed for T. Cadell & W. Davies in the Strand.

- *20cm x 28cm*
- **Guide price $2,580**

Book Sizes

The Folios – when a printed sheet is only folded once, normally used in large format books.

Quatro – Folded twice it forms eight pages and makes rather square-shaped editions.

Octavos – folded three times to make 16 pages.

Twelvemo – makes 24 pages with a complicated fold.

Sixteenmo – same as twelvemo but makes 32 pages.

Treasure Island

- 1890

Second illustrated edition of *Treasure Island* by Robert Louis Stevenson with original illustration by W.A. Page. Published by Cassell and Co. Ltd., London, Paris, New York, and Melbourne.

- *19cm x 14cm*
- **Guide price $850**

Harry Potter Set ▼

- **1997–2000**

An extremely scarce set of first editions of the *Harry Potter* series by J.K. Rowling, which includes: *The Philosopher's Stone, The Chamber of Secrets, The Prisoner of Azkaban* and *The Goblet of Fire*. Published by Bloomsbury, London. All signed.
- *20cm x 13cm*
- **Guide price $48,950**

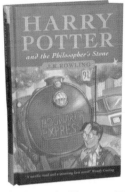

The Cat in the Hat ▼

- **1957**

First edition of *The Cat in the Hat* by Dr. Seuss. Original pictorial paper covered boards complete with dust wrapper. Illustrated throughout by the author.
- *29cm x 21cm*
- **Guide price $15,130**

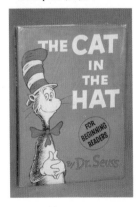

Peter Rabbit ▶

- **1902**

The Tale of Peter Rabbit by Beatrix Potter. First edition, and first issue of the flat spine.
- *14cm x 10cm*
- **Guide price $89,000**

Three Guineas ▲

- **1938**

First edition of *Three Guineas* by Virginia Woolf. Published by The Hogarth Press, London. Pale yellow cloth, gilt titles to spine, complete with dust wrapper. Illustrated with photographic plates.
- *18cm x 12cm*
- **Guide price $890**

Lady Chatterley's Lover ▲

- **1932**

First authorised UK edition of *Lady Chatterley's Lover* by D.H. Lawrence. Publisher's brown cloth with gilt title to spine. Complete with dust wrapper. Published by Martin Secker, London.
- *19cm x 12.4cm*
- **Guide price $800**

Little Lord Fauntleroy ▼

- **1886**

First UK edition of *Little Lord Fauntleroy* by Francis Hodgson Burnett. London: Frederick, Warne and Co. With 26 illustrations after Reginald B. Birch.
- *22cm x 14.5cm*
- **Guide price $370**

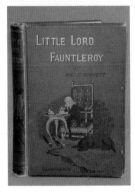

The Hound of Death and Other Stories ▼

- **1933**

The Hound of Death and Other Stories by Agatha Christie. First edition. Published by Odhams Press Limited, London.
- *18.5cm x 13cm*
- **Guide price $630**

Expert Tips

Most paper items are susceptible to damage from ultraviolet (UV) and visible light. If UV is present it should be eliminated using filters over windows and bulbs.

Map of Huntingdonshire ▲

• *1645*

Map of Huntingdonshire by J. Willem Blaeu with the inscription, "Hvntingdo-Nensis Comitatvs, Huntington-shire". Published in Amsterdam. Decorated with a ribanded display of coats or arms, the Stuart Royal Arms, and a hunters and hounds title-piece, with stags, falcon, boar, hare and rabbit. Originally produced by Blaeu in 1645.

• **Guide price $620**

City of London, Westminster and Southwark ▼

• *1720*

A New Plan Of The City Of London, Westminster And Southwark. Published in London: in 1720. Originally produced to accompany John Strype's revised edition of John Stow's 'Survey of London'. The map is dedicated to Sir George Thorold, Lord Mayor in 1719-1720.

• *48.5cm x 66cm*
• **Guide price $1,690**

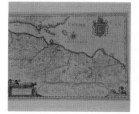

Map of Northumberland ▼

• *1645*

Map Of Northumberland by J. Willem Blaeu, entitled, "Comitatvs Northvmbria; Vernacule Northumberland" and produced in Amsterdam in1645. Decorated with shields, the Royal Arms, a draped title-piece, ships, cherubs, and a scale-bar showing a 17th-century surveyor at work. Copper line engraving on paper. Full contemporary hand colour.

• *41cm x 49cm*
• **Guide price $620**

Map of Lothian ◄

• *circa 1500s*

A map depicting the area of Lothian in Scotland, by the Dutch cartographer Joannes Janssonius, 1646, Amsterdam. A fine example of this well-known map of the Edinburgh region.

• *36.5 cm 54cm*
• **Guide price $710**

Binding Fit for a King ▼

• *1620–1630*

Extremely rare Renaissance gold binding, jewelled and enamelled. Possibly made for King Christian IV of Denmark. Enamelled with a design of different flowers, and a central plaque with the nativity, and decorated with 52 diamonds.

• *9.1cm x 6.4cm*
• **Guide price $151,300**

Map of the Orkney & Shetland Isles ▲

• *1654*

Map of the Orkney and Shetland Isles by Willem Janszoon Blaeu, Amsterdam, 1645. With the inscription, "Oradvm Et SchetandiE Insvlarvm Accuatissima Descriptio". The maps are finely decorated.

• *40.5cm x 53cm*
• **Guide price $620**

London ▲

• *1673*

An early map of London by Wenceslas Hollar, with the coat of arms of the City of London, 15 of the great Livery and Merchant Companies and those of Sir Robert Vyner of Viner.

• **Guide price $710**

Expert Tips

Ensure your hands are clean and dry before handling paper items, as oily skin can cause staining on paper.

Map of Essex ▲

- **1636**

The rare first issue of the
Janssonius map showing Essex,
entitled,"Essexi Descriptio. The
Description Of Essex". First
published in Amsterdam,
Holland, by the Dutch master
Janssonius (1588–1664) in the
"Atlas Appendix" of 1636. With
copper line engravings on paper.
In full contemporary hand colour.
- *38cm x 49cm*
- **Guide price $980**

Map of Norfolk ▼

- *circa 1646*

A fine seventeenth century map
of the county of Norfolk,
England, from the Dutch master
Joannes Janssonius (1588–1664).
The map is highly decorated with
a pastoral cartouche, shields,
putti, sailing ships and a sea
monster. This was originally
produced for the "inovus atlas..."
(Amsterdam 1646).
- *38cm x 49cm*
- **Guide price $700**

Expert Tips

*Providing good storage
conditions and safe handling
are critical to preserving book
collections.*

Map of Scotland ▼

- **1630s**

A decorative map of Scotland by
the Dutch cartographer
Janssonius entitled, "Scotia
Regnvm, Amsterdam" and dated
1636. This map was originally
produced for the "Janssonius
Atlas Appendix" of 1636. It is
decorated with the royal arms,
sailing ships, and a cartouche
featuring unicorns, sheep and
thistles.
- *38cm x 49.5cm*
- **Guide price $880**

Seutter British Isles ◄

- **18th century**

Original hand-coloured map of
the British Isles by Matthaeus
Seutter. A scarce antique map of
the British Isles, with an elegant
military lion and unicorn
cartouche. In another corner an
angel with a trumpet bears aloft
the arms of the four nations, and
sailing ships off the coast.
Originally engraved by Tobias
Conrad Lotter (1717–1777) for
Seutter's Atlas Minor in the
1740s.
- **Guide price $360**

Map of Somerset ▲

- **1630s**

An amorial map of the county of
Somerset, in England by
Janssonius entitled "Somerset-
Tensis Comitatvs Somerset
Shire". Amsterdam: G.Valk & P.
Schenk, 1636. This was first
published by Janssonius (1588-
1664).The map appears here in
its final form, with the addition of
grid lines to the original
Janssonius image.
- *37.5cm x 49cm*
- **Guide price $700**

Merian Map of the
British Isles ▼

- *mid 17th century*

Map of the British Isles from
Mathaus Merian the Elder
(1593–1650). With a baroque
title piece draped in cornucopia,
the Royal Arms and sailing ships.
Originally produced for the
"Neuwe Archontolgia Cosmica"
(Frankfurt 1638) and here in a
later issue, with Merian's name
removed.
- **Guide price $710**

Our Mutual Friend ▼

- **1860**

Our Mutual Friend by Charles Dickens with illustrations by Marcus Stone, published by Chapman & Hall, Piccadilly. Eighteen copies in original condition in two boxes, a further two boxes available.

- *22cm x 19cm*
- **Guide price $2,230**

Second Edition Cook's Voyage ▼

- **1823**

Atlas Volume of *Cooks Voyage*, part of the Earl of Harewoods volume of *Discoveries of the Southern Hemisphere*, illustrating a Lady from Otahiete.

- *57cm x 43cm*
- **Guide price $10,680**

Führer fur Pilzfreunde ▶

- **1897**

Führer fur Pilzfreunde by Edmund Michael, a book on mushrooms with 68 coloured illustrations.

- *20cm x 12cm*
- **Guide price $490**

Polar Seas ▲

- **1823**

Franklin's *Journey to the Polar Seas* by John Franklin Captain R.N. FRS. and Commander of the expedition, including an account of the progress of a detachment to the eastward by John Richardson. MD. FRS. FCS. and surgeon and naturalist to the expedition illustrated with plates and maps. Published by authority of the Right Honourable secretary of State for Colonial Affairs John Murray, London, printed by William Clowes.

- *29cm x 23cm*
- **Guide price $11,120**

Journey through Bootan ▲

- **1806**

A very rare second edition of *A Narrative of a Journey through Bootan, and part of Tibet*, by Samuel Turner with added views by Lieutenant Samuel Davis consisting of 13 folded plates, and one folding map.

- *30cm x 24cm*
- **Guide price $2,580**

African Game Trails ▲

- **1910**

African Game Trails an account of the African wandering of an American hunter-naturalist by Theodore Roosevelt, published by Charles Scribner & Sons, New York. With photographs and foreword by T. Roosevelt, Kartoum, March 15th, 1910.

- *28cm x 20cm*
- **Guide price $760**

First Edition Cook's Voyage ▲

- **1823**

First edition of *Cook's Voyage*, from the *Discoveries in the Southern Hemisphere*, compiled from the journal which was kept by the Commander and from the papers of Joshua Banks ESQ. Printed by W. Stahan and T. Cadell, London.

- *30cm x 23cm*
- **Guide price $10,680**

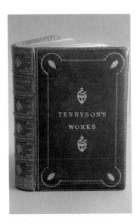

Tennyson's Works ▲
- *1882*

Tennyson's Works published in London by Kegan Paul. Finely bound by Sangorski & Sutcliffe in full-green morocco, spine faded to antique brown, gilt title and decoration to spine. With a fore-edge painting showing "The Lady of Shalott" after William Holman Hunt, and a portrait of Tennyson.
- *18cm x 13cm*
- **Guide price $620**

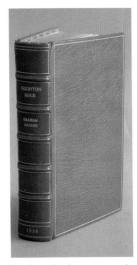

Brighton Rock ▲
- *1938*

First edition of *Brighton Rock* by Graham Greene, published by William Heinemann Ltd London, bound by the Chelsea Bindery.
- *18.5cm x 13cm*
- **Guide price $1,690**

The Poetical Works of Percy Bysshe Shelley ▼
- *1908*

The Poetical Works of Percy Bysshe Shelley. Macmillan and Co., Limited London. Bound by Riviere in full tree calf, and gilt lettered green morocco label and gilt decoration to spine with marbled end papers, all edges gilded.
- *18cm x 12cm*
- **Guide price $850**

La Reine des Neiges ▼
- *1911*

Hans Christian Andersen, *La Reine des Neiges et Quelques Autres Contes*. Illustration by Edmund Dulac. Publishers decorated vellum, with 29 full colour illustrations by Edmund Dulac. Published by H. Piazza. Paris.
- *20.5cm x 24cm*
- **Guide price $1,520**

Kew Gardens ▶
- *1919*

Kew Gardens by Virginia Woolf with woodcuts by Vanessa Bell. There were only 150 copies made and Virginia Woolf set the type.
- *23cm x 14cm*
- **Guide price $32,040**

The Tempest ▲
- *1926*

Deluxe edition of Shakespeare's *The Tempest*, illustrated by Arthur Rackham. Published by William Heinemann Ltd. London. Limited to 520 copies of which this is No. 128. Signed by Rackham.
- *32cm x 26cm*
- **Guide price $5,790**

The Kingdom of the Pearl ▲
- *1920*

The Kingdom of the Pearl by Leonard Rosenthal, illustrated by Edmund Dulac. Limited edition of 675 copies of which this is No. 67. Published by Nisbet & Co. London, with ten captioned tissue-pasted colour illustrations.
- *30cm x 24cm*
- **Guide price $1,070**

Arabian Horse ▶

- *1914*

The Arabian Horse His Country and People by Major General W. Tweedies. C.S.I. with fine coloured illustrations published by William Blakwood and sons, Edinburgh and London bound in green leather.
- *31cm x 25cm*
- **Guide price $3,200**

Hunting with Eskimos ▲

- *1911*

Hunting with the Eskimos by Harry Whitney, a unique record of a sportsman's year among the northernmost tribe. Illustrated with photographs, published by The Century Co., New York.
- *19cm x 15cm*
- **Guide price $130**

The Compleat Angler ▼

- *1866*

The Compleat Angler or The Contemplative Man's Recreation by Charles Cotton and Isaac Walton, published by Henry G. Bolton, Covent Garden, London. Bound in green leather.
- *11cm x 19cm*
- **Guide price $310**

Fishing Stories ◀

- *1913*

First edition of *A Book of Fishing Stories* by F .G. Aflaco. Published by JM Dent and Sons Ltd., Aldine House, Covent Garden and E.P. Dutton & Co., New York
- *30cm x 23cm*
- **Guide price $670**

Expert Tips

A few tips to look after your collection. You can store editions on book shelves but do remember dry heat and sunlight are damaging, as are damp and condensation. If a book needs rebinding leave it to the experts. And remember, book worms come in two forms: don't forget the ones eat the paper paste!

Our Native Songsters ▼

- *1804*

Our Native Songsters by Anne Pratt, author of *Wild Flowers*, published in Brighton, New York by E. and JB Young and Co.
- *6cm x 12cm*
- **Guide price $170**

Mr. Punch on the Links ▼

- *1929*

Mr. Punch on the Links by E.V. Knox consisting of 8 volumes with 32 illustrations, numerous golf anecdotes, and green cloth cover. Published in New York, Rue D Hendle Co. Inc.
- *23cm x 17cm*
- **Guide price $440**

Fruits from the Garden ◀

- *1850*

Fruits from the Garden and Field beautifully illustrated and bound in original tan leather with embossed foliate design.
- *18cm x 14cm*
- **Guide price $400**

Uncle Tom's Cabin ▼

- 1852

Uncle Tom's Cabin or *Life Among the Lowly* by Harriet Beecher Stowe. Boston, John P. Jewett & Company. First edition. Two volumes finely bound by Bayntun-Riviere.

- *height 18cm*
- **Guide price $6,230**

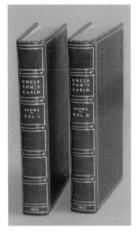

Letters by Mary Wollstonecraft ▼

- 1796

The first account of a business trip made by a woman, Mary Wollstonecraft, written during her short residence in Sweden, Norway and Denmark. Published by J.J. Johnston, St. Paul's Churchyard, London. First edition bound in full tan calf, with gilt lettered and a burgundy label.

- *height 21.5cm*
- **Guide price $2,230**

Gerard Mercator Atlas ▲

- 1632

Gerardi Mercatoris Atlas sive Cosmographicae Meditatones. Amsterdam, Johann Cloppenburg, with fine hand-coloured copperplate "architectural" title and 179 fine recent hand-coloured copperplate maps.

- *22cm x 28cm*
- **Guide price $48,950**

Decline and Fall of the Roman Empire ▲

- 1777

Six volumes of *The History of the Decline and Fall of the Roman Empire,* by Edward Gibbon published London, printed for W. Strahan and T. Cadell. Six volumes four, five and six are first editions. With author's frontis portrait in volume one.

- *height 29cm*
- **Guide price $6,230**

Blackstone Commentaries ▼

- 1765–1769

Blackstone Commentaries by Sir William Blackstone. A rare first edition. With the engraved "Table of Consanguinity" and the "Table of Descents" in Vol II. The date is stamped in black at the base of each spine.

- *28cm x 22cm*
- **Guide price $17,360**

Gone with the Wind ▼

- 1936

Gone with the Wind by Margaret Mitchell. First edition. Macmillan Company, New York. Original publisher's grey cloth, complete with dust wrapper.

- *height 22cm*
- **Guide price $7,030**

Winnie the Pooh ◄

- 1926

Limited to 1/350 *Winnie the Pooh* by A.A. Milne, with wonderful onlaid binding, and decorations by Ernest H. Shephard. Methuen & Co. London, numbered copies, signed by Milne and Shephard.

- *23cm x 17cm*
- **Guide price $15,130**

Natural Order of Plants ▶

- *1868*

One of two volumes of *The Illustrations of the Natural Order of Plants* by E. Twinning with 160 colour plates, published by Sampson Low & Son, Maston.
- *25cm x 17cm*
- **Guide price $1,510**

Rubaiyat ▲

- *1922*

First edition of the *Rubaiyat of Omar Khayyam*. English verse by Edward Fitzgerald with illustrations by Fish. Published by John Lane, London. Plates by Geo. Givvons & Co., Leicester.
- *29cm x 23cm*
- **Guide price $110**

Fragonard ▲

- *1906*

Fragonard, a limited edition of 500 copies with good quality sepia illustrations by Pierre de Nothac Groupil & Co. Editors Manz Joyant & Co. Bound with original red leather.
- *33cm x 28cm*
- **Guide price $980**

Archery ▼

- *1926*

Archery by Robert P. Elms former champion archer of the United States. Published by The Penn Publishing Co., Philadelphia.
- *18cm x 14cm*
- **Guide price $170**

Brazilian Wilderness ▼

- *1914*

Through the Brazilian Wilderness by Theodore Roosevelt, published by Charles Scribner's and Sons, 332 illustrations and map of the entire South American journey and River of Doubt.
- *28cm x 10cm*
- **Guide price $880**

Tess of the D'urbervilles ▼

- *1890*

First edition of *Tess of the D'urbervilles: A Pure Woman* by Thomas Hardy in three volumes. By James R. Oswool McIlvaine & Co., London.
- *18cm x 12cm*
- **Guide price $6,590**

Constant Gardener ◀

- *2001*

The Constant Gardener signed first edition by John Le Carre. Published by Hodder and Stoughton, London.
- *25cm x 18cm*
- **Guide price $150**

Don Quixote ▼

- **1920**

Don Quixote de le Mancha by
Cervantes with 206 illustrations
by Sir John Gilbert R.A. in
original hand back cover.
Published by G. Routledge &
Sons Ltd., New York, E. P. Dutton
& Co.
- *21cm x 18cm*
- **Guide price $80**

The Hobbit ▶

- **1951**

First edition of *The Hobbit or
There and Back Again* by J.R.R.
Tolkien illustrated by Aland Lee,
published by Harper Collins.
- *26cm x 20cm*
- **Guide price $270**

Spaniard in the Works ▲

- **1965**

A Spaniard in the Works, First
edition by the singer songwriter
John Lennon, published by
Jonathan Cape, London.
- *14cm x 10cm*
- **Guide price $250**

Tarantula ▶

- **1966**

First edition of *Tarantula* by the
singer and songwriter Bob Dylan.
- *18cm x 12cm*
- **Guide price $130**

Jane Eyre ▼

- **1847**

First edition of a set of three
leather-bound volumes of *Jane
Eyre: An Autobiography*, published
by Smith Eder & co. Cornhill
London.
- *20cm x 12cm*
- **Guide price $4,450**

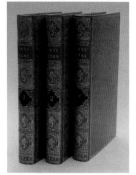

Old French Fairy Tales ◀

- **1920**

Old French Fairy Tales by
Comtesse de Segar illustrated by
Virginia Frances Sterrett,
published in Philadelphia by
Penn Publishing Co.
- *30cm x 26cm*
- **Guide price $1,160**

George and the Dragon ▲

- **1951**

Manifeste Mystique a pen and ink
drawing within a book of *George
and the Dragon*, together with
original etching from a drawing of
the famous Christ of St. John on
the Cross, signed and dated by
Salvador Dali.
- *40cm x 27cm*
- **Guide price $26,700**

The Lion, the Witch and the Wardrobe ▲

- *1950*

The Lion, the Witch and the Wardrobe by C.S. Lewis. First edition. Illustrations and colour frontispiece by Pauline Baynes. The first and best known of the Narnia chronicles. Post 8vo. Bound in an elegant recent green quarter-morocco, banded and gilt. Published by Geoffrey Bles.
- **Guide price $1,510**

Cooke's View of the Thames ▲

- *circa 1811*

Views of the Thames, from the Source to the Sea by Samuel Owen and William Bernard Cooke. London: by W. B. Cooke. Eighty-four tissue guarded etched plates. Contemporary full morocco, all edges gilt.
- **Guide price $1,330**

Expert Tips

When purchasing an illustrated book, make sure that you check that it still contains all the original plates, because if one is missing it could seriously devalue the item.

The Greater London ▼

- *circa 1884*

The Greater London: A Narrative of its History, its People, and its Places by Edward Walford. London: Cassell & Co. Heavily illustrated with 400 wood engravings. Two volumes Crown 4to. Original decorative cloth. gilt.
- **Guide price $350**

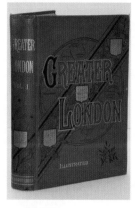

History of Lace ▼

- *1900*

A History of Hand-Made Lace by Emily Jackson. Dealing with the origin of lace, the growth of the great lace centres. Published by Upcott Gill. First edition. Plates and numerous illustrations. Original decorative cloth gilt in an eye-catching lace and cobweb design.
- **Guide price $330**

Sea Kings of Crete ▶

- *1910*

The Sea Kings of Crete by James Baikie. Publishers: Adam & Charles Black, London. First edition. Plates. Maps. Original decorative cloth, top edge gilt.
- **Guide price $130**

Alone ▲

- *1938*

Alone by Richard E. Byrd. Published by Putnam, London. First British edition. Admiral Byrd's harrowing account of his Antarctic sojourn. Decorations by Richard E. Harrison. Demy 8vo.
- **Guide price $110**

Brighton Rock ▲

- *1938*

Brighton Rock by Graham Greene. First edition. Crown 8vo. Bound in a striking full crimson morocco, banded and extra gilt by Bayntun-Riviere. All edges in gilt. Published by William Heinemann.
- **Guide price $1,510**

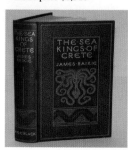

Carpets & Rugs

**European needlework carpets of the nineteenth century have become
an interesting area for the collector.**

Carpets and rugs have a long history, with the oldest surviving pile-knotted rug dating back two-and-half thousand years ago in Siberia. By the Dark Ages, rug-weaving industries had flourished in Egypt, Baghdad, Damascus, Aleppo, and China, but it was not until the seventeenth century that Oriental rugs became popular in European households and were collected and imported. There are few reliable guidelines in this area and success depends greatly on experience and a good eye. However, collectable carpets and rugs are not as expensive as most expect and there are many opportunities to attain woven masterpieces at very reasonable prices.

Persian Jozan Rug ▼
- *circa 1890*
A rare Persian Jozan rug in perfect condition decorated with deer and an angular floral design in ochre, red, blue, green and black.
- *137cm x 204cm*
- **Guide price $8,010**

Baluchi Carpet ▲
- *1860*
Section of a Baluchi carpet from Baluchistan.
- *length 280cm*
- **Guide price $4,980**

Bakhtiari Rug ▼
- *circa 1940*
Bakhtiari rugs woven by nomads and villagers of Luri, Kurdish and other ethnic origins from the Chahar Mahal region of Iran. Featuring a medallion design.
- *140cm x 228cm*
- **Guide price $4,090**

French Panel ◀
- *circa 1760–1780*
French needlepoint panel with central figured cartouche in petit point.
- *51cm square*
- **Guide price $3,470**

Indian Durrie
- *circa 1880*
Indian cotton durrie made by prisoners in the North Indian gaols. Dyed with indigo and turmeric.
- *length 203cm*
- **Guide price $1,320**

Tekke Rug
- *circa 1920*
Acha-Tekke are woven by the famous tribesmen from the Tekke tribe who are noted for their fine work. A geometric design in reds, cream and black.
- *20cm x 200cm*
- **Guide price $2,490**

Melas Rug ►
- *1880*
Melas prayer mat from Turkey, with a central design of a red mosque bordered with rosettes and stars.
- *length 125cm*
- **Guide price $2,230**

Kashan Rug ◄
- *circa 1920*
Kashan pictorial rug with peacocks in red, blue and green design surrounding a central vase.
- *137cm x 207cm*
- **Guide price $8,010**

Kashan Medallion Rug ▲
- *circa 1920*
Kashan rug with classical elongated medallion designs in coral and dark blue and corner decorations. Extremely good example of a curvilinear Persian floral rug.
- *137cm x 207cm*
- **Guide price $8,010**

Anotonian Kilim
- **1920**
Western Anotonian kilim
covering a beechwood chest.
- **50cm x 90cm**
- **Guide price $1,340**

North Persian Runner ▶
- *circa 1890*
Runner from northern Persia.
- **2.5cm x 91cm**
- **Guide price $4,450**

Western Anotonian Kilim Cushion
- **1920**
Western Anotonian kilim
converted into a cushion cover.
- **35cm square**
- **Guide price $80**

Luri Gabbeh Rug
- *circa 1880*
Exceptional Luri Gabbeh banded
design rug from south west Persia
with incredible use of natural
dyes contrasted by woven bands
of cotton pile.
- **length 148cm**
- **Guide price $5,790**

Sharshavan Cushion ▶
- **1920**
Cushion made from a Sharshavan
rug, which was originally part of a
cradle.
- **35cm square**
- **Guide price $120**

Bibibaff Quajquoli ▲
- *circa 1940*
An unusual and fine example of a
Bibibaff Quajquoli.
- **80cm x 118cm**
- **Guide price $1,960**

Karabagh Cushion
- **1920**

Karabagh kilim converted into a cushion cover.
- *35cm square*
- **Guide price $90**

Luri Gabbeth Rug
- ***mid 20th century***

A Luri Gabbeth rug from the Zagros mountains of southern Persia. With bold design of red, blue, brown and cream, the borders with red squares and cream centres.
- *length 180cm*
- **Guide price $2,580**

Turkaman Cushion
- **1860**

Fragment of a Turkaman used as a cushion cover.
- *47cm square*
- **Guide price $270**

Kilim Stool
- **1930**

Anotonian kilim upholstered stool.
- *30cm x 40cm*
- **Guide price $220**

Turkish Yurik Runner
- **1870**

A section of a Turkish Yurik runner with four hexagonal designs of blue, red, green, and gold in the centre panel, surrounded by a pink border with blue flowers.
- *length 300cm*
- **Guide price $3,200**

Bakhtiari Rug ▶
- *circa 1940*

Bakhtiari rug with a glorious central medallion design in blue, green, coral and cream. The reverse of the carpet shows a very open weaving technique with wefts which may have a bluish hue.
- *127cm x 207cm*
- **Guide price $870**

Bownat Marriage Rug
- *circa 1920*

Bownat marriage rug, produced by a small tribe in Southern Iran. The rug shows courting birds and the name and date in Arabic of the couple to be married. These rugs are some of the most beautiful tribal weaving produced today.
- *210cm x 293cm*
- **Guide price $2,940**

Shuli Gabbeth Rug ◄
- **early 20th century**
  Shuli Gabbeh wool rug.
- *length 163cm*
- **Guide price $1,100**

Anotonian Kilim Stool ▲
- **1930**
  Western Anotonian kilim
  covering a stool.
- *width 65cm*
- **Guide price $430**

Thracean Rug ▲
- **circa 1870**
  Thracean kilim from Turkey with
  geometric pattern.
- *119cm x 107cm*
- **Guide price $2,670**

Malayer Runner ▲
- **circa 1880**
  Malayer runner made by the
  Malayers who live 60 miles south
  of Hamadan in West Central
  Persia. The rug is decorated with
  blue, red, ochre and burnt orange
  vegetable dyes.
- *100cm x 490cm*
- **Guide price $5,250**

Luri Jijim Rug ▲
- **20th century**
  Luri Jijim rug with brown, navy,
  blue and cream, woven striped
  design, and navy, blue and red
  binding on the edge.
- *length 283cm*
- **Guide price $1,760**

Expert Tips

*The carpets of Turkoman tribes
are distinguished by a rich and
sombre palette, with different
shades of red, blue and brown,
a geometric design with totemic
symbolism and multiple rows of
medallions known as "guls", a
Persian word for flower.*

Kilim Cushion ►
- **1870**
  Fragment of a kilim from Turkey
  used as a cushion cover.
- *47cm x 38cm*
- **Guide price $270**

Tent Trappings ▲
- **1920**
  Tent trappings in red, purple,
  orange and cream with red,
  yellow and brown tassels.
- *height 50cm*
- **Guide price $120**

Tent Trappings
- *1940*

Tent trappings in red, purple, orange and cream with beaded tassels.
- *55cm x 13cm*
- Guide price $120

Tibetan Wool Rug
- *circa 1890*

Tibetan rug of natural dyes with a red background with three circles in the centre. Wool on warp and weft.
- *length 145cm*
- Guide price $1,690

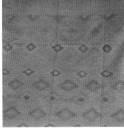

Indian Dhurrie
- *circa 1860*

Indian cotton dhurrie with a blue background with pink and yellow geometric designs and a pink key pattern design, on a yellow background with a yellow border.
- *269cm x 251cm*
- Guide price $4,980

Sarouk Rug
- *circa 1940*

Typical Harati design with a large medallion in the centre, the ground colour is coral with blue, pink and cream. Sarouk is a small village of approximately 1,000 houses, west of Iran.
- *89cm x 118cm*
- Guide price $1,960

Hammadan Runner
- *1870*

Section of a Hammadan runner.
- *length 300cm*
- Guide price $2,670

Western Anotonian Kilim
- *circa 1900*

Western Anotonian kilim converted into a cushion cover.
- *width 65cm*
- Guide price $220

Indian Dhurrie
- *1850*

Indian dhurrie, a blue foliate design and gold torchieries, on a pink background.
- *156cm x 230cm*
- Guide price $1,690

Ceramics

Condition is a major factor when estimating the value of a ceramic as it is very easy for a piece to become damaged.

Ceramics incorporates porcelain, which is translucent, and pottery, which is opaque. Porcelain tends to be more highly valued than pottery, which was often made for practical use, although some highly decorated pottery pieces can be found. Sought-after English pieces include items from the Chelsea factory, Empire-style cabinet wares made by Worcester and Victorian Staffordshire figures. Interest in minor English factories is growing, but collectors need to be familiar with the confusing system of factory markings used.

The eighteenth century was the golden age for European ceramics, when factories in Germany, France and Italy produced a beautiful array of decorative and domestic wares. Oriental porcelain has continued to be very desirable since the seventeenth century, and includes Japanese Imari porcelain, which is noted for its distinctive blue colouring and red gilding, and the traditional Chinese blue-and-white pattern pieces as well as the more colourful pieces they produced for export to the West.

English Ceramics

Pineapple Creamware ▼
- *circa 1765*
A Creamware vase with pineapple and leaf pattern.
- *13cm x 9cm*
- **Guide price $4,360**

Staffordshire Teapot ▲
- *circa 1755*
A small moulded Staffordshire blue and brown agate ware teapot standing on three lion's feet with a reclining lion on the lid.
- *16cm x 20cm*
- **Guide price $7,830**

Green Glazed Jug ◄
- *circa 1670*
Small green jug "Border ware".
- *12cm x 8cm*
- **Guide price $2,230**

Expert Tips

English and European porcelain is increasing in value and is an international commodity. Condition is critical and perfection is the order of the day.

Worcester Mug ▲
● **1780**
Cylindrical Worcester porcelain
tankard decorated with a painted
urn in purple enamel, with
garlands and sprays of
polychrome flowers between
underglaze blue and gilt bands.
Crescent mark.
● *height 13.5cm*
● **Guide price $1,870**

Painted Cup and Saucer ▲
● *circa 1850*
English cup and saucer centred
with a landscape showing a
classical ruin, within a gilded
floral border.
● *height 6cm*
● **Guide price $2,230**

Wileman & Co. Trio ▲
● *circa 1895*
Wileman & Co. The Foley china,
English white cup, saucer and
plate with gilt borders, hand
painted with swallows and
flowers.
● *height 6cm*
● **Guide price $150**

Wedgwood Figure ▼
● *circa 1810*
Unusual English Wedgwood
figure of a young boy feeding a
biscuit to a spaniel on a plinth
base.
● *height 18.5cm*
● **Guide price $1,340**

Worcester Sauce Boat ▼
● **1756**
Worcester cos lettuce moulded
sauceboat, painted with scattered
floral sprays, and a twig moulded
handle. Unmarked.
● *length 8.75cm*
● **Guide price $2,230**

Coalport Cream Jug ▲
● *circa 1835*
Coalport cream jug with gilded
floral designs on a blue ground
with small hand painted panels of
birds.
● *height 12.5cm*
● **Guide price $290**

Caughley Plates ▲
● *circa 1785–90*
One of a pair of Caughley plates
with scalloped edges and
underglaze blue border, probably
painted and gilded at Worcester.
"S" mark in underglaze blue.
● *diameter 23cm*
● **Guide price $1,160**

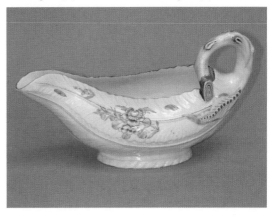

Cauliflower Teapot ▲

- *circa 1765*
Small Staffordshire teapot styled
as a cauliflower, with rustic
handle.
- *height 12cm*
- **Guide price $2,940**

Wedgwood Cup ▲

- *1910*
Wedgwood cup and saucer with
separate silver gilt holder.
- *height 7cm*
- **Guide price $220**

Fulham Pottery ▲

- *circa 1695*
Dwight period tankard with silver
rim from Fulham Pottery.
- *height 15cm*
- **Guide price $5,250**

Goat Jug ▲

- *circa 1750*
Very rare small saltglaze
Staffordshire milk jug styled as
two goats and a bee.
- *height 9cm*
- **Guide price $4,630**

Posset Pot ▼

- *circa 1690*
Staffordshire slipware posset pot,
inscribed with the initials M.S. and
decorated with a jewel-like glaze.
- *13cm x 17cm*
- **Guide price $68,530**

Handwarmer ▼

- *circa 1685*
London or Brislington white tin
glazed handwarmer in the shape
of a book.
- *height 15.2cm*
- **Guide price $34,710**

Crown Ducal Cup and Saucer ◄

- *1930*
Crown Ducal yellow glaze cup and
saucer with a gilded interior.
- *height 5cm*
- **Guide price $130**

Expert Tips

*Staffordshire figures often took
their inspiration from popular
paintings or prints and were
based on actual events such as
the theatre.*

Miniature Ewer and Stand ▼

- *circa 1835*

English ceramics miniature ewer and stand with original porcelain stopper and a painted floral panel set within gilded borders.

- *height 11cm*
- **Guide price $750**

Staffordshire Violinist ▼

- *circa 1840–45*

Staffordshire figure of a violinist in theatrical costume wearing a pink plumed hat.

- *height 21cm*
- **Guide price $460**

Staffordshire Boy Piper ▶

- *1820*

Staffordshire spill holder showing a group with a seated piper playing to a pig and a duck.

- *height 17.2cm*
- **Guide price $1,170**

Chimney Sweep ▲

- *circa 1810*

Early Staffordshire pottery figure of a chimney sweep decorated in overglaze colours.

- *height 18cm*
- **Guide price $790**

Staffordshire Cats ▲

- *circa 1870*

Pair of Staffordshire cats, painted black and white, with yellow collars.

- *height 8cm*
- **Guide price $850**

Staffordshire Spill Vase ▼

- *1815*

Staffordshire pottery "Game Spill" vase of unusual and fine quality in the form of a hollow tree, hung with various game and a hunter's satchel. Pearlware with overglaze enamel colours.

- *height 22cm*
- **Guide price $710**

Staffordshire Country Gentleman ▼

- *1870*

Staffordshire figure of a country gentleman, presenting a basket of trout, whilst standing on a naturalistically styled base.

- *height 25.5cm*
- **Guide price $530**

Staffordshire Figure ▼

- *1890*
Staffordshire model of a lady
seated on a wall, with a swan at
her feet.
- *height 18cm*
- **Guide price $270**

Staffordshire Pheasants ▼

- *1860*
Pair of Staffordshire pheasants
with unusual orange and blue
markings on the wings standing
on a rusticated base.
- *26cm x 12cm*
- **Guide price $2,670**

Leopard Spill Vases ▶

- *1845*
Pair of Staffordshire spill vases
showing two leopards with
bocage, standing on a
naturalistically formed base.
- *16cm x 11cm*
- **Guide price $6,410**

Sailor with Parrot ▲

- *1880*
Staffordshire figure of a man in
theatrical dress with a plumed
hat, holding a parrot.
- *height 20cm*
- **Guide price $310**

Elephant Spill Vases ▲

- *1830*
Pair of grey elephant spill vases
with pink saddles.
- *15cm x 10cm*
- **Guide price $4,800**

Dinner Plate ▼

- *circa 1880*
Blue and white dinner plate
decorated with classical ruins
with a scrolled floral border.
- *diameter 25cm*
- **Guide price $260**

Staffordshire Gardeners ▲
- *circa 1860–70*
Staffordshire spill vase group of two figures, probably gardeners, the man is holding a basket of flowers and there is a potted plant behind the seated girl.
- *height 21cm*
- **Guide price $330**

Staffordshire Soldier ▲
- *1880*
Staffordshire figure of an officer in a blue uniform with gilt buttons and a floral sash, within a bocage.
- *height 15cm*
- **Guide price $310**

Theatrical Dancers ▼
- *1850*
Staffordshire group of theatrical dancers depicting Miss Glover and Mrs Vining as Yourawkee and Peter Wilkins.
- *height 20cm*
- **Guide price $530**

Staffordshire Group ▼
- *1880*
Staffordshire group showing a gentleman with a dog under his arm and a lady wearing tartan.
- *height 17cm*
- **Guide price $400**

Staffordshire Inkwell ▶
- *1880*
Staffordshire inkwell showing a boy and his sister seated on an orange base.
- *height 11.5cm*
- **Guide price $310**

Staffordshire Figure ▲
- *1880*
Staffordshire figure of a girl wearing a blue dress seated on a large, horned goat.
- *height 12cm*
- **Guide price $430**

Staffordshire Children ▲
- *1880*
Staffordshire spill vase with two children seated by the trunk of a tree with a bird resting on a garland of orange flowers.
- *height 14cm*
- **Guide price $400**

Carlton Ware Cup and Saucer ▲

- *circa 1900*

Carlton Ware orange lustre cup and saucer with stylised birds and gilding.
- *height 6cm*
- **Guide price $290**

Hammersely Floral Cup and Saucer ▲

- *circa 1930*

Pink floral Hammersely cup and saucer with floral decoration.
- *height 4cm*
- **Guide price $120**

Green Crown Devon Cup and Saucer ▲

- *circa 1930*

Crown Devon cup and saucer with a green pearlised interior.
- *height 6cm*
- **Guide price $170**

Butterfly Handle Cup ▲

- *1930*

Unusual primrose yellow Ainsley cup with gilt rim on cup and saucer with unusual butterfly handle.
- *height 6cm*
- **Guide price $220**

Royal Worcester ▼

- *circa 1930*

Royal Worcester cup and saucer with a trailing foliate decoration with clusters of berries.
- *height 5.5cm*
- **Guide price $130**

Expert Tips

When washing china or pottery look carefully for old restoration work as immersion in warm water can soften old glues and lead to the undoing of repair work. Ultraviolet light can be used to pick out such defects.

Spode Copeland Cup and Saucer ▼

- *circa 1930*

Spode Copeland cup and saucer with floral sprays.
- *height 4cm*
- **Guide price $120**

Royal Winton ◀

- *circa 1920*

Blue Royal Winton with sprays of apple blossom on a royal blue background.
- *height 6cm*
- **Guide price $170**

Spill Vases ▼
- *1860*

Pair of Staffordshire spill vases modelled as foxes with chickens in there mouths, standing on a foliate base.
- *height 25cm*
- **Guide price $2,850**

St Mark ▲
- *1850*

Staffordshire figure of St Mark with a lion recumbent at his side, on a rock moulded base.
- *height 24cm*
- **Guide price $800**

Little Red Riding Hood ▼
- *1860*

Staffordshire figure of Little Red Riding Hood seated with a fox.
- *height 26cm*
- **Guide price $330**

Staffordshire Actor ▲
- *1855*

Man in theatrical dress sitting on a branch, with a parrot on his shoulder and a spaniel at his side, with gilding on a green foliate base.
- *height 37cm*
- **Guide price $800**

Staffordshire Children ▲
- *1850*

Pair of Staffordshire figures modelled as children playing with rats, raised on oval moulded bases with gilding.
- *height 15cm*
- **Guide price $1,420**

Queen Victoria's Children ▲
- *1880*

Staffordshire group depicting Queen Victoria's children.
- *height 41cm*
- **Guide price $490**

Expert Tips

Some Staffordshire figures were inspired by the famous Newfoundland dog rescuing a child from a river – one of the many faithful and heroic hounds who abound in Victorian literature and art.

Staffordshire Zebras ▲
- *1865*

Pair of prancing Staffordshire zebras on a foliate oval base with gilding.
- *height 16cm*
- **Guide price $1,290**

Staffordshire Group ▲
- *1880*

Ivory Staffordshire group modelled as a cow with her calf, standing on an oval moulded base with gilding.
- *16cm x 21cm*
- **Guide price $620**

Shelley Ceramic ◀

- *1920*

Shelley made cup and saucer with green and black geometric design Art Deco.
- *height 9cm*
- **Guide price $350**

Green Jug ▼

- *circa 1775*

Finely rouletted creamware jug with a green glaze fitted with a double strap handle attributed to the Yorkshire Potteries.
- *height 18cm*
- **Guide price $7,970**

The Tea Party ▼

- *circa 1770*

Wedgwood jug with Liverpool printed cartouche of a tea party on one side and a pastoral scene on the other.
- *14cm x 10cm*
- **Guide price $330**

Shield Toby Jug ▼

- *circa 1775*

Very rare Shield Toby Jug. Derives its name from the applied plaque on the side, which reads "It is all out then fill him again".
- *23cm x 18cm*
- **Guide price $25,810**

Staffordshire Lions ▼

- *circa 1820*

Staffordshire lion and lioness, standing on an oval base.
- *8cm x 12cm*
- **Guide price $5,070**

Shelley Cup and Saucer ▲

- *1930*

Hand-painted Shelley dainty shape cup and saucer with orange and yellow floral spray of flowers.
- *height 10cm*
- **Guide price $330**

Wedgwood Teapot ▲

- *circa 1765*

Liverpool Wedgwood creamware teapot with a cartouche of a gentleman giving a gift to a lady and child seated beneath a tree.
- *13cm x 19cm*
- **Guide price $1,170**

Blackware Teapot ▼

- *circa 1765*

Small blackware teapot, with ear shaped handle and a raised floral design, on pad feet, with a bird finial lid.
- *height 8cm*
- **Guide price $850**

Saltglazed Jug ▼

- *13th century*

Saltglazed jug of bulbous form, with strap handle and turned decoration to the neck.
- *height 22cm*
- **Guide price $2,310**

Blackware Bowl ▲

- *circa 1765*

Blackware bowl decorated with a raised design of gilt fruit and trailing foliage.
- *diameter 14cm*
- **Guide price $1,175**

Blackware Coffee Pot ▲

- *circa 1765*

Blackware coffee pot, raised on three feet with a pinched lip, moulded handle and a bird finial cover.
- *height 15cm*
- **Guide price $980**

English Sauce Tureen ◄

- *circa 1820*

English blue and white sauce tureen and cover on fitted base with a landscape depicting grazing rabbits within a country setting.
- *height 17cm*
- **Guide price $670**

Earthenware Jug ▼

- *12th century*

English earthenware vessel with a dark green glaze and circular design around the neck found at Sible Headingham, Essex.
- *height 29cm*
- **Guide price $9,790**

Sauce Tureen ▼

- *circa 1820*

India flowers sauce tureen and cover, with floral sprays on a red ground with gilding and acanthus leaf decoration (known as clobbered).
- *height 17.5cm*
- **Guide price $930**

Creamware Teapot ▼

- *circa 1795*

Creamware teapot with a foliate pattern in green and a central cartouche painted with a basket of wild flowers.
- *height 17cm*
- **Guide price $840**

Creamware Teapot ▶
- *circa 1775*
Small creamware teapot with a red and black mottled design, twig spout and handle and a red finial cover.
- *14cm*
- **Guide price $1,340**

Davenport Tureen and Cover ▲
- *circa 1820*
Davenport polychrome sauce tureen and cover, on fixed stand with chinoiserie designs within a key pattern border, with gilt-banding and a leaf-shaped finial.
- *height 17cm*
- **Guide price $410**

Wedgwood Teapot ▲
- *circa 1790*
Small Wedgwood teapot decorated with a tulip pattern in magenta, with designs on spout and handle with a flower finial cover.
- *height 12.5cm*
- **Guide price $750**

Swansea Pinwheel Pepperpot ▲
- *1870*
Swansea blue and white "Pinwheel" pepperpot of bulbous form raised on a splayed foot.
- *height 11cm*
- **Guide price $480**

Stone China Vase ◀
- *circa 1825*
One of a set of four stone china vases decorated with an apple blossom design with gilt-banded decoration.
- *height 11cm*
- **Guide price $640**

Swansea Moulded Jug ▼
- *circa 1825*
Swansea daisy pattern, moulded jug, with "C" scroll handle and shaped lip with red, blue, green and white stripes and a black diagonal stripe across the body.
- *height 22cm*
- **Guide price $270**

Pearlware Jug ▼
- *circa 1815*
Pearlware moulded jug decorated with pink roses, cornflowers and leaves, with black-banded decoration.
- *height 12cm*
- **Guide price $220**

Pearlware Mug ▼

- *circa 1780*
Baddeley-Litter Staffordshire
Pearlware mug.
- *height 13cm*
- **Guide price $2,760**

Red Barn ►

- *circa 1828*
A Staffordshire table group of the
"Red Barn".
- *height 23.5cm*
- **Guide price $25,810**

Dr. Syntax ◄

- *circa 1820*
Staffordshire figure of Dr. Syntax
modelled as a seated figure
holding a book and pen.
- *height 14cm*
- **Guide price $1,760**

Dr. Syntax ▲

- *circa 1820*
Staffordshire figure of Dr. Syntax
modelled with his hands tied to
a tree.
- *height 15cm*
- **Guide price $1,510**

Royal Doulton Cup and Saucer ◄

- *circa 1930*
Cream Royal Doulton cup and
saucer with sprays of violets and
gilding to rim of cup and handle.
- *height 9cm*
- **Guide price $100**

Paragon Art Deco Cup and Saucer ▲

- *circa 1920*
Fine Paragon pink floral Art
Deco cup and saucer.
- *height 10cm*
- **Guide price $80**

Queen Anne Shelly Cup and Saucer ◄

- *circa 1927*
White hand-painted Shelley cup
with saucer with black trailing
vine and yellow pink and blue
stylised flowers.
- *height 8cm*
- **Guide price $150**

Derby Squab Tureen ▶

- *circa 1760*

Finely painted Derby Squab tureen, naturalistically styled as a bird, with floral encrustation.
- *height 10cm*
- **Guide price $6,050**

Charles Bourne Vase ▲

- *circa 1820*

Charles Bourne vase with a band of finely painted flowers, between gilded floral borders on a blue ground.
- *height 15cm*
- **Guide price $860**

Yates Egg Cups ▼

- *circa 1820*

An early and rare set of six egg cups with stand by Yates, with finely painted flowers between scrolled cartouches, centred with birds.
- *height 5cm*
- **Guide price $1,340**

Chelsea Dish ▲

- *circa 1750*

Chelsea lozenge-shaped dish decorated with floral sprays of pink roses, with a scalloped edge with gilt trim and scrolling.
- *diameter 25cm*
- **Guide price $2,580**

Worcester Dish ▼

- *circa 1750*

Worcester dish in the form of a leaf, centred with a floral spray of roses and wild flowers, with a soft green border.
- *diameter 18cm*
- **Guide price $3,520**

Chelsea Derby Mug ◀

- *1770*

Chelsea Derby white mug delicately painted in a soft palette with a spray of pink roses, with scrolled handle and gilt rim.
- *height 10cm*
- **Guide price $1,960**

Derby Figures ▼

- **1765**

Pair of Derby figures of a young girl holding a basket and her companion holding a lamb under his arm, standing on a scrolled base scattered with flowers.
- *height 24cm*
- **Guide price $6,410 the pair**

Worcester Creamer ▼

- *circa 1765*

Worcester cream jug with a central cartouche of two Chinese men in a landscape carrying a lantern, and a blue floral design on the inside of the moulded rim.
- *height 7cm*
- **Guide price $1,350**

Derby Figure ▲

- *circa 1770*

Derby figure of a young maiden wearing a white dress and bonnet holding a basket of green and red grapes under her arm, on a circular base with gilt banding.
- *height 14cm*
- **Guide price $2,100**

Bow Candleholder ◄

- *circa 1760*

Bow candleholder encrusted with yellow and pink flowers around the trunk of a tree with two pheasants perched on the top and a central flower candleholder.
- *height 23cm*
- **Guide price $3,290**

Expert Tips

Slip combing is the technique of applying two colours of slip and combing one over the other to produce a feathered surface.

Bow Plates ▼

- *circa 1760*

One of a pair of octagonal Bow plates decorated with the Quail pattern, showing a chinoiserie tree with terracotta and gold flowers and a terracotta trim linked with gold.
- *diameter 22cm*
- **Guide price $2,990**

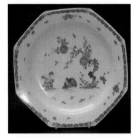

Bow Grape Sellers ▲

- *circa 1760*

Pair of Bow figures, of a young girl wearing a pink hat with finely painted dress of pink flowers and boy seated with matching breeches, and outstretched arm holding grapes.
- *height 16.5cm*
- **Guide price $6,760 pair**

English Danielle Cups with Saucer ◀

- *circa 1830*
Trio of two cups and one saucer early English Danielle, hand painted blue with cartouches of pink and yellow flowers with sprays of gilt folia with gilt rim and handle.
- *height 7cm*
- **Guide price $240**

Coalport Trio ◀

- *circa 1900*
Coalport cup, saucer, and plate with sprays of roses and blossom with gilding to rim of cup and handle.
- *height 7cm*
- **Guide price $220**

Royal Paragon Trio ▲

- *circa 1930*
Royal Paragon cup, saucer and plate painted with yellow blue and pink flowers and three green circular green bands and stylised handle.
- *height 9cm*
- **Guide price $150**

Paragon Trio ▲

- *circa 1920*
Paragon trio with octagonal plate with orange floral sprays, dramatic black and orange handle.
- *height 7.5cm*
- **Guide price $200**

Foley Trio ▲

- *circa 1920*
Trio of cup saucer and plate with orange flowers and banding with an unusual geometric handle.
- *height 8cm*
- **Guide price $130**

Expert Tips

Doulton was made from about 1820 to 1854 – go for named artists like George Tinworth, Hannah Barlow and Frank Butler.

Burleigh Ware Cup and Saucer ▲

- *circa 1930*
Burleigh Ware cup and saucer with painted daffodils and leaves and rusticated leaf handle.
- *height 7cm*
- **Guide price $80**

Bell-shaped cup ▲

- *circa 1920*
Ainsley bell-shaped cup saucer and plate with a profusion of yellow and white flowers.
- *height 7cm*
- **Guide price $130**

Royal Doulton Pepper Pot ▲

- *1884*

Royal Doulton pepper pot with blue glazed neck decorated with a raised, repetitive design, above a turned body, raised on a moulded foot.

- *height 8cm*
- **Guide price $120**

Doulton Jug ▲

- *1876*

Royal Doulton Lambeth jug designed by Frank Butler with a silver lid and thumb piece, the body decorated with a stylised leaf pattern, with jewelling.

- *height 17cm*
- **Guide price $420**

Fruit Bowl ▲

- *1920*

Blue and white fruit bowl with a rural scene with cows in the foreground, within a bold floral border.

- *diameter 19cm*
- **Guide price $250**

Staffordshire Figure of Neptune ▼

- *1830*

Figure of Neptune with trident, standing on a rock encrusted with seashells with a sea monster at his feet.

- *height 18cm*
- **Guide price $880**

Davenport Stilton Dish and Cover ▼

- *1860*

Davenport blue and white stilton dish and cover decorated with a Chinoiserie harbour scene.

- *height 35cm*
- **Guide price $4,630**

Staffordshire Group ▶

- *1850*

Staffordshire figure of a lady wearing a pink top with a floral skirt holding a baby, with a child at her side.

- *height 23cm*
- **Guide price $700**

Staffordshire Group ▲

- *1850*

Staffordshire group seated on a mossy bank with a tree in the background.

- *height 25cm*
- **Guide price $1,060**

Staffordshire Musician ▲

- *1840*

Staffordshire figure of a musician wearing a yellow hat with blue plumes, holding a mandolin with a lamb and flowers at his feet.

- *height 24cm*
- **Guide price $760**

Newhall Jug ▲
● *1814*
Newhall cream jug with pinched lip, decorated with a floral ribbon design and raised on a moulded foot.
● *height 9.5cm*
● **Guide price $500**

Newhalls Walberton Teapot ▲
● *1810*
Newhalls Walberton patent teapot and cover, with a gilt finial lid and foliate designs. The body is profusely gilded and decorated with a painted landscape, with a blue enamelled band at the base of the spout.
● *height 16cm*
● **Guide price $2,300**

Pepper Pot ▼
● *1884*
Royal Doulton pepper caster of bulbous form, with pewter cover and finial top, the neck and body decorated with a stylised leaf design, with jewelling.
● *height 10cm*
● **Guide price $170**

Mason's Jug ▲
● *1812*
Small Mason's jug with scrolled handle and pink Imari design around the body, with gilt trailing foliage and banding.
● *height 7cm*
● **Guide price $300**

Derbyshire Bowl ▼
● *1810*
Derbyshire double-handled sugar bowl, decorated with a pink heart shaped pattern and gilt foliate designs and banding.
● *height 9cm*
● **Guide price $640**

Worcester Sauce Tureen ▲
● *1820*
Worcester double-handled sauce tureen, finely painted with a floral design on a yellow, white and grey enamel, with gilt acorn finial.
● *height 14cm*
● **Guide price $850**

Staffordshire Archer ▲
● *1840*
Staffordshire figure of a lady archer wearing a plumed hat and green coat, holding a bow and arrow, standing on a plinth base.
● *height 17cm*
● **Guide price $530**

Coral Firs Cup and Saucer ▼

- *circa 1930*

A Clarice Cliff "Coral Firs" design from the Bizarre range with stylised terracotta trees.
- *height 9cm*
- **Guide price $590**

Clarice Cliff Trio ▲

- *circa 1930*

Clarice Cliff orange green and cream star decoration cup, saucer and plate.
- *height 7cm*
- **Guide price $700**

Burleigh Ware Cup and Saucer ◄

- *circa 1930*

Burleigh Ware cup and saucer with painted daffodils and leaves and rusticated leaf handle.
- *height 7cm*
- **Guide price $80**

Pink Floral Trio ▲

- *circa 1930*

Royal Doulton trio with pink floral design and a blue and cream gilded background.
- *height 8cm*
- **Guide price $130**

Expert Tips

Minton was founded in 1793 and is one of the finest potteries. Early Minton has the letter "L" painted sometimes with a number under it. Tea and dessert services were beautifully decorated – names to look for are Joseph Bancroft, George Hancock, and Thomas Steel.

Pink Azalea Trio ◄

- *1950*

Pink Azalea cup, saucer and plate trio, by Susie Cooper.
- *height 8cm*
- **Guide price $100**

Susie Cooper Trio ◄

- *1950*

"Green Dresden Spray" two tone green cup, saucer and matching plate trio with floral entwined sprays by Susie Cooper.
- *height 5cm*
- **Guide price $90**

Crown Devon Trio ▲

- *1950*

Crown Devon cup saucer and plate, with exotic birds their wings outstretched on a red glazed background.
- *height 8cm*
- **Guide price $290**

Worcester Dish ▶

- *circa 1768*

Worcester oval Imari pattern dish with a central cartouche of a pagoda and a orange blossom tree with clouds to the side, and twig orange handles.
- *length 28cm*
- Guide price $20,470

Worcester Tea Bowl ▼

- *1760*

Small Worcester tea bowl decorated with a courting couple in a classical setting, a small dog and garden roller in the foreground.
- *height of bowl 5cm*
- Guide price $1,000

Worcester Jug ▼

- *circa 1765*

Small Worcester jug decorated with a spray of pink flowers, with an orange line and scalloping on the inside of the rim.
- *height 8.5cm*
- Guide price $1,740

Chelsea Dish ▼

- *circa 1760*

Chelsea dish in the shape of a peony encircled by a green leaf, with a turquoise handle in the shape of a branch with a bud.
- *diameter 19cm*
- Guide price $4,810

Longton Hall Plate ▼

- *circa 1755*

Longhton Hall plate decorated with a raised design of strawberries and flowers, with a central panel of birds and a parrot in a tree.
- *diameter 24cm*
- Guide price $3,360

Worcester Jug ▲

- *1805*

Worcester jug with terracotta, dark blue and white floral and scroll design, with gold trim on rim and handle.
- *height 18cm*
- Guide price $2,280

Crown Ducal Breakfast Set ◀

- *1930*
Crown Ducal breakfast set, in the Wild Rose design.
- *height 7cm*
- **Guide price** $80

Chrysanthemum Trio ▲

- *1895*
Charles Wileman chrysanthemum pattern cup and saucers
- *height 6cm*
- **Guide price** $120

Purple Iris Trio ◀

- *1920*
Royal Doulton trio decorated with purple irises, having unusual rusticated leaf design handle.
- *height 8cm*
- **Guide price** $260

Daisy-shaped Trio ▲

- *1897*
Daisy shape with Snowdrop design by Charles Wileman.
- *height 6cm*
- **Guide price** $170

Coalport Trio ▲

- *1920*
Coalport matching trio with blue floral design and gilding to rim cup and handle.
- *height 7cm*
- **Guide price** $170

Blue Floral Trio ◀

- *1920*
Matching cup, saucer, and plate by Royal Doulton with unusual blue floral design and bronze and gold sponge underglaze.
- *height 6.5cm*
- **Guide price** $130

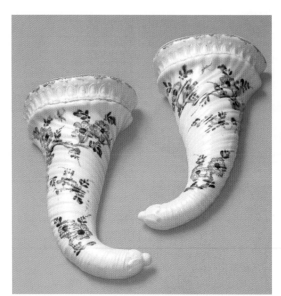

Worcester Cornucopias ◄

- *circa 1756–1758*

Pair of blue and white moulded Worcester cornocupias decorated with small blue flowers. Workman's mark.
- *height 22cm*
- **Guide price $8,010**

Large Worcester Mug ▲

- *circa 1805*

Large Worcester mug, with two yellow enamel bands between gilt banding and a central repetitive design of stylised feathers.
- *height 12cm*
- **Guide price $1,210**

Minton Cup ▼

- *circa 1805*

Minton cup decorated with three cartouches and a foliate design in terracotta, set amongst profuse gilding. With mark on base: M.205.
- *height 6.5cm*
- **Guide price $250**

Lowestoft Tea Bowl ▲

- *circa 1760*

Lowestoft tea bowl decorated with a blue and white chinsoserie scene depicting a house behind a wall with a tree and birds.
- *height of bowl 5cm*
- **Guide price $1,230**

Worcester Tea Bowl ▲

- *circa 1740*

Worcester octagonal tea bowl with finely painted sprays of flowers and insects with gilding, from the studio of James Giles.
- *height 5cm*
- **Guide price $750**

Pinxton Jug ►

- *circa 1805*

Small Pinxton cream jug with a scrolled handle and shaped rim with blue banding. Delicately painted body with three fuchsia sprigs.
- *height 10cm*
- **Guide price $1,230**

Grindly Floral Trio ◀

- *1920*

Hand-painted Grindley cup,
saucer and plate with yellow
floral decoration and a pale pink
raised background.
- *height 9cm*
- **Guide price $100**

Limoges Cup and Saucer ▼

- *circa 1875*

Limoges cup, saucer and plate,
gilded, with clusters of roses.
- *height 7cm*
- **Guide price $80**

Melba Nasturtium Trio ▲

- *1931*

Unusual octagonal Melba trio
with yellow and orange
nasturtiums and floral handle.
- *height 8cm*
- **Guide price $100**

Shelley Vogue Trio ▲

- *1930*

Shelley Vogue trio with various
shades of green with a triangular
shape handle.
- *height 7cm*
- **Guide price $490**

Spode Copeland Trio ▲

- *1910*

Spode Copeland trio with pale
pink roses, gilding on a dark blue
background.
- *height 6.5cm*
- **Guide price $120**

Charles Wileman Snowdrop Trio ◀

- *circa 1895*

Charles Wileman trio shaped as
snowdrops.
- *height 8cm*
- **Guide price $200**

Crescent Trio ◄

- *circa 1900*

English Crescent china trio with garlands of pink roses, gilding to cup and handle.
- *height 7cm*
- Guide price $100

Ainsley Trio ▲

- *circa 1900*

Ainsley royal blue trio with gilding.
- *height 7cm*
- Guide price $80

Ainsley Floral Trio ▶

- *circa 1895*

A Victorian Ainsley ceramic trio with a cluster of roses and foliage.
- *height 7.5cm*
- Guide price $70

Wedding Band Cup and Saucer ▲

- *circa 1930*

Susie Cooper coffee cup with a wedding band pattern.
- *height 7cm*
- Guide price $80

Staffordshire Jug ▶

- *1830*

A transfer printed rare Staffordshire jug with a verse for each month of the year and pictures of a mother and her children.
- *20cm x 17cm*
- Guide price $1,960

Drabware Urns ◄

- *1828*

A pair of Drabware urns with blue and white flowers on a green underglaze pattern.
- *20cm x 15cm*
- Guide price $1,510

Expert Tips

Spode was started in 1770 by Josiah Spode, whose son invented bone china (made with bone ash). The most collected are enamel, painted items by Henry Daniel.

Soup Tureen
- 1827

Soup tureen manufactured by Jones to celebrate the Coronation of George IV.
- *height 31cm*
- **Guide price $2,270**

Leeds Egg Cup
- 1820

Leeds blue and white egg cup decorated with two boys fishing beside a river within a parkland setting.
- *height 7cm*
- **Guide price $350**

Dresden Sauceboat
- 1225

Dresden sauceboat with scrolled handle, shaped lip, vase and floral decoration, raised on a moulded, splayed foot.
- *height 8cm*
- **Guide price $210**

Platter
- 1820

Blue and white platter with a moonlit naval battle scene surrounded by tropical shells and fauna.
- *width 53cm*
- **Guide price $2,400**

Tea Bowl and Saucer
- 1790

Pearlware tea bowl and saucer, with finely fluted decoration, painted with a dark blue trailing band with stylised flowers.
- *diameter 8.5cm*
- **Guide price $350**

Ewer and Bowl
- 1820

Blue and white ewer and bowl decorated with a view of Worcester, and the word "Worcester" inscribed on the base.
- *height of jug 20cm*
- **Guide price $870**

King of Prussia Teapot ▶
- *1765*

Staffordshire salt glaze teapot with black arrow pattern, and a cartouche of the King of Prussia with stylised twig handle, spout and finial top.
- *height 9cm*
- **Guide price $6,850**

Creamware Teapot ▲
- *1765*

English creamware teapot with farm hands resting in a pastoral setting, and a cottage on the reverse, with leaf designs to the handle and spout.
- *height 10cm*
- **Guide price $1,960**

Saltglaze Teapot ▲
- *circa 1765*

Staffordshire salt glaze teapot decorated with pink wild flowers on a crimson ground, with twig handle and spout.
- *height 10cm*
- **Guide price $3,740**

Staffordshire Teapot ▲
- *circa 1765*

Staffordshire salt glazed teapot with a musician wearing a pink jacket and a black hat, in chinioserie style, playing a flute, whilst seated on a riverbank.
- *height 9.4cm*
- **Guide price $6,500**

Staffordshire Creamer ▼
- *circa 1765*

Early Staffordshire creamer with the inscription "William Dixson" within a cartouche of flowers. The side of the jug is a painted figure of a musician wearing a red jacket and black tri-cornered hat.
- *height 18.4cm*
- **Guide price $12,190**

Staffordshire Sauceboat ▼
- *circa 1745*

Staffordshire sauce boat with a scrolled handle, decorated with a pink house and clouds, with shaped rim and foot.
- *height 8cm*
- **Guide price $3,290**

Saltglazed Stand with Teapot ▼
- *circa 1755*

Staffordshire teapot decorated with green and yellow vases and foliate design around the handle and spout, and standing on three raised feet.
- *height 8cm*
- **Guide price $7,030**

Staffordshire Greyhounds ▼
- *1860*
Pair of terracotta greyhounds recumbent on a cobalt blue base.
- *height 9cm*
- **Guide price $530**

Terracotta Greyhounds ▼
- *1890*
Pair of Staffordshire terracotta greyhounds sitting attentively on a circular moulded base.
- *height 10cm*
- **Guide price $530**

Staffordshire Group ▼
- *1830*
Unusual Staffordshire group depicting a dog with puppies and a cat with kittens.
- *height 11cm*
- **Guide price $4,450**

Staffordshire Giraffes ▼
- *1900*
Pair of Staffordshire giraffes reclining by a palm tree, on an oval moulded base.
- *height 14cm*
- **Guide price $4,800**

Staffordshire Lions ▲
- *1860*
Pair of Staffordshire lions with a lamb resting at their side, reclining on an oval moulded base, with gilding.
- *27cm x 17cm*
- **Guide price $11,570**

Spill Vases ▲
- *1845*
Staffordshire spill vases modelled as a pair of lions with bocage, standing on an oval base with gilding.
- *height 14cm*
- **Guide price $4,270**

Expert Tips

Functional redwares made from alluvial clay, were first made in America from around 1625 and continued well into the nineteenth century. New England pieces tend to be plain, though often with richly coloured glazes.

Creamware Baskets ◀

- *circa 1820*
One of a pair of Spode creamware baskets with oval stands.
- *8cm x 26cm*
- **Guide price $1,160**

Vegetable Tureen ▲

- *circa 1830*
A Masons ironstone vegetable tureen with lid, orange chrysanthemums and pink roses and gilding to handle.
- *21cm x 35cm*
- **Guide price $620**

Blue and White Footbath ◀

- *circa 1820*
English footbath with a figure of a seated shepherd playing a musical instrument to his sheep.
- *24cm x 51cm*
- **Guide price $4,450**

Wedgwood Plaque ▶

- *circa 1800*
A black and white Wedgwood plaque depicting Domestic Employment by Lady Templeton. Unrecorded.
- *16cm x 47cm*
- **Guide price $6,230**

Ironstone Vases ▼

- *circa 1830*
One of a pair of Ironstone Vases with lids, terracotta and royal blue flowers and gilding.
- *41cm x 23cm*
- **Guide price $3,290**

Blue and White Platter ▶

- *circa 1830*
English blue and white platter.
- *45cm x 53cm*
- **Guide price $980**

Staffordshire Group ▼

- *circa 1850*
Early Staffordshire brown and
white spaniel with puppy, resting
on an oval white base with
gilding.
- *height 8.5cm*
- **Guide price $820**

Copper Lustre Jug ▼

- *circa 1840*
Large copper lustre jug with
moulded band of shamrocks and
thistles in pale blue relief.
- *height 19cm*
- **Guide price $370**

Ralph Wood Group ▲

- *1785*
Fine quality Ralph Wood group of
the "Vicar and Moses" showing
two seated figures, painted in
brown and grey hues.
- *height 23.5cm*
- **Guide price $2,940**

Staffordshire Stag ▼

- *1810*
Fine quality Staffordshire pottery
stag shown recumbent on a
naturally formed oval base.
- *height 19cm*
- **Guide price $1,320**

Samuel Alcock Spaniel ▲

- *circa 1835*
Samuel Alcock model of a brown
and white spaniel sitting
attentively on a yellow base.
- *height 14cm*
- **Guide price $780**

Staffordshire Figure ▲

- *circa 1810*
Staffordshire pottery figure of
Iphegenia shown gathering her
skirts with her head to one side
- *height 18.5cm*
- **Guide price $1,510**

Musician ▲

- *circa 1840*
Small figure of a boy musician,
playing a penny whistle with a
poodle at his side.
- *height 16cm*
- **Guide price $380**

Waterloo Jug ▲

- *circa 1830*

English water jug with floral
pattern with the words "Waterloo
Band".

- *25cm x 22cm*
- **Guide price $2,230**

Fruit Dish ▲

- *circa 1805*

Fruit dish with blue flowers and
gilding.

- *11cm x 38cm*
- **Guide price $1,690**

Calypso Pot ◄

- *circa 1980*

Black and turquoise lustreware
Poole Calypso range pottery.
Owned by Lord Queensbury.

- *height 25cm*
- **Guide price $1,070**

Festival of Britain ▲

- *1952*

Tulip-shaped vase designed by
Alfred Reed for the Festival of
Britain with cream stripes and
oblong design circling the vase.

- *height 20cm*
- **Guide price $410**

Honiton Pottery
Water Jug ▲

- *circa 1930*

Bulbous-shaped water jug by
Honiton pottery with a foliate
and a floral design.

- *height 55cm*
- **Guide price $200**

Cruet Set ◄

- *circa 1950*

Festival of Britain cruet set
designed by Alfred Reed with a
lattice pattern.

- *height 8cm*
- **Guide price $100**

Pink Lustre Jug ▼
- *1825*

Pink lustre jug which is part of a set of ten cups and saucers with cream jug and two small bowls.
- *height 7cm*
- **Guide price** $500

Swansea Mug ▼
- *1870*

Blue and white Swansea mug with chinoiserie decoration and a bamboo moulded handle.
- *height 18cm*
- **Guide price** $610

Winchester Measure Jug ▲
- *1815*

Winchester measure jug with scrolled handle and pinched lip, with moulded leaf design around the neck and blue banded decoration.
- *height 14cm*
- **Guide price** $520

Blue and White Jug ▲
- *1817*

Large blue and white jug decorated with an Indian hunting scene with elephants and hounds giving chase to a tiger.
- *height 28cm*
- **Guide price** $3,030

Lustreware Jug ▼
- *1826*

Pink lustreware jug inscribed "John Evendon aged 17, 1826" with a view of the River Wear in Sunderland.
- *height 12.5cm*
- **Guide price** $250

Wine Jug ◄
- *circa 1820*

Large blue and white wine jug, with a scene depicting wine makers at the press, with vine and fruit decoration.
- *height 24cm*
- **Guide price** $2,050

Sugar Bowl ▼
- *1825*

Dawson Squire and Lackey blue and white sugar bowl, with cover and finial lid, decorated with a scene depicting a castle in a parkland setting.
- *height 10cm*
- **£435**　　　　　• **Libra**

Reed Bowl ◄
- **1950**

Alfred Reed design bowl with grey glaze and a lattice design in red and white.
- *diameter 20cm*
- **Guide price $370**

Butter Dish ◄
- *circa 1930*

Cream Poole Pottery butter dish designed by Truda Carter with yellow and red flowers.
- *height 9cm*
- **Guide price $130**

Biscuit Jar ▲
- **1930**

Poole pottery biscuit jar painted by Claire Heath with lid and wicker handle in original condition.
- *height 18cm*
- **Guide price $340**

Rye Pottery ►
- *circa 1950*

A Rye pottery jug with light grey glaze decorated with a trailing stylized foliate design.
- *height 20cm*
- **Guide price $220**

Expert Tips

Staffordshite figures are the most inexpensive of factory ware – pure Victoriana. Mat-backed and early figures are modelled completely – no flat backs. Very rare are examples of figures of Jenny Lind and Mrs Bloomer.

Poole Pottery ▼
- *circa 1930*

A Truda Carter design vase from Poole Pottery by Rene Hayes.
- *height 18cm*
- **Guide price $590**

Ironstone Bowl ▼
- *circa 1820*

Nineteenth century ironstone "Japan" pattern bowl.
- *5cm x 30cm*
- **Guide price $530**

Floral Vase ▲
- **1930**

Fine Poole Pottery vase painted by Ruth Paverley with stylized tulips and roses.
- *height 20cm*
- **Guide price $750**

European Ceramics

Frechen Earthenware Jug ▷

- *circa 1650*
Brown German earthenware jug modelled by Frechen.
- *height 22cms*
- **Guide price $2,400**

German Tankard with Pewter Lid ◄

- *circa 1697*
Small German tankard with E.R. 1697 inscribed on the pewter lid.
- *height 19cms*
- **Guide price $8,630**

Blue and White Bottle Vase ▷

- *circa 1700*
Dutch Delft blue and white bottle vase, decorated in the Chinese Transitional style, the body with flowers and birds, the neck with stiff pendant leaves.
- *height 28cm*
- **Guide price $1,030**

Bloor Derby Figures ◄

- *circa 1830*
Pair of Bloor Derby figures of a rural couple – the man holds a basket of fruit and the woman, a basket of flowers.
- *height 15cm*
- **Guide price $620**

Dresden Cup ▲

- *circa 1900*
Dresden cup and saucer enameled and gilded with cartouches of a romantic scene.
- *height 9cm*
- **Guide price $200**

Blue and White Plate ◄

- *1728*
Blue and white Delftware plate with the inscription "TDM" and "1778" surrounded by a foliate design.
- *diameter 12cms*
- **Guide price $4,900**

Expert Tips

Crazing, a network of patterns appearing when a lead glaze warps, can be faked but is easy to spot once compared to genuine items.

Limoges Plate ▲
- *1895*

Limoges plate enamelled with a floral spray of crimson and pink flowers with green and gold leaves, within a heavily gilded border.
- *diameter 23cm*
- **Guide price** $200

Meissen Shell Salt ▲
- *circa 1755*

Meissen shell salt in the form of an upturned shell the interior painted with a spray of puce, iron-red and yellow flowers with scattered sprigs, on scroll moulded feet, blue crossed swords mark.
- *diameter 10.2cm*
- **Guide price** $2,140

Nudenmiller Sauce Boat ▲
- *1780*

Nudenmiller sauce boat with scrolled handle and shaped rim, with floral sprays and gilding.
- *width 15cm*
- **Guide price** $710

Irish Belleek Basket ▲
- *circa 1880*

Irish Belleek moulded cream latticework basket with three bunches of roses and daisies.
- *height 5cm*
- **Guide price** $280

French Cup and Saucer ▲
- *circa 1860*

French cup, saucer and plate, centred with a cartouche of a chateau with gilt-banding.
- *plate diameter 18.5cm*
- **Guide price** $250

Dutch Delft Kylins ▼
- *1860*

One of a pair of Dutch Delft Kylins decorated with a blue and white floral design, seated with their mouths open.
- *height 32cm*
- **Guide price** $1420

Sèvres Dinner Plate ▲
- *circa 1814*

Sèvres dinner plate decorated with cherubs holding roses, on the side is the royal crest of M Imple de Sèvres, lst Empire.
- *diameter 24cm*
- **Guide price** $400

Faenza Maiolica Albarello ▼

- *circa 1530*
Painted with label inscribed in blue with "u.agrippa" against a background of scrolling foliage in green, blue, yellow and ochre.
- *height 16.5cm*
- **Guide price $3,290**

Apothecary Jar ◀

- *18th century*
Dutch Delft apothecary jar with moulded spout above scrolled Peacock and fruit cartouche marked "Rosarum".
- *height 20.3cm*
- **Guide price $2,400**

Faience Tankard ▲

- *1805*
Frankfurt pewter-mounted faience tankard decorated with figures in a garden above a band of stiff stylised leaves, with pewter lid.
- *height 27cm*
- **Guide price $1,600**

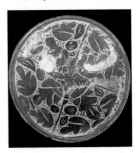

Neptune Plate ▲

- *circa 1815–30*
Blue-printed plate decorated with Neptune riding an eagle.
- *diameter 25cm*
- **Guide price $210**

Dish with Leaves ▲

- *17th century*
Hispano Moresque dish, 17th century, divided into four compartments and decorated with leaves.
- *diameter 28cm*
- **Guide price $1,570**

Expert Tips

Restoration reduces the value of an object. Repairs are acceptable but only when they are done well. Some repairs are obvious; staples are the best kind of honest repair, while modern glues can destroy a piece. When an antique ceramic is damaged, the current orthodoxy is to leave the damage showing. Certainly do not try to overpaint and never file away original surfaces to make repair work easier.

Russian Palace Plate ◀

- *circa 1815–30*
Blue-printed plate decorated with Russian Palace pattern.
- *diameter 25cm*
- **Guide price $230**

Miniature Flower Pot ▼

- *circa 1900*

Miniature flower pot decorated with flowers, a bird, insects and a butterfly. Made in Paris, France.
- *height 11cm*
- **Guide price $90**

Continental Figurative Group ▼

- *circa 1880*

Continental romantic figurative group modelled as a gentleman seated beside a small round table, wearing a finely painted floral brocade jacket, accompanied by a lady and her mother, on a serpentine base with a central Royal Crest and a gold "D".
- *22cm x 25cm*
- **Guide price $450**

Westerwald Ewer ▲

- *1630*

Westerwald blue and white ewer with pewter cover, a central cartouche of Jesus on the cross with two figures to either side, ten angels each side of the handle and lion mask decoration on lip.
- *height 23cm*
- **Guide price $5,870**

Meissen Figurative Group ◄

- *circa 1880*

Meissen figurative group with two children seated around a central column encrusted with flowers, a central cartouche of gilt scrolling, and blue and pink flowers on a circular moulded base with a conversion for an electric light.
- *height 26cm*
- **Guide price $860**

Expert Tips

Imari refers to a type of Japanese porcelain made from the beginning of the 17th century, which featured decoration based on native textiles and brocade.

Meissen Teapot ▶

- *circa 1735*
Meissen billet-shaped teapot and
cover with a painted cartouche
on each side, within a purple
lustre and gilt scrollwork,
encircling a Kauffahoftei scene of
merchants and their wares.
- *height 10cm*
- **Guide price** $11,570

Royal Vienna Huntsman ▲

- *circa 1890*
Royal Vienna prancing white
horse with a huntsman and
hounds on a white base.
- *height 20cm*
- **Guide price** $570

Dresden Coffee Pot ▲

- *circa 1800*
Dresden white coffee pot
decorated with yellow and lilac
floral swags and gilt-scrolling
around the base, handle and
spout. With Crown and Dresden
on the base.
- *height 19cm*
- **Guide price** $320

Saltglazed Jug and Cover ▲

- *17th century*
Westerwald blue and cream
saltglazed stainwear jug of
bulbous form with a pewter
handle with cartouches of
cherubs with wings and a
gentleman with a wig, wearing
a hat.
- *height 23cm*
- **Guide price** $4,980

Royal Vienna Plate ▲

- *circa 1870*
Royal Vienna plate hand-painted
with a scene of lovers in a boat,
with one cherub holding a basket
and the other has his arm around
the lady, to the side is a man
pulling up the anchor.
- *diameter 24cm*
- **Guide price** $670

Dresden Cup and Saucer ▼

- *circa 1880*
Dresden tall moulded cup and
saucer decorated with lilac and
orange flowers, with gilt-scrolling
to the rim and handle, and
saucer.
- *height 9cm*
- **Guide price** $2,000

Meissen Tea Bowl and Saucer

- *circa 1735*

Meissen tea bowl and saucer painted with a continuous scene of a merchant's encampment beside an estuary and the interior with a quayside scene.
- *height 5cm*
- **Guide price $4,360**

Dresden Teapot

- *circa 1843*

Dresden blue miniature square teapot of bulbous form, with a central cartouche of a courting couple in a pastoral setting on a white background, marked A.R. Helena Wolfsohn Dresden.
- *height 9cm*
- **Guide price $260**

Gilded Plate

- *circa 1814–60*

Meissen plate with heavily gilded water serpents with shells, and a central flower, within a gilt rope border. Blue cross swords.
- *diameter 22cm*
- **Guide price $290**

Westerwald Tankard

- *circa 1600*

Blue and cream saltglazed stainwear tankard with three cartouches depicting scenes of Frankfurt, with turned decoration, pewter lid and thumb piece.
- *height 17cm*
- **Guide price $4,450**

Dresden Trembleuse

- *circa 1880*

Dresden "trembleuse" cup and saucer decorated with pink, yellow and orange flowers. The saucer has a lattice container to hold the cup in place for trembling hands. Blue crown and "D" on the base, by Helena Wolfsohn.
- *height 11.5cm*
- **Guide price $4,140**

Expert Tips

Sèvres porcelain has been extensively faked. Many minor French factories used the interlaced "Ls" mark on their wares. They are identifiable through their inferior quality.

Meissen Salts

- *circa 1750*

Pair of Meissen salts of a lady and gentleman with tri-cornered hats seated on a pair of baskets.
- *height 15.5cm*
- **Guide price $1,390**

Polychrome Plate with Birds ▶

- *circa 1740*
Dutch Delft polychrome plate decorated with birds in a fenced garden, has mark of Jan Jansz Van der Laen.
- *diameter 22.4cm*
- **Guide price $500**

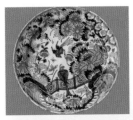

Venice Drug Jar ▲

- *circa 1550*
Venice drug jar with portrait of figure with orange hair.
- *height 16cm*
- **Guide price $3,920**

Hispano Moresque Dish with Bird ▼

- *17th century*
Hispano Moresque dish decorated with a bird in the centre.
- *diameter 20cm*
- **Guide price $320**

Pair of Italian Maiolica Wet Syrup Jars ▼

- *early 17th century*
Jars with ovoid bodies surmounted with a slightly flared rim, the handles in the form of stylised snakes, decorated in the beritinno style with blue scrolling foliage on a light blue ground.
- *height 19.8cm*
- **Guide price $5,880**

Italian Maiolica Deruta Tazza ◀

- *circa 1710*
Painted by the Maestro Del Reggimento with a biblical scene of Virgin Mary with other figures including a saint kissing the Christ child.
- *diameter 32.2cm*
- **Guide price $5,340**

Italian Maiolica Savona Flask ▲

- *late 17th century*
Rare flask with sides painted with ships or houses or plants; the base with the Savona shield in underglaze blue.
- *height 19cm*
- **Guide price $3,200**

- *circa 1736–40*
Meissen salts modelled by J.F.
Eberlein, basket shaped bowl with
rope twist handles painted with a
bird, supported by three male
caryatid figures terminating in
gilt-edged double scroll feet.
Completed by Eberlein for the
Sulkowsky service. Listed in the
factory records of June 1736.
- *height 10cm*
- **Guide price** $3,470

Saltglazed Stainwear Tankard ▲

- *1690*
Westerwald saltglazed stainwear
tankard with a pewter cover and
cartouches of royalty.
- *height 17cm*
- **Guide price** $2,940

Dresden Goblet ▶

- *circa 1880*
Dresden goblet with saucer
decorated with cherubs and
children playing, with a blue
iridescent interior and gilt leaves
circling the base and saucer
marked with a Crown and
Dresden.
- *height 9cm*
- **Guide price** $830

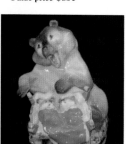

Russian Bear ▲

- *circa 1890*
Russian mother bear with two
baby bears in a cradle covered
with an orange cover with white
spots, set on a circular floral and
green base.
- *height 20cm*
- **Guide price** $450

Parisian Porcelain Plates ▲

- *1830*
Part of a set of six Parisian
porcelain plates with a green
border and gilt foliate designs
with dragonflies and central
cartouche of flowers.
- *diameter 16cm*
- **Guide price** $1,750

Dresden Group ▲

- *circa 1870*
Dresden group of young girl and
two men around a pillar with a
cherub holding a rose, on the
base is a basket overflowing with
pink roses and garlands.
- *height 30cm*
- **Guide price** $1,200

Sicilian Maiolica Albarello ▲

- *Early 18th century*
Sicilian maiolica albarello of waisted cylindrical form, painted in green, yellow, and manganese with gothic foliage.
- *height 24cm*
- Guide price $1,560

Multiple Tulip Vase ◀

- *early 18th century*
Blue and white Dutch Delft multiple tulip vase, heart-shaped on a stepped rectangular pedestal foot with eight flower holders arranged symmetrically at the top.
- *height 20.5cm*
- Guide price $12,460

Dutch Polychrome Tile ▲

- *17th century*
Dutch Delft polychrome tile decorated with central diamond surrounding a vase of flowers.
- *12cm x 12cm*
- Guide price $130

Hispano Moresque Dish with Stylized Bird ▼

- *17th century*
Hispano Moresque dish decorated with stylized image of a bird.
- *diameter 28cm*
- Guide price $1,420

Kraak Tile with Unicorn ▲

- *17th century*
Dutch Delft blue and white Kraak tile with a unicorn in the centre.
- *12cm x 12cm*
- Guide price $120

Kraak Tile with Flowers ▲

- *17th century*
Dutch blue and white Delft Kraak tile featuring a vase of flowers in the centre.
- *12cm x 12cm*
- Guide price $120

Expert Tips

Most tiles of value will probably be Dutch delft. The pattern was set up in Antwerp in 1512 and the factory was destroyed by a gunpowder explosion in 1654. It produced a massive output of tiles, wall panels, shop signs and the most collected are the composite tile pictures. From the early 17th century the potttery had an eastern influence and emulated Chinese porcelain.

Coffee Pot and Teapot ▲
- *circa 1800*
Meissen coffee and teapot, part of a set including milk jug, sugar bowl, cups and saucers, cake plates and one large plate.
- *height 27cm*
- **Guide price $ 4,540**

Meissen Figurative Group ▲
- *circa 1880*
Meissen figurative group of Diana the Huntress seated on a lion holding a cornucopia of flowers, with cherubs holding a key and garlands.
- *26cm x 24cm*
- **Guide price $2,810**

Westerwald Storage Jar ▶
- *17th century*
Rhineland blue salt glazed stainwear jar, with pewter cover and handle, with a cartouche on each side depicting William III, within a raised floral design.
- *height 27cm*
- **Guide price $8,630**

Dresden Europa and the Bull ▲
- *circa 1860*
Dresden group of Europa and the Bull, the lady wearing a lilac tunic, and the bull with a garland of flowers around its neck.
- *height 22cm*
- **Guide price $620**

Neptune ▲
- *1760*
Meissen figure of Neptune astride a sea horse with trident.
- *height 15cm*
- **Guide price $1,740**

Dresden Cup and Saucer ▲
- *circa 1880*
Dresden cup standing on three paw feet and saucer decorated with orange borders and a central cartouche of boats in a harbour.
- *height 10cm*
- **Guide price $510**

Expert Tips

Originating in the Kangxi period, famille vert is a palette of enamels in which a strong green predominates. It influenced the decoration of English soft paste porcelain in the 18th century, before being overtaken by famille rose colours.

Italian Castelli Dish ◀

- *circa 1720*
Fine Italian Castelli dish
romantically painted by Grue
with figures by classical ruins in a
wooded landscape.
- *diameter 17.5cm*
- **Guide price $3,200**

**Sicilian Tall
Waisted Albarello** ▶

- *circa 1700*
Decorated with scrolling foliage
and flower heads in yellow and
blue against a blue background
- *height 13.7cm*
- **Guide price $2,400**

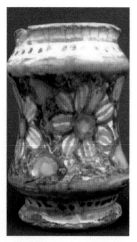

Sicilian Albarello ◀

- *16th century*
Sicilian albarello decorated with
yellow flower heads against a blue
background.
- *height 11.5cm*
- **Guide price $1,570**

**Italian Abruzzi, Waisted
Albarello** ▲

- *circa 1700*
Small albarello decorated with a
cartouche containing a label
below cross keys inscribed
"TROCIRCADIA.RODM".
- *height 11.4cm*
- **Guide price $1,600**

**Hispano Moresque Dish
with Three Lines** ◀

- *17th century*
Hispano Moresque dish decorated
with scrolling foliage divided in
the centre by three lines.
- *diameter 18cm*
- **Guide price $620**

Delft Punch Bowl ▲

- *circa 1750*
Dutch Delft blue and white
punch bowl featuring exterior
decorated with swirling panels of
flowers and interior with a
stylised foliate motive.
- *diameter 26.2cm*
- **Guide price $1,570**

Meissen Tea Bowl and Saucer ◄

- *circa 1750*

Meissen tea bowl and saucer painted with a central cartouche of merchants' boats, with a yellow background and purple flowers.
- *height 5cm*
- **Guide price $3,470**

Saltglazed Vessel ▼

- **1670**

Westerwald saltglazed stainwear vessel of bulbous form, with turned decoration and floral designs between courtly figures.
- *height 20cm*
- **Guide price $1,160**

Limoges Plate ▲

- **1895**

Limoges plate enamelled with a floral spray of chrysanthemums on a cream ground within a heavily gilded border.
- *diameter 23cm*
- **Guide price $200**

Lion and the Hare ▲

- *circa 1890*

A Russian lion seated and holding a white hare by the scruff of its neck.
- *height 15cm*
- **Guide price $430**

Dresden Cup and Saucer ◄

- *circa 1900*

Dresden cup and saucer standing on three paw feet decorated with pink panels of courting couples and flowers divided by gilt-scrolling design.
- *height 4cm*
- **Guide price $420**

Dresden Groups ▶

- *circa 1870*

A pair of Dresden groups showing amorous courting couples.
- *height 22cm*
- **Guide price $890**

Expert Tips

English slipwares and German stonewares have been honestly copied as well as faked. Copies of Raeren Brown stoneware are often very close to the style of the originals but are marked by the maker, for example, H.S. for the pottery-maker Hubert Schiffer.

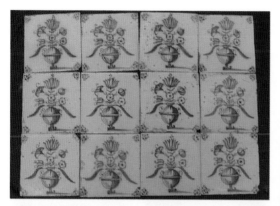

Delft Blue and White Tiles ◀

- *18th century*

Dutch Delft blue and white tiles featuring vase with flowers in the centre.

- *12cm x 12cm*
- **Guide price $800**

Stoneware Tankard ▲

- *18th century*

German stoneware tankard with pouring lip and flat pewter cover, decorated with applied blossoms and flowers connected by engraved stems with embossed diamond pattern above and below.

- *height 23cm*
- **Guide price $1,160**

Castelli Beaker ◀

- *18th century*

Castelli beaker decorated with a putto resting in woodland.

- *height 7.7cm*
- **Guide price $1,160**

Majolica Chestnut Dish ▼

- *1863*

Victorian Minton majolica chestnut dish and ladle.

- *length 26cm*
- **Guide price $2,230**

Faïence Sconces ▶

- *circa 1860*

Very attractive pair of Italian 19th century Faïence wall brackets molded with bust heads and swags.

- *43cm x 28cm*
- **Guide price $4,450**

115

Oriental Ceramics

Famille Rose Charger ◄

- *circa 1760*
Chinese export *famille rose* charger in the silver form. Qianlong period.
- *width 39cm*
- **Guide price** $1,510

Kutani Cup ▼

- *1890*
Rare Japanese Kutani opaque cup and saucer with hand-painted face of geisha girl on the saucer.
- *height 6cm*
- **Guide price** $100

Hexagonal Tea Jars ▶

- *circa 1849*
Chinese export blue and white hexagonal tea jars decorated with dragons chasing flaming pearls, in good condition.
- *height 36cm*
- **Guide price** $8,020

Gros de Bleu Temple Jars ▼

- *circa 1830*
Fine massive pair of Chinese export *gros de bleu* temple jars and covers in the Qianlong style. Exceptional gilding bright and unrubbed.
- *height 65cm*
- **Guide price** $16,910

Late Ming Punchbowl ▶

- *1573–1620*
Extremely rare late Ming (Wanli period) punchbowl in the Kraak style with European inspired decorations of figures amid landscapes.
- *16cm x 36cm*
- **Guide price** $5,700

Chinese Vase ▼

- *circa 1770*
A fine quality Chinese export porcelain two-handled vase, decorated with a turquoise chicken skin ground and bright "Mandarin" panels. Quianlong Period.
- *height 24cm*
- **Guide price $750**

Chinese Spoon Dish ▲

- *circa 1760*
Miniature Chinese export spoon dish with shaped rim and a central panel of fruit and flowers in a bowl.
- *length 13cm*
- **Guide price $430**

Cylindrical Hat Stand ▲

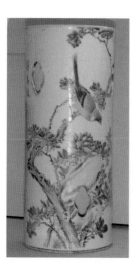

- *circa 19th century*
Cylindrical shape porcelain hat stand painted with a pink cherry blossom tree with a song bird, sitting above a pond, with a poem dedicated to the owner with leaf shape openings for airing. Seal of manufacturer on the base. Ex-Guonxi period.
- *height 29cm*
- **Guide price $690**

Famille Rose Teapot ◄

- *circa 1790*
Famille rose teapot with a scene after Watteau of Europe, in a garden watched by Pierot. Qianlong Period.
- *height 12cm*
- **Guide price $1,780**

Annamese Dish ▲

- *12th century*
Annamese dish with scalloped edge with a bold chrysanthemum in the centre, under an olive-green glaze.
- *diameter 15cm*
- **Guide price $450**

Chinese Sauce Tureen ►

- *circa 1760*
Very rare Chinese export sauce tureen and cover, modelled as a sitting quail on its nest and painted in iron red, black and green. From the Qianlong period.
- *height 9cm*
- **Guide price $11,930**

Expert Tips

To authenticate a piece of Ming blue and white ware, it is necessary to study the following aspects of the piece: painting techniques, wash methods, lines, brush strokes, form and shape, clay and glazes used and the evolution of motifs.

Meiping Vase ▶

- *circa 1745*

Famille rose "Meiping" vase of globular form, boldly painted with a phoenix among branches of prunus blossom. From the Qianlong period.
- *height 34cm*
- **Guide price** $16,200

Lemonade Jug ▲

- *circa 1780–1820*

Extremely rare (so far only one known) Canton enamel lemonade jug decorated with a pastoral scene and figures. The yellow background is decorated with foliate designs and pink blossom, with a lip incorporating a blue foliate design, with a chrysanthemum to the centre.
- *height 18cm*
- **Guide price** $2,140

Glazed Jug ▲

- *11th century*

Globular-shaped jug with strap handle, wide splayed neck, lobbed body and spout, raised on a circular foot with stops to the base.
- *height 24cm*
- **Guide price** $1,690

Octagonal Meat Dish ▼

- *circa 1760*

Famille rose octagonal meat dish, brightly enamelled with butterflies feeding from fruit and flowers within a motttled border of pale green and brown. From the Qianlong period.
- *length 33cm*
- **Guide price** $2,310

Famille Rose Plate ◀

- *circa 1760*

Chinese export porcelain *famille rose* pattern plate.
- *diameter 32cm*
- **Guide price** $610

Chinese Coffee Cup ▲

- *circa 1760*

Chinese export coffee cup of unusual size with ear-shaped handle and a *famille rose* pattern.
- *height 8cm*
- **Guide price** $170

Incense Burner ▼
- **5th century**

Green circular incense burner of two tiers with a dog on the upper section, the whole resting on three feet.
- *height 7cm*
- **Guide price $270**

Chinese Export Vases ▲
- *circa 1780*

A pair of Chinese export vases and stands in Mandarin palette on turquoise ground, each with a tapering square section and butterfly handles. Qianlong period.
- *height 24cm*
- **Guide price $42,720**

Sawankalok Bowl ▲
- **15th century**

Tia Sawankalok green bowl with a wide lip with a moulded rim, above a stylised lotus flower design, centred with a chrysanthemum.
- *diameter 26cm*
- **Guide price $500**

Chinese Teapoy ▲
- *circa 1790*

Chinese export polychrome teapoy and cover with a scene after Watteau of Europeans in a garden, watched by a Pierrot. From the Qianlong period.
- *height 16cm*
- **Guide price $3,120**

Chinese Bowl ▼
- *circa 18th century*

Elegant blue bulbous bowl supported on three button feet.
- *diameter 24cm*
- **Guide price $850**

Quianlong Plates ▼
- **1760**

One of a pair of Chinese export porcelain plates, painted with elaborate scenes within border in famille rose enamels.
- *diameter 21.5cm*
- **Guide price $1,340**

Sung Dynasty Bowl ◄
- **11–12th century**

Sung Dynasty bowl with an incised repetitive design of stylised flowers, under a green glaze.
- *diameter 20.4cm*
- **Guide price $710**

Expert Tips

Early Ming potters used calligraphic strokes to draw the motifs. The pieces are thicker and more translucent than late Ming pieces which have a thinner, transparent glaze.

Famille Rose Meat Dishes

- *circa 1760*
Pair of Chinese export *famille rose* meat dishes.
- *21cm x 29cm*
- **Guide price $2,490**

Japanese Imari Jars ▶

- *circa 1850*
Good pair of Japanese Imari jars with moulded bodies and unusual decoration of braid on the necks.
- *height 30cm*
- **Guide price $1,690**

Tureen and Stand ▲

- *circa 1770*
Excellent Chinese export *famille rose* tureen and stand from the Qianlong period. Decorated with a pretty floral motif.
- *20cm x 28cm*
- **Guide price $10,320**

Samson Armorial Wine Cooler ▶

- *circa 1850*
Samson Armorial wine cooler decorated in the Imari colours
- *height 19cm*
- **Guide price $1,510**

Imari Fish Dishes ◀

- *circa 1850*
Pair of 19th century Japanese Imari fish dishes.
- *height 29cm*
- **Guide price $1,690**

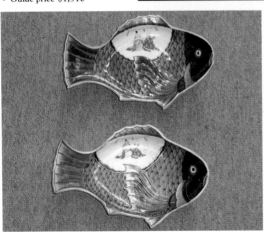

Expert Tips

On of the most famous copiers was Edme Samson, who worked in France from 1845. Samson copied Bow, Worcester, Meissen and Chinese and Japanese ware. His wares are often marked with an "S", which can appear with the factory mark – sometimes the "S" is tampered with and removed. His pieces are collectable in their own right.

Chinese Tankard ▼
- *circa 1770*
Export Chinese porcelain tankard with "Mandri"-style panel depicting a courtly scene.
- *height 24cm*
- Guide price $420

Oriental Cup ▼
- *16th century*
Blue and white cup with a wide splayed rim, with a blue lattice design running around the exterior, above a song bird with prunus blossom.
- *height 5cm*
- Guide price $800

Sauce Tureen and Cover ▶
- *circa 1765*
Rare Chinese export sauce tureen, cover and stand of English creamware form. Painted with the arms of Parker imp. Nesbitt, within a diaper border. Qianlong period. Made for the widow of the second Earl of Macclesfield (Parker), she was a Nesbitt.
- *height of tureen 13cm*
- Guide price $28,480

Desk Set ▲
- *circa 1760*
Rare and unusual *famille rose* desk set from the Qianlong period. Comprising five quill holders, two inkwells with pewter liners and a covered box.
- *height 6cm*
- Guide price $8,540

Chinese Marriage Plate ▲
- *circa 1750*
Exceptionally rare Chinese export marriage plate made for the Dutch market, with a polychrome depiction of the ship Slooten, from the Qianlong period.
- *diameter 36cm*
- Guide price $22,250

Tea Bowl and Saucer ▲
- *circa 1735*
Chinese export porcelain tea bowl and saucer, profusely gilded with floral sprays and cartouches of prunus with a central panel of a Chinese gentleman.
- *diameter of cup 6cm*
- Guide price $400

Nanking Bowl and Saucer ▲
- *1790*
Nanking blue and white bowl and saucer with pagoda scenes and later English gilding.
- *diameter of saucer 13cm*
- Guide price $220

Chinese Dinner Plate ◄

- *circa 1740*

Fine Chinese export *famille rose* dinner plate from the Qianlong period, painted with the "Arbour Pattern" after Cornelis Pronk.
- *diameter 23cm*
- **Guide price $9,260**

Chinese Candlesticks ▼

- *circa 1770*

Pair of *famille rose* candlesticks of European silver form, on octagonal bases, painted with Chinese domestic scenes on a gilt ground. Qianlong period.
- *height 18cm*
- **Guide price $19,050**

Storage Jar ▼

- *1640*

Blue and white storage jar of bulbous proportions decorated with a repetitive pattern of blue flowers on a white ground.
- *height 35cm*
- **Guide price $980**

Stoneware Jar ▲

- *Tang 618–906 AD*

Stoneware jar of globular form, with a flared neck and an uneven straw coloured glaze around the middle from the Tang Dynasty, raised on a circular foot.
- *height 12cm*
- **Guide price $630**

Famille Rose Ewer ▼

- *circa 1760*

Famille rose ewer and cover with "C" shape handle and matching basin all painted with flowering chrysanthemum growing from rockwork. Qianlong period.
- *height of ewer 22cm*
- **Guide price $8,900**

Expert Tips

The early Ming period is marked by a strict control of political and cultural development, for example, a decree was issued in 1371 during the reign of Hong Wu forbidding certain subjects such as previous emperors, queens, lions or saints on porcelains.

Fo Dogs on Bases ▼

- *circa 1850*

Large pair of *famille verte* figures of Fo dogs and puppies with detachable square bases in the Chinese Kangxi period style, by Samson de Paris.
- *height 48.5cm*
- **Guide price $5,160**

Kangxi Bowl ▶

- *18th Century*

Beautiful Chinese export Kangxi period moulded bowl. Finely moulded and decorated with a swirling design of flowers.
- *11cm x 22cm*
- **Guide price $4,450**

Kangxi Ewer ◀

- *circa 1675*

Exceptionally rare Chinese export Kangxi period ewer. Originally made for the Islamic market copying earlier metal forms. There are similar examples in the Topkapi museum in Istanbul.
- *28cm x 23cm*
- **Guide price $13,350**

Kangxi Temple Jar ◀

- *circa 1670*

Superb Kangxi temple jar. Cover decorated with a scrolling peony motif and a biscuit Fo dog finial.
- *height 60cm*
- **Guide price $9,790**

Famille Verte Vase ▼

- *circa 1850*

19th century *famille verte* vase decorated on the biscuit.
- *height 18.5cm*
- **Guide price $4,000**

Blanc de Chiné Fo Dogs ◀

- *circa 1710*

Pair of Kangxi period *blanc de chiné* taper stick holders of Fo dogs standing on square bases.
- *28cm*
- **Guide price $2,850**

Chinese Chocolate Pot ◀

- *circa 1775*

Unusual Chinese export bulbous chocolate pot.
- *height 19.5cm*
- **Guide price $16,020**

Tea Bowl and Saucer ▲

- *circa 1770*

Famille rose tea bowl and saucer, decorated with a group of European figures in a garden within a gilt, pink and grisaille border. Qianlong period.
- *height of cup 4.5cm*
diameter of saucer 13cm
- **Guide price $1,690**

Famille Rose Plate ▼

- *circa 1740*

One of a pair of fine and rare *famille rose* botanical plates, each vividly painted with a cornucopia of European flowers, made in the Qianlong period.
- *diameter 23cm*
- **Guide price $19,050**

Chinese Export Plate ▲

- *circa 1760*

Chinese export *famille rose* porcelain plate with floral sprays and gilding.
- *diameter 15cm*
- **Guide price $670**

Expert Tips

During the early Ming period the majority of the wares produced tended to be of a functional nature such as bowls, plates, covered jars and incense burners, with only a narrow range of motifs.

Chinese Hat Stand ▶

- *circa 19th century*

Porcelain hat stand of cylindrical form with a polychrome glaze of scholarly objects, flora and Buddhist symbols. The stand has a six-leaf shape opening for airing. Seal at the base. Ex-Guonxi period.
- *height 29cm*
- **Guide price $630**

Lobed Imari Dish

- *circa 1870*
Koransha Imari lobed dish
showing Kintaro on his carp in
the centre.
- *width 29cm*
- **Guide price $1,690**

Kangxi Charger

- *1662–1722*
Chinese *famille verte* charger,
decorated with flowers and leafy
tendrils within a conforming
border.
- *diameter 38cm*
- **Guide price $800**

Rouge de Fer Plates

- *1736–95*
Chinese *rouge de fer* plates
decorated with prunus blossoms
issuing from a branch and
chrysanthemums in a vase.
- *diameter 21.5*
- **Guide price $390**

Famille Verte Ginger Jar

- *1662–1722*
Chinese *famille verte* ginger jar
decorated with birds peonies and
flowers on rockwork.
- *height 22cm*
- **Guide price $3,200**

Famille Verte Plate

- *1662–1722*
Chinese *famille verte* plate
decorated with eight horses.
- *diameter 21.5cm*
- **Guide price $1,340**

Famille Rose Plate ▲

- *circa 1760*

One of a pair of Chinese export plates, painted with elaborate scenes within borders in *famille rose* enamel.
- *diameter 22cm*
- **Guide price $1,340 for pair**

Chinese Soup Plate ▲

- *1775*

Octagonal Chinese export soft paste porcelain soup plate.
- *diameter 23cm*
- **Guide price $270**

Oriental Jar ▲

- *circa 16th century*

Small blue and white jar with an inverted rim and tapered body, decorated with a repeated design of fir trees.
- *height 5cm*
- **Guide price $430**

Inkwell ▲

- *11–12th century*

Inkwell from the Sung Dynasty. Designed in a compressed globular form with a stylised flower pattern in relief, under a green glaze.
- *height 10cm*
- **Guide price $620**

Chinese Export Basin ▲

- *circa 1725*

Yongzheng period Chinese export basin, richly decorated in rouge de fer and gilt, with the arms of Mertins imp. Peck. The border is decorated with *famille rose* flower heads.
- *diameter 39.5cm*
- **Guide price $15,130**

Grisaille Chinese Plate ▶

- *circa 1750*

Important Chinese export plate decorated en grisaille with a portrait of Martin Luther above a panel of Christ and his disciples all within a gilt scroll border. Qianlong Period.
- *diameter 24cm*
- **Guide price $4,000**

Blue and White Teacaddy ▲

- *1736–95*
Chinese blue and white teacaddy
of shouldered rectangular form
and decorated with willow
pattern.
- *height 11cm*
- **Guide price $500**

Blue and White Chinese Dish ▲

- *circa 1600*
Chinese blue and white dish with
two hairline cracks.
- *diameter 27.2cm*
- **Guide price $680**

Qianlong Teacaddy ◄

- *1736–95*
Chinese blue and white teacaddy
of shouldered rectangular form
decorated with flowers and
without cover.
- *height 11cm*
- **Guide price $440**

Famille Verte Dish with Gardens ▼

- *1662–1722*
Chinese *famille verte* dish
decorated with a central basket of
peonies and daisies within shaped
panels of flowering gardens,
mythical beasts, vases of flowers
and precious objects.
- *diameter 35cm*
- **Guide price $8,010**

Famille Verte Charger with Battle Scene ◄

- *1662–1722*
Chinese *famille verte* charger
decorated with a battle scene
showing soldiers charging each
other on horseback with spears
and swords. The scalloped rim has
landscape cartouches.
- *diameter 37cm*
- **Guide price $4,980**

Famille Rose Teapot with Flowers ▶

- *1736–95*
Chinese *famille rose* teapot decorated with scattered flowers.
- *height 12.5cm*
- **Guide price $270**

Famille Verte Bowl and Cover ▲

- *1662–1722*
Chinese *famille verte* bowl decorated with floral patterns and matching lid with raised knob topped by red flower.
- *diameter 35cm*
- **Guide price $1,510**

Blue and White Tea Bowl and Saucer ▶

- *1662–1722*
Chinese blue and white tea bowl and saucer with small hairline crack to tea bowl.
- *diameter 15cm*
- **Guide price $250**

Famille Rose Punch Bowl ▲

- *1736–95*
Large magnificent Chinese *famille rose* punch bowl, finely painted with large Mandarin figures.
- *diameter 38cm*
- **Guide price $3,920**

Pair of Famille Rose Scalloped Bowls ◀

- *1736–95*
Pair of *famille rose* scalloped bowls decorated with floral sprays.
- *diameter 27cm*
- **Guide price $1,340**

Swato Dish ▼

- **15th century**

A slip decorated Swato dish, raised from a shipwreck off the coast of East Timor, from the late Ming Dynasty. The centre is decorated with a spray of chrysanthemums, in a stippled and feather technique, the simple scroll border with stippled blooms, all on an even cobalt-blue ground. The underside is plain, with a grit base.

- *diameter 38cm*
- **Guide price $1,160**

Mandarin Vases ▲

- **circa 1780**

Pair of Mandarin vases and covers with figurative scenes reserved on a gilt ground with *rouge de vert* with diaper covers showing small landscape scenes and dogs. With Fo. Qianlong period finials.

- *height 37cm*
- **Guide price $35,600**

Satsuma Vases ▲

- **circa 1870**

A pair of gold Satsuma vases of baluster form, painted with holy men and a dragon who keeps away the evil spirits and brings prosperity to the family.

- *height 23cm*
- **Guide price $800**

Ming Dish ▲

- **16–17th century**

Ming dish with scalloped rim and a raised floral design under a green glaze.

- *diameter 15cm*
- **Guide price $6,760**

Transitional Food Jar ▼

- **1640**

Blue and white transitional food jar of ovoid form, with a floral design running around the shoulders and figures in a pastoral setting running around the body.

- *height 16cm*
- **Guide price $980**

Chinese Bowl ◄

- **circa 1736–1795**

Rare salesman's bowl showing different patterns available to customers ordering from China. Qianlong Period.

- *diameter 11cm*
- **Guide price $5,340**

Clocks, Watches & Scientific Instruments

The world of the scientific instrument is fascinating and the subject is still in its infancy as far as collectors are concerned.

Clocks and other timepieces are some of the most personal antiques, often passing down through families for generations. This, and the fact that most English and some European clocks bear maker's marks, is very helpful for collectors wanting to know the history of their pieces. However, clocks and other scientific instruments are mechanical objects that require periodic attention and maintenance in order to function. Neglected clocks can be extremely expensive to repair and though removing worn wheels or pinions is acceptable, replacement of other original parts such as a dial can greatly reduce the overall value. Whenever possible, request a condition report on the case, movement and dials of an item that you are considering purchasing.

On a brighter note, even non-working clocks are beautiful pieces that can be used to adorn a home. Fine mahogany longcase clocks with painted faces, complex skeleton clocks and decorative carriage clocks are currently much sought-after items that are likely to increase in value.

Clocks

French Louis XV Clock ▶
- *circa 1765*
A magnificent French Louis XV transitional, ormolu mantel clock on ormolu-mounted ebonised base. Finely chased bronzework. Swan's head handles, rosettes and guilloche decoration to the base. English purpose-made chain fusee movement signed on dial and backplate, "Barwise, London".
- *height 40cm*
- **Guide price $35,380**

Lyre Clock ◀
- *circa 1890*
Fine Louis XV style *bleu du roi* porcelain and ormolu Apollo lyre clock with moving gridiron bezel pendulum with brilliants. Eight-day bell strike. Floral sprays painted on dial and bronze hands.
- *height 48cm*
- **Guide price $17,360**

Boy Riding a Dolphin Clock ▼
- *circa 1880*
Outstanding French ormolu and blue porcelain mantel clock, surmounted by a boy riding a dolphin. Depicted on each panel are a merman, a woman, the dial and Venus in her chariot. Silver highlights to the original ormolu, eight-day bell striking movement.
- *height 35cm*
- **Guide price $7,030**

Cupid Clock ▼

- *circa 1860*

Fine and unusual glove clock
with ormolu cupid resting on a
white marble circular base. Eight-
day bell strike lever movement.
- *35cmx 18cm*
- **Guide price $4,900**

Brass Clock ▲

- *circa 1880*

Unusual brass clock in the style
of Cole signed Hancock. Fine
English lever escapement.
- *height 41cm*
- **Guide price $11,130**

Louis XV Style Clock ▲

- *circa 1820*

Outstanding English double-fusee
mantel clock in the style of Louis
XV by the eminent maker James
McCabe, with a fine rococco
case, standing upon original base.
Superbly cast, chased and gilded.
Double fusee movement with
original chains and pendulum
strikes the hours on a bell.
- *height 14.5.cm*
- **Guide price $13,800**

Desk Compendium ▼

- *circa 1880*

Fine quality English gilt bronze
and enamel desk compendium in
the form of a satchel with deep
blue enamel buckles to the straps.
Inside a watch in the manner of
Cole, together with an inkwell
stamp box, pin holder and pen
rest.
- *9.5cm x 17.5cm*
- **Guide price $4,360**

Cloisonné Clock Set ▲

- *circa 1900*

A very attractive three piece gilt
bronze cloisonné clock set. The
side pieces in the form of urns
each with handles and a cupid.
Eight-day lever escapement
movement.
- *height 27cm*
- **Guide price $8,190**

Expert Tips

*A specialist should carry out the
cleaning and oiling of a clock's
mechanism. Wheels and pinions
should never be oiled.*

Mahogany Longcase Clock ▼

• *circa 1770*
A George III mahogany five pillar brass dial longcase clock with eight-day brass dial movement with silver chapter ring. Subsidiary seconds and date with separate engraved makers name plaque. Chimes hourly on a bell.
• *2.24m x 56cm*
• **Guide price $16,910**

English Bracket Clock ▼

• *circa 1840*
Mahogany English bracket clock by Taylor of Bristol. The twin gut fusee movement with shoulder plates and hour strike on a bell. White painted convex dial signed Taylor of Bristol with black spade hands.
• *53.5cm x 30cm x 18cm*
• **Guide price $6,230**

Victorian Bracket Clock ▲

• *circa 1870*
An English triple-fusee, black ebonised, quarter-chiming Victorian bracket clock. The three train movement striking the quarters on eight bells with hour strike on a gong. The brass dial with silvered and engraved chapter ring, silvered strike/silent ring and finely chiselled brass spandrels.
• *38cm x 30.5cm*
• **Guide price $9,790**

Bracket Clock ▲

• *circa 1850*
Burr walnut double fusee English bracket clock by Payne & Co, 163 New Bond Street, London. Numbered clock No.3234. The double chain fusee eight-day numbered and signed English movement.
• *43.5cm x 30.5cm*
• **Guide price $11,570**

Grand Sonnerie Bracket Clock ▼

• *circa 1750*
Oak cased original verge escapement Austrian Grand Sonnerie bracket clock. The triple fusee Austrian movement of short duration (30-hour) with original verge escapement. Makers name plague signed "Augustin Heckel".
• *53.5cm x 25.5cm*
• **Guide price $6,940**

Timepiece Clock ▼

• *circa 1830-35*
Victorian flame mahogany, unnamed, single-fusee timepiece clock, the single gut fusee eight-day English movement with original pendulum holdfast.
• *29cm x 17.5cm*
• **Guide price $3,200**

Queen Anne Clock ▼

- *circa 1860-1890*

Fine bracket clock in the Queen Anne style in blonde tortoiseshell and lacquered bronze. Eight-day movement having steel suspended pendulum and striking the hours and halves on a gong.
- *height 33cm*
- **Guide price** $13,800

Apollo's Lyre Clock ▼

- *circa 1817*

Fine French Empire clock in the form of Apollo's lyre, the case resting on four bun feet and with a trumpet mount to a rectangular base. Eight-day striking movement with silk suspension. Attributed to André Galle. Superb dial.
- *height 48cm*
- **Guide price** $12,020

Ormolu Clock ▶

- *circa 1860*

Cut and engraved ormolu English strut clock in the manner of Cole silvered dial with blue steel hands. Eight-day lever movement.
- *height 28cm*
- **Guide price** $4,360

Ormolu Clock ▲

- *circa 1870*

French original ormolu and blue celeste porcelain clock. Surmounted by an ormolu mounted porcelain urn, eight-day bell striking movement.
- *height 43cm*
- **Guide price** $6,140

White Marble Clock ▼

- *circa 1780*

French white marble and ormolu Directoire mantle clock in Gout d'Egypte. Sphynx figures to the sides of the clock. Brickwork column holding an ormolu fountain eight-day bell strike with silk suspension.
- *height 39cm*
- **Guide price** $7,570

French Lyre Clock ▲
- 1880
French Ormolu mounted birds-eye maple, lyre clock with foliate ormolu mounts.
- *height 44cm*
- **Guide price $3,560**

Skeleton Clock ▲
- *circa 1860*
English cathedral two-train skeleton clock modelled as a cathedral encased in dome-shaped glass case on a moulded marble base.
- *height 65cm*
- **Guide price $7,120**

French Zodiac Clock ▼
- 1885
French clock made for the Spanish market with barometer, thermometers and revolving signs of the zodiac. The clock is encased within a globe of the world with a silver cloud formation running through the centre of the piece.
- *height 43cm*
- **Guide price $5,340**

German Porcelain Clock ▼
- *circa 1880*
German porcelain clock modelled as a cherub sitting in a chariot drawn by two lions, raised on a painted rectangular base with a painted panel of a landscape.
- *51cm x 46cm*
- **Guide price $6,230**

French Clock Set ▲
- 1800
French slate mantle clock set, with eight-day movement and inlaid with brass. With two side urns, the base of each urn decorated in brass with a scene of children playing within a forest setting with animals.
- *height 46cm*
- **Guide price $670**

Viennese Clock ▲
- 1880
Vienna clock with porcelain cartouches of celestial scenes with blue enamelled architectural pillars and gilding, raised on gilt ball feet.
- *height 40cm*
- **Guide price $7,120**

Folding Clock ▶

- *circa 1927*
English silver and enamel folding
travelling clock Birmingham.
- *height 4cm*
- **Guide price $1,200**

Knight Mantel Clock ▲

- *circa 1880*
A French mantel clock in the
style of a knight's helmet with
white porcelain dial.
- *23cm x 18cm*
- **Guide price $2,230**

Silver and Blue Clock ▲

- *circa 1930*
Silver and blue enamel Art Deco
strut clock with Swiss dial.
- *height 11cm*
- **Guide price $1,360**

Chinoiserie Clock ▼

- *circa 1930*
Art Deco chinoiserie-decorated
clock with mother-of-pearl dial
with geometric blue enamelling.
- *height 10cm*
- **Guide price $2,630**

Blue Enamel Clock ◀

- *circa 1930*
Art Deco blue enamel guilloche
clock.
- *height 11cm*
- **Guide price $1,200**

French Lyre Clock ▼
- *circa 1900*

A satinwood and gilt ormolu mounted French timepiece lyre clock retailed by "Howell and James", Paris. eight-day French movement with original English lever escapement, convex cream enamel dial with hand painted swags of roses boarding black arabic numerals.
- *25.5cm x 12.5cm*
- **Guide price $2,850**

Three-Piece Clock Garniture ▼
- *circa 1870*

French gilt bronze and cloisonne-enamelled three-piece clock garniture. Eight-day movement, chiming hours and half hours on a bell. Urn-shaped side pieces in gilt bronze and blue porcelain with fine cloisonne-enamelling to match.
- *40.5cm x 22.5cm*
- **Guide price $6,590**

Three-Piece Clock Garniture ▲
- *circa 1860*

A gilt bronze and jewelled pink porcelain three-piece clock garniture with porcelain panels surmounted by an urn. Eight-day French movement, chiming hours and half hours.
- *43cm x 30.5cm*
- **Guide price $9,790**

Mantle Clock ▲
- *circa 1890*

A white Paris Bisque French timepiece mantle clock with small French eight-day timepiece movement, white convex enamel dial with roman numerals and counter poised moon hands.
- *25.5cm x 15.5cm*
- **Guide price $1,340**

Black Marble Clock ▼
- *circa 1860*

French black marble mantle clock with a gilt bronze figure of a maiden reading a book resting on a column with a lyre beside her, eight-day French movement. Half hour strike on a bell.
- *61cm x 56cm*
- **Guide price $6,230**

French Four Glass Clock ▼
- *circa 1870*

A polished brass French four glass clock with diamonte bezel. Eight-day movement with hour and half hour strike on a gong and mercury pendulum, the white enamelled dial is painted with pink music sheets.
- *25.5cm x 5cm*
- **Guide price $2,850**

Mantle Clock ◄
- *circa 1880*

French gilt metal and porcelain mantle clock, the gilt ormolu case swags to the sides, acanthus cast gallery to the base raised on toupie feet. The pink porcelain panels with gilt-bordered white reserves painted with flowers.
- *51cm x 25.5cm*
- **Guide price $4,090**

Chinoiserie Clock ▼

- *circa 1930*
A brass dial with a blue
chinoiserie figurative frame
resting on a brass stand.
- *20cm x 20cm*
- **Guide price** $750

Travelling Timepiece ▲

- *circa 1930*
Art Deco silver with enamel
travelling clock stamped Levi
Nande.
- *2.5cm x 2cm*
- **Guide price** $1,470

Boudoir Clock ◄

- *circa 1930*
A rare silver and enamel clock
with watch inset.
- *6cm x 8cm*
- **Guide price** $4,360

Eight-Day French Clock ▲

- *circa 1930*
Unusual boulle mantel clock with
French eight-day movement
regulated by a cylinder
escapement.
- *height 15cm*
- **Guide price** $2,270

Art Deco Timepiece ►

- *circa 1930*
Art Deco silver clock with
enamel flying birds in the
chinoiserie style.
- *11cm x 8cm*
- **Guide price** $2,270

Carriage Clock ▲
- *circa 1880–90*
French polished brass corniche cased timepiece with alarm, the eight-day movement with alarm sounding on a bell.
- *11cm x 7.5cm*
- **Guide price $980**

French Carriage Clock ▲
- *circa 1890–1900*
French miniature polished brass Corniche cased eight-day carriage clock timepiece with eight-day movement and silvered English lever platform escapement.
- *7.5cm x 5cm*
- **Guide price $1,690**

French Carriage Clock ▼
- *circa 1880–90*
Carriage clock with eight-day French timepiece movement and original silvered cylinder platform escapement, the polished brass corniche style case with solid cast scroll shaped carrying handle.
- *10.4cm x 10cm*
- **Guide price $980**

Brass Carriage Clock ▼
- *circa 1880–90*
French polished brass Anglaise Riche case chiming carriage clock. The eight-day French chiming movement striking the hours and half hours on a gong with original silvered English lever platform escapement.
- *12.5cm x 8.2cm*
- **Guide price $3,200**

English Bracket Clock ▲
- *circa 1860*
A solid mahogany and brass inlaid English bracket clock with quarter striking triple fusee. Retailed by Dixon of Norwich chiming every quarter on four bells. With eight day triple-fusee movement.
- *68.5cm x 41cm*
- **Guide price $9,790**

Gothic Bracket Clock ▲
- *circa 1839*
An early English flame mahogany silvered dial gothic bracket clock. The eight-day two-train gut fusee movement with hour and half hour strike on a large nickel bell. Signed and dated D. Shaw, Leicester, 1839.
- *71cm x 46cm*
- **Guide price $6,940**

Rosewood Clock ◀

- *circa 1860*
Fine balloon-shaped rosewood
mantel clock inlaid with brass
and copper with a porcelain dial
with blued steel moon hands.
Eight-day striking movement.
- *height 25cm*
- **Guide price $5,250**

Black Forest Clock ▼

- *circa 1860*
German Black Forest clock in the
style of a church with bell tower,
monk chime on the half hour and
hour standing on a rusticated base
- *70cm x 37cm*
- **Guide price $6,230**

French Clock ▲

- *circa 1890*
Mahogany French Art Nouveau
clock with floral fruitwood inlay
standing on four brass-turned
feet.
- *31cm x 9cm*
- **Guide price $1,070**

Asprey Dial Clock ▲

- *circa 1920*
Rosewood with satinwood inlays
and the dial signed by Asprey.
French eight-day cylinder
escapement.
- *height 45cm*
- **Guide price $3,030**

Regency Clock ▶

- *circa 1800*
A Regency ebonised Bracket
clock by Thos. Moss with brass
geometrical inlay and lion head
handles, standing on four brass
ball feet.
- *84cm x 24cm*
- **Guide price $8,460**

Revolving Lighthouse Clock ▶

- *circa 1880*

An unusual brass clock representing a lighthouse with a thermometer and revolving movement.

- *height 39cm*
- **Guide price $5,700**

Skeleton Clock ▲

- *circa 1880*

A brass skeleton clock in the style of a Cathedral with silvereddial standing on a marble base with original glass dome.

- *48cm x 33cm*
- **Guide price $3,290**

French Timepiece ▼

- *circa 1900*

French mahogany clock with fruitwood inlay and surmounted by a brass finial.

- *26cm x 13cm*
- **Guide price $1,060**

Ebonised Mantel Clock ▼

- *circa 1880*

Fine ebonised French clock, standing on four pillars with brass trailing encrusted vines and a young girl on a swing.

- *53cm x 33cm*
- **Guide price $2,760**

Expert Tips

The springs from which pendulums are suspended are easily broken in transit. Secure or remove them for journeys.

French Mantel Clock ▼

- *circa 1860*

A fine French ebonised mantel clock with four pillars and brass trailing foliage. White porcelain dial flanked by cherubs and scrolling gilt foliate design.

- *49cm x 23cm*
- **Guide price $2,400**

Green Enamel Clock ▶

- *circa 1931*
Silver and green Art Deco
guilloche enamel clock.
  - *10cm x 11cm*
  - **Guide price $1,560**

Gray of Paris Mantel Clock ◀

- *circa 1870*
Gilt mantel clock with foliate
scrolling and grapes by Gray of
Paris, signed on the VI, of the
white porcelain and navy blue
numerals.
  - *30cm x 20cm*
  - **Guide price $2,400**

Brass Travel Clock ▼

- *circa 1870*
Brass travelling carriage clock
with compass and thermometer
on the top with brass handle for
carrying.
  - *25cm x 15cm*
  - **Guide price $2,400**

Globe Clock ◀

- *circa 1920*
Unusual globe converted to a
clock with circular timepiece on a
mahogany stand with attached
movement, made in Leipseig.
  - *61cm x 30cm*
  - **Guide price $3,920**

Elephant Clock ▲

- *circa 1880*
Fine French patinated bronze and
original ormolu elephant clock.
Surmounted by a China-man
holding a parasol. Eight-day bell-
striking movement with a steel
suspended pendulum.
  - *height 30cm*
  - **Guide price $10,240**

Watches

Gold Skeletonised Swiss Verge ▼

- *1780*

Swiss verge in a gold and stone set double sided consular case. The plate and barrel cover pierced and engraved to reveal the train and blue steel mainspring.
- *diameter 40mm*
- **Guide price $3,380**

Skull Watch ▼

- **mid 19th Century**

Swiss verge in a silver case in the form of a skull with matching silver chain. Small full plate gilt fusee movement with pierced and engraved bridge cock.
- *diameter 6cm*
- **Guide price $8,900**

Mandolin Watch ▶

- *circa 1820*

Austrian verge form watch in a gold and enamel case in the form of a mandolin.
- *length 5cm*
- **Guide price $2,850**

Rare Agate and Gold Watch with Chatelaine ◀

- *circa 1740*

A rare English agate watch in gold settings with matching chatelaine. Full plate fire gilt movement with square baluster pillars.
- *diameter 51mm x 17mm*
- **Guide price $13,350**

Iron Fusee Drum Timepiece ▼

- *1540*

A rare German verge fusee timepiece in a gilt metal drum case. Deep circular movement constructed of iron with three pillars.
- *54mm x 39mm*
- **Guide price $44,500**

Ladies Swiss Watch ▼

- *1920s*

Ladies Swiss made 18ct gold with a white enamelled dial with Roman numerals.
- *diameter 2.7cm*
- **Guide price $710**

Gentleman's Rolex Watch ▼

- *1960*

Gentleman's Rolex Oyster perpetual explorer wristwatch on a Rolex Oyster expandable bracelet.
- *diameter 3cm*
- **Guide price $4,270**

Hexagonal Watch ▲

- *1920s*

Ladies silver hexagonal wristwatch with white enamel dial, auxiliary sweep seconds and a red number 12.
- *diameter 2cm*
- **Guide price $450**

Tiffany & Co. Watch ▲

- *1920s*

Ladies Tiffany & Co. Set in 9ct rose gold white enamelled dial with Arabic numerals and a red number 12.
- *diameter 2cm*
- **Guide price $890**

Rolex Oyster Watch ◄

- *1920s*

Rolex Oyster precision auxiliary sweep seconds white dial. Two, four, eight, ten and 12 in Arabic numerals, set in stainless steel.
- *diameter 1.6cm*
- **Guide price $1,160**

Omega Watch ▼

- *1950s*

Swiss made men's Omega 18ct gold mechanical movement watch with auxiliary sweep seconds and a gold dial with gold hands and gold digits.
- *diameter 3.1cm*
- **Guide price $1,160**

Expert Tips

Pocket watches date back to 1675. Engraved or hand-painted pictures of rural or hunting scenes add value, as do those of classical mythology, so keep a look out for these.

Ladies Movado Watch ▼

- *1940s*

Ladies Movado Swiss made 8ct rose gold wristwatch with a square face and two-tone dial with Arabic numerals.
- *diameter 1.9cm*
- **Guide price $800**

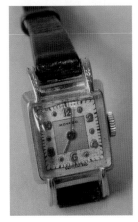

Omega Watch ▼
- *1950s*

Gentleman's Omega watch set in 9ct gold on a white dial with gold Arabic numerals and auxiliary sweep seconds.
- *diameter 2.9cm*
- **Guide price $620**

Lemania ▲
- *1953*

An Air Ministry RAF issue, pilots high grade one button chronograph with a steel case. The dial signed "Lemania &" with MOD Arrow, minute recording dial and sweep second dial. The case with fixed bar lugs and back with ordinance marks, "Arrow AM/6B/551 333/53".
- **Guide price $3,200**

Romer Wristwatch ▲
- *1950s*

Ladies Swiss made Romer wristwatch set in 9ct gold on a 9ct gold bracelet with safety chain. White dial with three, six, nine and 12 in Arabic numerals.
- *diameter 1.2cm*
- **Guide price $450**

Vacheron Constantin Watch ▼
- *1960s*

Gentleman's Vacheron Constantin 18ct white gold wristwatch with oblong design black dial with white digits.
- *diameter 1.9cm*
- **Guide price $2,310**

Omega Seamaster Watch ▲
- *1950s*

Gentleman's Omega seamaster wristwatch set in stainless steel with a black dial with white Roman numerals. Mechanical movement and a screw back case. Red second hand.
- *Diameter 2.9cm*
- **Guide price $530**

Bulova Wristwatch ▲
- *1920s*

Ladies Bulova wristwatch set in 18ct gold with white dial. three, six, nine and 12 in Arabic numerals with serrated lugs, on a black leather cocktail strap.
- *diameter 1.1cm*
- **Guide price $360**

Universal Geneve ▶
- *circa 1939*

An early 18ct gold Compax two-button chronograph with subsidiary seconds, minute and hour recording dials.
- **Guide price $6,940**

Rolex Watch ▼

• *circa 1920s*
Silver Tonneau shaped
gentleman's wristwatch. The
white enamel dial signed Rolex,
with luminous numerals and
hands and subsidiary seconds.
The 3pc case signed Rolex 7
Worlds Records Gold Medal
Geneva Suisse (RWC Ltd)
#64948. The lever movement
signed Rolex Swiss made. 15
Rubies.
• **Guide price $4,540**

Omega Watch ▼

• *circa 1938*
An 18ct gold wrist chronograph
with subsidiary seconds and 30
minute register dial. The main
dial with outer tachymeter scal.
Inner pulsations scale and base
1000 scale. The case signed
Omega & with Swiss control
marks. CS #9174757. The
movement signed Omega Watch
Company. 17 Jls #9388131.C333.
• **Guide price $11,570**

Aviator's Chronograph ▲

• *circa 1968*
An aviator's "Navitimer"
chronograph by Breitling, with
subsidiary dials for sweep seconds,
minute and hour recording. Outer
rotating bezel allowing various
aviation calculations. Case #
1307320 Ref # 806.
• **Guide price $3,200**

Hunting Chronograph ▲

• *1907*
Swiss made Hunting Split
Secondsi Chronograph with
subsidiary minute recording
and sweep second dials.
Case ~ 130519. The white
enamel dial signed S. Smith
& Son 9. The Strand London
Maker to the Admiralty.
142B 68.Non Magnetizable
Swiss Made.
• **Guide price $5,250**

Flightmaster Chronograph ▼

• *circa 1978*
A steel aviator's "Flightmaster"
chronograph by Omega, with
multifunction dial and internal
rotating bezel. This watch comes
with the original box and papers.
• **Guide price $3,200**

Propelling Pencil ▼

• *circa 1920*
French propelling pencil with
timepiece in engine turned body.
With Swiss lever 15 jewelled
movement. French control marks
and struck. 925 monogram to
case "MA".
• **Guide price $3,470**

Gentleman's Pocket Watch ▶

• *circa 1890*
Gold gentleman's pocket by
Balbi, Buenos Aires. With black
Roman numerals on a white face
with a subsidiary second dial. The
front of the case is engraved with
a house with mountains in the
background, surrounded by a
floral design, with diamonds.
• *2.5cm*
• **Guide price $1,690**

Ladies Oyster Watch ▲
- *1930s*
Rolex Oyster precision ladies stainless steel wristwatch with a white dial and trianglular digits.
- *diameter 1.8cm*
- **Guide price $1,160**

Benson Watch ▲
- *1940s*
J.W. Benson ladies wristwatch set in 9ct gold with fancy lugs amd white dial with Arabic numerals.
- *diameter 1.7cm*
- **Guide price $450**

Oyster Wrist Watch ▼
- *1950s*
Gentleman's Rolex Oyster Royal watch set in stainless steel with a white mottled dial with three, six, nine in Arabic numerals, Mercedes hands and mechanical movement.
- *diameter 2.6cm*
- **Guide price $1,420**

Rolex Wristwatch ▼
- *1918*
Ladies Rolex wristwatch with white enamelled dial set in 9ct gold. Black Arabic numerals.
- *diameter 2cm*
- **Guide price $1,030**

Gentleman's Longines Watch ▶
- *1930s*
Gentleman's Longines oblong design set in 14ct. rose gold, with white dial set with gold Arabic numerals and auxiliary sweep seconds.
- *diameter 1.8cm*
- **Guide price $1,690**

Fly-Back Chronograph ▲
- *circa 1970*
A rare German air force issue aviator's "Fly-Back" chronograph by Heuer in steel. The black dial with subsidiary seconds and minute recording dial 1 and red "3H" in circle, case # 6445-12-146-3774 and stamped "BUNDWEHR".
- **Guide price $3,920**

Omega Seamaster Wristwatch ▲
- *1940s*
Gentleman's Omega Seamaster wristwatch set in stainless steel automatic movement, two-tone dial with gold digits.
- *diameter 2.9cm*
- **Guide price $530**

Rock Crystal Clockwatch ▶
- *1620*

German verge clockwatch with the bell under the dial in a gilt metal and rock crystal case. Simple small silvered dial, with engraved Roman numerals, later single blue steel hand.
- *37mm x 77mm x 35 mm*
- **Guide price $29,370**

Gold and Enamel French Cylinder ▲
- *1790*

A French cylinder in a gold and enamel case with protective outer. Polychrome scene of two figures in a garden painted on translucent dark blue enamel over an engine turned ground.
- *diameter 36mm*
- **Guide price $4,360**

Turquoise Set Gold French Verge ▼
- *1820*

A French verge with gold cartouche dial in a turquoise set gold case. Decorative gold open face case, the bezels and middle set with turquoise.
- *diameter 41mm*
- **Guide price $1,740**

Silver Explorer's Watch ▼
- *1878*

A 19th century keyless fusee English lever with up and down dial in a watertight silver case. Comes in a green morocco travelling case with easel stand.
- *diameter 59 mm*
- **Guide price $6,770**

Small Early English Verge ▼
- *1655*

A pre-balance spring English verge in a silver gilt case deeply chased and engraved with a representation of a mythical animal amongst profuse foliage.
- *27mm x 10mm*
- **Guide price $15,220**

Expert Tips

Check that the case of a pocket watch labelled gold really is gold, particularly when purchasing an American watch. Also ensure the mechanism is in good working order.

Jaeger Le Coultre Watch ▲

- *circa 1960*

Jaeger Le Coultre Memovox (alarm) Stainless steel wrist watch with silver digits on a silver face and automatic movement.

- *diameter 4cm*
- **Guide price $2,670**

Rolex Cushion Watch ▲

- *1920s*

Gentleman's Rolex cushion wristwatch set in 9ct gold. With white enamel dial, auxiliary sweep seconds and a red number 12. Rolex signature underneath the dial.

- *diameter 2.5cm*
- **Guide price $1,690**

Ladies Rolex Wristwatch ▼

- *1940*

Ladies 18ct rose gold Rolex wristwatch with original expanding strap with the Rolex symbol on the buckle square face with scalloped lugs. Gold digits on a white face.

- *diameter 2cm*
- **Guide price $3,200**

Ladies Oyster Watch ▼

- *1920s*

Ladies Rolex Oyster wristwatch set in 14ct gold With mechanical movement, a sunburst dial, auxiliary sweep seconds and a white face with gold numbers.

- *diameter 2cm*
- **Guide price $2,670**

Ladies Swiss Watch ▶

- *1920s*

Ladies Swiss made wristwatch in 18ct rose gold with enamel dial with old cut diamonds on the bezel, on an expandable 18ct rose gold bracelet.

- *diameter 1.7cm.*
- **Guide price $890**

Air King Wristwatch ▲

- *1960s*

Gentleman's Rolex Oyster perpetual Air King Model wristwatch in steel and gold. Automatic movement, white dial with gold digits, with a sunburst bezel.

- *diameter 3cm*
- **Guide price $2,490**

Oyster Speedking Watch ▲

- *1950s*

Boys size Rolex Oyster Speedking. Stainless steel mechanical movement with silver digits and expandable Rolex Oyster bracelet.

- *diameter 2.8cm*
- **Guide price $1,690**

Gunmetal World Time Watch ▼

- *circa 1910*

A Swiss lever with world time dial in a gunmetal open face case. White enamel dial with gold decoration.

- *diameter 52mm*
- **Guide price $3,120**

Small Gold Hunter Coin Watch ◄

- *circa 1910*

A Swiss cylinder in a small gold full hunter case, the lids formed from the two halves of a French 20 franc coin dated 1908. When closed the watch resembles a stack of three gold coins.

- *diameter 21mm*
- **Guide price $1,740**

Swiss Digital Dial Lever ▲

- *circa 1895*

Swiss lever with digital dial in a nickle open-face case marked "Acier Garanti" in an oval, gilt winding button.

- *diameter 53mm*
- **Guide price $1,380**

Gold Half Hunter Wrist Watch ▼

- *circa 1880*

A Swiss cylinder by Patek Philippe in a gold half hunter case with blue enamel chapter ring, applied twisted wire lugs for a cord strap.

- *diameter 32mm*
- **Guide price $3,380**

French Oignon Watch and Clock Stand ▲

- *circa 1695*

A French verge oignon watch and ormolu and tortoiseshell stand for use as a clock. Standing on four gilt feet the case has an arched door bordered and decorated with gilt metal.

- *57mm x 22mm*
- **Guide price $10,640**

Silver and Tortoiseshell Verge ◄

- *circa 1688*

An English verge by Tompion in silver and tortoiseshell pair cases with silver pendant and stirrup bow.

- *56mm x 18.5mm*
- **Guide price $14,150**

Gold Half Hunter by Benson ▲

- *circa 1899*

An English lever by Benson in a gold half hunter case. Plain 18ct half hunter case with blue enamel chapter ring, maker's mark "JWB" in an oval.

- *diameter 49mm*
- **Guide price $2,140**

Gold and Enamel Quarter Repeater with Chatelaine ▼

- *circa 1780*

An French quarter-repeating verge in a gold and enamel consular case, decorated with an oval enamel cartouche depicting two cupids. Matching gilt metal and enamel chatelaine.

- *46mm x 11mm*
- **Guide price $12,280**

Gold Minute Repeating Half Hunter ▶

- *circa 1890*

A Swiss minute repeating lever in a gold half hunter case with blue enamel chapter ring, gold slide in the band.

- *diameter 48mm*
- **Guide price $5,700**

Expert Tips

Pocket watches date from 1675 – look out for hand-painted pictures of rural or hunting scenes.

Enamelled Centre Seconds English Verge ▶

- *circa 1789*

An English centre seconds verge in gilt metal. Outer case with engraved gilt bezels and set with a row of green paste stones.

- *64mm x 15mm*
- **Guide price $8,010**

Silver Swiss Half Hunter ▼

- *circa 1910*

A Swiss lever in a silver half hunter case. White enamel dial with subsidiary seconds, Arabic numerals and blue steel hands.

- *diameter 52mm*
- **Guide price $880**

Marine chronometer ◀

- *circa 1870*

A two-day marine chronometer by Dent with a 24 hour dial in a brass bound mahogany box with brass corners. Engraved signed and numbered silvered brass dial with Arabic numerals for 24 hours.

- *175mm x 175mm x 170mm*
- **Guide price $8,720**

Miniature Gold and Enamel Turkish Market Verge ▼

- *circa 1780*

An English verge made for the Turkish market in gold and enamel pair cases, the two halves meeting at a scalloped edge, faces decorated in light blue enamel.

- *34mm x 12mm*
- **Guide price $8,010**

Trench Guard Watch ▼
- *circa 1915*

A First World War large size officer's wristwatch with original mesh "Trench Guard". The white enamel dial with subsidiary seconds, signed Omega. The case struck Omega Depose No. 9846 case # 5425073. The movement with Swan Neck Micro Reg. Signed Omega # 211504.
- *diameter 4.2cm*
- **Guide price $4,000**

Cushion-shaped Watch ▼
- *1924*

Gentleman's silver cushion-shaped wristwatch. The movement signed "Rolex 15 Jewels Swiss Made" Cal 507 Rebberg Depose. The case back signed RWC Ltd. (Rolex Watch Company). The case frame # 655. The dial signed "Rolex Swiss Made". Lug size 22.5mm.
- *width 2.3cm*
- **Guide price $5,070**

Gold Rolex Watch ▲
- *1935*

A 9ct gold gentleman's Rolex wristwatch. The dial signed Rolex Swiss Made, with subsidiary seconds. The case signed Rolex 25 World Records Geneva Suisse R.W.C. Ltd. # 19736 ref # 2356. Movement Sig Rolex Precision 17 Rubis Patented Superbalance Swiss Made.
- **Guide price $8,010**

Oyster Royal Watch ▲
- *circa 1947*

An Oyster "Royal" waterproof Rolex wristwatch, with centre seconds. The case signed "Rolex Geneve Suisse" with screw down Oyster button and case # 506021. Ref # 4444.
- **Guide price $2,760**

Pocket Watch ▶
- *circa 1920*

A high grade fully jewelled minute repeating open face pocket watch, with dial with subsidiary seconds. The case with Swiss control marks for 18ct gold and case # 62837. Repeating activated by a slide on the band.
- **Guide price $8,540**

Peerless Wristwatch ▼
- *1934*

A gentleman's wristwatch, the movement jewelled to the centre signed "Peerless" Swiss Made # 332257 with S & Co Logo. The case # 331618-2 & FB fo Francis Baumgartner Borgelle case designer Enamel dial subsidiary seconds.
- *diameter 3.3cm*
- **Guide price $4,900**

Rolex Officer's Wristwatch ▼
- *circa 1916*

An early First World War officer's wristwatch. The silvered dial signed Rolex & Swiss Made. The movement # 4636 and signed Rolex Swiss 15 Jls. Case signed with "W & D" for Wilsdorf & Davis, the original founders of the Rolex empire. Case # 769936.
- **Guide price $4,450**

Scientific Instruments

French lluminated Globe ▶
- *circa 1950*
French globe made of glass on a
wooden stand in teak finish.
- *30cm x 20cm*
- **Guide price** $1,690

Famous Explorers Globe ▲
- *1807*
Made by Dudley Adams of
London, this globe shows the
accomplishments of the most
famous late 18th century
explorers; for example, the
discoveries of Captain Cook are
carefully marked. Three stretchers
hold a central compass with blued
steel needle.
- *58cm x 30cm*
- **Guide price** $29,370

Terrestrial and
Celestial Globe ▼
- *circa 1820*
Pair of tabletop globes with
wooden four-legged stands and
cross stretchers made by James
Kirkwood of Edinburgh.
- *46cm x 30cm (both)*
- **Guide price** $34,710

Desktop Political Globe ▼
- *1918*
Political globe by Peter
Oestergaard. Warm and cold
ocean currents and steamer routes
are marked. On wooden stand
with a mahogany finish.
- *64cm x 36cm*
- **Guide price** $2,580

Clock Globe ▲
- *circa 1890*
Globe shows the position and
path of the sun over the earth
with working clock and calendar
ring enclosed in a glass dome.
House of Delamarche, France.
- *56cm x 23cm*
- **Guide price** $44,500

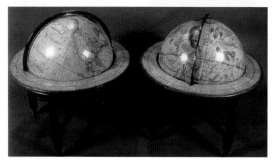

Terrestrial Globe ▼
- *1824*

Eight-inch terrestrial globe by
Delamarche is supported on an
ebonised beech stand which has
four quadrants giving the names
and latitudes of various different
cities.
- *height 20cm*
- **Guide price $13,350**

Travelling Thermometer ▼
- *circa 1810*

Fisherman's or travelling
thermometer in original wooden
Morocco case. Signed:
Richardson, 1 Drury Lane,
Holborn, London.
- *height 12cm*
- **Guide price $1,560**

Boxwood Nocturnal ▲
- *mid 18th century*

Fine boxwood nocturnal. The
central volvelle marked for the
Great Bear G and Little Bear L
constellations, the centre scale
marked with a calendar and hour
scale. The reverse of the
instrument is marked with the
polar distance correction for the
Pole star for both the Great and
Little Bear constellations when
finding the latitude marked Sam
Bosswell Fecit on the fiducial arm
and David Boswell on the handle.
- *height 25cm*
- **Guide price $19,140**

Pocket Globe ▼
- *mid 19th century*

Unsigned but probably German.
Composed of 12 engraved, hand
coloured gores with the
continents outlined in primary
colours. Housed in a blue card
box, the lid marked: "The Earth
and its inhabitants". The box
contains a folded engraved and
hand coloured illustration of 16
males from various parts of the
world in their national costumes,
labelled in English, French and
German.
- *diameter 5cm*
- **Guide price $6,230**

Noon-Day Cannon Dial ▼
- *early 19th century*

Fine noon-day cannon dial by
Boucar, 35 Q de L'Horloge, Paris.
The marble base supports a brass
cannon, adjustable magnifier and
calendar scale. The sun dial
graduated from five to 12 to
seven, correct for latitude 48.5 and 13 minutes.
- *height 26cm*
- **Guide price $10,240**

Map Measure ▼
- *early 19th century*

Map measure by W. & S. Jones,
30 Holborn, London. The gilt
brass case incorporates an enamel
dial graduated in Arabic
numerals, housed in its original
leather case.
- *height 8cm*
- **Guide price $6,680**

Expert Tips

*The original finish is what gives
a scientific item its value, so be
careful as many instruments
have been ruined by the lavish
use of metal polishes combined
with the buffing wheel.*

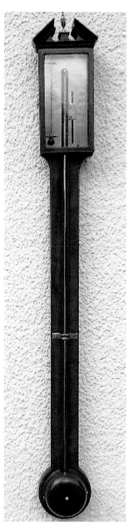

Admiral Fitzroy Barometer ▶

- *circa 1880*
Simple cased oak Admiral Fitzroy antique barometer with thermometer.
- *91.5cm x 14cm*
- **Guide price $1,340**

Mahogany Barometer ▼

- *circa 1840*
Mahogany with boxwood and ebony stringing and with thermometer, hygrometer, convex mirror and level dials.
- *96.5cm x 25.4cm*
- **Guide price $1,340**

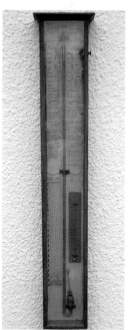

Mahogany and Brass Stick Barometer ▲

- *circa 1810*
Mahogany barometer with door over silver engraved brass scales. The scales always signed by a maker or retailer.
- *96.5cm x 10cm*
- **Guide price $4,720**

Dial Barometer ▶

- *1810–1820*
Mahogany barometer with inlay of flowers and shells. Main dial signed by maker.
- *96.5cm x 25.4cm*
- **Guide price $1,960**

Oak Case Barograph ◀

- *circa 1900*
Simple oak case barograph.
- *19cm x 20cm x 35.5cm*
- **Guide price $1,510**

Six-Drawer Telescope ▲
• *1854*
Miniature travelling six-drawer telescope signed: "Baker, 244 High Holborn, London". Housed in its original leather case with extra eye-piece and folding stand.
• *height 9cm*
• **Guide price $2,760**

Boxwood Quadrant ▲
• *circa 18th century*
English boxwood quadrant incorporating five star positions.
• *height 12.5cm*
• **Guide price $11,570**

Pocket Globe ▶
• *circa 1834*
Fine three-inch pocket globe by Newton Son & Berry, 66 Chancery Lane, London. Housed in its original simulated fish-skin case. The interior with celestial gores for the northern and southern celestial poles.
• *height 7.5cm*
• **Guide price $11,570**

Sand Glasses ▼
• **mid-17th century–early 19th century**
Group of three sand glasses. Manufactured from glass, brass and wood. Each glass has a different time duration and would have been used for a number of timing uses including marine, business, legal and ecclesiastical use.
• *height 27cm*
• **Guide price $5,340**

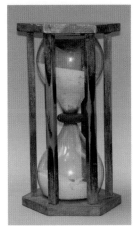

French Armillary Sphere ▲
• **late 19th century**
French armillary sphere signed on the enamel charter ring Grivolat Horloger, Paris. The dial is constructed of steel and brass.
• *height 61cm*
• **Guide price $10,240**

Collector's Items

From car boot to old boots, collectables continue to mesmorise and captivate the serious and amateur rummager alike.

In this disposable age, or perhaps because so much is disposable, the artefacts of today are valued more highly by modern collectors than their equivalents were by previous generations, who generally considered anything owned by their parents to be not worth having.

The old saying still holds true that what one throws away today will be collectable tomorrow. From soap packets to mobile phones, all have their place in the collector's market. But beware of fads that start with a splash and are just as soon forgotten. The most collectable items are those that were, in some way, ground-breaking or revolutionary at the time, such as radios, TVs or telephones. Look out, too, for items that are becoming obsolete in the digital age, such as records or cassette tapes. The great advantage when buying collectables is that they need not be especially old or cost a great deal to be considered valuable.

Advertising & Packaging

Bisto Tin ▼
- 1960

Tin of Bisto with a girl wearing a green hat and a boy with a red hat, both sniffing the aroma from a gravy boat.
- *height 19cm*
- **Guide price $25**

My Fair Lady Talc ▲
- 1960

Cusson's My Fair Lady talc, showing a photograph of a blonde-haired lady.
- *height 14cm*
- **Guide price $25**

Castle Polish ▲
- 1930

Red tin of Castle Ballroom floor polish with a picture of a castle.
- *height 11cm*
- **Guide price $20**

Pearce Duff's Custard Powder ◄
- 1950

Tin of Pearce Duff's custard powder with a picture of a bowl of custard and pineapple, plums and pears on each side.
- *height 11.5cm*
- **Guide price $20**

Ashtray ▼

• **1955**
Ashtray with "Don't forget your Anadin tablets" written in white writing on a red background and decorated with a two-tone green Anadin packet.
• *15cm square*
• **Guide price $20**

Thorne's Creme Toffee ▲

• **1924**
Royal blue tin with gold scrolling and the words, "Thorne's Extra Super Creme Toffee and British Empire Exhibition Souvenir".
• *height 5.5cm*
• **Guide price $50**

Huntley and Palmers Biscuits ▼

• **1927**
A British toy tank containing Huntley & Palmers biscuits.
• *height 9.5cm*
• **Guide price $1,420**

Sandwich Tin ▲

• **1930**
Yellow French sandwich tin with a red handle and trim, showing Mickey Mouse offering Pluto some sweets on the lid.
• *8cm x 18cm*
• **Guide price $270**

Aero Chocolate ▲

• *circa 1930*
Unused bar of Aero chocolate in a brown wrapper with cream writing by Rowntrees.
• *width 11cm*
• **Guide price $35**

Gray Dunn's Biscuits ▶

• **1915**
Yellow ochre bus with red roof and wheels with figures looking out of the window and a bus conductor. With the letters "Gray Dunn's Biscuits" in red and "Lands End to John O' Groats".
• *height 9.5cm*
• **Guide price $2,670**

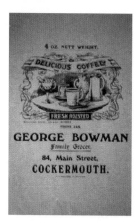

Coffee Packet ▲
- **1920s**

A packet of "delicious coffee", "fresh roasted" by George Bowman of 84 Main Street, Cockermouth. 4oz nett weight.
- *24cm x 19cm*
- **Guide price $10**

Probyn's Sign ▲
- **circa 1930**

An enamel sign for Probyn's Guinness's Stout – the Harp label. From the Argus Brand showing a picture of two stout bottles.
- *65cm x 40cm*
- **Guide price $710**

Cherry Blossom Shoe Stand ▶
- **circa 1930**

A tin and wood shoe stand advertising Cherry Blossom shoe polish in dark tan, with printed transfer on its sides.
- *height 30cm*
- **Guide price $270**

McVities & Prices Digestive Biscuits ▼
- **1930**

Small red tin with a cream lid and a boy seated on a red tin of McVitie & Price's Digestive Biscuits.
- *diameter 8cm*
- **Guide price $20**

Redbreast Tobacco Tin ▼
- **1930**

Ogden's Redbreast Flake tobacco tin, made in Liverpool, decorated with a robin shown perched on a branch.
- *width 14cm*
- **Guide price $20**

Pot Lid ▲
- **1890s**

Areca Nut toothpaste for "Beautiful White Teeth" with black and white underglazing, made in London.
- *diameter 6cm*
- **Guide price $150**

Show Card ▲
- **circa 1890**

Greensmith's Derby dog biscuits showcard (chrono lithograph) showing a clown holding a hoop for a dalmatian to jump through.
- *45cm x 34cm*
- **Guide price $350**

Book Mark ▼

- *circa 1910*

A book mark advertising
giveaways for Wright's Coal Tar
Soap. The Nursery Soap,
inscribed with the words "The
Seal of Health and Purity".

- *length 15.4cm*
- **Guide price $20**

Player's Ash Tray ▼

- *1930*

Pottery Player's ashtray showing
an interior scene with a man
seated smoking a pipe, a lady in a
green dress, a hound, and the
words "Player's Tobacco Country
Life and Cigarettes".

- *width 11.5cm*
- **Guide price $45**

Golden Leaf Tobacco Tin ▲

- *circa 1912*

Golden leaf navy cut tobacco tin,
manufactured by Louis
Dobbelmann, Rotterdam.
Showing an angel blowing a horn
and flying on wings in the center
of the tin, surrounded by flowers
and the Dutch flag.

- *width 8cm*
- **Guide price $110**

Grimbles Brandy ◀

- *circa 1900*

Grimbles royal cognac brandy of
Albany St, London. 3s per bottle.
Set in a red shield with gold foliate
design.

- *height 45cm*
- **Guide price $50**

Senior Service Tobacco ▲

- *1940*

Red plaque with the written
inscription "Senior Service
Satisfy – Tobacco at its best".

- *height 28cm*
- **Guide price $25**

Ceramic Coaster ▼

- *1890s*

A white beer coaster advertising
The Cannon Pale Ale, from the
Cannon Brewery Co Ltd and
bottled by Plowman & Co Ltd,
London.

- *diameter 16cm*
- **Guide price $310**

Bottles

Porcelain Snuff Bottle ▼
- *circa 1900*
Chinese porcelain snuff bottle with topaz stopper and silver rim.
- *height 7.5cm*
- **Guide price $120**

Opaque Bottle ▲
- *circa 1900*
Chinese opaque glass snuff bottle decorated with emerald green flowers and an oriental bird. With a cornelian stopper set within a silver rim.
- *height 7.5cm*
- **Guide price $310**

Pagoda Snuff Bottle ▲
- *circa 1900*
Chinese white snuff bottle decorated with crimson fish underneath a pagoda roof. Green stone stopper set in silver.
- *height 7cm*
- **Guide price $310**

Snuff Bottle ▼
- *circa 1900*
Opaque glass Chinese snuff bottle with a stylised sepia leopard chasing its tail.
- *height 6cm*
- **Guide price $260**

Blue Glass Bottle ▲
- *circa 1900*
Blue glass Chinese snuff bottle with green stone stopper set in silver.
- *height 6cm*
- **Guide price $170**

Chinese Bottle ▲
- *circa 1900*
Chinese snuff bottle decorated with a panda and palm trees with a semi precious stone stopper set in silver.
- *height 8cm*
- **Guide price $170**

Shalimar Scent Bottle ▲

• *1960*
Shalimar clear glass perfume
bottle with scrolling and bee
design, one of a limited edition of
a 100 manufactured.
• *height 20cm*
• **Guide price** $270

Saturday Night Lotion ▼

• *1940*
Saturday Night Lotion in clear
glass bottle with circular gilt
stopper.
• *height 14cm*
• **Guide price** $120

Schiaparelli Perfume ▲

• *1960*
Clear glass bottle in the form of
a female model. In a moulded
glass case.
• *10cm x 6cm*
• **Guide price** $450

Eau de Cologne ▲

• *1950*
Scrolling glass bottle with
burgundy flame stopper.
• *height 16cm*
• **Guide price** $210

Lancôme Bottle ◄

• *1960*
Lancôme perfume bottle with a
foliate design on the stopper
complete with original box.
• *10cm x 4cm*
• **Guide price** $150

Expert Tips

Sealed bottles with their original contents and carton are king. Also inventive forms and good makers.

Gold Tassle Bottle ▼

- *circa 1920*

Art Deco clear glass perfume bottle with yellow spots, and royal blue leaf design around the base and gilt stopper and gold tassle.
- *height 15cm*
- **Guide price $450**

Prince Matchabelli Bottle ▼

- *circa 1930*

Prince Matchabelli perfume bottle in the shape of a ceramic crown with gilt cross stopper, in original box.
- *height 4cm*
- **Guide price $220**

Cut Glass Bottle with Black Banding ▶

- *circa 1920*

Art Deco cut glass oval bottle with black enamel banding.
- *4cm x 11cm*
- **Guide price $330**

Art Deco Bottle ▲

- *circa 1930*

European Art Deco glass bottle with fine floral and foliate engraved stopper.
- *height 22cm*
- **Guide price $450**

Black Tassle Bottle ▼

- *circa 1920*

Moulded Art Deco glass bottle with black circular design and black tassle.
- *height 14cm*
- **Guide price $210**

Wedgwood Bottle ▼
- *circa 1930*
Wedgwood blue bottle with silver plate stopper.
- *height 4cm*
- Guide price $150

Silver Bottle ▼
- *1893*
Small silver bottle ornately engraved with a floral design.
- *height 5cm*
- Guide price $280

Ruby Red Bottle ▶
- *1880*
Ruby red double-ended perfume bottle with silver stoppers.
- *height 12.5cm*
- Guide price $330

Candy Stripe Bottle ▲
- *circa 1850*
Candy stripe pink glass perfume bottle with a rose gold stopper.
- *height 6cm*
- Guide price $510

Ruby Bottle ▶
- *1911*
Ruby red perfume bottle with a foliate design engraved in the silver stopper.
- *height 7cm*
- Guide price $170

Green Double Bottle ▲
- *1880*
Green perfume bottle with pinch back stoppers.
- *length 13cm*
- Guide price $300

Hallmarked Bottle ▶

- *1889*

Dual-ended cut glass Victorian
bottle with silver gilt stopper
hallmarked London, 1889.
- *length 14cm*
- **Guide price $440**

Victorian Bottle ▲

- *circa 1880*

Purple glass scent bottle with
silver stopper.
- *length 9cm*
- **Guide price $440**

Joy de Jean Patou Scent Bottle ▲

- *circa 1950*

Large black plastic bottle, large
red stopper, Joy de Jean Patou.
- *height 15cm*
- **Guide price $170**

Silver Case ◀

- *circa 1899*

Clear glass perfume bottle inside
a fine silver case.
- *height 4cm*
- **Guide price $500**

Twisted Glass Bottle ▲
- *1890*
Twisted glass perfume bottle with an opal and diamond stopper.
- *length 6.5cm*
- **Guide price** $980

Bloodstone Bottle ▲
- *19th century*
Bloodstone snuff bottle and stopper from China.
- *7.5cm x 3.2cm*
- **Guide price** $390

Cameo Bottle ▼
- *1860*
Thomas Webb cameo bottle in original box.
- *height 11cm*
- **Guide price** $4,900

Perfume Bottle ▼
- *1870*
Glass perfume bottle with a silver gilt stopper with amethyst stones, inscribed "M.S.V.".
- *height 9cm*
- **Guide price** $760

Heart Shaped Bottle ▶
- *1870*
Silver heart-shaped bottle with scrolled design.
- *height 9cm*
- **Guide price** $930

Silver Scent Bottle ▲
- *1760*
Silver lozenge shaped perfume bottle with a foliate design.
- *height 11.5cm*
- **Guide price** $1,160

Cranberry Perfume Bottle ▲
- *1870*
Cranberry glass perfume bottle with moulded bubbles with a silver lid.
- *height 10cm*
- **Guide price** $710

Cameras

Kodak Advertisement ▶

- *circa 1950*

An advertisement in the shape of
a yellow box of film with the
words "Kodak Verichrome Safety
Film" with black and red check
border.

- *41cm x 43cm*
- **Guide price $180**

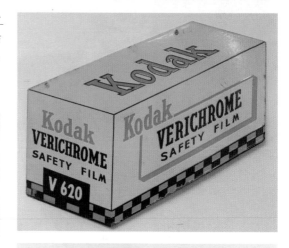

Ikonta Camera ▲

- *circa 1950*

Ikonta model no.524/2. Novur
Lens. F stop 4.5.

- *16cm x 10cm*
- **Guide price $270**

French Sign ▲

- *circa 1940*

Advertisement with a picture of a
camera and the words "*Film
appareils Lumiere – En Vente Ici*".

- *85cm x 80cm*
- **Guide price $360**

Sign for Photos ▶

- *circa 1950*

Cream metal sign with the word
"Photo" in red with red and
yellow border.

- *40cm x 59cm*
- **Guide price $90**

Zeiss Strut Camera ▲

- *1928*

A 4.5 x 6cm Strut-type camera,
with compur shutter.

- *10cm x 9cm*
- **Guide price $360**

Camera Sign ◀

- *circa 1950*

Yellow sign with red writing with
the words "*Appareils Pellicules*" a
sign for cameras and films.

- *26cm x 93cm*
- **Guide price $170**

Retina Kodak Camera ▲
- *circa 1960*
Retina-Xenar F2.8 45mm lens by Kodak.
- *height 8cm*
- Guide price $130

Franke & Heidecke Rolly Camera ▲
- *1921–40*
Frank & Heidecke Braunschweig, Germany, Rolley Heidoscop three lens stereo camera including its own case. 7.5cm F4.5 Tessar Lens.
- *height 17cm*
- Guide price $1,250

Soligor Camera ▲
- *circa 1960*
Soligor 50mm lens, Japanese made auto lens.
- *height 7cm*
- Guide price $130

Expert Tips

When purchasing an antique camera ensure, that it is in good working order and check the quality of the lens. Remember to ask the dealer which film type the camera uses as some films are no longer manufactured.

Robin Hood Camera ▼
- **1930**
Black marbelised bakelite Robin Hood camera with a picture of Robin Hood by Standard Cameras of Birmingham. Takes darkroom loaded single sheets of 45 x 107mm film. Originally came with film, paper and darkroom safelight. Sometimes seen in England, but rarely seen elsewhere.
- *height 5cm*
- Guide price $120

Miniature Tessina ▼
- **1960**
Swiss-made miniature Tessina camera in the style of a watch, with meter and strap. It took exposure on 35mm film, which was divided up in special cartridges.
- *width 6.8cm*
- Guide price $1,600

Mamiya ▲
- **1959**
Japanese Mamiya 16 camera.
- *width 11.5cm*
- Guide price $90

Contina Zeiss Camer ▲
- *circa 1960*
Zeiss Contina camera with an F2.8 45mm Novica lens.
- *height 7cm*
- Guide price $50

Rajar Bakelite Camera ▼
- *1929*

Rajar black bakelite No.6.
Folding camera. With 120 roll
film, with 6 x 9cm negative size.
- *height 17cm*
- **Guide price $90**

Rolleiflex Camera ▼
- *circa 1955–65*

Rolleiflex camera with a Tessar
1.3.8. F7.5mm lens.
- *height 19cm*
- **Guide price $120**

Revere Stereo 33 ▲
- *1950*

Revere Stereo 33 made in the
U.S.A. 35mm F3.5 Amaton.
Complete with its original leather
case.
- *width 19cm*
- **Guide price $450**

Ensign Cupid Camera ▼
- *1922*

Ensign Cupid simple metal-
bodied camera. 4 x 6cm exposures
on 120 film. The design is based
on a 1921 prototype for a stereo
camera, which was never
produced. Mensicus achromatic
F11 lens. Available in black, blue,
grey and some other colours.
- *height 8cm*
- **Guide price $160**

Tennents Lager Can Camera ▲
- *1980*

Promotional Tennents lager can
camera.
- *length 12cm*
- **Guide price $70**

The New Special Sybil ▶
- *1914–35*

The new special Sybil. Ross
Xpress F4.5 112mm. N & G
special shutter.
- *height 16cm*
- **Guide price $270**

Kodak Camera ▲
- *circa 1960*

Kodak 35 camera with an F4.5
51mm lens.
- *height 6cm*
- **Guide price $90**

Weston Master Light Meter ◀

- *circa 1940*

English Weston Master light meter.
- *9cm x 6cm*
- **Guide price $35**

Lizars Challenge ▶

- *circa 1903*

Lizars Challenge made in Glasgow mahogany frame and brass fittings, Bush and Long Lens.
- *17cm x 21cm*
- **Guide price $450**

Speed Graphhic ▲

- *circa 1948*

Miniature "Speed Graphic" camera. Optar Lens 101mm.
- *23cm x 16cm*
- **Guide price $530**

Meopta Admira 8F Camera ▶

- *circa 1960*

Meopta Admira 8F- similar to the A8G but with BIM.
- *16cm x 16cm*
- **Guide price $50**

Newman Sinclair ▲

- *circa 1946*

A Newman Sinclair, London. Used generally in the Antartic. London 35mm spring-driven movie camera. Polished patterned Duralumin body. Ross Xpres F3.5 lens.
- *24cm x 25cm*
- **Guide price $3,560**

Bolex H 16 ▶

- *circa 1950*

Swiss-made Paillard Bolex H16 Cine camera still used by students today for animation. Black leather body.
- *23cm x 24cm*
- **Guide price $530**

Ensign Auto-speed Camer ▼
- *1932*

Ensign auto-speed camera inscribed on the side, 100mm F4.5 lens, with focal plane shutter speed of 15–500 sec.
- *height 20cm*
- **Guide price $350**

Zenit B Camera ▲
- *circa 1960*

Zenit B camera with 300mm lens.
- *height 8cm*
- **Guide price $120**

Bolex Camera ▼
- *circa 1960*

A Bolex P1 zoom cine camera.
- *height 38cm*
- **Guide price $260**

Bolex Projector ▲
- *circa 1960*

An M.A. Bolex projector.
- *height 50cm*
- **Guide price $270**

Newman & Guardia ▼
- *1913*

The ideal Sybil camera by Newman & Guardia with an unusual Ross Express 136mm F4.5 Lens. The camera takes 3.25 x 4.25 inch film.
- *height 23.5cm*
- **Guide price $440**

Kodak Eastman ▲
- *circa 1920*

No.2 Hawkette brown tortoiseshell effect bakelite folding camera by Kodak.
- *height 18cm*
- **Guide price $120**

Contax G1 Camera ▲
- *circa 1990*

Contax G1, 35mm camera with an F2 Planar lens by Carl Zeiss.
- *height 8cm*
- **Guide price $90**

Hasselblad 550c Camera ▼
- *circa 1970*

A Hasselblad. Model 500c, 18mm
with 2.8 planner lens.
- *17cm x 10cm*
- **Guide price $1,250**

Super Nettle Camera ▼
- *circa 1920*

Zeiss Super Nettel. 11. F2.8.
Black leather covered press
camera.
- *9cm x 14cm*
- **Guide price $890**

Franke & Heideck
Rolleiflex Camera ▲
- *mid 20th century*

A Rolleiflex 2.8F Lens Zeiss,
made by Franke & Heideck.
- *13cm x 12cm*
- **Guide price $1,070**

Perkeo Camera ▼
- *circa 1954*

A Perkeo with rangefinder Color
Skopar lens in Prontor SVS
shutter. Voigtlander.
- *6cm x 12cm*
- **Guide price $360**

Expert Tips

*The condition of a camera body
and its shutter mechanism is
very important. Likewise, the
lenses must be free of scratches
for them to be worth collecting.*

Nikon Red Spot Camera ▼
- *1965*

Nikon F known as Red Spot.
Lens 50mm F1.4.
- *height 14cm*
- **Guide price $620**

Petie Vanity Camera
and Compact ▶
- *circa 1956*

Petie camera housed in a make up
compact. Front door opens to
reveal mirror and powder. One
top knob contains a lipstick,
another provides storage for an
extra roll of film. Beautiful Art
deco marblelized finish in either
red, green or blue made by Kreher
and Bayer Offenbach, Germany.
Kigu a British make of powder
compacts. Highly collectable.
- *8cm x 10cm*
- **Guide price $890**

171

Chess Sets

Silver and Enamel Chess Set ◀

- *circa 1940*
A fine Austro-Hungarian silver and enamel chess set.
- *height 8cm*
- **Guide price $9,790**

Dieppe Bone Chess Set ▼

- *circa 1790*
A polychrome bone "Dieppe" bust set. The pawns and bishops having lacquered paper hats.
- *height 7.5cm*
- **Guide price $12,100**

Indian Chess Set ▲

- *circa 1835*
Chess set by John Co. Rooks from India.
- *height 11cm*
- **Guide price $7,030**

Ebony Fruitwood Chess Set ▲

- *circa 1805*
Rare inverted lyon French chess set, made of ebony and fruitwood with carved bone mounts and horses heads.
- *height 8cm*
- **Guide price $4,360**

Ivory Chess Set ◀

- *circa 1830*
Finely carved ivory Indian chess set.
- *height 12cm*
- **Guide price $3,470**

Napoleon & Frederick the Great Chess Set ◄

- *circa 1850*

Rare German cast iron figural chess set of Napoleon verses Frederick the Great.
- *height 6.7cm*
- **Guide price $4,180**

South East Asian Ivory Chess Set ▲

- *circa 1880*

South East Asian natural and red stained figural ivory chess set.
- *height 4cm*
- **Guide price $9,790**

Blue and Green Bakelite Chess Set ◄

- *circa 1930*

Unusual blue and green Bakelite chess men with board and box.
- *height 7cm*
- **Guide price $1,210**

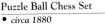

Puzzle Ball Chess Set ▼

- *circa 1880*

Cantones ivory Puzzle Ball chess set with a lacquer stand.
- *height 13.5cm*
- **Guide price $4,450**

Mysore Chess Set ▼

- *circa 1845*

Superb quality carved sandalwood and rosewood Indian Mysore chess set on a Hindu theme.
- *height 7cm*
- **Guide price $12,190**

War of Independence Chess Set ▲

- *circa 1830*

A French monobloc ivory American War of Independence polychromed figural chess set.
- *height 10cm*
- **Guide price $27,590**

Expert Tips

The very earliest chess sets were made in India in 600 AD or earlier. By 1000 AD the game had spread through Europe and as far as Scandinavia.

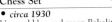

Coins & Medals

German Long Service Cross ▶
- **1936–1945**
NSDAP Long Service Cross, German Third silver for 25 years. GVF
- *Diameter 5cm*
- **Guide price $400**

WWI Iron Cross ▲
- **1870**
Iron Cross 2nd class, maker's mark "KO" which denotes it as a rare WWI made piece.
- *Diameter 4cm*
- **Guide price $530**

Order of the Bath ▶
- **1867–68**
A fine civil order of the Bath and Abyssinian campaign group of three consisting of Civil 1st type gold with gold pin buckle, Coronation 1902 in silver, and Abyssinian War Medal 1867–68 . All mounted for wear by Spink & Son London.
- *Diameter 6cm*
- **Guide price $510**

Third Lufwaffe ◀
- **1936–45**
German Third Lufwaffe Wireless Operator Air Gunners' Badge.
- *Diameter 3cm*
- **Guide price $400**

Kitzbuhel Shooting Badge ▲
- *1943*
Attractively enameled Kitzbuhel shooting badge, maker's mark "Ges Gesch" and the inscription Meisterklasse Kitzbuhel
- *Diameter 4cm*
- **Guide price $290**

Naval Service Medal ▲

- *1914–19*

Naval Distinguished Service medal with GVR bust, as awarded to: A8654. J. Crorkran. Sea. R.N.R. Mediterranean Service, 23 March, 1918. This award was mentioned in the London Gazette on 7.8.1918, and was approved for services in action with enemy submarines.
- *diameter 4cm*
- **Guide price $700**

DSO Miniature Medal Group ▲

- *1895–1902*

An unattributable contemporary group of three miniatures comprising: Distinguished Service Order, VR Gold Type, Delhi Durbar medal 1902, and India General Service medal with 3 clasps; Punjab Frontier 1897–98, Samana 1897, Tirah 1897–98. Medals mounted for wear with attachment pin by Spink & Son, London.
- *diameter 6cm*
- **Guide price $260**

Khedive's Star ▼

- *circa 1890*

Khedive's star dated 1882. Unnamed as issued.
- *diameter 4cm*
- **Guide price $100**

Purple Heart Award ▼

- *1932–present*

Purple heart medal of the Vietnam period. This is awarded for gallantry, the wounded or those killed in action in the service of the military forces of the United States of America.
- *diameter 4cm*
- **Guide price $40**

British Victory Medal ▲

- *1914–19*

British Victory medal, as awarded to Lieutenant J.C Holmes RAF, and Ceylon Planters Rifle Corps medal. Inscribed on rim with: "Marathon Race, L.C.P.L.J.C. Holmes Kandy 1913". This man was killed in action on Sunday the first September 1918 in Egypt, aged 29. Having served in the Ceylon Planter's Rifle Corps, transferred on 17/11/1915 to the Yorkshire Regiment, was later commissioned as a second Lieutenant and joined the Royal Flying Corps and latterly the Royal Air Force.
- *diameter 12cm*
- **Guide price $580**

Military Cross ▲

- *1914–19*

Military Cross, GVR, unofficially named on reverse: A. Melville Kennedy. 8th BN. Royal Scots Fusiliers June 1917.
- *diameter 4cm*
- **Guide price $700**

Inter-Allied Victory Medal ◀

- *1914–19*

Inter-allied Victory medal for the Great War, this is the Italian version, with maker's mark: "Sacchimi – Milano".
- *diameter 4cm*
- **Guide price $25**

Indian Army Long Service Medal ▶

- **1910–1936**
Indian Army Long Service and
Good Conduct Medal for Indians.
GVR Kaisar-i-hind bust.
- *Diameter 4cm*
- **Guide price $50**

Naval Reserve ▲

- **Pre-1914**
Royal Naval Reserve Decoration,
GV type with pre-1914 plain
green ribbon.
- *Diameter 3cm*
- **Guide price $45**

Q.S.A. ▲

- **1899**
Q.S.A. with two fixed clasps,
O.F.S. swivel suspension, and
contact marks.
- *Diameter 4cm*
- **Guide price $45**

Lapland Shield ▼

- **1939–45**
Lapland shield made from zinc on
a cloth backing.
- *Diameter 3cm*
- **Guide price $530**

Efficiency Decoration ▶

- **1936–1952**
The Efficiency Decoration, GV1,
with second award long service
bar, territorial top bar, and
Honourable Artillery Company
ribbon.
- *Diameter 3cm*
- **Guide price $70**

Volunteer Officer Medal ▼

- **1897**
Volunteer Officer's Decoration
V.R. cypher complete with top
bar pin and hallmarks for London
1897–98.
- *Diameter 3cm*
- **Guide price $170**

Third Lufwaffe ▼

- **1936–45**
German Third Lufwaffe Wireless
Operator Air Gunners' Badge.
- *Diameter 3cm*
- **Guide price $400**

Royal Air Force Brooches ▼
- *circa 1918*
Pair of Royal Air Force
sweetheart brooches made from
15 carat gold, with original box.
- **Guide price $350**

Masonic Collar Jewel ▼
- *1920*
Thirtieth degree Masonic collar
jewel with hinged crown above a
double-headed phoenix clutching
a double-edged sword.
- **Guide price $110**

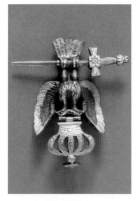

Edward VII Florin ▼
- *1802*
Edward VII florin. A scarce
example in enamel, centred with
Britannia.
- **Guide price $270**

George IV Shilling ▲
- *1826*
A George IV shilling. Unusual
because both sides are enamelled.
- **Guide price $450**

Masonic Jewel ▲
- *1930*
St John's Lodge whole Masonic
jewel. This hallmarked jewel
bears a good quality enamel of St
John the Martyr.
- **Guide price $130**

Victoria Crown ▲
- *1845*
1845 crown with the head of the
young Queen Victoria, centred
with enamel bearing the Royal
Standard.
- **Guide price $180**

Grand Master Jewel ▼
- *1850*
A jewel of the Grand Master's
Masonic Lodge, with a face with
rays of light radiating behind,
within an enamel blue circle.
- **Guide price $90**

Half Crown ▼
- *1854*
Enamel Victorian half crown
with the Royal Standard within a
laurel border.
- **Guide price $60**

Rose Cross ▼
- *1900*
Fifteen carat gold exceptionally
rare Rose Cross with coloured
jewel and a swan within degrees
and dividers surmounted by a
hinged crown with seven stars.
- **Guide price $620**

Boer War Medal ▼
- **1899–1900**
Queen's South Africa medal,
1899–1900 with six clasps; Relief
of Kimberley, Paardeberg,
Driefontein, Johannesburg,
Diamond Hill, Wittebergen, as
awarded to: 82180 Bomb:
WHLR: H. BlissEett. "P" BTY:
R.H.A. This man was wounded
during a Victoria Cross action at
Nooitedacht on the 13th of
December 1900.
- *diameter 4cm*
- **Guide price $670**

Campaign Service Medal ▼
- **1970–82**
Campaign Service medal with
one clasp; Northern Ireland,
South Atlantic medal 1982, with
rosette, UN Cyprus medal
(UNFICYP), as awarded to:
24501637 Gunner J.C Howe
Royal Artillery. Group mounted
court style for wear.
- *diameter 12cm*
- **Guide price $620**

Victorian Crown ▼
- **1887**
Mounted example of a Victorian
crown with fine enamels.
- **Guide price $170**

Air Force Cross ▲
- **1960–present**
US Airforce, Air Force cross.
- *diameter 5cm*
- **Guide price $80**

Distinguished Service Medal ▲
- **1970–present**
US Defence Distinguished
Service medal.
- *diameter 5cm*
- **Guide price $80**

Victoria Half Crown ▲
- **1876**
Enamel half crown
commemorating the reign of
Queen Victoria with fine
enamels.
- **Guide price $440**

Five Mark ▼
- **1875**
Unusual five mark coin. Well-
defined example centred with the
Habsburg Eagle.
- **Guide price $620**

George II Crown ▼
- **1743**
Rare example of George II crown
with fine enamels representing
England, Scotland and Ireland.
- **Guide price $710**

British Medal ▼
- **1890–97**
British South Africa Company
medal without clasp. Inscribed on
the reverse: Rhodesia, 1896. As
awarded to: 93593 Shoeg.Smith
W.Didoe. 10.B.Y.R.A. Died in
South Africa on 26th May, 1900.
- *diameter 4cm*
- **Guide price $530**

Military Cross ▶
- **1910–1936**
The Military Cross, GV, with inscribed name on reverse N.P. Spooner.
- *Diameter 4cm*
- **Guide price $60**

Sede Vacante ▼
- **1758**
Silver coin from the Papal states, *Sede Vacante 1 Scudo* from the Rome Mint.
- *Diameter 3.5cm*
- **Guide price $710**

Cyprus Coin ▶
- **circa 1928**
First Colonial Crown Cyprus coin, 45 Piastres.
- *Diameter 3.5cm*
- **Guide price $210**

Cape Colony Medal ◀
- **1902**
South African Cape Colony Medal – Coldstream Guards.
- *Diameter 4cm*
- **Guide price $130**

Crimea Medal ▲
- **1854–56**
Crimea Medal with no clasp, issued without a name.
- *Diameter 4cm*
- **Guide price $170**

Victoria Cross ▼
- **2003**
A modern example of a Victoria Cross in good condition.
- *Diameter 4cm*
- **Guide price $50**

SS Long Service ▼
- **1936–45**
German World War Two SS Long Service Medal for eight years. Bronze with original blue moire silk ribbon.
- *Diameter 4cm*
- **Guide price $610**

Expert Tips

Condition: FDC (mint), UNC (uncirculated), EF (extremely fine), VF (very fine), F (fine). "Fine" coins have considerable wear but you can still see the main features and inscriptions.

Zodiameterc Wheel Coin ▼

- **238–161 AD**
Copper drachma coin from
Roman Egypt featuring Antonius
Pius with zodiacmeterc wheel on
reverse.
- *Diameter 2.5cm*
- **Guide price $6,680**

Alexander the Great Coin ▶

- **336–323 BC**
Gold coin with the head of
Alexander the Great from the
Mileus Mint.
- *Diameter 1.5cm*
- **Guide price $2,940**

Bithynian Kingdom Coin ▼

- **124–94 BC**
Bithynian Kingdom silver
tetradrachm coin, featuring
Nicomedes III
- *Diameter 1.5cm*
- **Guide price $890**

Roman Gaius Coin ◀

- **24–37 AD**
Copper Roman coin, Gaius
Caligula Dupondius, from the
Rome Mint.
- *Diameter 2.5cm*
- **Guide price $710**

Roman Crispina Coin ▼

- **177–192 AD**
Roman coin featuring Crispina,
wife of Commodus Sestertius,
from the Rome Mint.
- *Diameter 3cm*
- **Guide price $320**

Ptolemaic Empire Coin ◀

- **30–81 BC**
Copper 80 drachna coin from the
Ptolemaic Empire Egyptian Mint,
Alexandria.
- *Diameter 1.5cm*
- **Guide price $2,310**

Maurice Tiberius Flollis Coin ▶

- **582–602 AD**
Maurice Tiberius flollis coin from
the Constantin Mint.
- *Diameter 2cm*
- **Guide price $50**

Constantine VII Coin ▶

- *945–9 AD*

Constantine VII and Romanus II
AV Solidus. from the
Constantinople Mint.
- *Diameter 1.5cm*
- **Guide price $470**

Crusader coin ▲

- *1275–1297 AD*

Crusaders of Tripoli coin,
Bohemond VII.
- *Diameter 2cm*
- **Guide price $160**

Peter III Gold Coin ▼

- *1336–1387*

Spanish gold coin from Barcelona
featuring Peter III.
- *Diameter 2cm*
- **Guide price $400**

German Third Spanish Cross ◀

- *1939–45*

Bronze German Spanish cross
with swords, no maker's mark.
- *Diameter 4cm*
- **Guide price $830**

Islamic Coin ▼

- *1201–1230 AD*

Rulers of Mardin al-Nasir Idirhm.
- *Diameter 2cm*
- **Guide price $70**

Ottoman Coin ▼

- *157–495 AD*

Murad III Sultani coin from
Gidrekipsine Mint.
- *Diameter 1.5cm*
- **Guide price $130**

Spanish Coin ◀

- *1556–1598 AD*

Spanish coin, Phillipe II, from
the Seville Mint.
- *Diameter 3cm*
- **Guide price $850**

Expert Tips

*Beware! There is more damage
done cleaning coins than
by anything else. If you
absolutely have to wash coins,
use slightly soapy water, never
use metal polish. A scratch
can cost you a mint!*

Knight Templar Collar ▲
- *1850*
Unusual Knight Templar's collar jewel with enamelled double cross in silver, gold, red, black and white.
- **Guide price $180**

Founder Jewel ▲
- *1940*
Hallmarked silver founder jewel with Masonic symbols painted on the enamel, set between two pillars
- **Guide price $70**

George IV Shilling ▲
- *1820*
Attractive example of the George IV shilling with enamel centre, with the Crown and Lion.
- **Guide price $70**

Victorian Shilling ▼
- *1897*
Victorian shilling with enamel standard and the date 1897.
- **Guide price $40**

Diamond Jubilee Medal ▼
- *1897*
Commemorative medal for the Diamond Jubilee of Queen Victoria decorated in silver, gilt and paste settings. The central cartouche of Queen Victoria is set within 24-paste diamonds, within the angle and the divider.
- **Guide price $110**

Canada General Service Medal ▼
- *1866–70*
Canada General Service medal 1866–70, with one clasp; Fenian Raid 1866, as awarded to: 311 Pte. A. Carroll, 7th Bn. Royal Fusiliers.
- *diameter 4cm*
- **Guide price $530**

Gold Post Master Jewel ▲
- *1930*
Nine carat gold Post Master jewel representing the guild of Freeman Lodge, decorated with the City of London's coat of arms.
- **Guide price $250**

Burmese Rupee ▲
- *1920*
Burmese rupee centred with a peacock. Whilst of exceptionally high quality this example is one of the more common seen on the market.
- **Guide price $210**

Victorian Crown ▲
- *1897*
A Victorian crown with a strong depiction of George and the dragon highlighted in enamel. Reasonably common example.
- **Guide price $110**

WWI Death Plaque ▲
- **1917**
World War One Death Plaque for Albert James Donovan 35th Battalion, Australian Infantry.
- *Diameter 4cm*
- **Guide price $120**

Royal Red Cross ▲
- **1913**
Royal Red Cross, second class (Associate), ARRC, GVR initials engraved on the reverse. In Garrad and Co. titled case of issue, with wearing pin.
- *Diameter 4cm*
- **Guide price $180**

Order of Medjidiek ▶
- **1916–17**
Order of Medjidie together with Royal Society of Arts Silver Medal awarded to A. J. Todd, Professor of the Khedivial School of Law.
- *Diameter 4cm*
- **Guide price $690**

Imperial Service Medal ▼
- **1901–1910**
Early star-shape EVII Imperial Service Medal, unnamed in case of issue.
- *Diameter 4cm*
- **Guide price $130**

Luftschutz Cross ◀
- **1938**
Luftschutz Cross, first class, in gold with original loop and ring suspender and pin-back ribbon. Rare, with less than 150 awarded.
- *Diameter 4cm*
- **Guide price $1,200**

Order of the War Cross ▲
- **1936–39**
Order of the War Cross "Cruz de guerra", second class, breast star in silver, awarded during the Spanish Civil War of 1936–39. In deluxe box of issue with the makers name, "Insustrias Egana" Motrico.
- *Diameter 4cm*
- **Guide price $350**

Sports Badge ▲
- **circa 1937**
Weightlifting bronze athlete's sports badge.
- *Diameter 3cm*
- **Guide price $580**

War Merit Cross

- *1939*

War Merit Cross, first class, with maker's mark.
- *Diameter 4cm*
- **Guide price $130**

Khartoum Medal

- *1897*

Khedive's Sudan Medal with one clasp.
- *Diameter 4cm*
- **Guide price $180**

Jubilee Medal

- *1897*

Silver jubilee medal in Wyon of Regent Street case, complete with wearing pin.
- *Diameter 4cm*
- **Guide price $180**

Hitler Youth Medal

- *1939*

Hitler Youth Kreisseiger 1939 bronze and enamel medal, maker's mark H. Aurich, Dresden.
- *Diameter 4cm*
- **Guide price $350**

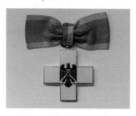

German Red Cross

- *1934*

German Red Cross, second class, white enameled cross with eagle in black and without swastika. The ribbon is in the style of a lady's bow.
- *Diameter 4cm*
- **Guide price $220**

German Iron Cross Bar

- *1939*

Second-class Bar badge of an eagle clutching a wreath.
- *Diameter 4cm*
- **Guide price $280**

Army Roll of Honour Clasp

- *1941–45*

Very rare Army Roll of Honour Clasp. An actual presentation award piece, the clasp is a superb fire-gilt tombak swastika in very high relief with slight wear.
- *Diameter 3cm*
- **Guide price $1,510**

Commemorative Ware

Patriot Jug

- *circa 1855*
Crimean War Royal Patriot jug by
Hill Pottery.
- *height 21cm*
- **Guide price $530**

Queen Victoria
Earthenware Mug ▶

- *circa 1887*
Golden Jubilee earthenware mug
to commemorate Queen Victoria.
Made for Cardiff Sunday school
children, presented by the Mayor.
- *height 8.5cm*
- **Guide price $140**

Doulton Beaker ▲

- *circa 1897*
Royal Doulton Queen Victoria
Diamond Jubilee beaker.
- *height 9.5cm*
- **Guide price $230**

Corn Laws Plate ◀

- *circa 1845*
Small hexagonal ceramic plate to
commemorate the abolition of
the corn laws, with the
inscription "Our bread untaxed
our commerce free".
- *diameter 11cm*
- **Guide price $210**

Diamond Jubilee
Chinaware Mug ▼

- *circa 1897*
A bone chinaware mug
celebrating the Diamond Jubilee
with a portrait of Queen Victoria
with all the Commonwealth
countries inscribed.
- *height 9cm*
- **Guide price $220**

Boer War Pin Tray ▼

- *circa 1900*
Carlton Ware circular pin tray to
commemorate the Boer War
depicting Lord Kitchener, Lord
Robert, and Buller.
- *diameter 11cm*
- **Guide price $200**

Doulton Beaker ▼

- *circa 1887*
Unusual-shaped bone china
beaker to commemorate the
Golden Jubilee of Queen Victoria.
- *height 10cm*
- **Guide price $200**

Golden Jubilee Plate ▼

- *circa 1887*
Royal Worcester blue and white
earthenware plate of Queen
Victoria's Golden Jubilee.
- *diameter 27cm*
- **Guide price $220**

Mason's Jug ▼

- **1935**

Mason's ironstone jug commemorating King George and Queen Mary, a limited edition of 1,000. With King George and Queen Mary in profile within a wreath border.
- *height 19cm*
- **Guide price $490**

Memorial Plaque ▶

- **1972**

An oval basalt plaque of the Duke of Windsor in memoriam.
- *8.3cm x 10.8cm*
- **Guide price $90**

Commemorative Plaque ▼

- **1914–15**

Bone china plaque commemorating the alliance between Germany and Austria, Kaiser Wilhelm II and Franz Joseph.
- *diameter 23.5cm*
- **Guide price $300**

Royal Albert Commemorative Mug ▲

- **1935**

Bone china Royal Albert commemorative mug of the Silver Jubilee of King George V and Queen Mary.
- *height 7cm*
- **Guide price $100**

Loving Cup ▼

- **1936–37**

Loving cup to commemorate the proposed Coronation of Edward VIII.
- *height 25.3cm*
- **Guide price $240**

Copeland Mug ▼

- **1936–7**

Earthenware mug for the proposed Coronation of Edward VIII, made by Copeland for Thomas Goode of London.
- *height 9.8cm*
- **Guide price $170**

Wedgwood Mug ▼

- **1939**

Wedgwood mug to commemorate the visit of King George and Queen Elizabeth to America with the inscription "Friendship makes Peace".
- *height 10cm*
- **Guide price $290**

Jubilee Jug ▼
• 1897
Doulton commemorative jug of
Queen Victoria's Diamond
Jubilee with a silver rim and olive
green cartouches showing Queen
Victoria.
• *height 16cm*
• **Guide price $430**

Doulton Mug ▼
• 1901
Doulton bone china mug
depicting Queen Victoria in
memoriam with purple
decoration around the rim, and
decorated with a prayer book,
inscribed below with the words,
"She wrought her people lasting
good".
• *height 7.6cm*
• **Guide price $850**

Diamond Jubilee Beaker ▲
• 1897
Goss white bone china beaker
celebrating Queen Victoria's
Diamond Jubilee.
• *height 9.7cm*
• **Guide price $200**

Royal Wintonia Mug ▲
• 1911
Royal Wintonia earthenware mug
for the Investiture of Edward
Prince of Wales made for the City
of Cardiff.
• *height 8cm*
• **Guide price $160**

Royal Doulton Beaker ▼
• 1902
Royal Doulton earthenware
King's coronation beaker
celebrating the coronation of
Edward VII in rare purple.
• *height 9.8cm*
• **Guide price $170**

Princess Mary Mug ▼
• 1929
Earthenware mug to
commemorate the visit of
Princess Mary Viscountess
Laschelles to Castleford.
• *height 8.6cm*
• **Guide price $310**

Coronation Mug ▼
• 1911
Green and white coronation mug
of George V. Manufactured by
Booths.
• *height 7.5cm*
• **Guide price $120**

Balance of Payments Plate ▶

- *1887*
Octagonal earthenware Golden Jubilee plate commemorating the Balance of Payments.
- *diameter 24cm*
- **Guide price $230**

Joseph Chamberlain Plate ▲

- *1904*
Ridgeway earthenware plate commemorating Joseph Chamberlain.
- *diameter 25cm*
- **Guide price $120**

King Edward Coronation Earthenware Jug ▲

- *1902*
Royal Doulton earthenware jug from the Lambeth factory to commemorate the Coronation of King Edward VII.
- *height 21cm*
- **Guide price $270**

King's Beaker ▼

- *1902*
Royal Doulton beaker commemorating the King Edward VII's Coronation Dinner, with a silver hallmarked rim, presented by His Majesty.
- *height 10cm*
- **Guide price $230**

Child's Plate ▼

- *1897*
A child's plate commemorating Queen Victoria's diamond jubilee.
- *diameter 16cm*
- **Guide price $120**

Princess of York Mug ▼

- *1937*
Royal Doulton bone china mug depicting a picture of Princess Elizabeth as a young girl.
- *height 9cm*
- **Guide price $710**

William Gladstone Charger ▼

- *1898*
Commemorative charger of William Gladstone with a cartouche of Hawarden Church and of his home Hawarden Castle.
- *diameter 25cm*
- **Guide price $130**

Edward VII Earthenware Mug ▼

- *1910*
An earthenware mug to commemorate the demise of Edward VII.
- *height 10cm*
- **Guide price $200**

King George & Queen Mary Beaker ▲

- *circa 1911*
Enamel on tin beaker to commemorate the Coronation of King George V and Queen Mary and also the investiture of the Prince of Wales.
- *height 10cm*
- **Guide price $120**

Lions' Heads Beaker ▲

- *2002*
Limited edition beaker of 2500 from the Royal Collection to commemorate the Golden Jubilee of Queen Elizabeth II.
- *height 22cm*
- **Guide price $90**

Booths Coronation Mug ▲

- *circa 1911*
Ceramic coronation mug to commemorate King George V and Queen Mary, by Booths.
- *height 9cm*
- **Guide price $110**

Prince William Bone China Mug ▲

- *2003*
Royal Collection English bone china mug to commemorate the 21st birthday of Prince William.
- *height 15cm*
- **Guide price $35**

Loving Cup ◄

- *1977*
Limited edition of 250 loving cup for the Silver Jubilee of Elizabeth II.
- *27cm x 37cm*
- **Guide price $2,230**

Paragon Mug ▼

- *circa 1935*
Silver Jubilee bone china paragon mug of George V and Queen Mary.
- *height 8cm*
- **Guide price $130**

Hammersley Bone China Mug ▼

- *circa 1935*
Bone china mug to commemorate the Silver Jubilee of King George V and Queen Mary – transfer with enamel colours.
- *height 10cm*
- **Guide price $170**

Prince William Porcelain Mug ◄

- *1982*
Porcelain mug by J. & J. May to commemorate the birth of Prince William depicting a pram with the royal crest.
- *height 9cm*
- **Guide price $120**

Expert Tips

Check that the painting or transfer has not been defaced in any way by harsh cleaning or chips on the porcelain. Also check the provenance as this contributes to the item's value.

Brass Shield Plaque ▼
• *1897*
Brass plaque of Queen Victoria in
the shape of a shield to
commemorate the Diamond
Jubilee of Queen Victoria.
• *43cm x 32cm*
• **Guide price $310**

Imperial Beer Stein ▼
• *1870*
Imperial half-litre size beer stein
with attractive painted enamelled
panel of Ulanen, of the Imperial
Lancers, hunting in a
mountainous landscape. Inscribed
with the following undamaged
lettering: "Zur Erinnerung an
meine Dienstzeit".
• *height 24cm*
• **Guide price $880**

Blue and White Plaque ▲
• *1898*
Blue and white plaque of William
Gladstone to commemorate his
death. Maker Burgess and Lee.
• *39cm x 25.8cm*
• **Guide price $410**

Gordon Highlanders ▲
• *1890*
One of a pair of Gordon
Highlander commemorative
plates. Decorated with a picture
of a soldier standing guard, with
the words "Gordon Highlander"
inscribed around the figure.
• *height 21cm*
• **Guide price $130**

Crown Devon Jug ▼
• *1937*
Crown Devon jug musical "Super
Jug" to commemorate the
coronation of King George VI
and Queen Elizabeth. Limited
edition. With a lion handle.
• *height 30.5cm*
• **Guide price $4,000**

German Knight ▼
• *1918*
German bronzed spelter figure of
a knight in armour on a stained
wood plinth, with a dedication
plate on the side to Major
Niemann from his brother
officers of the 39 Field Artillery
Regiment, 22 March to 16
November, 1918.
• *height 45.5cm*
• **Guide price $580**

Wall Plaque ◄
• *1938*
German black ash wall plaque
with metal relief of Artillery crew
serving their gun, and metal
label reading: "Res. battr. Opel 39.8.38.
11.10.38".
• *23cm x 32.5cm*
• **Guide price $200**

Fans

Ostrich Feather Fan ▶

- *circa 1900*
Ivory fan with fine ostrich feathers.
- *26cm x 41cm*
- **Guide price** $100

Child's Fan ▲

- *circa 1920*
Child's cream lace fan with sequins at the centre of the flower and a bone handle with gilt-scrolling.
- *14cm x 25cm*
- **Guide price** $80

Romantic Spanish Fan ▲

- *circa 1900*
Hand-painted Spanish or French fan of two ladies and a gentleman holding a garland of roses in a pastoral setting.
- *26cm x 49cm*
- **Guide price** $200

Dancing Figures Fan ▲

- *circa 1920*
Small ivory fan with a pierced ivory foliate design and featuring a silhouette of two figures dancing.
- *13cm x 23cm*
- **Guide price** $50

Pink Feather Fan ▲

- *1920*
Pink feather fan with ivory handle, painted with birds and floral design.
- *22cm x 30 cm*
- **Guide price** $45

Union Castle Cruise Fan ▼

- *circa 1900*
Hand-painted flowers on parchment with delicate wood frame inscribed "Union Castle Line souvenir".
- *21cm x 35cm*
- **Guide price** $40

Expert Tips

The earliest of all fans were palm leaves in Biblical times, but for the collector the late seventeenth century fan would be seen as the birth of European fans and Victorian fans can still be found today. Look out for fine painting on the parchment, silk, or paper and the better the sticks (arms) the more valuable. Ivory, mother-of-pearl and tortoiseshell are the most common.

Benedictine Fan ◀

- *1920*
An advertisement fan featuring a figure in red holding a lamp sitting beside a bottle of Benedictine.
- *23cm x 34cm*
- **Guide price** $40

Spanish Fan ▲

- *circa 1920*
Satin Spanish silk fan with ivory stick featuring a hand-painted romantic man giving a rose to a lady.
- *24cm x 29cm*
- **Guide price** $100

Gentlemen's Accessories

Maiden with Rifle Tobacco Jar ▶

- *circa 1890*

A very rare German Conta and Boheme porcelain jar modelled as a young woman standing before a drum holding a rifle.

- *26cm x 18cm*
- **Guide price $1,510**

Laughing Cavelier Tobacco Jar ▲

- *circa 1880*

Conta and Boheme porcelain jar modelled as a cavelier seated on a half-barrel holding a goblet.

- *25cm x 14cm*
- **Guide price $1,320**

Devil Tobacco Jar ▼

- *circa 1900*

Terracotta devil head tobacco jar by Johann Maresch.

- *14cm x 18cm*
- **Guide price $690**

Entertainer Tobacco Jar ▼

- *circa 1880*

Porcelain jar modelled as an entertainer, sitting on a large drum, his dog beside him.

- *height 38cm*
- **Guide price $1,140**

Girl on Trunk Tobacco Jar ▼

- *circa 1880*

Conta and Boheme porcelain jar modelled as a young woman with trumpet in hand seated on a trunk.

- *height 26cm*
- **Guide price $1,140**

Victor Hugo Tobacco Box ▼

- *circa 1890*

Conta and Boheme porcelain figural tobacco box.

- *height 35cm*
- **Guide price $1,030**

Expert Tips

Tobacco jars were mostly made in the nineteenth century from terracotta or majolica, but rare versions come in bronze or wood.

Jack on Guard Tobacco Jar ▼

- *circa 1890*
Appealing polychrome painted terracotta figure of a golass-eyed begging dog wearing a straw hat.
- *39cm x 27cm*
- **Guide price $5,870**

Mother-of-Pearl Desk Set ▶

- *circa 1810*
A fine quality Palais Royal mother-of-pearl and gilt-bronze inkstand having elaborately scrolling handles and a base enriched with tiles of mother-of-pearl.
- *9cm x 24cm*
- **Guide price $29,370**

Bloch Tobacco Jar ◀

- *circa 1900*
Polychrome and painted terracotta jar from a series produced by Bernhard Bloch of a black man at the races.
- *height 33cm*
- **Guide price $2,760**

Frog Tobacco Jar ▲

- *circa 1900*
Tobacco jar of Phylias Fogg seated in a top hat holding a book by Bernhard Bloch.
- *37cm x 15cm*
- **Guide price $2,580**

Pair of Monteiths ▲

- *circa 1810*
A pair of Regency red tole monteiths decorated with classical urns, swags and vine leaves.
- *11cm x 27.5cm x 20cm*
- **Guide price $11,570**

Jack Russell Tobacco Jar ▲

- *circa 1910*
Part polychrome painted terracotta jar modelled as a barrel with a black and white Jack Russell forming the lid. Maker Johann Maresch.
- *height 20cm*
- **Guide price $1,200**

Folding Bagatelle Table ▲

- *circa 1890*
Victorian mahogany folding games table with green baize interior, complete with a cue, cue rest and a set of balls.
- *13cm x 92cm x 51cm*
- **Guide price $490**

Bowler Hat ◀

- *circa 1930*
Black bowler hat with original box from James Lock & Co. Ltd., 6 St James Street, London SW1.
- *height 32cm*
  - **Guide price $80**

Top Hat ▲

- *circa 1940*
Grey top hat by Army and Navy, London.
- *height 14cm*
- **Guide price $80**

Travelling Mirror ▲

- *1930*
Travelling mirror in original leather case with the letter H.R.B. inscribed on the lid.
- *diameter 23cm*
- **Guide price $70**

Miniature Tool Kit ▲

- *1920*
Miniature travelling tool kit in a leather case with "Bonsa" on flap.
- *width 14.5cm*
- **Guide price $530**

Shaving Brush ▲

- *1903*
Gentlemen's travelling silver shaving brush.
- *length 14.5cm*
- **Guide price $710**

Spirit Flasks ▶

- *1920*
Pair of silver-plated spirit flasks housed in original leather case.
- *height 15cm*
- **Guide price $530**

Grey Top Hat ▲

- *1930*
Grey top hat with original box by Herbert Johnson of New Bond St, London.
- *height 16cm*
- **Guide price $130**

Horn Beakers ◀

- *1873*
Nest of six horn beakers with hall marked solid silver collars in original leather case.
- *height of case 14,5cm*
- **Guide price $3,560**

Handbags

Pink Velvet Bag ▶

- *circa 1820*
Pink velvet ladies evening bag,
with ormolu ornate foliate frame
and rosette base.
- *10cm x 8cm*
- **Guide price** $130

Victorian Leather Handbag ▲

- *circa 1860*
Rare and unusually small
Victorian fine leather handbag
with silver frame and clasp in
excellent condition.
- *15cm x 16cm*
- **Guide price** $290

Austrian Silver Tapestry Bag ▲

- *1850*
Black tapestry bag with rose pink
floral pattern, a fine Austrian
silver frame with unusual figures
of ladies entwined in the
scrolling.
- *25cm x 26cm*
- **Guide price** $490

Dogs Head Clasp Handbag ▼

- *circa 1920*
Silver lame rose fabric with lilac
silk lining and an unusual dog's
head clasp with ruby eyes.
- *21cm x 20cm*
- **Guide price** $190

Gold Scrolling Purse ▼

- *circa 1860*
Cream felt purse with gold
embroidered scrolling design.
- *height 21cm*
- **Guide price** $260

Buffalo Skin Purse ▼

- *1903*
Art Deco buffalo skin purse with
a silver chain and frame,
hallmarked with unusual silver
circular ring handle for use with a
chatelaine.
- *9cm x 10cm*
- **Guide price** $130

Chinese Silk Purse ◀

- *1920*
Delicate rose Chinese silk and
gold thread overlay handbag with
enamel and green stone clasp.
- *26cm x 25cm*
- **Guide price** $170

Blue Beaded Bag ▼
- *circa 1940*

Blue beaded circular bag with an unusual gilt ball clasp and generous beaded looped handle.
- *diameter 16.5cm*
- Guide price $530

Bakelite Bag ▼
- *1950*

American silver grey bakelite bag with lucite top. With a flower and foliate design standing on ball feet.
- *height 15cm*
- Guide price $470

Pink Sequinned Bag ▼
- *1960*

English baby pink beaded and sequinned small evening bag.
- *width 22cm*
- Guide price $290

Two Owls Bag ▲
- *1930*

Brown leather bag with strap decorated with two owls with beaded glass eyes, surrounded by a foliate design.
- *width 21cm*
- Guide price $260

Leather Handbag ▶
- *1930*

Brown leather handbag with chrome and orange bakelite clasp.
- *width 21cm*
- Guide price $530

Cream Beaded Bag ▲
- *1880*

Victorian cream beaded bag depicting a basket of pink flowers with emerald green and pink beaded tassels, gilt clasp and chain handle.
- *height 21cm*
- Guide price $1,240

Laurel Leaf Handbag ▼
- *18th century fabric and 19th century frame*
Woven silk bag with a gilt laurel leaf design frame inset with pearls.
- *27cm x 21cm*
- **Guide price $470**

Coral Clasp Purse ▶
- *circa 1780*
Tapestry bag with gilt and delicate coral inlay, cameo glass clasp and gilt chain.
- *25cm x 25cm*
- **Guide price $470**

Cocktail Mirror Bag ▼
- *circa 1950*
Ladies black cocktail oval silk bag with handle and small square mirrored sides.
- *8cm x 15cm*
- **Guide price $110**

Beaded Roses Purse ▲
- *circa 1850*
Large beaded bag with rose design and a gilt frame with chain.
- *30cm x 28cm*
- **Guide price $650**

Tapestry Bag ▼
- *circa 1760*
Early romantic tapestry bag of birds and crest on one side and a floral and foliate cartouche with the portrait of a young handsome gentleman on the reverse – silver frame and handle.
- *18cm x 15cm*
- **Guide price $270**

Belgian Crewell Handbag ▼
- *1910*
Belgian crewell work of pink roses and purple flowers with a blue scrolling design on black silk and a floral gilt frame and jewelled clasp.
- *19cm x 20cm*
- **Guide price $280**

Black Beaded Bag ▼
- *1890*

Fine black beaded Victorian bag with floral design of pink roses, blue cornflowers and daisies, with a filigree frame and paste jewels.
- *height 25cm*
- **Guide price** $880

Clear Perspex Bag ▼
- *circa 1950*

Clear perspex American bag with foliate design on the lid.
- *height 11cm*
- **Guide price** $440

Petit Point Handbag ▶
- *circa 1940*

A handbag with black petit point background decorated with flowers in a vase.
- *width 21cm*
- **Guide price** $490

Moiré Silk Evening Bag ▲
- *circa 1940*

Brown moiré silk evening back with a geometric gilt clasp by Josef.
- *height 17cm*
- **Guide price** $470

Wicker Bag ▼
- *1950*

Wicker bag made by Midas of Miami, decorated with birds, and green, orange and blue sequins.
- *width 37cm*
- **Guide price** $240

Velvet Bag ▲
- *circa 1860*

Black velvet bag with cut steel beading of a heraldic design. With metal clasp and chain.
- *height 28cm*
- **Guide price** $1,590

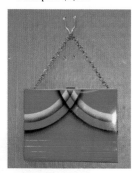

Red Plastic Bag ▲
- *1930*

Red plastic bag with a gold and black geometrical design, with a gilt chain handle.
- *width 19cm*
- **Guide price** $700

Velvet Strawberries Purse ▼
- *circa 1960*

Plastic cream wicker bag with
handle with pink and red velvet
strawberries on the lid, pearls set
in the green velvet leaves and
pink velvet and gold trim.
- *18cm x 26cm*
- **Guide price $230**

Pink Beaded Bag ▼
- *circa 1930*

Very unusual soft pink beaded bag
with circular beaded tassels.
- *height 25cm*
- **Guide price $200**

Flowers and Butterflies Handbag ▶
- *circa 1960*

Woven wool bag with butterflies
and floral design with carrying
handles.
- *27cm x 25cm*
- **Guide price $130**

Beaded Deco Purse ▲
- *circa 1920*

Black Art Deco silk ladies bag
with a scrolling design of silver
and black jet beads.
- *11cm x 17cm*
- **Guide price $120**

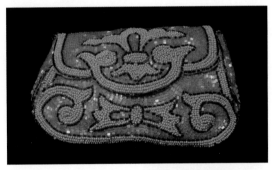

Chrome Velvet Bag ▶
- *circa 1960*

Velvet ladies evening bag with
chrome stripes and handle.
- *height 25cm*
- **Guide price $220**

Plastic Strawberries Purse ▼
- *circa 1950*

Woven wicker bag with plastic
strawberries and white flowers on
the lid with red velvet trim.
- *height 20cm x 26cm*
- **Guide price $140**

Sequined Bag ▼
- *circa 1930*

Small ladies Art Deco sequined
bag with fine cream beaded
scrolling and ribbon design.
- *10cm x 14cm*
- **Guide price $100**

Beaded Bag ▲
- *circa 1920*
Gold metal beaded bag with pink lotus flowers and a green and pink geometric design, with a metal clasp and gold and silver looped fringing.
- *height 20cm*
- **Guide price $700**

Bulaggi Bag ▼
- *circa 1950*
Bulaggi plastic bag with gold metal fittings and handle, with the inscription Bulaggi on the right-hand side.
- *width 17cm*
- **Guide price $150**

English Handbag ▶
- *1831*
English leather handbag with floral design. Inside the inscription reads "His Majesty King William the Fourth to his dutiful subject and servant John Singleton Lord Lyndhust AD 1831".
- *width 19cm*
- **Guide price $310**

Brown Bakelite Bag ◀
- *1950*
America brown bakelite bag with lucite cover with faceted foliate design, made by Solar.
- *height 15cm*
- **Guide price $700**

Wicker Bag ▲
- *1950*
Simulated wicker bag with a fabric head of palomino horse made by Atlas of Hollywood.
- *width 32cm*
- **Guide price $290**

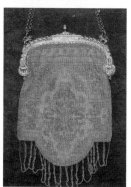

Metal Beaded Bag ▼
- *circa 1920*
Metal beaded bag with a blue, pink and gold floral design and a gilt frame and chain.
- *height 22cm*
- **Guide price $1,240**

Petit Point Bag ◀
- *circa 1940*
Petit point bag decorated with figures on horseback outside a castle, with an opaline beaded and enamel frame.
- *width 21cm*
- **Guide price $700**

Victorian Beaded Bag ▲
- **1890**
Cream Victorian fine beaded bag with pink and yellow roses, with a silver gilt frame and pink and green glass beaded tassles.
- *height 25cm*
- **Guide price $880**

Ken Lane Handbag ▲
- **1960**
Ken Lane brown handbag with a dramatic coral circular diamante handle.
- *height 15cm*
- **Guide price $530**

Floral Handbag ▲
- *circa 1940*
Petit point floral design bag with black enamel frame with gilt scalloped edge and gilt chain.
- *width 19cm*
- **Guide price $530**

Clochette Evening Bag ▶
- *circa 1920*
Clochette shaped beaded evening bag, with rows of blue and pink with a black metal filigree clasp and silver and black handle.
- *height 18cm*
- **Guide price $700**

Chain Link Bag ▼
- **1900**
Gilt chain link bag with an Art Nouveau lady on the rim inset with sprays of berries inset with red stones and foliate design.
- *height 14cm*
- **Guide price $700**

Velvet Bag ▼
- *circa 1860*
Victorian cream velvet evening bag with a silver filigree frame, and fine cut-steel looped fringing.
- *height 23cm*
- **Guide price $880**

French Beaded Bag ▼
- *circa 1950*
French beaded bag decorated with pink roses and a gold and white beaded frame inset with enamel roses.
- *width 22cm*
- **Guide price $1,240**

Silk Evening Bag ▲
- *circa 1920*
Black silk evening bag decorated with flowers in blue, red and green with steel chips decoration.
- *height 18cm*
- **Guide price $530**

Pink Suede Purse ▼
- *circa 1960*

Pink suede handbag with gilt oval clasp.
- *height 26cm*
- **Guide price** $290

Chain Coin Purse ▲
- *circa 1900*

A fine chain mail coin purse with expanding clasp.
- *height 6cm*
- **Guide price** $130

Silver Mesh Bag ▼
- *circa 1930*

Silver mesh bag with a delicate pink and orange floral design, a silver foliate design frame and chain handle.
- *height 18cm*
- **Guide price** $400

Belgian Art Deco Purse ▲
- *circa 1920*

Belgian Art Deco silk leaf design with gold overlay and gilt foliate. The styled frame is inset with green stones and the purse has a blue stone clasp.
- *19cm x 20cm*
- **Guide price** $310

Whiting & Davis Purse ▲
- *circa 1920*

Art Deco chain-mail bag with pink, blue, and cream design and a grey and silver frame by Whiting and Davis.
- *height 16cm*
- **Guide price** $35

Amethyst Clasp Handbag ▼
- *circa 1910*

Art Nouveau ladies evening bag of finely woven material with delicate silver scrolling frame, silver chain handle and an amethyst clasp.
- *18cm x 19cm*
- **Guide price** $290

Kitchenalia

Bakelite Cruet ▶

- *1960*

Salt and pepper pots made from Bakelite styled as a red pepper and green chilli.

- *height 9cm*
- **Guide price** $20

Kenwood Mixer ▲

- *1952*

Classic design steel Kenwood "Chef" food mixer with red dial and red lid, together with a steel bowl.

- *36cm x 37cm*
- **Guide price** $110

Kosy Kraft Teapot, Sugar Bowl, and Water Jug ▲

- *1958*

Pale pink china and stainless steel teapot, sugar bowl, and water jug. Unused in their original with "Kosy Kraft Ever-Hot: The Greatest Name in Thermal Tableware" box and wrapper.

- *35cm x 35cm*
- **Guide price** $130

Expert Tips

Bakelite is a synthetic plastic with properties that make it ideal for kitchenware. It was very popular in the 20s, 30s and 40s.

Milk Shake Mixer ▼

- *circa 1940*

Classic stainless steel café milk shake mixer, with wood handle and metal stand.

- *height 47cm*
- **Guide price** $130

Bovril Cup ▲

- *1960*

Red plastic cup with "Bovril warms and cheers" in white writing.

- *height 9cm*
- **Guide price** $35

Weighing Scales ▲

- *1950*

Beige Salter ten lb kitchen scale.

- *height 24cm*
- **Guide price** $20

Enamel Coffee Pot ▼
- *1890*

White enamel coffee pot in two sections with purple flowers and red banding.
- *height 33cm*
- **Guide price** $130

Enamel Utensil Rack ▼
- *1890*

French utensil rack painted red and black with a shaped top, white tray, and grey utensil.
- *height 54cm*
- **Guide price** $120

Metal Weighing Scales ▲
- *1890*

Metal kitchen weighing scales with metal base and copper scoop and weights, inscribed "To weigh 2lbs".
- *height 22cm*
- **Guide price** $180

Worcester Ware Cake Tin ▲
- *1950*

Worcester Ware tin with a red lid and "Cakes" in red letters on the front and "Worcester Ware made in England" on the base.
- *diameter 22cm*
- **Guide price** $50

Copper Dish ▲
- *1920*

Medium size copper dish with cover and brass handles.
- *9cm x 22cm*
- **Guide price** $100

Small Iron ▲
- *circa 1920*

Small iron with a moulded base made by W. Cross and Son.
- *length 12cm*
- **Guide price** $30

Sucre and Café Pots ◄
- *1920*

French enamel blue and white marbled pots printed in black with the words "sucre" and "café".
- *height 23cm*
- **Guide price** $80

Metal Weighing Scale

- *1950*

Metal Hanson five lb.weighing
scale.
- *height 25cm*
- **Guide price** $100

Storage Jar ▼

- *1930*

Hanging enamelled storage jar
with a wooden lid and flue and
white check design.
- *height 24cm*
- **Guide price** $70

French Enamel Rack ▼

- *1890*

French pale blue enamel utensil
rack with shaped top and blue
and white sunshine border with
two pale blue utensils.
- *height 52cm*
- **Guide price** $130

Porcelain Jars ▶

- *1910*

Five French cream pottery storage
jars in three different sizes for
cafe, sucre, farine and poivre,
each one decorated in blue with
wild flowers.
- *height 22cm*
- **Guide price** $170

Enamel Storage Tin ▶

- *1890*

French enamel storage tin with
yellow and blue marbled pattern.
- *height 15cm*
- **Guide price** $40

Blue and White Coffee Pot ▲

- *1890*

French enamel coffee pot, white
with blue banding and a white
scrolling pattern.
- *height 29cm*
- **Guide price** $140

Bread Board ▼

- *circa 1940*

Circular wood bread board with
the inscription "Bread" and a
foliate design surrounding a
central flower.
- *diameter 28cm*
- **Guide price** $50

Large Brass Kettle ▼

- *1920*

Oversized brass English kettle.
- *height 20cm*
- **Guide price** $120

Plastic Container Set ▶
- *circa 1959*

A set of flour, sugar, rice, tea and coffee containers in variegated sizes, each one having a figurative design, and also a set of five smaller containers on a plastic shelf.
- *height 26cm*
- **Guide price $150**

Cornish Ware Jug ▲
- *1959*

Blue and white-striped Cornish Ware milk jug
- *height 18cm*
- **Guide price $150**

Set of Egg Cups ▶
- *circa 1930*

A set of four green Bakelite egg cups on a circular tray.
- *height 8cm*
- **Guide price $20**

Bakelite Egg Cups ▼
- *circa 1950*

A set of four Bakelite egg cups: two yellow, one blue and one red.
- *6cm x10cm*
- **Guide price $10**

Spice Containers ▲
- *circa 1950*

A set of five cream Australian Bakelite spice containers with red lids on a shelf.
- *height 8cm*
- **Guide price $160**

Sputnik Egg Cups ◀
- *circa 1950*

Set of red, yellow, grey, black, blue, and green Sputnik egg cups with matching spoons.
- *height 3cm*
- **Guide price $35**

Expert Tips

Most kitchenalia is nineteenth and twentieth century and a good start for collectors with a budget.

Fruitwood Flour Scoop ▶

- **1940**
Fruitwood flour scoop carved
from one piece of wood with a
turned handle.
- *length 28cm*
- **Guide price $35**

Enamel Casserole Dish ▲

- **1910**
French enamel casserole dish
with painted cornflowers and
variegated blue, white and
turquoise, with white handles.
- *height 18cm*
- **Guide price $120**

Green Thermos ▲

- **1950**
Green Vacwonder metal thermos
painted with a selection of
sportsmen including runners,
cyclists, shot putters and
swimmers, made to commemorate
the Olympic Games.
- *height 27cm*
- **Guide price $120**

Art Deco Allumettes ▲

- **1920**
Art Deco allumettes storage box
decorated with a purple floral and
geometric design with red spots.
- *height 13cm*
- **Guide price $80**

Peugeot Frères Coffee Grinder ▲

- **1950**
Wooden coffee grinder with the
makers mark in brass, Peugeot
Frères Valentigney (Doubs) with
a large metal handle and wood
knob.
- *height 19cm*
- **Guide price $90**

Butter Press ▲

- **circa 1890**
Wooden butter press with an oak
leaf mould.
- *height 19cm*
- **Guide price $100**

French Water Jug ▶

- **1880**
Large white French enamel water
jug with red banding and a red
pattern of squares and a central
diamond with four gold bands.
- *height 29cm*
- **Guide price $100**

Blue Enamel Candleholder ▶

- **1880**
French blue enamelled
candleholder with gold-banding
on the handle.
- *diameter 16cm*
- **Guide price $35**

Hoover Janitor ◄
- *circa 1950*
Classic metal and cloth Hoover
Janitor.
- *height 106cm*
- **Guide price $60**

Kitchen Material ▲
- *circa 1950*
Unused kitchen curtain fabric
with red coffee grinders and
assorted containers and floral
arrangements in baskets on a
white background.
- *width 94cm*
- **Guide price $130**

Sputnik Butter Dish ▼
- *circa 1950*
Red plastic Sputnik-style butter
dish with white spots, standing on
three legs.
- *height 12cm*
- **Guide price $15**

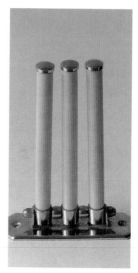

Tea Towel Rail ▲
- *circa 1960*
Metal tea towel rail coated with
yellow plastic.
- *length 16cm*
- **Guide price $15**

Sugar Shaker ▼
- *circa 1950*
Glass sugar shaker with metal lid
and spout.
- *height 18cm*
- **Guide price $20**

Cheese Dish ►
- *circa 1950*
Clear plastic cheese dish with
plastic stand and geometric plastic
handle.
- *10cm x 18cm*
- **Guide price $30**

Ham Stand ▼
- **1910**
English white pottery ham stand.
- *height 20cm*
- **Guide price $70**

English Sugar Jar ▲
- **1950**
English white porcelain sugar jar
with a circular wood lid with a
royal blue geometric design with
the words "Sugar" in black.
- *height 17cm*
- **Guide price $50**

Metal Salad Sieve ▲
- **1920**
Metal salad sieve with handles
and two feet.
- *height 24cm*
- **Guide price $25**

Enamel Utensil Rack ◀
- **1880**
French Royal and light blue
enamel wall hanging utensil rack,
with two utensils.
- *height 52cm*
- **Guide price $130**

Copper Kettle ▼
- **1850**
Large English rose copper kettle
with original patina.
- *height 30cm*
- **Guide price $220**

Porcelain Wall Box ▲
- **1950**
Porcelain wall box with wooden
lid and decorated with fruit and
blue banding with "Allumettes"
in gold writing.
- *height 15.5cm*
- **Guide price $70**

Bread Bin ▲
- **1890**
French enamel red and white
marbling bread bin with handles
each side and a handle on the
cover.
- *height 23cm*
- **Guide price $90**

Toast Rack ▶

- *circa 1950*
Yellow plastic toast rack with
black spots.
- *length 12cm*
- **Guide price $15**

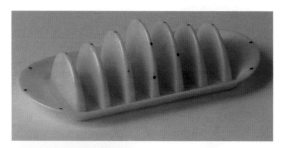

Metal Saucepans ▲

- *circa 1940*
Blue and grey metal saucepan
with lid.
- *height 30cm*
- **Guide price $25**

Pink Pyrex Dish ◀

- *circa 1950*
Pink Pyrex casserole dish with
snowflake design, set on a metal
stand with two burners.
- *15cm x 36cm*
- **Guide price $20**

Ceramic Cruet Set ▼

- *circa 1960*
White ceramic cruet decorated
with pink fish.
- *height 16cm*
- **Guide price $25**

Dessert Knives ▲

- *circa 1960*
A set of six pink, green, blue,
purple, white and yellow Sheffield
stainless steel dessert knives.
- *length 22cm*
- **Guide price $20**

Sugar Shaker ▲

- *circa 1950*
Pale blue plastic sugar shaker with
star-pierced design on the lid and
handle.
- *height 10cm*
- **Guide price $10**

Caldor Ware ▶

- *circa 1950*
Green ceramic casserole dish with
white lid decorated with a yellow
cooker, blue sink, whisk, spatula,
blue kettle and a frying pan.
- *height 13cm*
- **Guide price $100**

Rocket Ice Crusher ▶
• *1950*
American rocket ice crusher
made from aluminium with red
plastic handle and container.
Made by Fortuna.
• *height 32.5cm*
• Guide price $270

Enamel Coffee Pot ▲
• *1890*
French cornflower blue
enamelled coffee pot with turned
fruitwood side-handle.
• *height 22cm*
• Guide price $130

Scales ▲
• *1920*
European cast iron weighing
scales with copper pans and iron
weights.
• *height 32cm*
• Guide price $80

Café and Chicorée Pots ▲
• *1920*
Café and chicorée brown
enamelled pots with white
writing and banding.
• *height 20cm*
• Guide price $80

Enamel Funnel ▶
• *1890*
French blue and white enamel
funnel.
• *height 12cm*
• Guide price $20

Wood Butter Pat ▲
• *1910*
Wood butter pat moulded one
side with a handle.
• *length 19.5cm*
• Guide price $20

Small Metal Mould ▲
• *1890*
Small metal mould in the shape
of a fish.
• *length 9.5cm*
• Guide price $20

French Storage Jar ▼
• *1920*
French hanging storage jar with a
wood lid with red and white
panels and the word "Sel" in
black.
• *height 27cm*
• Guide price $120

Wagon Train Teapot, Sugar Pot, and Milk Jug ▶

- *circa 1958*
Teapot, sugar pot and milk jug stylised to represent vehicles from the Wagon Train TV programme
- *height 14cm*
- **Guide price $230**

Diamond-cut Honey Jar ▲

- *1820*
Heavily diamond-cut honey jar and cover with star-cut foot.
- *height 16.5cm*
- **Guide price $880**

Cut Star and Vine Engraving Cream Jug ▼

- *1870*
Charming English cream jug with cut star and fruiting vine engraving.
- *height 15.3cm*
- **Guide price $400**

Victorian Pastry Roller ▼

- *1860*
Victorian pastry roller and pie crimper.
- *length 15cm*
- **Guide price $120**

Herb Chopper ▲

- *19th century*
A lovely herb chopper, steel and brass with horn handle.
- *width 15cm*
- **Guide price $150**

Bristol Blue Egg Cups ▼

- *1800*
Two rare "Bristol Blue" eggcups with gilded rim.
- *height 8.9cm*
- **Guide price $350 for pair**

Fox-shaped Vegetable Chopper ▲

- **Early 19th century**
A European vegetable chopper in the form of a fox. Original horn and brass handle and complete with original brass eye.
- *length 34.3cm*
- **Guide price $1,070**

Luggage

Foxcroft Suitcase ▶

- *circa* **1950**
Cream plastic suitcase with
leopard skin print on one side by
Foxcroft.
- *45cm x 77cm*
- **Guide price $130**

Antler Vanity Case ▲

- *circa* **1950**
Plastic leopard skin design vanity
case by Antler with carrying
handle.
- *height 30cm*
- **Guide price $120**

Leather Briefcase ▶

- *circa* **1900**
Leather briefcase with brass
fittings and "M. D Amoso" on the
lock.
- *26cm x 36cm*
- **Guide price $210**

Leather and Hide
Vanity Case ▶

- *circa* **1970**
Morocco leather and hide vanity
case.
- *32cm x 23cm*
- **Guide price $160**

Leather Suitcase ▼

- *circa* **1940**
Leather suitcase with two straps
and covered with labels of various
destinations.
- *42cm x 74cm*
- **Guide price $90**

Teenage Case ◀

- *circa* **1950**
Blue and white plastic teenage
case with figure of a young girl
wearing jeans and a blue-check
shirt using the telephone.
- *30cm x 35cm*
- **Guide price $130**

Snakeskin Hat Box ◀

- *1912*
Lady's hardrock python snakeskin hat box with snakeskin handle, made in London for a family in Brunei.
- *23cm x 33cm*
- **Guide price $2,670**

Leather Suitcase ▼

- *1930*
Brown leather suitcase with leather straps.
- *width 73cm*
- **Guide price $210**

Gladstone Bag ▶

- *1930*
Lady's gladstone leather bag with brass fittings and leather handle.
- *width 37cm*
- **Guide price $130**

Army & Navy Hat Box ▼

- *1910*
Leather and canvas top hat box made by Army and Navy outfitters, comes with original top hat.
- *height 33cm*
- **Guide price $360**

Gentleman's Hat Box ▼

- *1910*
Leather gentleman's top hat box with leather handle, brass lock and leather strap.
- *height 23cm*
- **Guide price $280**

Crocodile Skin Case ▼

- *1930*
Indian crocodile skin case with handles at each end and silver nickel locks.
- *32cm x 61cm*
- **Guide price $800**

Tapestry Case ▶

- *circa 1950*

Circular zip-action tapestry case, with labels of Rome, Casablanca and Brussels.
- *diameter 40cm*
- **Guide price $130**

Black Circular Case ▲

- *circa 1950*

Black circular vanity case with zip-action and black plastic carrying handle.
- *diameter 42cm*
- **Guide price $100**

Tartan Plastic Case ▲

- *circa 1950*

Tartan plastic case with black plastic trim and handle.
- *diameter 35cm*
- **Guide price $170**

Fruitwood Case ◀

- *circa 1920*

Fruitwood gentleman's carrying case.
- *30cm x 42cm*
- **Guide price $210**

Black Crocodile Case ◀

- *circa 1920*

Black crocodile ladies vanity case relined with blue Moiré silk.
- *25cm x 32cm*
- **Guide price $620**

Brown Crocodile Case ▲

- *circa 1920*

Brown crocodile vanity case – relined with a new handle.
- *35cm x 40cm*
- **Guide price $1,510**

Leather Briefcase ▲
- *circa 1920*
Leather brief case with circular
brass fitting and leather straps
and handle.
- *length 40cm*
- **Guide price** $890

Louis Vuitton Case ▲
- *1920*
Louis Vuitton case with leather
trim and handle with brass
fittings.
- *width 70cm*
- **Guide price** $1,780

Expert Tips

*There is a steady rise in
auctions of original Louis
Vuitton luggage, leather hat
boxes and picnic hampers, with
their quality and durability
guaranteeing their popularity.*

Tan Hat Box ▼
- *1930*
Tan leather hat box with nickel
fittings and a leather handle.
- *diameter 41cm*
- **Guide price** $1,250

Hat Box ▶
- *circa 1890*
Tan leather top hat bucket with
brass fittings and leather handle.
- *height 23cm*
- **Guide price** $890

Cricket Case ▼
- *1930*
Tan leather cricket case with
brass fittings and leather handle,
the interior fitted with leather
straps for holding a tennis racket,
by Finnigans of Bond Street,
London.
- *length 73cm*
- **Guide price** $1,420

Dispatch Satchel ▲
- *circa 1900*
Leather dispatch satchel with a
good patina, one main leather
shoulder strap and three smaller
straps.
- *width 61cm*
- **Guide price** $1,420

Crocodile Hat Box ▶
- *circa 1920*
Crocodile skin hat box with gilt over brass locks, with brown Moiré silk lining.
- *26cm x 41cm*
- **Guide price** $7,120

Crocodile Case ▲
- *circa 1900*
Small crocodile case with handle and nickle fittings, with the letters L.T. on the lid.
- *width 35cm*
- **Guide price** $1,160

Attaché Case ▲
- *circa 1900*
Rare moulded Norfolk hide attaché case with original brass fittings, a leather handle, and a green leather interior.
- *10cm x 47cm x 32cm*
- **Guide price** $1,780

Goyard Hat Case ▶
- *1920*
Goyard canvas hat case with a painted chevron pattern and a tan leather trim with small brass nails, leather handle and brass fittings.
- *25cm x 49cm*
- **Guide price** $2,670

Lady's Travelling Case ▶
- *circa 1930*
Lady's green leather travelling case in two separate sections, fitted with a silk interior incorporating a turquoise enamel brush set, boxes with silver gilt lids and a travelling clock.
- *width 32cm*
- **Guide price** $1,070

Gladstone Bag ◀
- *1890*
Small leather Gladstone bag with brass fittings and leather handle.
- *24cm x 34cm*
- **Guide price** $890

Mechanical Music

Rock-Ola Princess ▲
- *1946*
American Rock-Ola Princess No.1422, manufactured in 1946, plays 20, 78 R.P.M. records. In good original condition with pheonilic pilasters and a central panel with decorative metal scrolling.
- *149cm x 54cm*
- **Guide price $9,260**

Eight Air Musical Box ▲
- *circa 1885*
Swiss eight air music box with five bells and drum by Paillard, in an inlaid rosewood case with brass handles each side standing on square ebonised feet.
- *23cm x 68cm*
- **Guide price $7,120**

Singing Bird Autometer ▼
- *circa 1880*
Rare French singing bird autometer in a brass and gilded cage with moving chicks and singing bird. The cage with foliate design and gilded panelling around the base. Coin-operated and in perfect working order.
- *58cm x 21cm*
- **Guide price $12,100**

Heart Musical Box ▼
- *1950*
Heart-shaped musical manicure box, lined with pink silk, with a circular mirror on the inside of the lid and a couple in evening dress dancing. Fitted with pink manicure set and two small circular metal boxes.
- *diameter 23cm*
- **Guide price $90**

Ami Continental ▲
- *1961*
American Ami Continental juke box, which has push button electric selection and plays both sides. In good working condition and fully restored.
- *170cm x 70cm*
- **Guide price $11,570**

Seeburg HF100R ▲
- *1954*
Seeburg H.F. 100R. Holds 60 records with push button electric selection. Plays both sides. Considered by many to be the best design of a series of jukeboxes made by Seeburg in the 50s and 60. Made in the U.S.A.
- *158cm x 87cm*
- **Guide price $12,460**

American Music Box ▲
• **1895**
Regina music box cased in light
oak with two rows of beading. On
the inside of the lid is a central
figure of a lady surrounded by
cherubs playing instruments.
• *28cm x 55cm*
• **Guide price $7,650**

Zodiac ▲
• **1971**
A Zodiac multi selector model
3500 phonograph, manufactured
by the Wurlitzer Company,
Tonawanda, New York, U.S.A.
with the slogan "Music for
Millions".
• *138cm x 74cm*
• **Guide price $1,780**

Swiss Music Box ▲
• **circa 1890**
Unusual Swiss music box with
convex glass lid by Mermod Freres.
• *27cm x 76cm*
• **Guide price $7,120**

Rock-Ola 1454 ▼
• **1956**
Rock-Ola 1454 juke box in
original condition. The cabinet
styling is based on a Seeburg
M100 from 1954.
• *143cm x 77cm*
• **Guide price $7,120**

Rock-Ola Princess ▼
• **1962**
Rock-Ola Princess stereophonic
juke-box, Model 1493. Takes 50
records. Stereo and auto mix,
(plays with or without centres).
In original condition. Made in
the U.S.A.
• *124cm x 76cm*
• **Guide price $7,120**

Swiss Music Box ▶
• **circa 1875**
Swiss music box playing ten airs
with 16-reed organ by Bremond.
• *29cm x 69cm*
• **Guide price $8,900**

Ami H ▲
• **1957**
American Ami H, one of the first
of the car influenced style of
jukebox with a wrap around glass.
It holds 100 records, with orange
and blue push button electric
selection, and plays both sides.
Fully restored and in original
condition.
• *159cm x 80cm*
• **Guide price $12,460**

Singing Bird Autometer ▲
• **circa 1900**
French singing bird, sitting on a
brass rail with white flowers in a
brass cage. Standing on a circular
base with foliate scrolling
decoration.
• *height 53cm*
• **Guide price $8,190**

Bal-Ami S100 ▲
- *1960*
The Bal-Ami Jukebox, made in Britain by Balfoure. Engineering, using *High Tech* parts manufactured in the U.S.A by Ami, to overcome import ban on luxury goods after the Second World War.
- *147cm x 80cm*
- **Guide price $6,230**

Key-Wind Musical Box ▲
- *1858*
Nicole Frères key-wind musical box playing six operatic airs by Bellini, in an inlaid rosewood case. No.37625.
- *11cm x 56cm*
- **Guide price $4,630**

Líepee Music Box ▲
- *circa 1880*
Six bell music box by Líepee, playing eight operatic airs in an inlaid rosewood case.
- *22cm x 58cm*
- **Guide price $7,120**

Ami J 200 ▼
- *1959*
Ami J.200. Holds 100 records. With pink plastic push-button electric selection, playing both sides. Made in U.S.A. Fully restored.
- *152cm x 83cm*
- **Guide price $10,320**

Birdcage Autometer ▼
- *1870*
French birdcage with two singing birds in rustic setting with roses, standing on a circular gilded base with a leaf design and circular feet. In perfect working order.
- *height 61cm*
- **Guide price $9,970**

German Symphonion ▲
- *1895*
German symphonion in a rococo walnut case carved with cherubs and a courting couple on the lid, with carved foliate design. Standing on bracket feet.
- *height 30cm*
- **Guide price $10,680**

Musical Jewellery Box ▲
- *1960*
Red plastic musical jewellery box in the form of a radiogram with turn-table that rotates when music plays, Blue interior, red drawers and a gold *fleur de lis*.
- *height 11cm*
- **Guide price $100**

Music Box ▲
- *circa 1875*
Music box by Nicole Frères playing eight operatic airs.
- *12cm x 58cm*
- **Guide price $4,450**

Photographs

Film Makers ▲
- **1960**
Three Italian neo-realist filmmakers, from l to r; Vittorio de Sica (1901–1974), Roberto Rossellini (1906–1977) and Federico Fellini (1920–1993) on the set of de Sica's film, "Generale delle Rovere". Black and white fibre, silver gelatin photograph. Limited edition: one of only four signed by the photographer Slim Aarons. Printed from original negative in Getty Images darkrooms.
- *length 25.4cm*
- **Guide price $2,670**

Bacall and Bogart ▶
- **24th December 1951**
American actor Humphrey Bogart (1899–1957) with Lauren Bacall and their son Stephen at their home in Beverly Hills on Christmas Eve. Black and white fibre, silver gelatin photograph from a limited edition: one of only four signed by the photographer Slim Aarons. Printed from original negative in Getty Images darkrooms.
- *length 61cm*
- **Guide price $2,670**

Take It ▼
- **September 1970**
Painter Salvador Dali (1904–1989) in a pose with his trademark walking stick, with some of his works at Port Ligat, Costa Brava, Spain. Colour Lambda photograph. Limited edition: one of only four signed by photographer Slim Aaron.
- *50.8cm x pro*
- **Guide price $4,270**

Groucho Marx ▼
- **circa 1954**
American comic Julius "Groucho" Marx (1895–1977), member of the Marx brothers, in bed with a joke cigar in Beverly HillS. Black and white, fibre silver gelatin photograph, from a limited edition: one of only four signed by the photographer Slim Aarons. Printed from original negative in Getty Images darkrooms.
- *length 61cm*
- **Guide price $2,670**

Capucine ▲
- **1957**
French actress Capucine, (Germaine Lefebvre) (1933–90) fanning herself at a New Years Eve party held at Romanoffs in Beverly Hills. By Photographer Slim Aarons. Black and white fibre, silver gelatin photograph. Limited edition: one of only four signed by the photographer. Printed from original negative in Getty Images darkrooms.
- *length 50.8cm*
- **Guide price $2,670**

Kings of Hollywood ▲
- **31st December 1957**
Film stars (left to right) Clark Gable (1901–1960), Van Heflin (1910–1971), Gary Cooper (1901–1961) and James Stewart (1908–1997) enjoy a joke at a New Year's party held at Romanoff's in Beverly Hills. A black and white, fibre silver gelatin photograph. Limited edition: one of only 250 signed by the photographer.
- *length 50.8cm*
- **Guide price $3,560**

Jackie K ▼

- *circa 1959*

Jacqueline Kennedy (Jackie Onassis 1929–1994), wife of Senator Jack Kennedy at an "April in Paris" ball. Colour Lambda photograph. Limited edition: one of only four signed by the photographer.
- *50.8cm x pro*
- **Guide price $4,270**

Sea Drive ▶

- *1967*

Film producer Kevin McClory takes his wife and family out in an "Amphicar" in the Bahamas. Colour Lambda photograph. Limited edition: one of only four signed by the photographer
- *length 1.52m*
- **Guide price $6,230**

The Rolling Stones ▼

- *January 1967*

British rock group The Rolling Stones; from left to right, Bill Wyman, Brian Jones (1942–1969), Charlie Watts, Keith Richards and Mick Jagger. Photographer: Keystone Collection. Modern black and white, fibre silver gelatin archival photograph printed in Getty Images Darkrooms. Limited edition: 300.
- *length 50.8cm*
- **Guide price $400**

Man's Work ▲

- *1960*

Hugh Hefner working at his typewriter surrounded by "bunny" girls. Publisher Hugh M Hefner at the Playboy Key Club in Chicago. He founded adult magazines, *Playboy*, *VIP* and *Oui*. Colour Lambda photograph. Limited edition: one of only four signed by the photographer.
- *length 50.8cm*
- **Guide price $4,270**

Victoria Bridge ▲

- *1859*

Victoria Bridge – Special limited edition. A lone man sitting on the Victoria Railway Bridge over the St Lawrence River in Montreal, during its construction. Photographer: William England/London Stereoscopic Company. PLATINUM Photograph. Modern platinum print made from original glass negative by Studio 31. Platinum Limited edition: ten only.
- *paper size: 40.7cm x 30.5cm image size: 23cm x 20.4cm*
- **Guide price $890**

Hitchcock Profile ▼

- *July 1966*

Film director Alfred Hitchcock (1889–1980) during the filming of "The Torn Curtain" by photographer Curt Gunther/BIPs Collection. Modern black and white, fibre silver gelatin archival photograph, printed in Getty Images Darkrooms. Limited edition: 300.
- *length 50.8cm*
- **Guide price $400**

Night Time New York ▼

- *1936*

Paramount Building in Times Square, New York, towers over Schenley's Chinese Restaurant. Photographer: Fox Photos Collection. Modern black and white, fibre silver gelatin archival photograph, printed in Getty Images darkrooms. Limited edition: 300.
- *length 50.8cm*
- **Guide price $400**

Chrysler Building ▲

- *3rd May 1957*
The Chrysler Building in New York by Photographer: Phil Burcham, Fox Photos. Modern black and white, fibre silver gelatin archival photograph, printed in Getty Images darkrooms. Limited edition: 300.
- *length 50.8cm*
- **Guide price $400**

Taylor Reclines ▲

- *1954*
American actress Elizabeth Taylor reclining in bed by the photographer Baron. Modern black and white, fibre silver gelatin archival photograph, printed in Getty Images darkrooms. Limited edition: 300.
- *length 50.8cm*
- **Guide price $400**

John Lennon Profile ▼

- *26th June 1967*
John Lennon (1940–1980), singer, songwriter and guitarist with the Beatles by photographer Peter King, Fox Photos. Modern black and white, fibre silver gelatin archival photograph, printed in Getty Images darkrooms. Limited edition: 300.
- *length 50.8cm*
- **Guide price $400**

Ali In Training ▼

- *August 1966*
American heavyweight boxer Muhammad Ali in training in London for his fight against Brian London. Photographer: R.McPhedran, Express Collection. Modern black and white, fibre silver gelatin archival photograph, printed in Getty Images darkrooms. Limited edition: 300.
- *length 50.8cm*
- **Guide price $400**

Commissionaire's Dog ◀

- *22nd October 1938*
A hotel commissionaire talking to a small dog in London. Photographer: Kurt Hutton, Picture Post. Modern black and white, fibre silver gelatin archival photograph, printed in Getty Images darkrooms. Limited edition: 300.
- *length 40.7cm*
- **Guide price $330**

The Beatles ▲

- *10th January 1964*
Paul McCartney, Ringo Starr, John Lennon (1940–1980) and George Harrison (1943–2001) of the Beatles. Photographer: Terry Disney, Express Collection. Modern black and white, fibre silver gelatin archival photograph, printed in Getty Images darkrooms. Limited edition: 300.
- *length 50.8cm*
- **Guide price $400**

Gorbals Boys ▲

- *31st January 1948*
Two boys in the Gorbals area of Glasgow. The Gorbals tenements were built quickly and cheaply in the 1840s. Conditions were appalling; overcrowding was standard and sewage and water facilities inadequate. The tenements housed about 40,000 people with up to eight family members sharing a single room, 30 residents sharing a toilet and 40 sharing a tap. By the time this photograph was taken 850 tenements had been demolished since 1920. Photographer: Bert Hardy, Picture Post. Modern black and white, fibre silver gelatin archival photograph, printed in Getty Images darkrooms. Limited edition: 300.
- *length 40.7cm*
- **Guide price $330**

Snow in the Park ▼

- **1947**

A man trudging through Central Park West, New York City, in a blizzard by photographer: Nat Fein/Courtesy of Nat Fein's Estate. Exclusive. Black and white, fibre silver gelatin archival photograph, printed from original negative in Getty Images darkrooms.
- *length 50.8cm*
- **Guide price $860**

Walking in the Rain ▲

- *circa 1955*

A man and his dog walking in the rain in Central Park, New York City by photographer: Nat Fein/Courtesy Of Nat Fein's Estate. Black and white, fibre silver gelatin archival photograph, printed from original negative in Getty Images darkrooms. Exclusive.
- *length 40.7cm*
- **Guide price $740**

Fair Fun ▲

- **8 October, 1938**

Two young women enjoying themselves on a roller coaster at Southend Fair, England by the photographer Kurt Hutton, Picture Post. Modern black and white, fibre silver gelatin archival photograph, printed in Getty Images Darkrooms. Limited edition: 300.
- *length 50.8cm*
- **Guide price $400**

Fonda in Town ▼

- **1951**

Film star Henry Fonda (1905–1982) on a balcony overlooking a street in New York by photographer Slim Aarons. Black and white, fibre silver gelatin photograph, printed from original negative in Getty Images darkrooms. Limited edition: 300.
- *paper: 40.7cm x 30.5cm image: 30.5cm x 30.5cm*
- **Guide price $330**

Guggenheim Window ▲

- *circa 1955*

The Guggenheim Museum of Modern and Contemporary Art in New York. Photographer: Sherman, Three Lions Collection. Black and white fibre, silver gelatin photograph, printed from original negative in Getty Images darkrooms. Limited edition: 300.
- *length 61cm*
- **Guide price $450**

Bright Lights ▲

- **1970**

Aerial view of the Manhattan skyline at night, looking southeast down Fifth Avenue, from the RCA Building Rockefeller Center, New York City by photographer: Lawrence Thornton. Modern black and white, fibre silver gelatin archival photograph, printed in Getty Images Darkrooms. Limited edition: 300.
- *length 50.8cm*
- **Guide price $400**

Jazz Scooter ▶

- **1949**

Lucille Brown takes control of the Vespa scooter as her husband Louis Armstrong (1898–1971) displays his musical appreciation of the ancient Coliseum in Rome. Black and white fibre, silver gelatin photograph, from a limited edition of 300 by photographer Slim Aarons. Printed from original negative in Getty Images darkrooms.
- *length 50.8cm*
- **Guide price $400**

Portrait Miniatures

Richard Cosway

- *circa 1790*

A portrait of Sir Charles Cockrell, in original gold frame, the reverse with gold monogram CC on blond plaited hair within gold mount and blue glass border.

- *height 5cm*
- **Guide price $14,240**

Kenneth Macleay

- *circa 1835*

A miniature of Lt. John Ure Donaldson wearing scarlet uniform with gold epaulettes and collar, white cross band with gold plate XLVI within laurel wreath and crown.

- *height 11 cm*
- **Guide price $3,470**

Samuel Shelley

- *circa 1790*

A miniature of Captain Edward Herriman of the HEICS, wearing blue uniform with black facings and gold lace, yellow waistcoat, his powdered hair en queue. Set in a gold frame.

- *height 7.5cm*
- **Guide price $11,570**

Christian Richter ▶

- *circa 1705*

Queen Anne, wearing ermine robes over a golden dress, a blue sash and order around her neck. On vellum, set in the original gold coloured frame with pierced spiral cresting.

- *height 7.5cm*
- **Guide price $10,410**

Charles Hayter ▼

- *circa 1790*

A portrait of a lady with powdered wig, wearing white dress, fichu and matching turban. Set in the original gold frame with shaped border, the reverse with locks of hair tied with split pearls and gold wire on ivory ground.

- *height 7.5 cm*
- **Guide price $4,800**

Andrew Plimer ▲

- *circa 1810*

Portrait miniature of Miss Abrams possibly Eliza (1772–1830) the sister of Harriet and Theodosia by artist Andrew Plimer. Set in the original ivory frame with gold mount and plaited hair reverse.

- *height 7cm*
- **Guide price $11,570**

George Engleheart ▶

- *circa 1790*

A miniature of a young lady with powdered hair wearing white dress with turquoise trimmings, ruff collar and pearl necklace, a turquoise ribbon entwined in her hair. Gold oval frame with plaited hair reverse.

- *height 6cm*
- **Guide price $12,190**

Posters

Salamander Brandy ▶

- *circa 1950*

Advertising poster for Salamander Brandy with a view of a village and the sea in the background and a cartouche of the factory, a large bottle of cognac, and a bunch of grapes in the foreground.

- *41cm x 36cm*
- **Guide price $260**

Ovaltine Nightcap ▲

- *circa 1950*

An Ovaltine advertisement of a young smiling lady holding a cup and saucer with the words "Ovaltine – The World's Best Nightcap".

- *37cm x28cm*
- **Guide price $130**

Marcella Cigars ▼

- *circa 1950*

Poster of a hand holding five Marcella cigars and the words "A Grand Shilling's Worth".

- *42cm x 36cm*
- **Guide price $210**

Metrovick Lamps ▼

- *circa 1950*

Advertising poster of a lady wearing a cream dress leaning over a red chair advertising Metrovick Lamps for Metropolitan.

- *48cm x 36cm*
- **Guide price $130**

Grapefruit Breakfast ▼

- *circa 1950*

Gentleman in a suit and bowler hat seated on a grapefruit with the slogan "Start the day on a Grapefruit".

- *26cm x 46cm*
- **Guide price $100**

Expert Tips

Poster collecting is now a major activity. Two tips: top condition and old film stars.

Monarch Whisky ◀

- *circa 1950*

The Monarch Old Scotch Whisky advertising poster.

- *37cm x 23cm*
- **Guide price $120**

Apocalypse Now ◄
- 1979

"Apocalypse Now" with Marlon Brando. German double panel.
- 85cm x 1.18m
- Guide price $2,310

Way Out West ▼
- 1937

"Way Out West" with Laurel and Hardy.
- 28cm x36cm
- Guide price $1,160

Ice Cold in Alex ▼
- 1958

"Ice Cold in Alex" with John Mills and Sylvia Syms. Directed by Bruce Robinson.
- height 1.02m
- Guide price $620

The Untouchables ▲
- 1987

"The Untouchables", with Kevin Costner, Sean Connery and Robert De Niro.
- 28cm x 36cm
- Guide price $130

Blade Runner ▲
- 1982

"Blade Runner" with Harrison Ford.
- 1.04m x 58cm
- Guide price $710

Sherlock Holmes Faces Death ▲
- 1951

"Sherlock Holmes Faces Death". Spanish one sheet.
- 1.04m x 29cm
- Guide price $800

The Birds ▲
- 1963

"The Birds" by Alfred Hitchcock, with Tippi Hedren and Rod Taylor.
- 1.02m x 79cm
- Guide price $890

Goldfinger ▲
- 1964

"Golfinger" starring Sean Connery.
- 28cm x 36cm
- Guide price $580

Cycles Favor Motos

- *circa 1950*
Advertisement for Cycles Favor
Motos featuring a mechanic
wearing a cap and blue overalls,
holding a bicycle in one hand
and a motor bike in the other.
- *46cm x 50cm*
- **Guide price** $130

Jaws II ▲

- *1961*
U.S. linen-backed "Jaws II" poster
with art work by Mick McGinty.
- *1.04m x 69cm*
- **Guide price** $890

Bay of Naples ◄

- *1950*
Lady holding a guitar seated on a
boat, with the words "A trip thro'
the Bay of Naples".
- *48cm x 54cm*
- **Guide price** $80

Cruising West Indies ▲

- *circa 1960*
"Southampton to the West
Indies" travel poster showing a
cruise liner, tropical fruit, and the
words "French Line – A Service
of Distinction".
- *80cm x 48cm*
- **Guide price** $150

Night of the Demon ◄

- *circa 1960*
"The Night of the Demon"/"La
notte del demonio" Italian linen-
backed poster.
- *1.4m x 99cm*
- **Guide price** $2,670

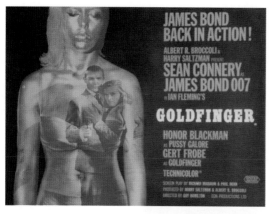

Goldfinger ◀

- *1964*

"Goldfinger" poster with Sean Connery as James Bond and Honor Blackman as Pussy Galore.

- *76cm x 1.01m*
- **Guide price $4,980**

Withnail and I ▼

- *1987*

"Withnail and I" starring Richard E. Grant and Paul McGann.

- *height 1.03m*
- **Guide price $710**

The Godfather ▲

- *1972*

"The Godfather" and "Italian Photobusta".

- *45cm x 65cm*
- **Guide price $620**

Alfie ▲

- *1966*

"Alfie", with Michael Caine.

- *28cm x 36cm*
- **Guide price $170**

Brigitte Bardot ▲

- *1963*

"Le Mepris", with Brigitte Bardot.

- *height 1.58m*
- **Guide price $2,670**

Goldfinger ▼

- *1967*

"Goldfinger" with Sean Connery.

- *56cm x 1.02m*
- **Guide price $2,140**

High Society ▼

- *1956*

"High Society" with Frank Sinatra, Grace Kelly and Bing Crosby.

- *28cm x 36cm*
- **Guide price $210**

Deserto Rosso ▶
- **1964**
Italian linen backed poster for "Deserto Rosso".
- 2.01m x 1.4m
- **Guide price $4,450**

Persona ◀
- **1966**
Swedish linen-backed poster for Ingmar Berman's "Persona" with Bibi Andersson and Liv Ullmann.
- 99cm x 69cm
- **Guide price $3,200**

Czerwona Pustynia ▲
- **1964**
Polish "Il Deserto Rosso"/ "Czerwona Pustynia" poster with art by Witold Janowski.
- 84cm x 58cm
- **Guide price $1,070**

Badlands ▲
- **1974**
British linen-backed film poster for "Badlands".
- 76cm x 1.02m
- **Guide price $670**

Expert Tips

Posters of the early twentieth century were not intended to last and were printed on very thin paper. Make sure the central image is unaffected by stains, folds and fading, though small tears are not a big problem.

Sporting Life ◀
- **1963**
British linen-backed poster for "This Sporting Life" with art by Renatop Fratini.
- 1.04m x 69cm
- **Guide price $530**

French Cancan ▶

- **1955**
Linen-backed "French Cancan"
poster with art by Rene Gruau.
  - *1.6m x 1.19m*
  - **Guide price $4,000**

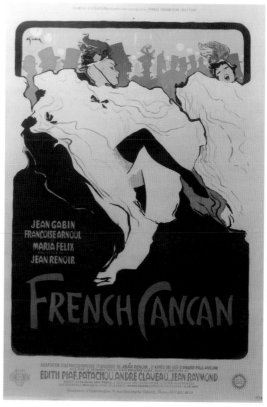

Battleship Potemkin ▲

- **1925**
Poster for first Japanese release of
"The Battleship Potemkin".
  - *76cm x 51cm*
  - **Guide price $1,070**

Forbidden Planet ▲

- **1956**
American linen-backed poster for
landmark science fiction film
"Forbidden Planet" with Leslie
Nielson.
  - *1.04m x 69cm*
  - **Guide price $13,350**

Apocalypse Now ◀

- **1979**
Australian linen-backed poster
for "Apocalypse Now".
  - *1.02m x 69cm*
  - **Guide price $620**

Italian Rififi ▶

- **1955**
Italian linen-backed poster for
"Rififi" by Jules Dassin.
  - *1.40m x 99cm*
  - **Guide price $2,230**

Pyscho
- *1962*
"Pyscho" 1962 re-issue U.S. sheet.
- *width 29cm*
- Guide price $1,070

Gilda
- *1946*
"Gilda", American insert.
- *92cm x 35cm*
- Guide price $2,850

Love is My Profession ▼
- *1959*
"Love is My Profession", starring Brigitte Bardot.
- *83cm x 60.5cm*
- Guide price $620

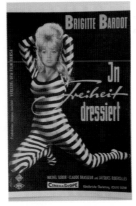

Breakfast at Tiffany's ▼
- *1961*
"Breakfast at Tiffany's", starring Audrey Hepburn.
- *28cm x 36cm*
- Guide price $850

Manhattan ▼
- *1979*
"Manhattan" Lobby Carl.
- *28cm x 36cm*
- Guide price $170

Revenge of the Creature ▲
- *1955*
"Revenge of the Creature" U.K. Quad John Agar Laurie Nelson.
- *1.02m x 60.5cm*
- Guide price $1,510

My Fair Lady ▲
- *1965*
"My Fair Lady" with Audrey Hepburn and Rex Harrison.
- *75cm x 1.37m*
- Guide price $800

The Enforcer ▲
- *1977*
"The Enforcer" with Clint Eastwood as Dirty Harry.
- *28cm x 36cm*
- Guide price $170

Yellow Submarine ▼

- **1969**

"Yellow Submarine" with the Beatles. U.S. One sheet.
- height 1.04m
- **Guide price $22,250**

Thunderball ▶

- **1965**

"Thunderball" with Sean Connery.
- 41cm x 27cm
- **Guide price $1,960**

The Italian Job ▲

- **1969**

"The Italian Job" with Michael Caine. U.K. Mini Quad.
- 31cm x 41cm
- **Guide price $10**

Expert Tips

If you decide to start collecting posters, it is best to start with the posters that depict your favourite old films and stars. As an amateur antique collector, posters are a good starting point because their cost is fairly reasonable.

The Apartment ▶

- **1960**

"The Apartment" starring Jack Lemmon and Shirley McLaine.
- 28cm x 36cm
- **Guide price $150**

Bullitt ▲

- **1969**

"Bullitt" with Steve McQueen. U. S. One sheet.
- 27cm x 21cm
- **Guide price $1,210**

Midnight Cowboy ▼

- **1969**

"Midnight Cowboy" with Dustin Hoffman. U.K. Quad.
- 76cm x 1.02m
- **Guide price $340**

Radios

Decca Gramaphone
- *1951*
Children's gramophone in original box with nursery rhyme pictures on each side and carrying handle.
- *18cm x 32cm*
- **Guide price $270**

Dansette Portable Radio
- *1961*
Grey plastic Dansette portable radio with beige plastic handle and large circular dial.
- *14cm x 21cm*
- **Guide price $80**

Isis Plastic Radio
- *circa 1960*
Isis white plastic radio in the form of the word "radio".
- *7cm x 25cm*
- **Guide price $100**

Calypso Radio
- *circa 1960*
Grey plastic Calypso radio with circular dial.
- *18cm x 23cm*
- **Guide price $50**

Kidditune Record Player
- *1962*
Red plastic battery-operated record player by Marx Toys in original box complete with original records.
- *13cm x 26cm*
- **Guide price $120**

Wrist Radio
- *1960*
Panasonic blue plastic radio worn around the wrist.
- *17cm x 18cm*
- **Guide price $90**

Panasonic Novelty Radio
- *1960*
Yellow plastic wrist radio by Panasonic.
- *17cm x 18cm*
- **Guide price $90**

Roberts Metal and Teak Radio
- *1968*
Roberts radio with metal and teak case and carrying handle.
- *23cm x 38cm*
- **Guide price $70**

P.Y.E. Record Player ▲
- **1955**
P.Y.E. record player in a bow-fronted teak case with cream turntable. Holds ten records on stack.
- *height 26cm*
- **Guide price $180**

Radio and TV Diary 1957 ▲
- **1957**
Radio and TV Diary for 1957 with photographs on each page of actors and musicians. Showing a photograph of David Attenborough.
- *height 12cm*
- **Guide price $20**

P.Y.E. Record Player ▼
- **1955**
P.Y.E. record player in a grey with white polka dot case, with unusual curved sides, white plastic carrying handles and a black and gold sparkling grill.
- *height 25cm*
- **Guide price $130**

Perdio Transistor ▶
- **1962**
Perdio Super Seven Transistor radio, inscribed with "Real Morocco leather made in England", on the back, with a dial for an aerial and phone or tape, and a large brass dial and gold writing.
- *height 12.5cm*
- **Guide price $70**

E.A.R. Triple Four ◀
- **1958**
E.A.R. Triple four record player in a blue and grey Rexine case with cream piping and handles.
- *height 27cm*
- **Guide price $140**

Hacker ▲
- **1964**
Hacker record player in a black and grey case with metal fittings.
- *height 27cm*
- **Guide price $90**

Roberts Radio ▲
- **1958**
Roberts radio in original condition with red Rexine case and handle and brass dials and fittings.
- *height 15cm*
- **Guide price $120**

Rock & Pop

Record Bag ▶
- **circa 1950**
Plastic multi-coloured bag for
carrying 45rpm records with
various musical instruments.
- *diameter 24cm*
- **Guide price $45**

ABBA Mirror ▲
- **circa 1970**
Mirror with photograph of the
band ABBA.
- *24cm x 20cm*
- **Guide price $30**

Record Case ▶
- **circa 1950**
White plastic carrying case for
45rpm records with jazz and
dancing design.
- *diameter 26cm*
- **Guide price $50**

Sex Pistols ▼
- **circa 1980**
Sex Pistols T-shirt with a picture
of the Queen and the words "God
Save the Queen".
- *50cm x 42cm*
- **Guide price $45**

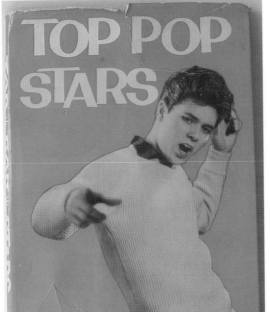

Top Pop Stars ◀
- **circa 1950**
"Book of Top Pop Stars" with
Cliff Richard on the cover.
- *28cm x 24cm*
- **Guide price $25**

Michael Jackson Doll ▼
- 1995

A singing Michael Jackson doll wearing a white shirt and black trousers in original box.
- **Guide price $90**

Pat As I See Him ▲
- 1966

"Pat As I See Him", a pen and ink portrait on an envelope by Joe Meek of his lover. Annotated in verso "Pat was Meek's boyfriend and was present at the landlady's shooting and Meek's subsequent suicide".
- **Guide price $9,350**

Stone Age ◄
- 1971

"Stone Age" by The Rolling Stones.
- **Guide price $1,030**

Instant Karma Lennon ▲
- 1971

John Ono Lennon "Instant Karma" produced by Phil Spector.
- **Guide price $210**

Andy Warhol ◄
- 1967

Andy Warhol- "Andy Warhol's Index Box". First hardback edition-Random House USA complete and in working order including the velvet underground flexi-disc. Reed's eye has not even popped!
- **Guide price $2,670**

Bob Dylan ◄
- *1961*
Bob Dylan's first recording produced by John Hammond.
- **Guide price $1,310**

Beatles Lady Madonna ▲
- *1968*
"The Inner Light, Lady Madonna" by The Beatles.
- **Guide price $130**

Time Will Pass ▲
- *1977*
"Time Will Pass" by the Spriguns. Distributed by The Decca Record Company Limited, London.
- **Guide price $310**

Equinoxe 4 ▼
- *1979*
"Equinoxe 4", an album by Jean Michel Jarre, with a signed autograph in black biro on front cover.
- **Guide price $110**

Agogo ▲
- *1963*
"Agogo", with Ray Charles, The Supremes, Petula Clark, and The Everly brothers.
- **Guide price $60**

Yellow Submarine ▼
- *1960s*
The Beatles "Yellow Submarine and Eleanor Rigby".
- **Guide price $130**

Status Quo ▲
- *1970*
"In my Chair/Gerdundula" Status Quo.
- **£Guide price $130**

The Monkees ▲
- *1968*
The Monkees. Original motion picture sound track "Head".
- **Guide price $170**

239

The Beatles

- *circa 1960*
"The Beatles:, An Illustrated Record" by R. Carr and T. Tyler.
- *23cm x 30cm*
- Guide price $35

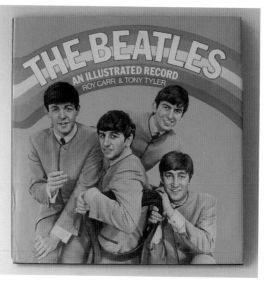

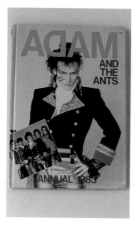

Adam Ant

- *circa 1970*
Annual of Adam and the Ants.
- *24cm x 20cm*
- Guide price $25

Slade in Flame

- *circa 1970*
Rare album and cover of Slade in Flame.
- *42cm x 42cm*
- Guide price $35

Donny Osmond

- *circa 1970*
Teen Pin-Ups dynamite colour comic featuring Donny Osmond.
- *23cm x 28cm*
- Guide price $20

Latin a la Lee

- *circa 1950*
Peggy Lee album and cover.
- *width 42cm*
- Guide price $10

The Police Box ▼
- *1997–87*

"The Police Box" (Sting, Stewart Copeland and Andy Summers) from 1977 to 1987.
- Guide price $270

Elvis ▼
- *1971*

"You'll Never Walk Alone" by Elvis. Manufactured and Distributed by RCA Limited.
- Guide price $3,200

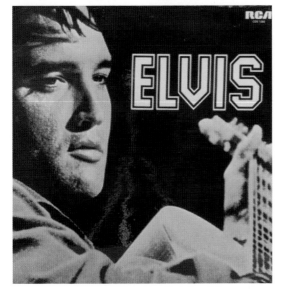

H. M. S. Donovan ▲
- *1971*

"H.M.S. Donovan" produced by Donovan Engineered by Mike Bobak at Morgan Studios London. All paintings by Patrick.
- Guide price $230

Sticky Fingers: Rolling Stones ▲
- *1972*

"Sticky Fingers", an album by The Rolling Stones.
- Guide price $390

Whitehouse Present Total Sex ▼
- *circa 1980*

Whitehouse present "Total Sex".
- Guide price $220

The Velvet Underground ▼
- *circa 1967*

Andy Warhol presents the "The Velvet Underground and Nico", original German Issue with Erice Emmerson Sleeve (No Banana).
- Guide price $440

Roy Harper Sophisticated ▼
- *1966*

Roy Harper "Sophisticated Beggar" Strike JHL 105. Test pressing. W/Proff Sleeve in excellent condition.
- Guide price $980

Sewing Items

Wicker Sewing Bag

- *1880*

Wicker sewing bag with green
wool panels, decorated with pink
silk flowers and lined with green
silk.
- *26cm x 20cm*
- **Guide price** $310

Silver Thimble

- *1912*

Silver thimble made in
Birmingham.
- *height 2cm*
- **Guide price** $80

Needle Case

- *circa 1900*

Hand-carved ivory needle case.
- *height 7cm*
- **Guide price** $140

Mother-of-Pearl Bobbin

- *circa 1900*

Small ivory bobbin with mother-
of-pearl.
- *height 3.5cm*
- **Guide price** $80

Needle Case

- *circa 1900*

Ivory needle case.
- *height 7cm*
- **Guide price** $100

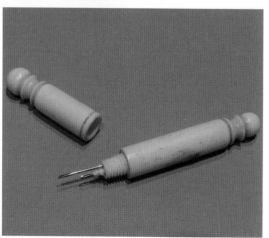

Expert Tips

*Thimbles are great fun to
collect, before you start view
collections ahead and decide
what type to collect.*

English Thimble ▶

- *circa 1880*

English mother-of-pearl thimble set inside case with velvet lining and clasp.
- *height 2cm*
- Guide price $390

Silver Bear Pincushion ▼

- *1908*

English silver articulated bear pincushion from Birmingham.
- *height 8cm*
- Guide price $1,510

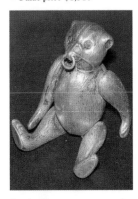

Sewing Box ▶

- *circa 1820*

Chinese export black lacquer sewing box with a scene showing a family group with a pagoda and landscape in the background, with fitted interior, standing on gilt claw feet.
- *34cm x 23.5cm x 14cm*
- Guide price $3,560

Filigree Scissor Case ▶

- *circa 1840*

Delicate silver filigree scissor case with scrolling.
- *length 6.5cm*
- Guide price $850

Musical Sewing Box ◀

- *circa 1850*

Palais Royale tortoiseshell and ivory-faced musical sewing box with a reverse glass painted pastoral scene on the lid, enclosing original inkwells, needle case, screw top pencil, scissors, thimble and other sewing implements. Most with the Palais Royale insignia. The music box is in working order.
- *10cm x 19cm*
- Guide price $6,140

Silver Filigree Case ▲

- *circa 1780*

French silver filigree case enclosing pincushion and blue glass bottle.
- *length 5cm*
- Guide price $2,050

Silk Winder ▶
- **circa1890**
Chinese carved hardwood double silk winder.
- *18cm x 2.5cm*
- **Guide price $60**

Ivory Pin Cushion ▲
- **circa 1900**
Small urn-shaped ivory pin cushion holder.
- *height 6cm*
- **Guide price $120**

Plum Blossom Silk Winder ▼
- **circa 1890**
Chinese hardwood silk winder carved with a plum blossom, a symbol of winter.
- *15cm x 4cm*
- **Guide price $40**

Red Lacquer Winder ▲
- **circa 1890**
Carved Chinese festive red lacquer winder with gilded flowers.
- *13cm x 8cm*
- **Guide price $40**

Chinese Scissors ▲
- **circa 1860**
Steel Chinese sewing scissors.
- *height 11cm*
- **Guide price $170**

English Bodkin Case ▲
- *circa 1780*
English lilac enamel bodkin case in two sections with a bird cartouche.
- *length 15cm*
- **Guide price** $930

Pig Pincushion ▲
- *circa 1880*
Ivory pig with brown velvet pincushion on the back.
- *height 3cm*
- **Guide price** $640

Ivory Needle Case ▼
- *circa 1870*
Fine ivory needle case with original needle packets and the inscription "T.H." on the cover.
- *height 11cm*
- **Guide price** $880

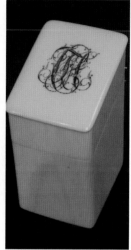

Oval Tortoiseshell Case ▼
- *circa 1880*
Oval tortoiseshell sewing case, complete with gold scissors, thimble, pick needle case and pencil.
- *length 12.5cm*
- **Guide price** $1,690

Gold Egg Sewing Case ▲
- *circa 1880*
French gold filigree case in the shape of an egg and lined with the original red velvet. With gold thimble scissors, needle case and pick.
- *height 8cm*
- **Guide price** $1,250

Tortoiseshell Box ▲
- *circa 1880*
Tortoiseshell needle case, with hinged cover.
- *height 5cm*
- **Guide price** $590

Bodkin Case ◄
- *circa 1780*
Purple bodkin case with white hexagonal spot design and six landscape cartouches, with gold banding.
- *length 15cm*
- **Guide price** $1,750

Fruitwood Winder ◀

- *circa 1900*

Finely carved fruitwood Chinese silk winder.
- *height 24cm*
- Guide price $50

Lacquered Needle Case ▶

- *circa 1870*

Carved wood red and gold lacquer needle case in the form of a flower.
- *12cm x 8cm*
- Guide price $180

Chinese Thimble ▲

- *circa 1860*

Silver Chinese thimble engraved with trailing blossom, worn as a ring.
- *diameter 1.5cm*
- Guide price $170

Silver Needle Case ▶

- *circa 1890*

Needle case of silver with trailing foliate banding.
- *length 8cm*
- Guide price $170

Carved Needle Case ▲

- *circa 1930*

Carved fruitwood winder and needle case.
- *length 26cm*
- Guide price $170

Satinwood Table Workbox ▶

- *circa 1820*

English hexagonal sewing workbox having triangular lidded compartments with small knob handles on either side of a central rectangular pin cushion.
- *7.5cm x 18.5cm x 28cm*
- Guide price $1,340

Silver Boot Pincushion ▼
- *circa 1870*

Silver boot pincushion.
- *height 5cm*
- **Guide price $500**

Silver Wool Winder ▼
- *circa 1780*

Silver wool winder in the shape of a ball made of fine foliate filigree, with small flowers on each leaf.
- *circumference 18cm*
- **Guide price $1,510**

Gold Chatelaine ▶
- *circa 1780*

French gold five piece sewing chatelaine, with heavily engraved design of flowers in baskets, ribboning, and scrolling joined by linked chains to a central foliate scrolled hook.
- *length 18cm*
- **Guide price $2,400**

Silver Scissors ◀
- *circa 1880*

Victorian silver case with scissors.
- *length 9.5cm*
- **Guide price $450**

Gothic Chair Pincushion ▲
- *circa 1900*

Gothic silver metal chair the red velvet seat being a pincushion.
- *height 6.5cm*
- **Guide price $240**

Walnut Sewing Case ▶
- *circa 1840*

French walnut sewing case in the form of a nut, lined with red satin and containing small scissors, thimble, needle case and pick.
- *width 5cm*
- **Guide price $1,230**

French Etui ▲
- *circa 1880*

French ebonised etui with silver gilt fitting.
- *length 12cm*
- **Guide price $980**

Snuff Boxes & Smoking Equipment

Horn Box ◄
- *circa 1890*

Horn snuff box with inlaid silver foliate design.
- *length 8cm*
- **Guide price** $120

Hampton Court Snuff Box ◄
- *circa 1890*

Oblong silver snuff box with Hampton Court on the lid, by G. Smith and Sons.
- *length 5cm*
- **Guide price** $120

Miniature Snuff Box ▲
- *circa 1890*

Miniature papier mâché snuff box with silver inlay of fleur-de-lys.
- *length 2cm*
- **Guide price** $50

Table Snuff Box ▲
- *circa 1890*

Table snuff box with the words "Help yourself" on the lid.
- *4cm x 13cm*
- **Guide price** $180

Huntsmen and Hounds Snuff Box ◄
- *circa 1890*

Silver snuff box by Fribourg and Treyer of London with huntsmen and foxes on the lid.
- *length 5cm*
- **Guide price** $100

French Gold Snuff Box ◄
- *circa 1750*
French oval snuff box with a
tooled striped pattern of gold over
tortoiseshell, and a roped effect
around the rim.
- *length 7cm*
- **Guide price $3,520**

Burr Walnut Snuff Box ▲
- *circa 1870*
Burr walnut circular snuff box,
with a painted landscape scene
on the lid and gold banding.
- *diameter 6.5cm*
- **Guide price $450**

Silver Gilt Snuff Box ►
- *circa Louis XIV*
French silver gilt snuff box with
shell design on the top and a
pastoral scene with a bird at the
bottom.
- *length 8cm*
- **Guide price $1,740**

Painted Snuff Box ►
- *circa 1890*
English oval papier mâché
snuff box painted with the head
of a young man on a red
background.
- *length 7cm*
- **Guide price $820**

Ebonised Snuff Box ▲
- *circa 1870*
Circular ebonised snuff box,
painted with a portrait of a
woman shown against a blue
background, by L. Fischer.
- *diameter 8.5cm*
- **Guide price $1,350**

Circular Painted
Snuff Box ►
- *circa 1790*
Circular tortoiseshell painted
snuff box showing a lady seated
playing a harp.
- *diameter 8cm*
- **Guide price $3,120**

Mother-of-Pearl Snuff Box ◀

- *circa 1890*
Oblong black lacquer snuff box
with inlaid banding of mother-of-
pearl pink.
- *length 7cm*
- **Guide price $70**

Silver Flower Snuff Box ▼

- *circa 1880*
Horn snuff box with ivory
banding and silver foliate
design.
- *length 4cm*
- **Guide price $120**

Horn Mull Snuff Box ▲

- *circa 1880*
Horn snuff box with silver
banding and shield with the
initials "L.M".
- *length 9cm*
- **Guide price $490**

Chinoiserie Snuff Box ◀

- *circa 1890*
Oval silver snuff box with
chinoiserie scene featuring a
pagoda and trees on the lid.
- *diameter 5cm*
- **Guide price $120**

Expert Tips

*Collecting snuff boxes is one
area where there are very few
period fakes or improvements –
nothing reasonably and
economically could be turned
into a snuff box. However,
during the eighteenth century,
snuff boxes were sometimes
turned into vinaigrettes,
portable containers for vinegar
to be used as a suppressant of
bad smells and as a disease
deterrent, by the addition of a
grill under the lid. These are
now rare and highly collectable.*

Silver and Enamel Cigarette Case ▶

- *circa 1896*

Silver cigarette case with an enamel picture showing a circus ring, with a lady in a pink dress astride a white horse, with a clown turning towards her.
- *length 9cm*
- **Guide price $2,400**

Tortoiseshell and Silver Snuff Box ▲

- *circa 1780*

An oval tortoiseshell snuff box with a silver floral and geometric design, with a mother-of-pearl background.
- *diameter 6.5cm*
- **Guide price $430**

Japanese Cigar Box ▲

- *circa 1880*

Japanese export cigar box with a dragon and Japanese characters on the lid characterising longevity and good fortune.
- *5cm x 18cm*
- **Guide price $210**

Mother-of-Pearl Snuff Box ▼

- *circa 1750*

Small bulbous snuff box with mother-of-pearl sections and silver banding.
- *height 5cm*
- **Guide price $1,340**

Satinwood Humidor ▲

- *circa 1910*

An elegant English rectangular satinwood humidor, with ivory banding and a fitted interior.
- *12.5cm x 23cm*
- **Guide price $880**

Dog Tobacco Jar ▲

- *circa 1900*

Carved mahogany tobacco jar in the shape of a comical dog with glass eyes, wearing a hat with a tassel and a bow tie.
- *height 18cm*
- **Guide price $1,070**

Telephones

Call Exchange Telephone ◄

- *circa 1950*

Black telephone cast in Bakelite with large central rotary dial and small drawer.
- *20cm x 26cm*
- **Guide price $240**

Black Bakelite Telephone ▲

- *circa 1930*

Black Bakelite telephone with large dial and drawer.
- *18cm x 25cm*
- **Guide price $290**

Expert Tips

The trimphone is now popular with collectors because it was so unpopular with users.

Red G.P.O. Telephone ▲

- *circa 1960*

Unusual G.P.O. telephone cast in red.
- *14cm x 18cm*
- **Guide price $90**

Trimphone ▶

- *circa 1970*

Two tone beige trimphone with push-button dialing.
- *10cm x 19cm*
- **Guide price $100**

Two Toned Telephone ▶

- *circa 1970*

Two toned, adjustable volume stone coloured British GPO telephone in plastic.

- *12cm x 10cm*
- **Guide price $90**

English Telephone ▲

- *circa 1950*

Cream Bakelite telephone with nickel rotary dial and black numerals, inscribed Portobello 4559, rare in any colour but black.

- *height 15cm*
- **Guide price $520**

Belgian Desk Telephone ▼

- *circa 1950*

European ivory desk telephone with large numerals and clear plastic rotary dial.

- *height 12.5cm*
- **Guide price $130**

Candlestick Telephone ▲

- *circa 1920*

Candlestick telephone with Steal handle with black bakelite top and brass and separate wood and brass ring box.

- *44cm x 15cm*
- **Guide price $700**

Ericsson Telephone ◀

- *circa 1950*

Cream bakelite Ericsson telephone with original handset and cord and large rotary dial with black numerals.

- *height 14cm*
- **Guide price $330**

Bakelite Telephone ▶

- *circa 1950*
Black bakelite British G.P.O.
telephone with ringing bell.
- *16cm x 24cm*
- **Guide price $190**

Gecophone Telephone ▼

- *circa 1930*
Gecophone black bakelite
telephone with bell ringing.
- *18cm x 24cm*
- **Guide price $330**

Genie Telephone ▼

- *circa 1970*
Red "Genie" designer telephone
by A. P. Besson manufactured by
British Telecom, with push
button dial.
- *11.5cm x 22cm*
- **Guide price $120**

Pyramid Telephone ▼

- *circa 1930*
Black bakelite pyramid telephone
with drawer and bell ringing.
- *16cm x 23cm*
- **Guide price $330**

Red Telephone ▲

- *circa 1960*
Red plastic British GPO
telephone.
- *13cm x 24cm*
- **Guide price $80**

Green Plastic Telephone ◀

- *circa 1960*
Green plastic British GPO
telephone. Slightly older than
telephone # 9965.
- *13cm x 24cm*
- **Guide price $80**

Expert Tips

*Ivory or coloured bakelite
telephones were more expensive
for the subscriber to rent and
are therefore now rarer and
more valuable to the present
day collector.*

Tools

Plumb Board ▶

- **1866**

A pine plumb board, probably Austrian, displaying punch decorations.
- *length 56cm*
- **Guide price $270**

Expert Tips

Although the best place to buy antique tools is from a good dealer, they can be very expensive in country auctions. You may have to buy a large lot, however, in order to acquire the one tool you want.

Router ▼

- **Early 19th century**

A European carved fruitwood router with flamboyant carved detail.
- *length 30.4cm*
- **Guide price $450**

Ebony-handled Hammer ▲

- **18th century**

Unusually-formed ebony-handled hammer with pleasing decoration.
- *length 17.8cm*
- **Guide price $180**

Iron Saw ▼

- **18th century**

An iron saw with ivory and ebony handle and iron ferrule.
- *length 51cm*
- **Guide price $710**

Bronze Brace ▼

- **18th century**

Bronze brace with fruitwood handles and ivory head button.
- *length 30.4cm*
- **Guide price $1,780**

Leatherworkers' Punch ▲

- **Early 19th century**

Beautiful leatherworkers' punch.
- *length 11.4cm*
- **Guide price $70**

Brass Trammels ▲

- *19th century*
A quality pair of steel-tipped brass trammels with keeps.
- *length 20.32cm*
- **Guide price** $150

Medical Forceps ▼

- *Early 19th century*
A pair of rare medical forceps with blackwood handles.
- *length 33cm*
- **Guide price** $130

Brass Bevel ▲

- *18th century*
A beautifully engraved brass and rosewood bevel.
- *length 17.8cm*
- **Guide price** $700

Shoe Rule ▲

- *19th century*
A boxwood shoe rule, nicely marked "Thomas Webb".
- *length 20.3cm*
- **Guide price** $160

Combination Tool Kit ▼

- *1850*
An extremely high quality gentlemen's tool kit by Timmins, figured rosewood handles and original carrying case.
- *10cm x 4cm*
- **Guide price** $700

Pump Drill ▼

- *17th century*
A primitive, stone and wood pump drill, extremely rare.
- *height 1m*
- **Guide price** $270

Bronze Dividers ◄

- *17th century*
A pair of steel tipped bronze dividers with a rare circular design.
- *length 12.7cm*
- **Guide price** $530

Chamfer Plane ▶

- **1890**
A solid boxwood chamfer plane
with lovely patina.
- *length 15cm*
- **Guide price $180**

Smooth Plane ▲

- **19th century**
A classic Scottish smoothing
plane with cove front, double
pierced lever cap and hardwood
infill.
- *length 25cm*
- **Guide price $710**

Beech Plough ▲

- **1880**
A beech plough by Mosely with
the rare internal stem adjustment
feature.
- *length 25cm*
- **Guide price $710**

Fiddlemakers Clamps ▲

- **19th century**
Eight hardwood Violinmakers
"Fiddlemakers" clamps.
- *length 20cm*
- **Guide price $50**

Drawing Instrument Set ▼

- **1910**
A quality set of drawing
instruments with two ivory rulers,
an ivory parallel rule, and brass
protractor.
- *15cm x 20cm*
- **Guide price $220**

Inuit Knife ▲

- **19th century**
An Inuit bone knife, typically
decorated with scrimshaw moose.
- *length 20cm*
- **Guide price $180**

Stanley Plane ▶

- **1925**
A Stanley 85 plane with original
decal.
- *length 20cm*
- **Guide price $1,070**

Planishing Hammer ▶

- *18th century*
A rare planishing hammer with a
few age cracks to the handle.
- *length 30cm*
- **Guide price $90**

Blueing Pan ◀

- *1880*
An extremely rare early Georgian
watchmakers' blueing pan used
for the oxidization of watch parts.
- *length 20cm*
- **Guide price $1,160**

Beech Ogee ◀

- *1910*
A little used handled beech ogee
by T. Hall, Newcastle.
- *length 7.6cm*
- **Guide price $130**

Bridle Plough ▲

- *1870*
A unique solid Brazilian rosewood
Mathieson brass stemmed bridle
plough.
- *length 30cm*
- **Guide price $7,120**

Styled Hammer ▶

- *Late 17th – early 18th century*
Silversmiths' or Goldsmiths'
hammer of wonderful style with
replaced ebony handle.
- *length 26cm*
- **Guide price $710**

Veterinary Tools ◀

- *19th century*
A travelling set of veterinary
instruments including some nice
horn-handled knives.
- *20cm x 30cm*
- **Guide price $130**

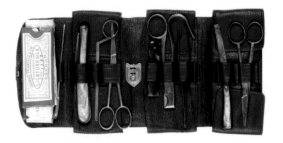

Expert Tips

*Many craftsmen, particularly
cabinet makers, made their own
tools. An expert can identify
the provenance by the
workmanship, but often there
is a maker's mark.*

Walking Sticks

Hand Holding Whistle Cane ▲

- *circa 1890*
Small carved ebony hand holding a metal whistle (probably for calling the dog), plain silvered collar, on ebonised hardwood shaft.
- *length 92cm*
- **Guide price $610**

Silver Vinaigrette ▲

- *circa 1880*
Rare scottish silver handle containing a vinaigrette. The hinged top covers a pierced silver gilt grill which lifts out by means of a small ring.
- *length 89cm*
- **Guide price $2,850**

Ivory Fighting Dogs Cane ▲

- *circa 1870*
Carved Victorian ivory handle depicting two fighting dogs artistically positioned. Plain silver collar mounted on dark brown hardwood shaft with light horn ferrule.
- *length 92cm*
- **Guide price $2,230**

Silver Gold Head System Cane ▲

- *circa 1880*
Golf club handle mounted on a fine snakewood shaft opens to reveal a compartment for cigarettes and is engraved with the monogrammed initials "EP".
- *length 90cm*
- **Guide price $3,200**

Jewelled Rock Crystal Cane ◄

- *circa 1890*
Rock crystal handle inset with a curtain of small gold set rubies in art nouveau taste, the wide gold collar overlaid with dark red guioche enamel, on ebonised hardwood shaft with light horn ferrule.
- *length 91cm*
- **Guide price $3,200**

Cane Display Stand ▲

- *circa 1880*
Polished Victorian cast iron cane stand, with a large decorative fretted back, and fitted with a removable drip tray.
- *71cm x 36cm*
- **Guide price $1,160**

Parrot Cane ▼
● *1870*
Oversized head of a parrot carved
from fruitwood, with fine detail,
mounted on a hardwood shaft,
with ornate gilt collar.
● **Guide price $1,510**

English Walking Stick ▼
● *1870*
Country walking stick with a
carved wood handle, modelled as
a hare with large glass eyes and
silver collar, mounted on a briar
wood shaft.
● **Guide price $1,030**

Ebony Cane ▲
● *1840*
Ebony cane with the handle
carved as the head of a Negro
with ivory teeth and boxwood hat
and collar, mounted on a
rosewood shaft.
● **Guide price $850**

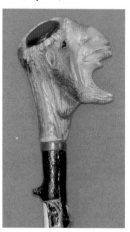

Stag Horn Cane ▲
● *1860*
Country walking stick carved as a
grotesque with a beard and glass
eyes, mounted on a knotted wood
shaft, with a silver collar and an
antler handle.
● **Guide price $700**

Victorian Cane ▼
● *1860*
Elegant Victorian cane with a
well carved handle depicting a
hunting dog with a bird, mounted
on a partridge wood shaft, with a
gilt collar.
● **Guide price $1,960**

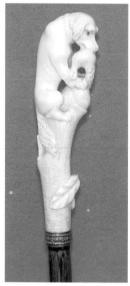

Hussar Head Cane ▼
● *1860*
A painted and carved wood cane
with the handle modelled as a
Continental hussar, with a
plumed helmet.
● **Guide price $1,690**

Decorative Arts

The term "decorative arts" is ambiguous and can be loosely defined as "the modelling or carving of stone, wood and bronze."

Decorative arts, as collected, tend to follow Oscar Wilde's maxim that "all art is completely useless", because decorative arts are those items that have no practical application whatsoever, but are there to be admired. Art for art's sake, in fact.

There is no doubt that collecting these items – particularly those relating to the excesses of the Victorian era – is often tinged with a degree of irony. Many would not be regarded today with quite the same reverence they had then and some are frankly hilarious.

On the other hand, items of the sheerest beauty, of wonderful craftsmanship and unique quality are to be found and, particulary in our eclectic age when homogeny is no longer regarded as a *sine qua non* of decoration, such beautiful objects of any period find themselves very much in demand. Interior designers have definitely enhanced the market for these items.

Another aphorism of Oscar's would now be seen as only partly true: "For there is no art where there is no style, and no style where there is no unity, and unity is of the individual."

Figures & Busts

Gnome with Axe ▶
- *circa 1900*
Delightful polychrome painted terracotta gnome chopping wood, Austrian.
- *height 47cm*
- **Guide price $3,120**

Art Nouveau Maiden Bust ◀
- *circa 1890*
Fine quality bisque porcelain bust of a stunning Nouveau maiden heightened with gilt and rouge, signed Andre Traggia.
- *height 31cm*
- **Guide price $3,020**

Gardening Gnome ▼
- *circa 1900*
Gnome holding a top hat with a rabbit, one of three.
- *height 58cm*
- **Guide price $10,150**

Augustus Caesar ▼

- *circa 1850*

Italian marble bust of Augustus Caesar raised on a marble plinth. This is taken from the bronze full-length figure of Augustus, circa 20 BC in the Vatican Museum. The breastplate is richly carved with mythological and historical scenes and the bust is supported on a panelled and moulded marble plinth of tapering form.

- *height 2.08m*
- **Guide price $17,440**

Bronze Centaur ▼

- *circa 1850*

Italian bronze of a centaur fighting a ram on marble.

- *height 17cm*
- **Guide price $1,590**

Pair of Maidens ▶

- *circa 1730*

One of a pair of white marble busts of maidens in the antique manner, attributed to Michael Rysbrach (1694–1770). With finely carved robes pinned at the shoulder with a brooch, the hair flowing loosely over one shoulder, supported on later Portoro marble socles.

- *76cm x 36cm*
- **Guide price $58,740**

Marley Horses ▲

- *circa 1880*

A small pair of French Marley horses after the model by Costeau. On black marble bases decorated with patinated friezes.

- *height 28cm*
- **Guide price $1,910**

Napoleon ▼

- *circa 1850s*

A fine well-finished momento mori of Napoleon in bronze from the mid-19th century.

- *height 13cm*
- **Guide price $850**

Maternity ◀

- *circa 1880*

A fine patinated, cold-painted parcel gilt bronze of a mother feeding an infant from the breast while holding a sleeping toddler, by Paul Dubois (1829–1905). Cast by the F. Barbedienne Foundry.

- *height 49cm*
- **Guide price $7,030**

Grand Tour Bronze ▲

• *circa 1860*
Unusual and small Italian grand
tour bronze of a man about to use
a sling.
• *height 12cm*
• **Guide price $760**

Marble Statue ▲

• *circa 1890*
An attractive Italian marble
statue of a young girl leaning
against a fountain playing a set of
panpipes. Signed "Pittaluga".
• *height 80cm*
• **Guide price $15,580**

Italian Bronze Boy ▶

• *1904*
A fine Italian bronze of a naked
young boy playing with kittens.
He holds one up while cuddling
the other. The bronze is signed
"Marcuse, Roma 1904". On a
chamfered marble base.
• *height 73cm*
• **Guide price $10,590**

Stone Roundels ▼

• *circa 1850*
A pair of Italian carved stone
roundels in the Renaissance
manner, each with a carved head,
one depicting Benvenuto Cellini
(1500–1571), Florentine sculptor,
goldsmith and amorist. The other
depicts Giulio Romano
(1499–1546), painter and
architect, one of the creators of
Mannerism, and chief assistant of
Raphael.
• *diameter 102cm*
• **Guide price $21,360**

Bronze Bust ▼

• *circa 1880*
Fine pair of bronze busts of
Albrecht Durer & Paul Romaine,
with two colour patination,
standing on bases of red and
black reeded marble, after the
style of Salmson.
• *height 40cm*
• **Guide price $5,250**

Beaux Arts Figure ▲

• *circa 1890*
French Beaux Arts statuary
marble figure of a young woman
emblematic of spring. Signed "F.
Palla".
• *76cm x 23cm*
• **Guide price $11,570**

Venus ▲

• *circa 1860*
A Victorian re-constituted stone
figure of Venus by the Farnley
Co. Standing by a pillar in
flowing chiffon, her hair dressed
in a chignon, on a rectangular
plinth.
• *1.34m x 55cm*
• **Guide price $1,340**

Boy Archer ▶

- *circa 1925*

Carved ivory figure of a naked young boy holding a bow raised on onyx base, signed "Ferdinand Preiss".
- *height 15cm*
- **Guide price $6,760**

Wolfhound Bronze ▲

- *circa 1920*

French cast of Gayrad's peaceful wolfhound, from the Susse Frères foundry.
- *8cm x 16cm*
- **Guide price $1,900**

Tiger Hunt Bronze ▲

- *circa 1890*

Cold-painted Austrian bronze of an elephant and a tiger.
- *height 24cm*
- **Guide price $10,320**

Bronze Spaniel Bookends ▲

- *circa 1930*

Cold-painted Austrian bronze spaniels, one black and the other liver and white.
- *13cm x 8cm*
- **Guide price $1,390**

Parrot on a Branch ▼

- *circa 1900*

Cold-painted Austrian bronze of a parrot perched on a branch.
- *height 28cm*
- **Guide price $5,870**

Arab on a Camel ▼

- *circa 1830*

Superb bronze model of an Arab on a camel.
- *height 30cm*
- **Guide price $8,540**

Nue Debout ▼

- *circa 1920*

Exquisite hand-carved ivory figure of a standing nude lady raised on a rouge marble base, signed "Joe Descomps".
- *height 27cm*
- **Guide price $6,760**

Austrian Hare Bronze

- *circa 1890*

Bronze with original paint of a hare with punishment in mind, aiming a stick at a youngster being held up by one ear.
- *height 4cm*
- **Guide price $1,250**

Mouse with Biscuit ▼

- *circa 1890*

Viennese novelty of a small mouse guarding the remains of a biscuit.
- *height 2cm*
- **Guide price $960**

Robin in a Basket ▲

- *circa 1890*

Austrian bronze of a pretty robin sitting in an oak-leaf basket, with original paint.
- *14cm x 16cm*
- **Guide price $1,390**

Ram with Horns ▲

- *circa 1890*

Austrian bronze of a ram with head down, huge horns, and undocked tail – with original paint.
- *5cm x 13cm*
- **Guide price $1,280**

Hare Musician ▼

- *circa 1890*

Austrian bronze of a hare playing a double base.
- *height 8cm*
- **Guide price $1,250**

Stag Bronze ▲

- *circa 1900*

Model of a standing stag with a good show of antlers and original paintwork.
- *height 10cm*
- **Guide price $1,140**

Maribou and Chicks ▲

- *circa 1900*

Austrian bronze figures of a family group of birds, a mother with her young, with original paint.
- *height 10cm*
- **Guide price $1,960**

Expert Tips

Spelter or bronze? One test is to "ping" it with your finger; bronze will ring, spelter will make a dull thud. Another test is to scratch the underside; spelter will reveal a silver colour, whereas bronze is golden. Most spelter pieces also tend to be hollow.

Winning Greyhound Bronze ▶

- *circa 1870*

Striking bronze figure of a winning greyhound with rich brown patina and excellent detail, signed by Paul Comolera.
- *height 36cm*
- **Guide price $6,400**

Poodle on a Cushion ▼

- *circa 1830*

A bronze French poodle on a cushion, after the original by Thomire.
- *height 30cm*
- **Guide price $4,090**

French Rabbit Bronze ◀

- *circa 1880*

Charming model of a rabbit by sculptor Isidore Bonheur. Cast by his brother-in-law Peyrol, signed and stamped.
- *height 5cm*
- **Guide price $2,490**

Bronze Duck ▶

- *1560*

Small finely cast bronze duck.
- *height 2cm*
- **Guide price $180**

Gilt Bronze Cat ▶

- *circa 1920*

Delightful gilt bronze model of a seated cat signed by Thomas Carter.
- *15cm x 13cm*
- **Guide price $2,490**

Napoleon III's Dogs ◀

- *circa 1900*

Napoleon III adored his two dogs. Ravagout and Ravageole, here depicted by E. Fremiet and cast by Barbedienne.
- *16cm x 17cm*
- **Guide price $6,760**

Bronze Dancer ▶

- *circa 1890*
French bronze figure of a naked
nymph with fine smooth surface
raised on rouge marble, signed
"August Moreau".
- *height 21cm*
- **Guide price $3,290**

Maiden with Scroll ▲

- *circa 1890*
Gilt bronze figure of a semi-clad
maiden holding a scroll and quill.
Signed by "George Baeau" and
inscribed.
- *height 27.5cm*
- **Guide price $5,250**

Expert Tips

*Another way to tell spelter from
bronze is simply to hold it in
your hand. If it warms up
quickly it is probably spelter.*

Dachshund and
Pups Bronze ◀

- *circa 1880*
Superb Clovis Masson bronze
group of dachshund and pups
with excellent detail and rich
brown patination sign.
- *height 19cm*
- **Guide price $10,320**

Bronze Study of
Rhinoceros ◀

- *circa 1920*
Detailed study of a rhinoceros
on a rectangular base.
Madlestickse of Germany.
- *6cm x 8cm*
- **Guide price $1,500**

Bronze Eagle ▶

- *13th century*
Fine bronze eagle standing on a
circular stand with a star-shaped
base.
- *height 15cm*
- **Guide price $1,420**

Alex Falguiere ▲

- *circa 1880*
Gilt bronze figure of a coy young
lady on a marble base, signed and
stamped with Siot foundry.
- *height 16cm*
- **Guide price $2,580**

Lighting

Column Table Lamp ▶

- **1870**

Tall English facet-cut column
table lamp with cut font and
gilded mounts.
- *height 56cm*
- **Guide price $3,200**

Student Lamp ▲

- *circa 1900*

Crossbanded student lamp in
gilded brass fitted with a marble
plinth and bell-shaped
crossbanded glass shade.
- *63cm x 15cm*
- **Guide price $2,140**

Wedgwood Lamp ▼

- *circa 1925*

Wedgwood desk lamp fitted with
a trough-shaped shade and
circular stepped base.
- *38cm x 23cm*
- **Guide price $2,310**

Tiffany Lamp ▼

- **20th century**

Bronze lamp with caged green
glass shade stamped "Tiffany
Studio".
- *height 50cm*
- **Guide price $10,500**

Chrome Wall Lights ▼

- *circa 1925*

Set of six wall lights in chromed
brass fitted with coolie-shaped
shades.
- *20cm x 15cm*
- **Guide price $4,450**

"Go To Bed" Candlestick ▲

- *circa 1850*

Victorian Tunbridge Ware and rosewood "go to bed" candlestick, and taper holder. The lid rises to reveal storage for candles and tapers.
- *height 11cm*
- **Guide price $650**

Italian Gilded Candlesticks ▲

- *circa 1880*

One of a pair of Italian gilded bronze candlesticks, with three foliate scrolled branches.
- *height 74cm*
- **Guide price $5,250**

Victorian Table Lamp ▼

- *1880*

Victorian brass pedestal lamp with a pink and glass shade with a cherry blossom painted design.
- *height 49cm*
- **Guide price $1,590**

French Student Lamp ▼

- *circa 1899*

French highly decorative adjustable library lamp with a frosted glass shade, standing on a reeded Corinthian column with laurel leaf decoration, standing on a rouge royale marble base.
- *height 65cm*
- **Guide price $2,140**

French Chandelier ◄

- *circa 1880*

French ormolu and cut-glass bag and waterfall eight-branch chandelier.
- **Guide price $4,270**

Victorian Bijou Lamp ▲

- *1880*

Victorian adjustable reading lamp with a pink glass tulip shade, metal rim and a curved brass stand, on a circular wooden base.
- *height 24cm*
- **Guide price $1,250**

Silver-Plated Table Lamp ▲

- *circa 1895*

Late Victorian silver-plated table lamp, fitted with feathered white glass lampshade, standing on a moulded silver column and base.
- *height 36cm*
- **Guide price $1,590**

Branch Chandelier ▲

- *circa 17th–18th century*

Chandelier with ten large branches and five smaller ones from the 17th century with some later additions.

- *height 1.86m*
- **Guide price $12,100**

French Prichet Sticks ▲

- *1780*

One of a pair of French prichet sticks standing on three feet.

- *height 55cm*
- **Guide price $1,690**

Black Tôle Lamp ▲

- *1870*

Black tôle lamp with gilt vases and floral swags around the base, and sprays of corn around the central column, with original patination.

- *height 74cm*
- **Guide price $1,030**

Victorian Ceiling Pendant ▼

- *circa 1889*

Victorian gas ceiling pendant in brass, fitted with two branches with acid-edged cranberry glass shades.

- *height 90cm*
- **Guide price $1,960**

Cast Brass Table Lamp ▼

- *circa 1890*

English cast brass table lamp fitted with a hand-painted glass lampshade decorated with a scene of birds and trailing foliage, supported by brass arms.

- *height 48cm*
- **Guide price $1,960**

Glass Wall Lights ▶

- *circa 1950*

Set of three Italian moulded glass wall lights fitted with vertical chrome bands.
- *20cm x 16cm*
- **Guide price $2,670**

Dutch Brass Six-Arm Chandelier ▲

- *circa 1900*

Brass chandelier with six arms attached to central shaft terminating in a sphere and hoop.
- *53.3cm x 50.8cm*
- **Guide price $2,230**

Swedish Brass and Glass Chandelier ▲

- *circa 1850*

Ornate chandelier with brass arms terminating in candle holders and tear-shaped glass pendants.
- *78.7cm x 61cm*
- **Guide price $5,340**

French Brass and Glass Chandelier ▼

- *circa 1850*

Chandelier with 16 light fittings profusely decorated with hanging faceted crystals.
- *1.07m x 63.5cm*
- **Guide price $7,120**

Brass Chandelier ▼

- *circa 1880*

A European six-armed chandelier with globe-shaped reservoir and curved foliate arms.
- *53.3cm x 71cm*
- **Guide price $3,200**

Bronzed Gas Wall Light
- *circa 1865*

An important English bronzed gas wall light fitted with opal glass gas shade with decorative motives.
- *height 45cm*
- **Guide price $2,140**

French Chandelier ▼
- *circa 1890*

One of a pair of gilt brass French Gothic revival chandeliers.
- *62cm x 91cm*
- **Guide price $6,230**

Three Light Ceiling Pendant ▶
- *circa 1899*

Edwardian three light ceiling pendant in brass, fitted with acid-edged cranberry glass shades.
- *height 43cm*
- **Guide price $2,670**

Wall Appliqués ▲
- *circa 1860*

A pair of gilt brass Neo-Classical wall appliqués.
- *length 81cm*
- **Guide price $2,670**

Brass Wall Lamp ▲
- *circa 1880*

One of a pair of English decorative gas brass wall lamps fitted with cut and acid-edged glass shades.
- *height 20cm*
- **Guide price $1,770**

French Candelabra ▼
- *circa 1840*

One of a pair of French four branch ormolu candelabra with a snake circling a tapered column, with scrolled acanthus leaf and shell decoration and a flame finial, the whole on a solid platform base.
- *height 60cm*
- **Guide price $6,850**

Wall Lantern ◄
- *circa 1880*

Wall lantern of copper and sheet iron, made by Faucon Frères, Paris.
- *58.4cm x 24cm x 30cm*
- **Guide price $1,510**

Expert Tips

There are a lot of copies on the market, so beware. Look for original wiring and original light bulb holders, as these were generally too difficult or expensive for imitators to copy.

Brass Lanterns ▼
- *1850–60*

A pair of English 19th century brass lanterns with conical roofs ending in brass hoops for hanging.
- *32cm x 15.2cm*
- **Guide price $980**

Tôle Lamp ▲
- *circa 1920*

One of a pair of French tôle lamps, cream with gilt decoration.
- *71cm x 35.5cm*
- **Guide price $3,290**

Column Lamps ◄
- *circa 1880*

One of a pair of bronze fluted French column lamps.
- *height 52cm*
- **Guide price $7,030**

Bouillotte Lamp ▲
- *circa 1840*

Red French tôle bouillotte lamp with two snuffers, painted later.
- *50.8cm x 38.1cm*
- **Guide price $2,230**

English Gas Wall Lamp ▲

- *circa 1875*
One of a pair of decorative glass brass wall lamps fitted with acid-edged glass shades.
- *33cm*
- **Guide price $1,770**

French Silver Plated Obliques ▲

- *circa 1860*
French silver plated three branch wall obliques with cut glass storm shades, mounted on a silver stylised shield with scrolled shell design.
- **Guide price $6,050**

Victorian Wall Lamp ▲

- *circa 1895*
One of a pair of Victorian gas wall lamps fitted with moulded peach-coloured glass shades.
- *34cm*
- **Guide price $1,590**

English Wall Lamp ▲

- *circa 1880*
One of a pair of English decorative cast brass gas wall lamps fitted with acid-edged glass shades.
- *35cm*
- **Guide price $1,770**

Gas Wall Lamp ▲

- *circa 1875*
One of a pair of highly decorative cast glass gas wall lamps fitted with cut glass shades.
- *22cm*
- **Guide price $1,770**

Expert Tips

Try to buy from a reputable dealer who will have rewired the gas lamp fittings with new electric cables, and check that the shades are not broken.

Electric Wall Lamp ▲

- *circa 1900*
One of a pair of decorative cast brass electric wall lamps fitted with blue vaseline glass shades.
- *20cm*
- **Guide price $1,590**

Wall Lamp ▶

- *circa 1890s*
One of a pair of English bronzed electric wall lights. Fitted with cut crystal glass shades.
- *height 28cm*
- **Guide price $3,200**

Metalware

Brass Ewers ▶

- *circa 1805*

Fine pair of patinated brass and overlay ewers by Naurio.
- *height 28cm*
- **Guide price $12,020**

Alex Vibert Ewer ◀

- *circa 1890*

Art Nouveau gilt bronze ewer with raised decoration of a naked nymph fishing in a pool.
- *height 44cm*
- **Guide price $7,920**

Victorian Tôle Coal Box ▶

- *circa 1850*

Victorian tôle coal box with gilt chinoiserie and pattern decoration on a most unusual malachite background.
- *54cm x 48cm x 33cm*
- **Guide price $1,510**

Bird Cage ▲

- *circa 1900*

Rare late 19th century triple singing birds in cage, having a penny-in-the-slot mechanism.
- *58.5cm x 25.5cm x 25.5cm*
- **Guide price $15,580**

Frog Candlesticks ▼

- *circa 1870*

Superb pair of bronze candlesticks with tri-form frogs to the base and lily bud sconces. Signed by August Cain.
- *height 36cm*
- **Guide price $4,270**

Pair of Bronze Hunting Trophy Lidded Vases ▼

- *circa 1870*

Fine pair of bronze hunting trophy lidded vases attributed to Auguste Cain (1822–1894) and decorated front and back with animal trophies in bold relief. Ormolu handles terminated in retriever heads.
- *height 45.5cm*
- **Guide price $5,250**

Ormolu Ewers ▲

- *circa 1795*

A pair of French Directoire period patinated bronze and finest original ormolu ewers. Of slender ovoid form, the sinuous lip continuing to an SOR-scroll arm with finely chased griffin and satyrs mask terminal, on a circular base with stiff leaf and engine turned decoration, resting on a square plinth.
- *height 38cm*
- **Guide price $20,030**

Ormolu Tazza ▼

- *circa 1815*

A fine quality fire gilded ormolu tazza or dish set on a porphry base. Almost certainly Swedish from early 19th century. With fine quality work to tazza and original ormolu.
- *25cm x 25cm*
- **Guide price $4,000**

Bronze Dolphins ▼

- *1880*

A pair of English stylized bronze dolphins with mounted seashells resting on their tails, on a rectangular marble base.
- *height 16cm*
- **Guide price $2,940**

Bronze Lady ▼

- *circa 1880*

Bronze lady with a pensive expression, one arm over a chair and the other at her spinet.
- *height 53cm*
- **Guide price $1,280**

Gothic Revival Splint Holders ▲

- *circa 1850*

An attractive pair of gothic revival splint holders in the style of Pugin. With fine original ormolu in superb condition. Probably French.
- *height 20.5cm*
- **Guide price $3,120**

Bronze Girl with Dragonfly ▲

- *circa 1880*

Painted spelter figure of a young laughing girl with a bow in her hair, one arm outstretched and the other holding a bowl with a dragonfly. Standing on a foliate rustic mound and circular wood base.
- *height 49cm*
- **Guide price $390**

Expert Tips

While condition is important, rust on ironwork is not a problem; it can be stripped, treated with an antirust agent and sympathetically repainted with metal paint.

French Empire Candlesticks ▼

- *circa 1815*

A fine pair of patinated bronze and original ormolu French Empire candlesticks. In the form of a classically draped vestal standing holding an oil lamp in her arms, with a very well formed candleholder on her head, with round ormolu socle.

- *height 38cm*
- **Guide price** $7,030

Bronze Young Girl ▼

- *circa 1880*

Bronze classical figure of a young girl semi-clad, holding her robe in one hand.

- *height 52cm*
- **Guide price** $2,350

Reclining Nude Plaque ▲

- *circa 1880*

Reclining nude with her head resting on her hand and Cupid at her feet.

- *width 51cm*
- **Guide price** $490

Boy Water Carrier ▲

- *circa 1870*

Gilt on bronze boy carrying two ewers on a yoke, standing on a circular bronze base, signed "Moreau".

- *height 23cm*
- **Guide price** $2,230

Orient ▶

- *circa 1900*

A good quality early 20th century French bronze bust of a woman inscribed "Orient", and stamped: E Villanis.

- *51cm x 34cm*
- **Guide price** $4,900

Bronze Figures ▲

- *circa 1870*

Very attractive pair of patinated bronze figures of negro slaves carrying produce. Produced and signed by Susse Frères from models by Charles Cumberworth an American born artist working in Paris. On reeded onyx bases.

- *height 50cm*
- **Guide price** $8,460

Fire Jambs ▶

- *1820–40*
Pair of bell metal fire jambs.
English or American.
- *18cm x 16.5cm x 14cm*
- **Guide price $680**

Fire Tools ◀

- *circa 1840*
Set of English polished steel fire
tools, comprising a shovel with
pierced lattice-work, poker and
tongs.
- *height 76.2cm*
- **Guide price $800**

Expert Tips

*Brass in the seventeenth and
early eighteenth century was
raised from the hammered sheet.
Later brass was made from
thin, rolled sheets giving a
smooth finish.*

Dutch Brass Andirons ▼

- *circa 1840*
Pair of Dutch cast brass andirons
with ornate bases incorporating
male head and crest.
- *45.7cm x 12.7cm x 26.7cm*
- **Guide price $1,340**

Brass Fender ▼

- *1780–1800*
Late 18th century English cast
brass fender with lattice design
raised on paw feet.
- *16.5cm x 20.3cm x 1.12m*
- **Guide price $700**

Fire Screen ▲

- *1890–1910*
Late 19th century or early 20th
century French fan fire screen in
brass with fine lattice work.
- *7cm x 15cm x 99cm*
- **Guide price $1,160**

Coal Scuttle ▼

- *1860–70*
English Brass repoussée coal
scuttle with original turned ebony
handles, foliate and scrolled
motifs and lion heads.
- *45.7cm x 32cm x 44.5cm*
- **Guide price $700**

Bacchante ▼

- *circa 1880*
A fine quality 19th century
French bronze figure of
Bacchante. Signed "Clodion".
Also stamped with the
Barbedienne foundry stamp.
- *55cm x 54cm*
- **Guide price** $5,330

The Kiss ▶

- *circa 1875*
A superb 19th century French
bronze bust of a couple kissing.
Signed "Houdon".
- *46cm x 39cm*
- **Guide price** $8,810

Celinius ▲

- *circa 1800*
Bronze figure of Celinius and the
infant Bacchus.
- *height 59cm*
- **Guide price** $6,680

Robert the Bruce ▼

- *circa 1890*
Impressive spelter figure of
Robert the Bruce wearing armour
and holding a shield, standing on
a square green marble base.
- *height 83cm*
- **Guide price** $2,670

Bronze of David ▼

- *circa 1880*
Bronze figure of David with the
head of Goliath. Stamped and
signed "A. Mercie Barbedienne
foundry".
- *height 70cm*
- **Guide price** $8,810

Bronze Chinese Roe Deer ◀

- *circa 1880*
Bronze study of a Chinese Roe
deer from the Chiurazzi foundry,
Naples.
- *height 56cm*
- **Guide price** $13,890

Boot Chimney Ornaments ▲

- **1850–60**
Pair of curious English cast bronze or bell metal chimney ornaments as buttoned boots.
- *13.3cm x 2.5cm x 12.7cm*
- **Guide price $320**

Lion Chimney Ornaments ▼

- **1840–60**
Pair of English cast iron chimney ornaments as recumbent lions on pedestals.
- *11.4cm x 2.54cm x 18cm*
- **Guide price $150**

Brass Wall Pocket ◄

- **1840–50**
Nineteenth century English brass wall pocket in a pleasing curved and pierced design.
- *16cm x 6.4cm x 23.5cm*
- **Guide price $390**

Brass Skimmer ◄

- **1910–20**
Early 20th century English brass skimmer with pierced eagle motif and lattice handle.
- *53.3cm x 20.3cm*
- **Guide price $390**

Lion Tool Rests ▲

- **1860–70**
Pair of English Victorian cast iron and brass fire tool rests figured as lions on brass egg and dart bases on eight-sided pedestal.
- *35.5cm x 17.8cm x 25.4cm*
- **Guide price $1,690**

French Brass Andirons ◄

- **circa 1880**
Large French 19th century cast brass andirons with original backs and scrolled and foliate bases.
- *63.5cm x 44.5cm x 30.5cm*
- **Guide price $1,510**

Furniture

The chest or coffer is the earliest form of furniture, made from planks and sometimes reinforced with iron bandings.

Almost since man started to use furniture in his home there has been another man who has made a career of trying to enhance it to increase the value. Because collecting furniture is something of a minefield, in this area more, perhaps, than any other it is most important to genuinely like the pieces that you buy. Then, when they turn out to be not quite what you thought they were, at least you don't mind living with them. Buying from reputable dealers is your best guarantee of authenticity, but it is always worth making your own checks. Furniture should be worn from use. Anything that seems unnecessarily distressed in unlikely places should be avoided. Similarly, anything that suggests uneven proportions should be treated with care – although taste will probably steer you away from it anyway. It may have been cut down or "married". When in doubt, trust your instincts.

Beds

Mahogany Bed ▶
- **1920**
Large, elaborately carved, mahogany bed with pointed headboard and footboard and posts with finial decoration.
- *width 1.96m*
- **Guide price $7,570**

Mahogany Four Poster Bed ▲
- *19th century*
Four poster bed with moulded and carved headboard and footboard and turned and fluted columns.
- *width 1.53m*
- **Guide price $4,450**

Walnut Louis Style Bed ▶
- *late 19th century*
An unusual French walnut Louis style bed in very good condition with quarter veneer design to the head and foot, carved mouldings, and detailed cabriole feet.
- *1.57m x 1.98m x 1.52m*
- **Guide price $3,740**

French Empire Bedstead ▼

- *circa 1870*
French empire flame mahogany
bedstead with pilaster moulding,
cross banded and inlaid designs
with ormolu mounts.
- *width 1.53m*
- **Guide price $11,570**

French Mahogany Bedstead ▼

- *circa 1880*
French mahogany Louis XVI bed
with a moulded headboard with a
gilt torchière in the centre with
two cherubs below, and gilt
finials.
- *length 1.78m*
- **Guide price $9,790**

Mahogany French Bedstead ▶

- *circa 1860*
Flame mahogany Louis XV
bedstead with highly decorative
floral and ribbon ormolu mounts.
- *width 1.37m*
- **Guide price $10,680**

French Louis XV Bedstead ▲

- *circa 1880*
French Louis XV solid walnut
single bed with moulded and
carved headboard and footboard.
- *length 1.84m*
- **Guide price $7,480**

Bow-Fronted Bedstead ▼

- *19th century*
Upholstered bow-fronted and
padded Louis XV bedstead with
original green paintwork.
- *1.48m*
- **Guide price $2,300**

Walnut Louis XVI Bedstead ◀

- *circa 1880*
Large French solid walnut Louis
XVI bed with carved ribboning
on the headboard, and floral
swags footboard, with fluted
posts.
- *length 1.79m*
- **Guide price $12,020**

Expert Tips

*If you come across a pair of
period bed posts for a four
poster bed, snap them up.
It is simple to make your own
bed as long as you have the
genuine posts.*

Mahogany Wall Bed ▲
- *late 19th century*
A French mahogany wall bed
with a beautifully carved super
top rail from left to right at each
end and mouldings that continue
down the side columns.
- *length 2.06m*
- **Guide price $2,050**

Scroll End Upholstered Bed ▲
- *late 19th century*
A French scroll end upholstered
bed with original rails, mouldings,
and gilding to highlight. The
upholstery is in good condition.
- *1.19m x 1.60m x 1.98m*
- **Guide price $4,000**

Painted Empire Bed ▼
- *late 19th century*
French kingsize Empire Henri
style bed restored and repainted
in its original style with carved
guilded mouldings. Part of a suite
with a pair of matching bedside
cabinets and a triple door armoire.
- *1.37m x 2.08m x 1.50m*
- **Guide price $4,900 for suite**

Louis Style Painted Bed ▲
- *late 19th century*
A good quality late 19th century
French Louis style painted bed
with a fitted base.
- *1.37m x 1.90m*
- **Guide price $2,050**

Regency Four Poster Bed ◄
- *circa 1810*
Decorated and giltwood Regency
period four poster bed attributed
to Thomas Hope.
- *2.97m x 1.88m x 2.18m*
- **Guide price $115,700**

Italian Bombe Bed ▲
- *early 20th century*
An unusual Italian "bombe" bed
made in solid walnut with
marquetry inlay incorporating
tireless attention to detail.
- *1.63m x 1.83m x 2.24m*
- **Guide price $5,960**

Cane Bergère Bed ▲
- *late 19th century*
A French solid walnut framed
cane bergère bed with beautiful
carving on the frame and cane in
excellent condition.
- *2.13m x 1.55m*
- **Guide price $3,470**

Louis XV Bedstead ▲
- *19th century*
Upholstered Louis XV pink
velvet button backed bedstead
with solid walnut frame and bow
fronted base, standing on cabriole
legs.
- *length 2.22m*
- **Guide price $2,660**

Louis XV Bedstead ▲
- *1880*
Painted, padded and upholstered
Louis XV bedstead with original
gilding to headboard and base.
- *length 1.85m*
- **Guide price $8,010**

Walnut Louis XV Bedstead ▲
- *circa 1880*
French solid walnut Louis XV
bedstead with carved floral swag
and moulded decoration.
- *width 1.53m*
- **Guide price $7,480**

Renaissance Style Bedstead ▶
- *circa 1880*
Extended Renaissance style
walnut bedstead with wreath and
torchière ormolu mounts.
- *width 2.22m*
- **Guide price $12,370**

Victorian Bedstead ▼
- *1895*
Victorian brass and black-painted
iron bedstead with unusual
tubular brass top and central
linked plaques on both the
headboard and base.
- *length 2.22m*
- **Guide price $4,450**

Cottage Bedstead ▼
- *1880*
Victorian hand-forged black iron
cottage bedstead.
- *length 2.22m*
- **Guide price $2,660**

Victorian Bedstead ▲
- *1885*
Victorian black cast iron bedstead
with brass rail and ball finials.
- *length 2.22m*
- **Guide price $2,300**

Spanish Bedstead ▲
- *1850*
A Spanish hand-forged iron
bedstead with large ornate cast
brass ornamentation.
- *length 1.83m*
- **Guide price $4,630**

Bookcases

George IV Mahogany Bookcase ▲

- *circa 1825*

A George IV cream-painted and parcel-gilt mahogany bookcase in the manner of William Kent. The rectangular moulded cornice above an egg and dart dentilled lower cornice above a foliate swagged frieze centred by a female mask and flanked by shells. There are four glazed panelled doors below, between Ionic pilasters. The base section with four panelled doors between plain panelled uprights, each enclosing an adjustable shelf.

- *3.08m x 2.1m*
- **Guide price $85,440**

Mahogany Bookcase ▲

- *circa 1840*

Fine flame mahogany secretaire bookcase with two glazed doors and fitted interior and two cupboards below on a square base.

- *2.36m x 1.04m*
- **Guide price $18,690**

Mahogany Bookcase ▼

- *1880*

Unusually large breakfront bookcase with mahogany and satinwood cross-banded decoration, swan neck pediment, galleried and moulded designs, raised on a plinth base.

- *2.33m x 3.13m*
- **Guide price $49,840**

Glazed Bookcase Cabinet ▼

- *circa 1760*

An early George III mahogany glazed bookcase cabinet. With a broken, moulded dentil work pediment, each door composed of two astragal glazed octagonal panels with glazing bars connecting to the door frames, the interior lined and fitted with glass shelves. The cabinet with figured timber, the doors each with a shaped fielded panel defined by ribbon and flower-head moulding. The cabinet fitted with a moulded lip at the base above.

- *2.33m x 1.17m*
- **Guide price $43,610**

Victorian Walnut Bookcase ▲

- *circa 1880*

Victorian walnut bookcase with moulded flat top pediment, glazed doors enclosing five shelves, two deep drawers above two moulded doors, standing on moulded bracket feet.

- *height 2.51m*
- **Guide price $5,070**

Secretaire Bookcase ▲

- *circa 1820*

Regency secretaire bookcase with Gothic glazed upper section, the fall opens to reveal a well fitted interior above matched flame veneer doors, the whole raised on splayed feet with shaped apron.

- *2.62m x 1.2m*
- **Guide price $33,380**

Mahogany Revolving Bookcase ▶

- *circa 1900*
Mahogany inlaid revolving bookcase with marquetry rosette.
- *68.6m x 46cm x 46cm*
- **Guide price $3,120**

Mahogany Waterfall Bookcase ▲

- *circa 1800*
Regency mahogany waterfall bookcase, the shelves over two drawers, with its original brasses and legs.
- *1.1m x 25cm x 76cm*
- **Guide price $6,680**

Mahogany Breakfont Bookcase ▲

- *circa 1780*
A fine George III mahogany breakfront bookcase. Provenance – made for Harborough House, signed "J. Johnson Price".
- *3.22m x 57cm x 4.34m*
- **Guide price $104,950**

Book Carrier ▲

- *circa 1820*
Regency period mahogany book carrier on wheeled feet.
- *43cm x 24cm x 82cm*
- **Guide price $7,030**

Regency Mahogany Bookcase Cabinet ▼

- *circa 1815*
A fine Regency period highly figured mahogany bookcase cabinet with surmounting Grecian style moulded cornice above two glazed doors, unusually fitted with brass astragal glazing bars enclosing three adjustable shelves, the base with two panelled cupboard doors on four square tapered peg feet.
- *2.18m x 44cm x 1.01m*
- **Guide price $20,920**

George III Breakfront Bookcase ▼

- *circa 1790*
George III mahogany breakfront bookcase, the moulded cornice with a flame-mahogany veneered frieze surmounted by a broken arch pediment, above four gothic glazed doors, the base section with a projecting top with a moulded edge above a narrow frieze, above four panelled cupboard doors. Provenance: Lord Oakley – JAT Bartsow, Esq, DSO TD.
- *2.61m x 54cm x 2.51m*
- **Guide price $86,330**

George I Bureau ▼

- *circa 1715*
George I walnut veneered double domed bureau cabinet, replacement glass plates and brass wear.
- *2.04m x 58.5cm x 1.02m*
- **Guide price $86,330**

Walnut Book Cabinet ◀

- *circa 1720*
George I walnut veneered bureau book cabinet, incorporating mirrored door.
- *2.02m x 48cm x 76cm*
- **Guide price $29,370**

Mahogany Bookcases ◀

- *circa 1800*

A rare pair of English mahogany bookcases of small size, with open upper shelves above a pair of small panelled doors.
- *1.1m x 32cm x 63.5cm*
- **Guide price $85,440**

Bamboo Chiffonier ▶

- *circa 1870*

Victorian bamboo chiffonier with lacquer and anaglypta paper panels.
- *1.8m x 41cm x 74cm*
- **Guide price $1,690**

Burr Walnut Bookcase ▲

- *circa 1720*

Tall George I bookcase with two large mirrored doors with brass key escutcheons. The interior has numbered folio shelves and is stamped in two places on the base GR VI surmounted by a crown.
- *2.58m x 67cm x 1.29m*
- **Guide price $471,700**

Oak Bookcase ▼

- *circa 1870*

Large Victorian bookcase with gothic influence, four shelves above two deeper base shelves with ledge.
- *2.3m x 40.6cm x 2.5m*
- **Guide price $10,590**

Rosewood Bookcase or Display Cabinet ▲

- *circa 1840*

French rosewood bookcase or display cabinet with a shaped scroll pediment, two glazed doors with cast gilt brass decorative edging, and a rosewood veneered lined drawer above two smaller glazed doors.
- *2.37m x 47.5cm x 1.1m*
- **Guide price $44,500**

Secretaire Bookcase ▲

- *mid 20th century*

Mahogany breakfront secretaire with brass fittings surmounted by glass-fronted bookshelves.
- *2.1m x 36cm x 1.7m*
- **Guide price $8,460**

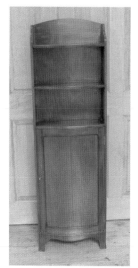

George II Mahogany Bookcase ▲

- *circa 1750*

George II mahogany bookcase, the bold swan neck pediment with foliate and rosette carving, above two astragal glazed doors opening to reveal a fitted interior. The lower section with sloping fall opening to reveal a finely fitted interior. The whole on bracket feet.
- *2.28m x 1m*
- **Guide price $48,950**

George III Bureau Bookcase ▼

- *circa 1765*

George III mahogany bureau bookcase, the astragal glazed doors enclosing adjustable shelves with fall front and well fitted interior of tulip wood. With letter slides and drawers.
- *width 1.09m*
- **Guide price $14,060**

Satinwood Secretaire Bookcase ▼

- *circa 1780*

Excellent secretaire bookcase of small elegant proportions. The whole veneered in satinwood heightened with cross banding in tulip wood, with shaped cornice and urn finials surmounting a corbelled frieze above two doors with moulded gothic glazing bars retaining their original glass.
- *1.94m x 52cm x 23cm*
- **Guide price $151,300**

Victorian Mahogany Bookcase ▲

- *circa 1880*

One of a pair of mahogany bookcases with open shelves and storage cupboards below, enclosed by bow-fronted doors.
- *1.35m x 13cm*
- **Guide price $3,290**

Regency Bookcase ▲

- *circa 1810*

English Regency period two door chiffonier/bookcase in a mixture of pine and fruit wood with galleried and turned designs.
- *1.07m x 63cm*
- **Guide price $5,250**

Regency Bookcase ▲

- *circa 1835*

Regency rosewood bookcase with glazed doors and two panelled doors below, standing on a plinth base.
- *1.93m x 84cm x 36cm*
- **Guide price $5,790**

Boxes

Jewellery Table Cabinet ▶
- *circa 1825*
Dutch mahogany jewellery table cabinet with hinged lid that opens to reveal a full-sized velvet lined interior and six small drawers fitted with small ivory knob handles.
- *30.5cm x 23cm x 32cm*
- **Guide price $2,670**

Mother-of-Pearl Coffret ▲
- *circa 1670*
Spa lace box with walnut ground inlaid with mother-of-pearl and silvered metal flowers and animals.
- *2.5cm x 24cm x 33cm*
- **Guide price $34,710**

Expert Tips

"Tea caddy" is a late eighteenth century term derived from the Malay word, "Kati" – a unit of weight slightly over 1lb.

Oval Lacquer Casket ▼
- *circa 1690*
A fine Japanese oval casket decorated on all sides with panels of raised lacquer depicting a fenced garden and rockeries. Nashiji interior mounted on an ormolu base in the rococo manner.
- *22cm x 21cm x 39.5cm*
- **Guide price $28,480**

Regency Tea Caddy ◀
- *circa 1820*
Regency maple wood tea caddy with two divisions and a mixing bowl inside.
- *43.2cm x 38cm x 78.7cm*
- **Guide price $1,510**

Red Casket ▲
- *1870*
Flashed ruby red Bohemian casket well-engraved with spa towns.
- *30cm x 15cm*
- **Guide price $2,140**

Wig Box

- *circa 1780*
French wig box with a domed lid
hand-painted with floral garlands
centred by a classical folly in a
heart shaped cartouche, flanked
by a lady to the right and a
gentleman to the left.
- *16cm x 30cm*
- **Guide price $1,870**

Document Box ▲

- *circa 1880s*
Late Meiji period sugi wood
cabinet for documents, in six
sections.
- *71cm x 46cm*
- **Guide price $2,480**

Box on Stand ▼

- *circa 1870*
Leather lacquered box on stand
with original brass lockplate with
"ruyi" head mounts and fittings.
Ex- Shanxi.
- *36cm x 48cm*
- **Guide price $1,020**

Jewellery Case ▲

- *circa 1880*
Black lacquered jewellery box
with a red interior and
polychrome paintings of flora and
fauna. Inside the lid is a folding
mirror. Ex Fuzhou.
- *20cm x 24cm*
- **Guide price $700**

Blackwood Box ▼

- *circa 1870*
Small box with a mirror fitted
under the lid, with double
handles, chrysanthemum-shaped
mounts and brass lockplate
fashioned as a butterfly. Ex
Shanghai.
- *10cm x 24cm*
- **Guide price $500**

Chinese Hat Box ▼

- *circa 1880*
Red lacquered cylindrical
Chinese hat box with original
brass fittings, the interior fitted
with two sandalwood plates for
the storage of hats.
- *41cm x 34cm*
- **Guide price $770**

Tortoiseshell Box ◄
- **1909**
A tortoiseshell and silver ring box with floral piqué.
- *height 3cm*
- **Guide price $420**

Tortoiseshell Trinket Box ▼
- *circa 1850*
An English miniature tortoiseshell trinket box with pagoda top.
- *3.8cm x 4.5cm x 6.3cm*
- **Guide price $700**

Trinket Box ►
- *circa 1860*
An English miniature tortoiseshell trinket box.
- *3cm x 3cm x 6.3cm*
- **Guide price $560**

Tortoiseshell Domed Box ▲
- *circa 1875*
A small English tortoiseshell dome topped box with silver feet.
- *2.5cm x 2.5cm x 7cm*
- **Guide price $510**

Ring Box ◄
- **1906**
A silver and tortoiseshell ring box with swag inlay "H Matthews", Birmingham.
- *height 3.8cm*
- **Guide price $590**

George III Ivory Tea Caddy ▲
- *circa 1790*
A George III ivory tea caddy with tortoiseshell stringing and mother-of-pearl inlay.
- *11.5cm x 8.9cm x 15cm*
- **Guide price $9,260**

Blonde Tortoiseshell Box ◄
- *circa 1860*
A miniature blonde tortoiseshell trinket box with ivory edging, English.
- *3.8cm x 5cm x 7.6cm*
- **Guide price $590**

Ash Tea Caddy ▶

- *circa 1850*

Tea caddy made from Mongolian ash, with lead receptacles and an oval enamel plaque with a painted cherub. This was a wedding present in 1869, and at that date tea cost 10/- per lb.
- *height 11cm*
- **Guide price $4,980**

Red Merchant's Trunk ▼

- *circa 1880*

Lacquered merchant's trunk with a moulded hinged lid over a conforming body, decorated with intricate brass-work of faceted and smooth rounded nails. The front lock is a large stylised butterfly – the symbol of longevity. Ex-Fuzhou.
- *27cm x 24cm*
- **Guide price $710**

Tortoiseshell Tea Caddy

- *circa 1800*

Rare George III red tortoiseshell single tea caddy with ebony line stringing. The cover and interior lid have the original silver-plated ball handles, with original silver-plated lock and hinges.
- *height 10cm*
- **Guide price $9,930**

Expert Tips

A tortoiseshell tea caddy is worth more if it is not restored. Sometimes slight wear and tear at the corners makes the tea caddy more valuble.

Regency Rosewood Tea Caddy ▶

- *circa 1810*

Regency rosewood tea caddy with brass foliate inlay, with a cushion moulded cover on a tapering body, standing on brass ball feet. The interior is fitted with the original cut glass mixing bowl and two brass inlaid tea containers.
- *height 21cm*
- **Guide price $2,360**

Tortoiseshell Box ▼

- *circa 1760*

Tortoiseshell Anglo Dutch box with ivory stringing and silver mounts, on silver bun feet.
- *16cm x 28cm x 20cm*
- **Guide price $5,340**

Satinwood Tea Caddy ▼

- *circa 1790*

A George III oval satinwood tea caddy with bats wing pattern to the front and cover and original axe head handle to lid.
- *height 12cm*
- **Guide price $3,470**

George III Cutlery Urn ▲

- *circa 1790*

One of a pair of George III mahogany cutlery urns, with chequered line stringing and barbers pole edging. The stepped lid with ivory finial rises to reveal the original fitted interior for twelve place settings. Standing on a platform base with barber's pole stringing.
- *height 66cm*
- **Guide price $19,540**

George III Mahogany Tea Caddy ▼

- *circa 1790*
A George III mahogany and inlaid oval tea caddy.
- *11.5cm x 9cm x 15cm*
- **Guide price $3,560**

Belgian Tea Caddy ▲

- *circa 1830*
A wonderful Belgian Spa pen work sycamore single cube tea caddy.
- *11.5cm x 10cm x 11.5cm*
- **Guide price $3,030**

Ivory Tea Caddy ▼

- *circa 1790*
A rare George III ivory tea caddy, strung in horn and mounted with three Wedgwood blue and white Jasper cameos. The centre cameo surrounded by silver piqué-clouté.
- *9.5cm x 7cm x 11.4cm*
- **Guide price $18,720**

Holly Tea Caddy ▲

- *circa 1795*
A Georgian mahogany tea caddy with holly oval panels and barber pole stringing.
- *11.5cm x 11.5cm x 11.5cm*
- **Guide price $1,560**

Cube Tea Caddy ▼

- *circa 1800*
A George III satinwood cube tea caddy with incised decoration.
- *12cm x 10cm x 12.7cm*
- **Guide price $2,600**

Green Tortoiseshell Tea Caddy ▲

- *circa 1825*
A rare green tortoiseshell double compartment tea caddy with pewter stringing and silvered ball feet, English.
- *14.5cm x 10cm x 17.7cm*
- **Guide price $16,050**

Tea Chest ▲

- *circa 1840*
A Victorian mahogany double tea chest, English.
- *16.5cm x 15cm x 30.5cm*
- **Guide price $1,560**

Mahjong Set ▲

- *1920*

Impressive and imposing
Mahjong set of the highest
quality in a solid oak case with
extensive brass work decoration
to the sides and top. With solid
brass handle and sliding front
panel revealing five similarly
decorated drawers containing
solid ivory tiles, game sticks and
dice. Provenance: The Right
Honourable The Viscount
Leverhulme, K. G. of Thornton
Manor.
- *29cm x 32cm*
- **Guide price** $10,590

Apothecary Box ▲

- *circa 1830*

Georgian mahogany apothecary
box with an almost complete set
of original bottles, some with
original contents. With lower
drawer with original scales,
weights, mortar, pestle and key.
- *13cm x 19cm*
- **Guide price** $3,470

Tortoiseshell Tea Caddy ▶

- *circa 1775*

Exceptional red tortoiseshell tea
chest with ivory stringing, silver
ball feet and top handle, the
interior with three original glass
canisters with silver plate lids and
original key.
- *height 14cm*
- **Guide price** $52,510

Georgian Knife Boxes ▼

- *circa 1790*

One of a pair of superb flame
mahogany Georgian knife boxes
with original interiors, silver plate
ring pulls and escutcheons.
- *height 48cm*
- **Guide price** $12,370

Regency Chinoiserie Box ▼

- *circa 1820*

English Regency penwork box
with trailing floral designs around
a central panel depicting a group
of hand-painted Chinese figures.
- *height 16cm*
- **Guide price** $2,940

Scholar's Parchment Box ▲

- *19th century*

Scholar's leather parchment box
embossed with the design of the
Buddhist swastika, the cover
designed with the character of
"Long Life". Ex-Shanghai.
- *18cm x 28cm*
- **Guide price** $830

Tea Tins ▲

- *1880*

Set of six cylindrical tea tins with
covers and a central cartouche of
a classical ruin surrounded by a
foliate design, each with a gilt
shield and numerals.
- *height 48cm*
- **Guide price** $4,450

Regency Tea Caddy ▶
- *circa 1820*
A Regency tortoiseshell tea caddy
with canted corners and double
cavetto top, English.
- *14cm x 8.9cm x 14cm*
- **Guide price $6,900**

Shagreen Box ▲
- *circa 1920*
An English Art Deco geometric
shagreen box with ivory stringing.
- *5cm x 10cm x 12.5cm*
- **Guide price $800**

Tortoiseshell Tea Caddy ▲
- *circa 1830*
A blonde tortoiseshell tea caddy
with ivory stringing and horn
edging, English.
- *14.6cm x 8.9cm x 15cm*
- **Guide price $6,280**

Satinwood Tea Caddy ▲
- *circa 1790*
A satinwood tea caddy with
conch shell inlays, chequer and
rosewood bandings, ebony
stringing.
- *12cm x 10.8cm x 19cm*
- **Guide price $3,030**

Mother-of-Pearl Tea Caddy ▼
- *circa 1875*
Late Victorian mother-of-pearl
double tea caddy with abalone
banding.
- *8.5cm x 8.5cm x 14cm*
- **Guide price $2,940**

Rosewood Tea Caddy ◀
- *circa 1850*
A Victorian rosewood tea caddy
with mother-of-pearl inlay,
relined with hand-made paper.
- *17.8cm x 12.7cm x 24cm*
- **Guide price $750**

Expert Tips

*Some of the most exquisite
boxes were produced during the
eighteenth century as containers
for snuff, patches or tobacco.
Price is usually determined by
quality and materials used.
Boxes of wood or papier mâché
are the most affordable and
generally available.*

Bombe-shaped Tea Caddy ▶

- *circa 1830*

A bombe-shaped tortoiseshell tea caddy with pewter stringing and ivory edging.
- *15cm x 10cm x 19cm*
- **Guide price $8,400**

Indian Box ◀

- *circa 1860*

An Indian tortoiseshell Vizagapatam box with bone edging and feet.
- *5cm x 6.4cm x 11.5cm*
- **Guide price $420**

Indian Box with Ivory Veneer ◀

- *circa 1780*

An Indian Vizagapatam box, ivory veneered on sandalwood, engraved with architectural scenes.
- *8.9cm x 22.8cm x 30.5cm*
- **Guide price $7,020**

Regency Tea Chest ▼

- *circa 1830*

A large Regency blonde tortoiseshell tea chest with lion claw feet and lion head handles.
- *17cm x 12.7cm x 28cm*
- **Guide price $12,100**

Vizagapatam Box ◀

- *circa 1785*

A very rare late 18th century Vizagapatam engraved and etched ivory tea caddy with floral banding and architectural scene on the lid.
- *width 12cm*
- **Guide price $8,450**

Georgian Tea Caddy ▲

- *circa 1790*

A rare Georgian fluted ivory octagonal single tea caddy with tented top and silver adornments, horn stringing and interior facing.
- *12cm x 7.5cm x 10.5cm*
- **Guide price $12,370**

Stag Horn Double Caddy ◀

- *circa 1800*

A very rare late 18th century stag horn double caddy with ivory hunting scene panels, ivory stringing and claw feet. The interior with rustic lids. Probably Austrian.
- *width 20cm*
- **Guide price $16,020**

Pagoda Top Tea Caddy ◀

- *circa 1835*
A fine William IV tortoiseshell tea caddy with inverted front and pagoda top.
- *12.7cm x 10cm x 17cm*
- **Guide price $6,490**

Regency Tea Caddy ▶

- *circa 1830*
A very rare late Regency mother-of-pearl veneered tea caddy of polygonal form with white metal and abalone engraved floral inlay and ivory banding to the interior with twin subsidiary covers. The base on six carved mother-of-pearl-feet.
- *width 18.4cm*
- **Guide price $32,930**

Spa Tea Caddy ▼

- *circa 1820*
A very rare early 19th century painted Spa tea caddy of inverted rectangular shape with cut out canted corners, each panel painted with scenes of the town, the top panel of an interior scene of a minstrel serenading a maiden. The interior with two compartments, each with a painted cover of a spa scene.
- *width 23cm*
- **Guide price $13,800**

"Melon" Tea Caddy ▲

- *circa 1790*
Late 18th century painted melon fruitwood tea caddy with original stalk.
- *12cm x 12cm x 12cm*
- **Guide price $25,810**

"Aubergine" Tea Caddy ▲

- *circa 1840*
Mid 19th century Chinese aubergine single tea caddy with screw top.
- *height 19cm*
- **Guide price $17,710**

"Pear" Tea Caddy ▲

- *circa 1790*
Very fine late 18th century George III fruit wood pear tea caddy with original escutcheon.
- *height 18cm*
- **Guide price $12,370**

Belgian Spa Tea Caddy ▶

- *circa 1800*
Late 18th century Belgian Spa single oval tea caddy in mint condition, the lid and four panels with hand-painted scenes of the town.
- *10cm x 10cm x 16cm*
- **Guide price $8,810**

Tunbridge Ware Tea Caddy ▶

- *circa 1860*

Excellent Tunbridge Ware marquetry inlaid single tea caddy with stick marquetry roses on lid.
- *width 13.5cm*
- **Guide price $880**

Tortoiseshell Jewel Casket ▼

- *circa 1860*

High quality 19th century French tortoiseshell jewel casket with bowed panels, extensive ormolu decorative mounts and original silk lined interior. The lustre effect of this casket is the result of a rare technique of gilding behind the tortoiseshell.
- *width 35cm*
- **Guide price $14,150**

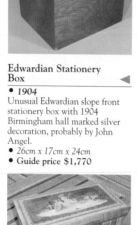

Edwardian Stationery Box ◀

- *1904*

Unusual Edwardian slope front stationery box with 1904 Birmingham hall marked silver decoration, probably by John Angel.
- *26cm x 17cm x 24cm*
- **Guide price $1,770**

Book Box ▲

- *circa 1900*

Italian inlaid book box with secret compartments.
- *11.4cm x 12.7cm x 23cm*
- **Guide price $330**

Regency Double Tea Caddy ▼

- *circa 1830*

A sarcophagus-shaped Regency beech double tea caddy with high quality hand painted decoration on every panel, the interior with matching subsidiary lids and original painted inner lid. All on decorative brass feet with matching brass side handles.
- *width 22cm*
- **Guide price $7,030**

Bohemian Box ▼

- *circa 1770*

Bohemian box with panelled top opening to reveal a simple interior, the front with split balusters and moulded decoration containing traces of the original flower decorated pattern.
- *58.4cm x 47.6cm x 75.6cm*
- **Guide price $6,410**

Brass-bound Military Coffer ▼

- *circa 1890*

Box strengthened with brass inlay on all edges, brass carrying handles and lock and key.
- *45.7cm x 37cm x 66cm*
- **Guide price $1,000**

Military Instrument Box ▶

- *circa 1890*
Wooden box with brass corners and handles.
- *49.5cm x 29cm x 38cm*
- **Guide price $610**

Oak and Brass Jewellery Box ▲

- *circa 1870*
Late Victorian oak and brass mounted box originally for letters now converted for jewellery, with lined interior. Bears Edinburgh maker's plaque.
- *width 20.3cm*
- **Guide price $700**

William IV Box ▲

- *circa 1835*
William IV rosewood and maple marquetry box converted for jewellery.
- *length 35cm*
- **Guide price $580**

Regency Card Boxes ▼

- *circa 1830*
Pair of Regency lacquer card boxes.
- *length 9cm*
- **Guide price $200**

Anglo Indian Box ▶

- *circa 1830*
Early 19th century Anglo-Indian ivory mounted box.
- *length 25.5cm*
- **Guide price $1,240**

Mahogany Stationery Case ▼

- *circa 1880*
Sloped stationery case with hinged compartments and original escutcheon.
- *33cm x 27cm x 37cm*
- **Guide price $700**

Expert Tips

Dates and inscriptions to famous people enhance value – the reverse is true of those who history has forgotten.

Glove Box ◀

- *circa 1835*
William IV rosewood and satin birch marquetry glove box with original interior.
- *length 20cm*
- **Guide price $330**

Bureaux

George I Bureau Bookcase ◄

- *circa 1720*

A walnut veneered oak bureau bookcase, with bevelled mirrors and original brass furniture.
- *2.3m x 1.07m*
- Guide price $133,500

Georgian Chippendale Bureau Bookcase ►

- *circa 1760*

Mahogany bookcase with glazed doors enclosing four shelves above a bureau with a sloping fall.
- *2.24m x 56.5cm x 1.13m*
- Guide price $44,500

William & Mary Walnut Bureau ▼

- *circa 1690*

Walnut bureau with fall opening to reveal an interior with a well and two secret compartments over three frieze drawers.
- *96.52cm x 58.4cm x 96.5cm*
- Guide price $50,730

French Bureau Plat ▶

- *circa 1850*

French ebony, tortoiseshell and
brass inlaid bureau plat. The
antique leather top with a
massive moulded gilt bronze edge,
above a large recessed central
drawer flanked by two smaller
drawers. Supported on four
cabriole legs, mounted above the
knees with a satyr's mask, and
terminating in hoof feet. With
chased and gilt bronze mounts.
The central drawer is mounted
with a large mask of Bacchus.
- *79cm x 2.02m*
- **Guide price $115,700**

Regency Secretaire ▲

- *circa 1805*

A Regency mahogany secretaire
cabinet enclosed by a pair of
astragal glazed doors. Fitted with
a secretaire drawer and an arched
frieze drawer below, on square
tapering legs terminating in spade
feet.
- *1.6m x 75cm*
- **Guide price $22,250**

Swedish Bureau ▼

- *1780*

Swedish bureau with original
paintwork and fall front with
stepped interior above three long
drawers, standing on original
scrolled bracket feet.
- *1.04m x 94cm x 54cm*
- **Guide price $11,040**

French Secretaire ▼

- *circa 1810*

Secretaire desk with serpentine
front, original paint, three long
drawers with oval iron handles,
brass escutcheon plates and a fall
front enclosing fourteen small
drawers, the whole raised on
gilded feet.
- *1.08m x 1.21m*
- **Guide price $16,020**

Druce of London Bureau ▲

- *circa 1880*

George III style mahogany bureau
with fall front, fitted interior and
original brass fittings, standing on
moulded bracket feet, with a brass
plate bearing the inscription,
"Druce & Co, Baker St, London"
inside the top drawer.
- *height 1.13m*
- **Guide price $6,230**

Walnut Secretaire ▲

- *circa 1880*

Fine Swedish secretaire, heavily
carved with a burr walnut veneer.
The fall front enclosing an
architectural fitted interior, above
three long drawers.
- *1.47m x 1.09m*
- **Guide price $11,570**

George I Walnut Bureau ▼

- *circa 1720*

George I walnut bureau, with a fitted interior veneered in walnut with line inlay.

- *1.05m x 51cm x 92cm*
- **Guide price $20,470**

Queen Anne Walnut Veneered Bureau ▼

- *circa 1710*

A bureau with fitted interior and later mirrored plate, with a secret well.

- *98cm x 43cm x 68cm*
- **Guide price $32,040**

Burr Walnut Bureau Bookcase ▲

- **1920**

Bureau bookcase with upper doors enclosing shelves and drawers above a bureau and base.

- *2.34m x 56cm x 1.12m*
- **Guide price $8,450**

Cylinder Bureau ▶

- *circa 1880*

A Louis XVI style gilt bronze mounted mahogany bureau with a pierced gallery above three drawers over a tambour retracting cylinder front. The bureau has three tiers of letter compartments above a sliding leather writing surface.

- *1.2m x 80cm x 1.52m*
- **Guide price $53,400**

Cabinets

George III Secretaire ▶
- *circa 1775*

A George III satinwood secretaire abattant decorated on all sides with panels of Chinese and Japanese lacquer and standing on carved feet enriched with foliate decoration.
- *1.42m x 41cm x 1.04m*
- **Guide price $97,900**

George III Bedside Cabinets ▲
- *circa 1790*

A pair of George III mahogany bedside cabinets, the tray tops with pierced carrying handles above a single cupboard door with brass drop handle, raised on square tapering legs.
- *77cm x 33cm x 46cm*
- **Guide price $53,400**

Mysore Table Cabinet ◀
- *1898-1905*

Solid rosewood and ivory inlaid "Mysore" table cabinet, made in India. Features a shaped pediment surmounted by three urn-shaped finials above two panelled doors enclosing a full-sized interior divided and a full-width drawer below.
- *78cm x 24cm x 45.5cm*
- **Guide price $7,120**

Coromandel Cabinets ▶
- *circa 1808*

A pair of coromandel wood side cabinets with brass star and scroll decoration in the Egyptian style.
- *1.07m x 39cm x 91.5cm*
- **Guide price $67,640**

Macassar Sideboard ▼
- *1929-30*

Art deco period Heal's Macassar ebony veneered sideboard having top panels of green shagreen and sides and front veneered in boldly figured timber supported on ivory feet.
- *89cm x 152.5cm x 51cm*
- **Guide price $52,510**

George III Bedside Table ◀
- *circa 1765*

A large mahogany bedside table raised on square chamfered legs, with pierced carrying handles and pull-out commode section with dummy drawer front.
- *81.5cm x 56cm x 51.5cm*
- **Guide price $18,690**

Mahogany Bow Fronted Georgian Sideboard ▲
- *circa 1790*

Sheraton period sideboard with a skirting board overhang above three drawers fitted with brass lion mask ring handles.
- *89.5cm x 61cm x 96.5cm*
- **Guide price $10,680**

Expert Tips

"China cabinets" are not strictly cabinets. A cabinet should be a case fitted with small drawers or cupboards, and with doors. The correct term for this glazed-fronted display case is "china cupboard".

Victorian Cabinet ▼

- *circa 1890*

Victorian walnut and planewood bedside cabinet, with moulded cupboard doors, raised on a plinth base.
- *height 85cm*
- Guide price $800

Chinese Medicine Cabinet ▶

- *circa 19th century*

One of a pair of black lacquer Chinese medicine cabinets with forty-five drawers with circular ring handles.
- *height 2.06m*
- Guide price $3,200

English Corner Cupboard ▲

- *1780*

English painted wall-mounted, corner cupboard, with carved moulded door panels and original blue paintwork.
- *1.08m x 81cm*
- Guide price $4,980

Continental Painted Cabinet ▼

- *circa 1880*

Continental fruitwood display cabinet with circular moulded pediments, two glazed doors, flanked by bevelled glass, below two cupboard doors painted with ribbons and flowers, surmounted with a pierced brass rail, standing on small cabriole legs.
- *1.75m x 1.35m*
- Guide price $6,230

Walnut Bedside Cabinet ▼

- *circa 1880*

One of a pair of Louis XV style walnut bedside cabinets with one single drawer above a carved and moulded cupboard door, raised on cabriole legs.
- *height 88cm*
- Guide price $2,940

Small Chinese Cabinet ◀

- *1880*

Small Chinese cabinet from Zhejiang Province, decorated with carvings of a phoenix and lotus plants.
- *81cm x 55cm*
- Guide price $980

Bow Fronted Sheraton Double Corner Cupboard ▲

- *circa 1790*
A two-part Sheraton double corner cupboard with two Gothic arched glazed doors enclosing three fixed shelves. A pull-out mahogany slide surmounts the base with two additional bow-fronted doors.
- *2.26m x 61cm x 95.5cm*
- **Guide price $44,500**

Domed Walnut Cabinet ▲

- *circa 1930*
Pretty walnut cabinet with domed bookcase, raised on cabriole legs.
- *60cm x 40.6cm x 58.4cm*
- **Guide price $4,000**

Pot Cupboard ▶

- *19th century*
A mahogany pot cupboard having inlaid marble top
- *71.1cm x 35.6cm*
- **Guide price $1,960**

Queen Anne Cabinet on Chest ▲

- *circa 1710*
Cabinet on chest with bevelled mirrored door opening to reveal ten chevron banded drawers and a bookshelf. The lower section with a secretaire drawer and three further drawers.
- *2m x 48.3cm x 76.2cm*
- **Guide price $80,100**

Painted Walnut Cabinet ▲

- *circa 1930*
Fine quality walnut cabinet with painted panel set into the door of still life with roses.
- *73.6cm x 43.2cm x 1.143m*
- **Guide price $5,790**

Open-fronted Walnut Cabinet ▼

- *circa 1930*
Open-fronted walnut corner display cabinet with shaped moulded pediment.
- *1.85m x 68.6cm*
- **Guide price $3,290**

Walnut Sideboard ▼

- *circa 1930*
Pretty serpentine-fronted walnut cabinet and sideboard with moulded panel doors.
- *81.3cm x 40.6cm x 81.3cm*
- **Guide price $4,000**

Dutch Walnut Display Cabinet ▲

- *circa 1780s*
A slim Dutch walnut display cabinet profusely decorated with floral and foliate motifs in marquetry, the shaped cornice above shaped glazed doors and canted corners to the upper section. The lower section of bombe form, the whole on turned and ebonised bun feet.
- *2.37m x 1.70m*
- **Guide price $40,050**

Dutch Display Cabinet ▲

- *circa 1780*
Dutch walnut display cabinet with foliate inlay and glass panels to front and doors.
- *height 85cm*
- **Guide price $8,630**

Japanese Lacquer Cabinet ▶

- *circa 1880*
Japanese lacquer cabinet with two doors decorated with mother-of-pearl floral inlay, two small drawers and one long drawer inlaid with boxwood.
- *39cm x 29cm*
- **Guide price $800**

Mahogany Chiffonier ▼

- *circa 1840*
Flame mahogany chiffonier with single long drawer, above two gilt brass grills with door silks, flanked by turned pilasters, raised on turned feet.
- *93cm x 91.5cm x 41cm*
- **Guide price $5,700**

Two Part Kortan Cabinet ▼

- *circa 1800*
A kortan cabinet of two parts made from elm, with four drawers above two cupboard doors with brass mounts.
- *1.45m x 1.05m*
- **Guide price $5,250**

George IV Display Cabinet ▲

- *circa 1825*
George IV mahogany display cabinet, the top section with two glazed doors, above a lower section with four octagonal tapering legs decorated with stylised palmetto.
- *1.91m x 94cm*
- **Guide price $15,580**

Swedish Mahogany Cupboard ▲

- *circa 1890s*
Swedish Louis XVI style mahogany cupboard with two doors, above one single drawer, with moulded apron and gilt ormulu mounts, on tapering slender legs.
- *1.06m x 59cm*
- **Guide price $3,470**

Walnut Display Cabinet ▲

- *circa 1920*
Walnut display cabinet with
doors opening to reveal shelves,
scrolled apron with central finial
on turned legs with double
stretcher
- *1.55m x 28.1cm x 99cm*
- **Guide price $7,030**

Regency Side Cabinet ▲

- *circa 1825*
A rosewood breakfront dwarf side
cabinet in the manner of Gillows
of Lancaster with four pleated
panel and glazed doors enclosing
adjustable shelves to a plinth base
with beadwork mouldings.
- *99cm x 36cm x 1.55m*
- **Guide price $17,440**

Red Lacquer Corner Cupboard ▼

- *Early to mid 18th century*
Red lacquer bow-fronted corner
cupboard in chinoiserie style with
three waterfall display shelves.
- *1.27m x 33cm x 48.3cm*
- **Guide price $4,000**

Black Lacquer Cabinet ▶

- *Early 20th century*
English lacquer cabinet in the
Chippendale style incorporating
fine peacock design, the whole
surmounted by a galleried
cornice.
- *1.80m x 43.2cm x 68.6cm*
- **Guide price $5,250**

Regency Chiffonier ◀

- *circa 1820*
Regency rosewood two door
chiffonier, the white marble top
with a reeded edge, above a pair
of pleated silk doors flanked by
spiral twist columns.
- *85.5cm x 33cm x 87cm*
- **Guide price $14,950**

Walnut Credenza ▲

- *circa 1870*
French walnut credenza with
inlayed oval artwork, fine gilt
mouldings and glazed display
cupboards at each side.
- *1.02m x 40.6cm x 1.65m*
- **Guide price $12,370**

Sheraton Revival Satinwood Side Cabinet ◀

- *circa 1900*
A Sheraton revival satinwood
cabinet of semi-elliptical form
inlaid and crossbanded
throughout. One central door
with circular decorative panel
encloses a single shelf.
- *91.5cm x 45.5cm x 99.5cm*
- **Guide price $16,730**

Expert Tips

*Large cabinets can have a
chequered past; quite often they
are "marriages". The two parts
may be from the same period,
but very often they have been
coloured in.*

Regency Rosewood Side Cabinet ▲

- *circa 1810*

A Regency rosewood and boxwood strung side cabinet with canted front corners incorporating two frieze drawers above twin glazed and pleated doors.
- *91.5cm x 38cm x 75cm*
- **Guide price $8,630**

Pine Table Cabinet ▼

- *Late 19th century*

A small, decorated table cabinet used for storing scrolls and books. Pine with dark burgundy stain and carved and gilded door panels depicting birds and flowers. The doors close to a central, removable post and internally there are two drawers at the base. Original brassware.
- *45cm x 65cm x 55cm*
- **Guide price $520**

George III Mahogany China Cabinet ▼

- *circa 1770*

China cabinet with swan-neck pediment and single arched astragal glazed door enclosing shelves with panelled cupboard door below.
- *2.04m x 1.14m x 51cm*
- **Guide price $41,830**

Regency Period Chiffonier ◄

- *circa 1820*

Regency ebonised chiffonier with double cupboard and silk panel doors, one drawer and two display shelves with scrolled edges, fine gilding and ball feet.
- *1.44m x 40.6cm x 90cm*
- **Guide price $17,530**

Decorated Lacquer Cabinet ▲

- *Late 19th century*

Four-door cabinet, pine with red lacquer and gilded, carved panels. Decoration and brassware are original.
- *1.65m x 1.24m x 54cm*
- **Guide price $2,850**

Satinwood Display Cabinet ▲

- *circa 1900*

A satinwood cabinet with a crossbanded frieze which features panel of decorative feathery veneers. The two glazed doors each have a lower panel with a distinctive oval motif in West Indian show-wood.
- *1.76m x 38cm x 1.1m*
- **Guide price $24,480**

Regency Rosewood Chiffonier ▲

- *circa 1820*

Regency period rosewood veneered chiffonier having raised super-structure with shelf and original brass gallery mirror. Supported on brass turned uprights below a two-door cupboard.
- *1.30m x 34cm x 1.08m*
- **Guide price $24,920**

Expert Tips

Backs of cabinets were not designed to be seen and are relatively crudely made. They should be dry and untouched and probably show some signs of shrinkage.

Regency Chiffonier ▼

- *circa 1820*

Regency mahogany chiffonier with silk panel doors, a pierced gallery and one long mirror, with two Corinthian columns, lions head ring handles and brass ormulu mounts.
- *1.18m x 1m*
- **Guide price $2,940**

Mahogany Corner Cupboard ▼

- *circa 1890*

Mahogany corner cupboard with double moulded panel doors, above three drawers with turned knob handles.
- *width 1.16m*
- **Guide price $2,820**

Victorian Cabinet ▲

- *circa 1880*

Victorian mahogany cabinet with two panelled doors, enclosing two small drawers with turned handles, raised on a plinth base.
- *width 1.34m*
- **Guide price $2,090**

George III Dressing Stand ▲

- *circa 1795*

George III mahogany gentleman's dressing stand with original mirror, and brass fittings.
- *89cm x 51cm*
- **Guide price $1,470**

Mahogany Chiffonier ▼

- *circa 1880*

Victorian mahogany chiffonier, with one long single drawer above two moulded panelled doors, flanked with carved pilasters.
- *1.05m x 1.14m*
- **Guide price $2,400**

Biedermeier Style Cupboard ▼

- *circa 1899*

Danish Biedermeier style cupboard in birchwood, with a central oval inlay in rosewood and satinwood of an urn with a spray of flowers.
- *1.28m x 55cm*
- **Guide price $9,970**

Swedish Sideboard ◄

- *circa 1800*

Louis XVI Gustavian painted pine sideboard with two centrally carved diamond panels on the doors.
- *98cm x 1.07m*
- **Guide price $8,010**

Campaign Furniture

Travelling Games Table ▶

- *circa 1830*
George IV mahogany campaign games table that dismantles to fit neatly into its folding chess board box top.
- *72.4cm x 33cm x 38.1cm*
- **Guide price $2,230**

Low Table ▼

- *Late 19th century*
Teak campaign low table by S.W. Silver & Co. Flat packs for travel.
- *58.4cm x 61cm x 61cm*
- **Guide price $1,060**

E. Ross Dining Chairs ▲

- *Mid 19th century*
Pair of mahogany Ross chairs with a stencilled maker's mark.
- *87.6cm x 50.5cm x 45.7cm*
- **Guide price $2,050**

Folding Armchair ◀

- *Third quarter 19th century*
Colonial folding teak armchair with brass straps.
- *73.7cm x 53.3cm x 52cm*
- **Guide price $1,420**

Campaign Double Mirror ▼

- *Early 19th century*
Mahogany oval campaign double mirror with both a standard and a magnifying looking glass.
- *1.9cm x 15.2cm x 23.5cm*
- **Guide price $350**

Campaign Cradle ◀

- *Early 19th century*
Mahogany campaign cradle that completely dismantles for travel.
- *1.23m x 63.5cm x 1.143m*
- **Guide price $3,920**

Powder Box ◀

- *Early 19th century*
Black powder box with copper canisters and double protective caps. This box would have provided safe storage for gun powder in between filling up a powder horn for everyday use.
- *23cm x 18.4cm x 28.6cm*
- **Guide price $2,580**

Railway Companion

• *Late 19th century*
Railway companion with
sandwich tin and decanter with
the drinking glass forming the
bottle stop.
• *18.4cm x 7.6cm x 10.2cm*
• **Guide price $610**

Campaign Commode

• *Second quarter 19th century*
Campaign commode in
mahogany with leather seat and
lead plumbing. Stamped
"Bonneels".
• *48.3cm x 53.3cm x 61cm*
• **Guide price $4,900**

Portable Desk

• *Early 19th century*
Three section portable desk with
brass strapwork and secret
drawers.
• *15.2cm x 24.8cm x 34.3cm*
• **Guide price $1,020**

Travel Flask

• *Early 20th century*
Travel flask with four beakers in a
two-part leather case.
• *19.7cm x 5.1cm x 8.9cm*
• **Guide price $350**

Folding Cutlery Set

• *Late 18th to early 19th century*
Prisoner-of-war bone and horn
folding cutlery set.
• *2.54cm x 4.4cm x 20.3cm*
• **Guide price $350**

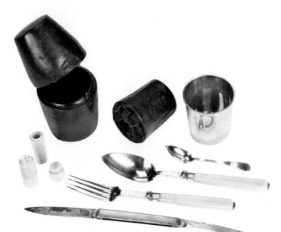

Campaign Cutlery

• *Second quarter 19th century*
French campaign silver cutlery in
leather barrel case.
• *13.2cm x 7.6cm x 7.6cm*
• **Guide price $2,050**

Canterburies

Mahogany Canterbury ◀

- *circa 1870*

Victorian mahogany canterbury
with three compartments. The
side drawer with turned knob
handles, finials and supports, with
original porcelain castors.
- *height 62cm*
- Guide price $1,770

Mahogany Canterbury ▶

- *circa 1830s*

Early Victorian mahogany
galleried and tiered dumb waiter,
with turned supports and single
drawer with turned handles, the
whole standing on bulbous turned
legs with brass castors.
- *1m x 38cm*
- Guide price $3,920

Rosewood Canterbury ▼

- *circa 1790*

Mahogany canterbury comprising
four sections with a single side
drawer with circular ring handle,
raised on square tapered legs with
original brass castors.
- *height 39cm*
- Guide price $3,470

Victorian Canterbury ▲

- *circa 1880*

Victorian walnut canterbury of
four sections, with pierced
scrolled decoration above a lower
shelf, on upturned scrolled legs.
- *height 55cm*
- Guide price $2,130

Walnut Canterbury ▶

- *circa 1880*

Victorian walnut canterbury with
four sections with heavily carved
and pierced floral designs, turned
handles, and a single side drawer,
the whole raised on turned legs
with brass castors.
- *height 54cm*
- Guide price $2,300

Chairs

Commode Armchair ▶

- *circa 1780*
George III mahogany commode
armchair with rounded shield
back above a slip-in upholstered
seat with shaped and concaved
moulded arms. Attributed to
Gillows.
- *99cm x 44.5cm x 56cm*
- **Guide price $2,670**

Metamorphic Library Chair ▲

- *circa 1815*
A Regency period metamorphic
library chair made by Morgan and
Saunders, specialists who
patented the design in 1811.
- *91.5cm x 63.5cm x 58.5cm*
- **Guide price $32,040**

Queen Anne Gilt Chinoiserie Side Chairs ▲

- *circa 1700*
Side chairs with caned rear panels
and stuffed overseat standing on
cabriole legs with stretcher.
- *height 1.09m*
- **Guide price $5,250**

Mahogany Regency Chairs ▼

- *circa 1815*
A set of eight Regency period
mahogany dining chairs (six
singles and two with arms) in the
style of Thomas Hope, featuring
sabre legs and top rails decorated
with Greek key patterns of
boxwood inlay.
- *84cm x 47cm x 56cm*
- **Guide price $31,150**

Arts and Crafts Chair ▼

- *circa 1880*
Mahogany hall chair by Liberty
& Co with original paper label
still under the seat.
- *height 95cm*
- **Guide price $2,230**

Pair of Walnut Chairs ◀

- *circa 1870*
Pair of French walnut chairs with
floral pattern seats and backs.
- *96.5cm x 48cm x 51cm*
- **Guide price $4,900**

Expert Tips

*The price of a set of chairs rises
exponentially with quantity.
Beware of sets made up of parts
of originals.*

Rosewood Chairs ▶

- *circa 1800*

A rare pair of French rosewood chairs with undecorated rectangular backs with square section upright supports. The shaped arms with low relief carved decoration to the upper surface, terminating in very well carved rams heads above scrolled supports with low relief carved decoration to the front. With a straight seat rail above an apron.
- *1m x 59.5cm*
- **Guide price $27,590**

Regency Mahogany Chair ▼

- *circa 1810*

Regency mahogany elbow chair, with curved arms and turned legs and leather seat.
- *height 89cm*
- **Guide price $1,770**

Elbow Chair ▼

- *1890*

One of a pair of mahogany elbow chairs with foliate carving on slender turned legs with cane back and set.
- *height 97cm*
- **Guide price $2,580**

Victorian High Chair ▲

- *circa 1860*

Victorian ash and elm child's high chair, with turned decoration.
- *height 99cm*
- **Guide price $700**

French Walnut Chair ▲

- *1890*

French walnut chair with carved mask decoration, standing on a cross stretcher base.
- *height 87cm*
- **Guide price $1,060**

Child's Chippendale Chair ▼

- *circa 1890*

Chippendale-style mahogany child's chair, with pierced back splat, serpentine top rail and raised on straight tapered legs.
- *height 78cm*
- **Guide price $850**

Victorian Nursing Chair ▼

- *1880*

Victorian nursing chair with a circular padded seat and a padded back.
- *height 74cm*
- **Guide price $980**

Leather Desk Chair ◀

- *circa 1920*
Walnut desk chair with leather upholstery.
- *94cm x 48cm x 58.4cm*
- **Guide price $1,690**

Wing Back Chair ▼

- *circa 1900*
Oak framed wing armchair, re-upholstered in Watts of Westminster fabric.
- *1.04m x 71cm x 71cm*
- **Guide price $4,360**

Empire Bergère ▲

- *circa 1815*
French mahogany Bergère chair with turned top rail and curved, padded arms.
- *92cm x 61cm*
- **Guide price $5,070**

Hepplewhite Armchair ▲

- *circa 1780*
Painted and decorated English Hepplewhite ebonised armchair, shield back with urn detail, curved arm supports and straight tapered legs with hand-painted designs of trailing foliage and ribboning.
- *97cm x 57cm*
- **Guide price $7,920**

Pair of Decorated Fauteuils ▲

- *circa 1760*
One of a pair of French beechwood painted and gilt decorated fauteuils stamped "Premy" with oval backs.
- *94cm x 61cm*
- **Guide price $13,880**

Library Bergère ◀

- *circa 1815*
Rare Regency period Irish library Bergere in burr yewwood with scroll arms standing on panelled legs decorated with Amthenions and reeded feet into brass cup castors, covered in black hide.
- *95.5cm x 73.5cm x 99cm*
- **Guide price $29,470**

Louis XV Fauteuil ▲

- *circa 1750*
Louis XV French giltwood
fauteuil, with carved floral
designs raised on cabriole legs.
- **Guide price $2,230**

Swedish Armchair ▲

- *circa 1880*
Swedish armchair, with gilded
floral decoration to the back rail,
carved and gilded supports to the
arms and original neutral paint.
Part of a set comprising a sofa,
armchair and four single chairs.
- *height 1.06m*
- **Guide price $32,930 set**

Mahogany Chair ▼

- *circa 1870*
Set of six mahogany and brass
inlaid dining chairs in the
manner of Gillows.
- **Guide price $5,700**

Swedish Dining Chair ▼

- *circa 1880*
Swedish dining chair, with lyre
shaped back, gilded with floral
designs, raised on straight tapered
front legs, with swept back legs.
- *height 83cm*
- **Guide price $32,930**

English Hepplewhite
Chairs ◀

- *circa 1780*
English Hepplewhite oval back
chairs, with three Prince of Wales
feathers carved into the back
splat, above a shaped front rail,
raised on elegant cabriole legs,
with floral and shell motifs.
- *height 84cm*
- **Guide price $9,790**

Directoire French Chair ▲

- *circa 1880*
One of a pair of French,
mahogany directoire style open
armchairs with carved finial
decoration, raised on tapered,
reeded legs.
- **Guide price $3,290**

George I Walnut Chair ▲

- *circa 1715*
One of a pair of George I walnut
side chairs with vase shaped
splats, the front cabriole legs and
back legs united by a turned wavy
stretcher.
- *height 96cm*
- **Guide price $12,100**

Sheraton Armchair ▶

- *circa 1880*

Sheraton revival decorated armchair of very good quality with interlaced splats, labelled for Druce & Co of Baker Street, with finely painted floral decoration.

- *85cm x 52cm x 55cm*
- **Guide price $4,900**

Cockfighting Chair ▼

- *circa 1835*

William IV oak and leather desk/cockfighting chair, with padded button back.

- *90cm x 61cm*
- **Guide price $3,470**

Georgian Dining Chairs ▲

- *circa 1800*

Set of eight (six chairs two carvers) late Georgian mahogany dining chairs. Having many interesting features.

- *84cm x 48.5cm x 51cm*
- **Guide price $25,810**

George II Dining Chairs ▼

- *circa 1740*

Two chairs from a set of four George II dining chairs in red walnut, on cabriole front legs to pad feet, front and back.

- *height 93.5cm*
- **Guide price $5,870**

Yew Wood Open Armchairs ▼

- *circa 1800*

Two from a set of six late George III armchairs, each with a pierced serpentine top rail with ball finials above a simulated-bamboo filled rectangular back and a pair of out-curved arms, the seat covered in green ribbed velvet.

- *96.5cm x 49cm x 61cm*
- **Guide price $22,700**

George III Mahogany Dining Chairs ▶

- *circa 1790*

Two from a fine set of twelve Hepplewhite design mahogany dining chairs, each with moulded top rails and uprights with leaf carved decoration, standing on tapering square section legs.

- *92.5cm x 43cm x 51cm*
- **Guide price $101,550**

Expert Tips

When buying any chair it is a good idea to stand back and assess its proportions. A good chair should "stand well" when looked at from all angles. Some are not at all well-proportioned and should be avoided. A good chair should be comfortable as well, so try it out.

Hepplewhite Armchair ▼

- **1785**

Hepplewhite mahogany armchair, with shield back and shaped arm rests with scrolled terminals on wavy supports, the whole raised on square tapered legs.
- *98cm x 57cm*
- **Guide price $46,280**

Court Chair ▼

- *circa 1810*

One of a pair of Chinese court chairs of simple elegant form.
- *1m x 61cm*
- **Guide price $5,520**

Victorian Mahogany Chair ▶

- *circa 1860*

Victorian mahogany button back chair, with scrolled arms and cabriole legs.
- *height 1.1m*
- **Guide price $2,400**

French Desk Chair ▲

- *circa 1880*

French mahogany desk chair in the Louis XV style, with gilt ormolu mounts and carved front rail.
- *height 95cm*
- **Guide price $3,470**

Horse Shoe Back Chair ▲

- **18th century**

One of a pair of Chinese antique horseshoe back chairs, each bearing a moon symbol.
- *97cm x 24cm x 18cm*
- **Guide price $4,770**

Elmwood Chairs ▼

- **19th century**

A pair of Chinese elmwood chairs.
- *1.02m x 56cm*
- **Guide price $1,590**

Lancashire Spindle Back Chair ▼

- *circa 1880*

One of a set of ten Harlequin Lancashire rush seat spindle back chairs.
- *height 98cm*
- **Guide price $12,020**

French Louis XV Suite ▼

- **1870**

French Louis XV suite with two armchairs and one sofa.
- *1.06m*
- **Guide price $18,690**

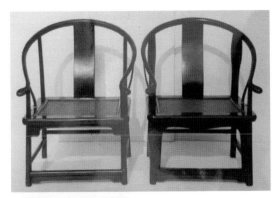

Georgian Wing-Back Armchairs ◀

- *circa 1760*
Georgian mahogany wing-back armchairs, raised on square chamfered legs, with an "H" stretcher, upholstered in a woven silk damask.
- *height 1.19m*
- **Guide price** $6,140

Georgian Fruitwood Chairs ▼

- *circa 1760*
Georgian fruitwood chairs of the Chippendale period, with unusual rosewood splat and square chamfered legs. Original colour and patina.
- *height 95cm*
- **Guide price** $860

French Walnut Bergère ▼

- *circa 1880*
French 2nd Empire bergère with a heavily carved walnut frame incorporating floral swags and fruit motifs, raised on cabriole legs.
- *height 1.01m*
- **Guide price** $3,920

Regency Armchair ▲

- *circa 1880*
Regency revival armchair with mahogany frame carved with honeysuckle and harebell motifs, raised on moulded bun feet.
- *83cm x 54cm*
- **Guide price** $2,480

Italian Walnut Chair ▲

- *circa 1740*
One of a pair of Italian armchairs. The walnut framwork carved with scrolled and moulded decoration, raised on cabriole legs with escargot feet.
- *height 1.14m*
- **Guide price** $24,920

Victorian Lacquered Chair ▲

- *circa 1860*
Small Victorian black lacquered chair with mother-of-pearl inlay, wicker back and seat and elongated arms, standing on turned legs with brass castors.
- *height 75cm*
- **Guide price** $1,770

Windsor Chair ▲

- *circa 1860*
Oak Windsor chair, with carved vase shaped back splat, turned supports and shaped seat.
- *height 1.07m*
- **Guide price** $1,340

Painted Fauteuil ▼
- *circa 1760*

One of a pair of beechwood
fauteuils with oval backs and gilt
foliate designs over cream paint.
Stamped "Premy".
- *height 83cm*
- **Guide price $13,880**

Regency Chair ▼
- *circa 1820*

One of a pair of Regency faux
rosewood chairs, with turned and
gilded designs, raised on sabre
legs.
- *height 82cm*
- **Guide price $4,900**

Ebonised Beechwood Chair ▲
- *circa 1880*

One of a pair of ebonised
beechwood chairs with rush seats,
influenced by William Morris.
- *height 84cm*
- **Guide price $390**

French Louis XV Fauteuil ▲
- *circa 1760*

One of a pair of Louis XV
fauteuils with curved top rail,
inverted arm supports,
serpentine front rail, raised on
cabriole legs.
- *height 84cm*
- **Guide price $9,350**

Mahogany Armchair ◄
- *1880*

One of a pair of mahogany
Chippendale-style armchairs,
with a heavily carved serpentine
top rail and pierced back splat,
raised on carved cabriole legs.
- *height 95cm*
- **Guide price $15,660**

Directoire Armchair ▼
- *circa 1795*

Fine directoire mahogany
armchair, with scrolled top rail,
pierced back splat, and turned
arm supports.
- *height 86cm*
- **Guide price $4,450**

Empire Bergère ▼
- *circa 1815*

Mahogany Empire bergère, with
turned top rail and curved,
padded arms.
- *height 94cm*
- **Guide price $5,070**

Expert Tips

*When buying antique furniture
always try to buy the item in
pristine condition and from a
good dealer, as restoration costs
could be a shock.*

Adam-style Chairs ▶
- *circa 1785*
Pair of George III Adam-style
carved mahogany elbow chairs
with anthemion carved splats and
foliate rails, on moulded legs with
miniature florets.
- *94.5cm x 61cm x 59.5cm*
- **Guide price $6,850**

Regency Hall Chairs ▲
- *circa 1815*
A pair of Regency mahogany hall
chairs with scrolled and leaf
carved backs to platform seats on
turned and fluted front supports.
- *90cm x 48.5cm x 44.5cm*
- **Guide price $4,000**

Mahogany Library Chair ▶
- *circa 1835*
William IV mahogany library
chair with beautifully shaped
back, recently re-leathered.
- *1.09m x 91.5cm x 71cm*
- **Guide price $7,740**

"Drunkards" Chairs ▶
- *circa 1775*
A matched pair of George III
mahogany hall chairs, sometimes
referred to as "drunkards" chairs.
- *86.5cm x 58.5cm 61.5cm*
- **Guide price $6,050**

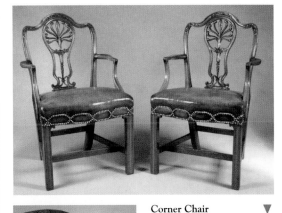

Corner Chair ▼
- *circa 1835*
William IV buttoned hide chair
on three turned legs, very
unusual, designed for a corner.
- *height 87.5cm*
- **Guide price $5,160**

Regency Dining Chair ◀
- *circa 1815*
Set of twelve Regency period
decorated dining chairs with cane
backs and fine gilding.
- *84.5cm x 48cm x 43cm*
- **Guide price $121,950**

Queen Anne Desk Chair ▼

- *circa 1705*
Queen Anne walnut single desk chair with interesting and boldly shaped front legs and back splat.
- *1.02m x 40cm*
- **Guide price $3,120**

French Fauteuil ▼

- *circa 1840*
A well proportioned French fauteuil. The carved beech frame retaining traces of original painted decoration.
- *1m x 73cm*
- **Guide price $9,790**

Ash Dining Chair ▲

- *18th century*
One of a set of ten ash dining chairs, decorated with floral marquetry and birds. The shaped top rail over a serpentine splat with shaped serpentine fronted seat rails and cabriole legs with pad feet.
- *92cm x 51cm*
- **Guide price $40,050**

English Windsor Chair ▲

- *circa 1750s*
Unusual rustic, mid 18th century, Windsor chair made from elm, with turned supports and solid seat, with good warm patina.
- *1m x 53cm*
- **Guide price $6,850**

Venetian Chair ◄

- *1820*
Venetian Rococo style carved fruitwood armchair, in original condition.
- *1.04m x 84cm*
- **£Guide price $14,240**

Directoire Side Chair ▼

- *1780*
One of a set of four French giltwood directoire dining chairs, with original cream paintwork and gilt pastel pink covers.
- *89cm x 43cm*
- **Guide price $12,100**

Elm Elbow Chair ▼

- *circa 1890s*
One of a pair of late 19th century elbow chairs in elm from southern China, of sculptural ox-bow form, from a good merchant's house.
- *1.25m x 60cm*
- **Guide price $10,680**

Ladder-back Chair ▲

- *circa 1780*
Well proportioned 18th century
ladder-back chair made from elm
with rush seat and good patina.
- *1.06m x 57cm*
- **Guide price $3,120**

English Elbow Chair ▲

- *circa 1900*
One of a stylish pair of English
elbow chairs in an Egyptian style,
with carved heads and paw feet
and hand-worked signed tapestry
upholstery in the Regency
manner.
- *95cm x 62cm*
- **Guide price $8,010**

Country Armchair ▶

- *circa 1700*
A rare traditional English country
armchair, with two vase-shaped
backsplats, down-swept arms on
two turned supports, solid seat
and turned front legs.
- *1.2m x 55cm*
- **Guide price $13,970**

Chinese Armchair ▼

- *circa 1850s*
One of a pair of Chinese
armchairs in padouk wood with
original seats, from the Meiji
period.
- *height 90cm*
- **Guide price $7,030**

Yew-wood Rocking Chair ▼

- *circa 1820s*
Yew-wood early 19th century
rocking chair, with carved and
turned decoration.
- *1.05m x 49cm*
- **Guide price $3,120**

Blade & Gilt Dining Chair ▲

- *circa 1840*
One of a set of eight harlequin
blade and gilt japanned
dining/salon chairs, with shaped
seat rails, turned baluster legs, the
black ground with pilwork
depicting flowers, foliage and
birds.
- *90cm x 46cm*
- **Guide price $10,320**

Hepplewhite Chair ▲

- *1785*
Hepplewhite mahogany chair.
The shield back with pierced
decoration above a concave
leather upholstered seat, raised on
square tapered legs.
- *98cm x 57cm*
- **Guide price $46,280**

George IV Hall Chair ▼

- *circa 1825*

A pair of George IV, mahogany hall chairs, with original painted armorials to the shaped and reeded backs, raised on reeded front legs with outswept rear legs.
- *85cm x 42.5cm*
- **Guide price $8,810**

Tub/Desk Chair ▶

- *circa 1880*

French flame mahogany "klismos" shaped tub/desk chair, the downswept arms decorated with gilt ormolu palmettos and supported by winged swans, raised on square tapered legs.
- *1.09m x 68cm*
- **Guide price $8,010**

English Regency Chair ▲

- *circa 1830*

English Regency mahogany chair, with a shield back and a "klismos" shaped seat, with carved and reeded designs.
- **Guide price $6,230**

Set of Dining Chairs ◀

- *circa 1835*

A set of eight William IV period mahogany dining chairs. Stamped: J. Porter, Cabinet Chairs & Sofa Manufacturer, Upholsterer, 166 High Street, Camden Town. Each consisting of a panelled klismos tablet back, supported by shaped uprights which are in the form of stylised ionic columns with leaf motifs to capitals. With turned reeded legs and sabre back legs.
- *89.4cm x 44cm*
- **Guide price $29,370**

George I Dining Chair ▲

- *circa 1720*

Set of walnut George I dining chairs, with shaped top rail, vase shaped back splat and moulded seat and rail, raised on cabriole legs, with turned cross rails.
- *97cm x 47cm*
- **Guide price $24,920**

William IV Library Chair ▲

- *circa 1835*

Outstanding William IV gentleman's library chair. The massive mahogany frame heavily carved with C scrolls and acanthus leaf designs. Supported on large brass castors.
- *1.02m x 98cm*
- **Guide price $14,150**

Regency Hall Chairs ▲
- *circa 1820*
Pair of Irish mahogany hall chairs from the Regency period, with shell backs and acanthus carved rail and sabre legs.
- *81.5cm x 48.5cm x 39.5cm*
- **Guide price $5,520**

George I Sidechairs ▲
- *circa 1725*
Pair of George I walnut sidechairs, veneered splat and rails, with old leather covers.
- *98cm x 40.5cm x 49.5cm*
- **Guide price $4,900**

Hepplewhite Sidechairs ◀
- *circa 1790*
A pair of Hepplewhite hoop back side chairs, having saddle seats and rope carving to the back and to the front legs.
- *94cm x 52.5cm x 54cm*
- **Guide price $3,920**

Wing Armchair ▶
- *circa 1890*
Late 19th century Georgian style mahogany wing armchair of good proportions.
- *1.09m x 71cm x 84cm*
- **Guide price $3,470**

Walnut Wing Chair ◀
- *circa 1740*
George II red walnut wing chair with scrolled arm rests and cabriole legs.
- *1.16m x 78cm x 69.8cm*
- **Guide price $12,190**

Walnut Armchair ▲
- *circa 1750*
George II solid walnut armchair, pierced splayed splat, upholstered seat on cabriole legs with pad feet.
- *95cm x 59.5cm x 56cm*
- **Guide price $5,790**

Regency Dining Chairs ▶

- *circa 1815*
Set of six Regency period
mahogany dining chairs, raised
on turned legs.
- *81cm x 48cm x 40cm*
- **Guide price $10,410**

Mahogany Dining Chair ▶

- *circa 1830*
Set of eight William IV
mahogany dining chairs, richly
carved front legs on scroll feet.
- *95cm x 48cm x 43cm*
- **Guide price $40,050**

French Library Chairs ▲

- *circa 1850*
A stylish pair of continental
mahogany library chairs, with
plumed escutcheon, on sabre legs.
- *94cm x 45.7cm x 56cm*
- **Guide price $4,900**

Regency Library Chair ◀

- *circa 1820*
Regency period mahogany library
chair with olive leather
upholstery.
- *84cm x 53cm x 68.5cm*
- **Guide price $6,230**

Pair of Swan Armchairs ◀

- *circa 1880*
Pair of 19th century gilt wood
and decorated continental swan
armchairs.
- *85cm x 67cm x 58.5cm*
- **Guide price $31,150**

Mahogany Library Chair ▲

- *circa 1820*
Early 19th century French
mahogany library chair with
scrolled arms and leather
upholstery.
- *95cm x 63.5cm x 56cm*
- **Guide price $13,970**

Folding Campaign Chair ▲
- *circa 1870*
A mid-Victorian folding campaign chair made from mahogany with cane seat.
- *70cm x 37cm*
- **Guide price $700**

Hepplewhite Carver ▲
- *1880*
One of a set of eight mahogany Hepplewhite-style, dining chairs including two carvers.
- **Guide price $19,580**

Arts & Crafts Chair ▶
- *circa 1890*
Russian Arts & Crafts chair of triangular outline, with a tablet back, profusely inlaid with numerous wood specimens including walnut, mahogany, satinwood and harewood in geometric patterns. Above a shaped back splat decorated with inlaid woods, with decorated arms issuing from tablet back, leading to an overstuffed shaped brown leather seat. Raised on turned legs of alternate specimen woods.
- *86.5cm x 58.5cm*
- **Guide price $6,050**

Oak Elbow Chair ▼
- *circa 1890*
Oak elbow chair from the late Victorian period, with padded and buttoned top rail.
- *90cm x 55cm*
- **Guide price $700**

Regency Chair ▼
- *circa 1830*
Regency rosewood chair with scrolled top rail, splayed back legs and turned front legs.
- *84cm x 51cm*
- **Guide price $1,750**

Oak Dining Chair ▲
- *circa 1890*
One of a set of four late Victorian oak dining chairs, in the Chippendale style, raised on square straight legs.
- *1m x 50cm*
- **Guide price $1,240**

Windsor Armchair ▲
- *circa 1810*
Beechwood Windsor armchair with elm seat, hooped back and arms, standing on turned legs.
- *87cm x 55cm*
- **Guide price $780**

Flemish Carved Walnut Chairs ▶

- *circa 1670*

A pair of 17th century Flemish carved walnut chairs. The carved crested top supported by twist uprights and caned back and seat with unusual carved decoration to the seat rails.
- *1.21m x 40.5cm x 53.3cm*
- **Guide price $15,800**

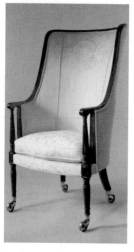

Rush Seated High Chair ▼

- *circa 1890*

Simple country-style child's rush seated high chair.
- *height 84cm*
- **Guide price $520**

Regency High-backed Bergère ◀

- *circa 1815*

A Regency period mahogany framed Bergère chair with swept high back, supported by a reeded mahogany frame and with turned reeded columns joining the arms to the ring turned front legs.
- *height 1.42m*
- **Guide price $15,800**

Elm Lady's Chair with Carved Panel ▲

- *Late 19th century*

A lady's chair made in the traditional style of a five-legged round stool with back. The back splat is divided into carved panels, the central one depicting a lady standing in a pavilion. Elm, stained to simulate hardwood, with caned seat.
- *height 95cm*
- **Guide price $490**

George III Wing Chair ▶

- *circa 1800*

A mahogany framed wing chair, with shaped back and wings and a single cushion. Supported on square taper and reeded front legs, with plain square swept legs to the back, joined by stretchers.
- *1.11m x 58cm x 76cm*
- **Guide price $10,320**

Grape and Leaf Carved Dining Chairs ▲

- *circa 1840*

A set of ten single solid rosewood dining chairs. with unusual panelled back with grape and leaf carving to the ears. Moulded shaped uprights joined by a leaf carved stretcher, contain later caned seats.
- *86cm x 40cm x 45cm*
- **Guide price $26,700**

Chinese Rocking Chair ▲

- *Early 20th century*

A rocking chair with turned legs and arm supports showing a very Western-influenced style. Blackwood with cane seat and back, with a simple floral motif carved into the back rail.
- *height 1.1m*
- **Guide price $870**

Court Chairs ▲

- *circa 1810*

Pair of Chinese court chairs of
simple elegant form.
- *1m x 61cm*
- **Guide price $5,520**

Italian Chair ▲

- *circa 1870*

One of a pair of Italian walnut
chairs, heavily carved with
depictions of Pan, ram's heads,
and griffins, raised on claw feet.
- *height 1.54m*
- **Guide price $32,040**

Horseshoe Shaped Chair ▲

- *circa 1800*

A single low horseshoe shaped
back rail chair. Originally low in
construction.
- *82cm x 57cm*
- **Guide price $2,640**

Syrian Folding Chair ▲

- *circa 1890*

Attractive and decorative,
folding, Syrian chair with inlaid
ivory stars, profusely carved with
scrolled, foliate designs
throughout.
- *height 1.05m*
- **Guide price $860**

Ladder Back Chair ▲

- *circa 1820*

One of a pair George IV ash and
elm ladder back chairs, with
domed top rail above four
graduated ladders, on turned legs
standing on pad feet.
- *height 94cm*
- **Guide price $1,910**

Regency Dining Chairs ◄

- *circa 1820*

One of a set of eight Regency
mahogany dining chairs, with
pierced back splats, raised on
turned legs.
- *height 84cm*
- **Guide price $21,360**

Cherry Dining Chair ▶

- *circa 1920*
One of six Provençal dining chairs in cherrywood with rush seats.
- *height 96.5cm*
- **Guide price $2,310**

Balloon Back Chair ▲

- *circa 1920*
One of six balloon back chairs with cane seats.
- *89cm x 38cm x 40.6cm*
- **Guide price $1,360**

Sabre Leg Chair ▲

- *circa 1820*
One of an attractive set of four regency mahogany sabre leg chairs.
- *height 92.7cm*
- **Guide price $2,400**

Lion's Head Chairs ▶

- *circa 1880*
English chairs standing on carved lion mask headed cabriole legs terminating in hairy paw feet. The open arms are finely shaped and terminate in eagles' heads, expressive of power and victory.
- *1.09m x 51cm x 74cm*
- **Guide price $25,810**

Edwardian Child's Chair ▼

- *circa 1910*
Simple country-style chair with shaped armrests, turned legs and cross rails, with good patina.
- *75cm x 34cm x 38cm*
- **Guide price $330**

Neo-classical Armchair ▶

- *circa 1880*
A satinwood inlaid and brass stung chair with a lyre-shaped back, upholstered seat, and square tapered legs terminating in spade feet. The cresting is finely inlaid with mother-of-pearl, ivory and brass decoration.
- *97cm x 52cm x 52cm*
- **Guide price $9,790**

Regency Chair ▼

- *circa 1810*
One of a pair of Regency chairs with sabre legs and new upholstery.
- *86.4cm x 45.7cm x 47cm*
- **Guide price $1,150**

Tub Chair with Cabriole Legs ▲

- *circa 1860*
A Victorian rosewood tub chair on cabriole legs, the arms terminating in carved scrolls.
- *91.4 cm x 53.3cm x 66cm*
- **Guide price $2,940**

English Bamboo Chair ▲
- *circa 1830*
One of a set of four English faux bamboo chairs, with cane seats, and splayed front legs.
- 85.5cm x 44.5cm x 38cm
- Guide price $4,900

French Walnut Chair ▼
- *circa 1780*
One of a pair of French walnut upholstered open bergère chairs, standing on cabriole legs.
- Guide price $6,770

Elm and Beech Chair ▼
- *circa 1890*
Elm and beech kitchen chair.
- *height 97cm*
- Guide price $120

First Empire Chair ▲
- *circa 1810*
French First Empire, giltwood chair in the manner of Dellenge, with carved stylised floral decoration.
- Guide price $6,770

Mahogany Hall Chairs ▲
- *circa 1775*
One of a pair of English mahogany hall chairs inspired by designs from Chippendale's pattern books, the circular carved and pierced backs in the form of spoked wheels, the dished seats shaped to reflect this pattern, the turned front legs decorated with ring turning.
- 95cm x 35cm
- Guide price $18,690

Gothic Revival Style Leather Library Armchairs ▶

- *circa 1900*
Library chairs upholstered in deep buttoned burgundy leather with slightly out-curved arms, resting on "C" scroll arc-shaped supports. Cabriole legs support the chair, terminating in pad feet.
- *99cm x 61cm x 69cm*
- **Guide price $22,250**

Biedermeier Style Satin Birchwood Arm Chairs ▲

- *19th century*
Armchairs with plume shaped top rails terminating in an ebonised fan shaped splat, above a stepped stretcher. The scrolling arms supported on "C" scrolls with ebonised ball finials.
- *97cm x 51cm x 61cm*
- **Guide price $13,350**

Black Lacquer Folding Chair ▲

- *Early 20th century*
A pair of folding chairs, black lacquer over elm with cane seat and back. Made in Shanghai, where a more Westernised style was popular.
- *height 90cm*
- **Guide price $700**

Sheraton-style Side Chairs ▼

- *circa 1870*
A pair of satinwood and painted chairs with pierced petal shaped and decorated splats forming an eight pointed flower within the chair backs, centred with charming and romantic paintings of young ladies.
- *97cm x 41cm x 46cm*
- **Guide price $18,690**

SOH Armchairs ▼

- *Mid 19th century*
One of a pair of elm wood "southern official's hat" chairs with original black lacquer, much of which has worn from the seat and footrest. The back splat has a carved medallion and the seat is paneled.
- *1.01m x 47cm x 60cm*
- **Guide price $2,140**

Horseshoe Back Chair ▼

- *Late 19th century*
A cross-legged armchair in elm with black lacquer and a caned seat. The back splat is carved with a cloud design and inlaid with bone figures.
- *height 85cm*
- **Guide price $850**

Indian Parcel Gilt Silvered Throne ▼

- *circa 1880*
The throne of His Highness The Thakore Saheb of Limbdi, with a shaped rectangular padded back and seat, surmounted by a coat of arms and gilt urn finials. Silvered recumbent lions guard each side, above a serpentine apron, centred to the front by a gilt lion's head.
- *1.49m x 69cm x 39cm*
- **Guide price $53,400**

Hall Chair ▼

- **1890**
One of a pair of mahogany hall
chairs, with carved shield back
and oval padded insert, raised on
cabriole legs.
- *height 87cm*
- **Guide price $1,560**

Walnut Armchair ▲

- *circa 1880*
George I, Chippendale-style
walnut armchair with pierced
back rest with scrolled designs,
supported by shaped, scrolled
arms above a serpentine front
rail, with scalloped motifs, raised
on cabriole legs with claw and
ball feet.
- *height 95cm*
- **Guide price $2,850**

George II Irish Armchair ▲

- *circa 1730*
A rare and exquisite George II
Irish mahogany open armchair of
outstanding quality and design.
The chair is beautifully carved
throughout and in exceptional
condition for its age.
- *height 98cm*
- **Guide price $11,570**

Walnut Chair ▲

- **1880**
One of a pair of fine George I-
style walnut chairs with pierced
backsplat and scrolled back,
raised on cabriole legs with
scalloped designs and claw and
ball feet, with original leather
and good patina.
- *height 95cm*
- **Guide price $3,120**

William IV Rosewood
Armchair ◄

- *circa 1830.*
William IV colonial rosewood
armchair, formerly the property
of Major Arthur Annesley.
- *height 89cm*
- **Guide price $6,850**

Small Swedish Chair ▶

- *1780*

Small Swedish pine nursing chair in original condition with moulded oval back, standing on turned legs.
- *height 92cm*
- **Guide price $1,510**

Oak Hall Chair ▼

- *1870*

Victorian oak hall chair with an architecturally carved back, raised on turned legs with good patina.
- *height 84cm*
- **Guide price $670**

Regency Mahogany Bergères ▶

- *circa 1820*

One of a fine pair of Regency mahogany bergères decorated with ebony mouldings and turnings, with later cane and hide coverings.
- *width 66cm*
- **Guide price $38,270**

Recumbent Easy Chair ◀

- *circa 1830*

One of a pair of rare matched English Regency "Daws" patent "Recumbent Easy Chairs", both bear the maker's stamp, with one chair bearing an original label for Bantings of Pall Mall.
- *height 79cm*
- **Guide price $32,930**

French Fauteuil ▲

- *circa 1870*

One of a pair of French fauteuils, with a high padded back and wings, with carved and gilded foliate decoration to the back and arms, raised on turned legs.
- *height 1.49m*
- **Guide price $3,290**

Chests of Drawers & Commodes

George III Mahogany Bow Fronted Chest of Drawers ▶

- *circa 1790*
A small bow-fronted chest of drawers of the Sheraton period with four full-width oak and pine lined cockbeaded graduated drawers with decorative brass circular plate ring handles.
- *93.5cm x 56cm x 80cm*
- **Guide price $7,120**

Bachelors Chest of Drawers ▶

- *circa 1780*
Mahogany chest of drawers with Georgian veneered and crossbanded caddy top over a fitted brushing slide with four graduated drawers all retaining the original handles, standing on original bracket feet.
- *78.7cm x 47cm x 86.4cm*
- **Guide price $12,020**

Welsh Oak Cwpwrdd Deuddarn ◀

- *mid 18th century*
A Welsh Oak Cwpwrdd Deuddarn from Cardiganshire the upper section with turned pendants and three panelled doors over frieze drawers with conforming cupboards below.
- *1.80m x 58.4cm x 1.5m*
- **Guide price $25,810**

William & Mary Walnut Chest on Stand ◀

- *circa 1690*
Walnut chest with veneered top and three crossbanded drawers standing on a three-drawer Gothic arched base with cup and cover turning to wavy stretchers.
- *1.55m x 53.3cm x 1.04m*
- **Guide price $30,170**

George III Tallboy ▼

- *circa 1780*
Tallboy with eight drawers having original ram's head plate handles and standing on bracket feet.
- *1.85m x 53.3cm x 1.22m*
- **Guide price $50,730**

Expert Tips

In the antiques world, bigger does not always mean better. Small chests of drawers from the eighteenth century consistently command three times the price of larger pieces.

Venetian Commode ▶

- *circa 1760*
Superb Venetian commode with
trailing foliate painted design
overall, two deep drawers large
metal handles painted marble
top, with moulded carved apron
on cabriole legs.
- *35cm x 1.01m*
- **Guide price $33,370**

Gustavian Commode ▲

- *circa 1800*
Louis XVI Swedish Gustavian
commode with three long drawers
and original brass handles,
standing on square legs.
- *86cm x 1.03m*
- **Guide price $11,930**

Indian Brass Chest ▲

- *circa 1890*
An Indian repoussé and
engraved, floral, banded design
brass chest with teak interior.
The slightly domed lid decorated
with studded bands interspersed
with repoussé floral stripes,
flanked by stripes decorated with
diamonds. The lid with brass
inscribed catch; the front panel of
grid design with repoussé
decorated squares within a
banded frame, standing on
concealed wooded wheels.
- *70cm x 97cm*
- **Guide price $6,230**

Ash Cupboard ▶

- *1870*
One of a small Hungarian pair of
pot cupboards, disguised as a chest
of drawers.
- *height 66cm*
- **Guide price $3,550**

George III Chest ▲

- *circa 1750*
George III mahogany chest of
drawers, of small proportions,
with four graduated drawers and
original brass handles, raised on
bracket feet.
- *86cm x 77cm*
- **Guide price $8,810**

Small Chest of Drawers ▼

- *circa 1780*
George III small chest of oak two
small and two long drawers
standing on moulded bracket feet.
- *height 50cm*
- **Guide price $9,790**

Japanese Chest ▼

- *circa 1880*
Large standing Meiji period
Japanese chest, possibly for futon
storage.
- *1.71m x 1.8m*
- **Guide price $8,890**

William & Mary Chest of Drawers ▲

- *circa 1690*

William & Mary chest of two short and three long drawers on turned bun feet, the whole in oyster laburnum with broad cross-banding to the side, top and drawer fronts.
- *84cm x 94cm x 26cm*
- Guide price **$43,610**

Mahogany Chest of Drawers ▲

- *circa 1860*

Flame mahogany, marble-topped chest of drawers with good colour and patination, one long single drawer above three deep drawers, standing on scrolled bracket feet.
- *92cm x 74cm*
- Guide price **$3,290**

Himalayan Kist ▶

- *circa 17th century*

Fine Himalayan pine chip slab Kist (chest) with deeply carved designs, from the Indian state of Himachal Pradesh.
- *56cm x 1.3m*
- Guide price **$1,390**

French Commode ▲

- *1880*

French marquetry commode of small proportions, with serpentine top and fine gilt ormolu mounts.
- *79cm x 74cm*
- Guide price **$9,790**

Biedermeier Tallboy ▶

- *1820–1830*

A rare narrow Swedish mahogany Biedermeier tallboy with one narrow and five wider drawers with ormulu mounts, standing on gilt paw feet.
- *1.36m x 67cm*
- Guide price **$8,010**

Wellington Chest ▼

- *circa 1835*

Unusually tall rosewood Wellington chest with finely figured rosewood, the rectangular top with moulded lip, with eight drawers with wooden pulls, with hinged and locking stile, the whole raised on a plinth.
- *56.5cm x 53cm*
- Guide price **$9,970**

Kusuri Dansu ▼

- *circa 1890s*

A Japanese Kusuri Dansu (storage chest) with small drawers, from the Meiji period.
- *50cm x 43cm*
- **Guide price $2,660**

Burr Walnut Tallboy ▶

- *circa 1740*

A good George II period burr-walnut tallboy with original metalwork. The top surmounted with a canted concave cornice above three short drawers and three graduated long drawers, all drawers having herringbone inlay and cross-banded with panels of distinctively figured walnut and fitted with open brass plate handles, with fluted canted corners terminating in an ogee point. The lower section with moulded lip above three long graduated drawers flanked by canted fluted corners headed and terminating in ogee points.
- *1.91m x 1.09m*
- **Guide price $45,390**

Mahogany Chest of Drawers ◀

- *circa 1890*

One of a pair of small Victorian mahogany chest of four drawers.
- *height 93cm*
- **Guide price $2,440**

Bombe Commode ▲

- *circa 1890*

Swedish serpentine-fronted, walnut bombe commode, with cross-banded designs and gilt brass mounts raised on splayed legs.
- *82cm x 92cm x 20cm*
- **Guide price $4,000**

Biedermeier Tallboy ▲

- *1842-1843*

Biedermeier birchwood tallboy with a gentleman's chest, interior signed and dated: Carl Christian Hoff, Trondhjem, Norway.
- *1.4m x 1.18m*
- **Guide price $15,660**

Brass Bound Chest of Drawers ▼

- **1890**
Mahogany and brass-bound military-style chest of drawers
- *width 87cm*
- **Guide price $1,340**

Scottish Chest ▼

- **1880**
Large Scottish mahogany chest of drawers with large wide drawers surmounted by five smaller ones.
- *width 1.3m*
- **Guide price $1,560**

George I Burr Walnut Chest of Drawers ▲

- *circa 1725*
Chest of drawers with quarter veneered and banded top over two short and three long chevron banded drawers, the sides walnut veneered and banded standing on bun feet.
- *91.4cm x 55.9cm x 1.02m*
- **Guide price $22,250**

Shaped Front Chest of Drawers ▼

- *circa 1920*
Walnut shaped front chest of drawers of lovely faded colour.
- *50.8cm x 40.6cm x 69cm*
- **Guide price $7,030**

Mahogany Chest on Chest ▲

- *circa 1790*
Fine mahogany inlaid chest on chest.
- *2.11m x 58.4cm x 1.194m*
- **Guide price $26,250**

Expert Tips

Drawer linings are usually of oak or pine. During the seventeenth century they tended to be chunky – the later the piece the thinner the drawer lining. Up until 1770, the drawer lining runs from front to back, from 1780 onwards it runs from side to side.

Walnut and Fruitwood Commode ▼

- *circa 1770*
North Italian walnut and
fruitwood three drawer serpentine
commode retaining its original
locks and brasses, with a poplar
carcass, probably Piedmont or
Lombardy.
- *81.5cm x 40.5cm x 96.5cm*
- **Guide price $12,020**

George III Commode ▶

- *circa 1770*
A George III figured mahogany
serpentine fronted commode of
three long drawers with shaped
apron on splayed bracket feet.
- *83cm x 49.5cm x 99cm*
- **Guide price $32,930**

William and Mary Oyster Chest ▼

- *circa 1695*
William and Mary chest with two
short and two long drawers,
veneered throughout in
olivewood oyster pieces, the top
drawer fronts outlined in
boxwood, the top decorated with
circles forming a flower.
- *84cm x 58.5cm x 96cm*
- **Guide price $40,940**

Walnut Chest of Drawers ◀

- *circa 1930*
Walnut chest of drawers on
cabriole legs.
- *86.4cm x 50.8cm x 76.2cm*
- **Guide price $4,900**

Expert Tips

*As a rule, the more dovetail
joints on the corners of drawers,
the later the piece. Fine
eighteenth century drawers may
have six dovetails, seventeenth
century pieces may have three.*

Victorian Chest of Drawers ▲

- *circa 1860*
Victorian walnut chest of drawers
in lovely condition.
- *86.4cm x 50.8cm x 91.4cm*
- **Guide price $5,790**

Dutch Chest of Drawers ▶
- *circa 1725*
An excellent early 18th century Dutch chest of drawers of serpentine form, with four graduated long drawers. The top quarter veneered and walnut strung. This is an exceptionally small example of this type of furniture.
- *75cm x 79cm*
- **Guide price $33,370**

Collector's Chest ▲
- *circa 1880*
Mahogany collector's chest of eight small drawers with wooden bar with lock and key.
- *28cm x 33cm*
- **Guide price $300**

Louis XV Style Commode ▲
- *circa 1880*
Louis XV style bombe commode, with violet marble top with three long drawers, veneered in rosewood and mahogany with marquetry panels, profusely gilded with foliate bronze ormolu mounts.
- *1.02m x 1.15m*
- **Guide price $9,790**

George III Oak Chest of Drawers ▶
- *circa 1817*
George III chest of drawers with two short and three long drawers, with boxwood banding and brass handles, standing on shaped bracket feet.
- *90cm x 88cm*
- **Guide price $2,540**

English Mahogany Chest of Drawers ▼
- *circa 1780*
Fine English mahogany chest of two small and three long drawers standing on plain bracket feet.
- *height 1.06m*
- **Guide price $4,540**

Oak Coffer ▲
- *circa 1780*
George III oak chest with carving to the front standing on square straight legs.
- *height 56cm*
- **Guide price $12,190**

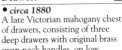

Mahogany Chest of Drawers ▲
- *circa 1880*
A late Victorian mahogany chest of drawers, consisting of three deep drawers with original brass swan neck handles, on low bracket feet.
- *85cm x 1.15m*
- **Guide price $2,670**

Mahogany Chest of Drawers ◄

- *1790*

One of a pair of small mahogany chests of drawers with three drawers with ebony moulding, brass handles, standing on bracket feet.
- *height 66cm*
- **Guide price $3,120**

Chest on Chest ▼

- *circa 1760*

Fine George III beautifully figured mahogany chest on chest, with dentil moulded cornice above an upper section of two short and six long drawers, supported on ogee bracket feet.
- *1.95m x 1.02m*
- **Guide price $22,700**

Georgian Chest of Drawers ▲

- *circa 1790*

Georgian chest of two short and three long drawers, with swan neck handles, standing on bracket feet,
- *1.13m x 98cm*
- **Guide price $2,630**

Walnut Chest of Drawers ▲

- *circa 1820*

Walnut chest of four drawers standing on bracket feet, with original handles.
- *height 98cm*
- **Guide price $8,540**

French Mahogany Commode ▲

- *circa 1840*

French flame mahogany commode with original marble top and one long and three deep drawers on a straight base with small plain bracket feet.
- *width 1.12m*
- **Guide price $4,000**

Walnut and Marquetry Chest of Drawers ▼

- *circa 1695*
Late 17th century walnut and marquetry chest of drawers, with two short and three long drawers. Fine ornate scrolled designs on front and top, raised on moulded bracket feet.
- *89cm x 54.6cm x 96.5cm*
- **Guide price $22,870**

Walnut Chest on Stand ◄

- *circa 1920*
Pretty walnut chest with seven drawers on cabriole legs.
- *1.27m x 43cm x 76.2cm*
- **Guide price $4,360**

George I Walnut Chest on Stand ▲

- *circa 1715*
George I chest on stand, the upper part with a cross grained cavetto cornice above five boxwood and ebony chevron inlaid drawers. The stand comprising a long central and two short side drawers, standing on walnut cabriole legs.
- *1.56m x 58.5cm x 1.06m*
- **Guide price $23,500**

William & Mary Walnut Chest on Stand ▲

- *circa 1700*
A walnut veneered chest on stand, the upper section with two short and three long drawers on a stand with one long central drawer flanked by two deep drawers above an arched apron.
- *1.58m x 56cm x 1.04m*
- **Guide price $26,430**

Chippendale Chest on Chest ▲

- *circa 1760*
Chippendale period mahogany chest on chest with dentil moulded cornice and finely carved frieze above an upper section of two short and six long drawers, supported on ogee bracket feet.
- *1.79m x 54.6cm x 1.11m*
- **Guide price $15,750**

George III Chest of Drawers ►

- *circa 1810*
Satinwood bow front chest of four drawers on a moulded apron with slay bracket feet and original fittings.
- *99cm x 58.4cm x 1.08m*
- **Guide price $24,650**

George I Walnut Veneered Chest of Drawers ▶

- *circa 1720*

George I chest of drawers with a well figured quartered top with chequered stringing and cross-banding. Five chequered strung standing on a plinth base with restored bracket feet.

- *95.3cm x 52.7cm x 95.3cm*
- **Guide price $24,030**

Oak Chest of Drawers ▼

- *circa 1760*

Mid 18th century chest of drawers of good proportions on ogee feet with very good original ormolu handles in the rococo taste.

- *81cm x 52cm x 92cm*
- **Guide price $8,810**

Mahogany Chest of Drawers ▼

- *circa 1750*

Chest of four graduated drawers with re-entrant corners, a brushing slide, and replacement handles. Unusually small and good colour.

- *74cm x 46cm x 76cm*
- **Guide price $7,920**

Chest On Chest ◀

- *circa 1760–70*

A chest on chest of the Chippendale period with original shaped swan neck handles and escutcheons; the top with reed canted sides and dentil cornice.

- *79cm x 55cm x 1.3m*
- **Guide price $10,240**

Olivewood Chest of Drawers ▲

- *circa 1860*

William and Mary oyster olivewood chest of drawers having a top with matching oysters and geometric circles of holly inlay. Two short and three long drawers similarly decorated supported on bun feet.

- *79cm x 54.6cm x 85cm*
- **Guide price $51,620**

Expert Tips

From the eighteenth century drawer fronts are flat with overlapping ovolo moulding. From c.1735 cock beading was introduced. Herringbone crossbanding was used from c.1690–1720 as was inlaid boxwood decoration.

Davenports

Victorian Davenport ▶
- *circa 1870*

An unusual Victorian burr walnut rising top davenport, enclosing a fitted interior and pull out ratcheted writing slope.
- 90cm x 60cm
- **Guide price $7,740**

Regency Davenport ▲
- *circa 1820*

A Regency style faux rosewood davenport with pen drawer to right hand side and a removable fire screen.
- 98cm x 51cm
- **Guide price $1,770**

Walnut Davenport ▲
- *circa 1860*

Fine walnut Victorian davenport with original leather, inlaid with satinwood, with four side drawers, pierced brass rail and maple interior.
- *height 88cm*
- **Guide price $3,470**

Burr Walnut Davenport ▼
- *circa 1860*

Burr walnut davenport with piano lid, central cupboard flanked by eight small side drawers with turned wood handles.
- 98cm x 62cm
- **Guide price $6,680**

Rosewood Davenport ▼
- *circa 1820*

Small Regency rosewood davenport, with pierced brass gallery and pen drawer to the side of a writing slope with unusual side action.
- 88cm x 34cm
- **Guide price $7,110**

Expert Tips

The name davenport came from an entry in the book of Captain Davenport in the 1790s. Look out for the following:

*fine veneer in walnut
panelled back
original inkwells
pen trays
mother of pearl escutcheons
secret drawers*

Up to 1840 their style was quite plain, but after 1840 davenports tended to be more feminine, with scrolled supports.

Walnut Davenport ◀
- *circa 1840*

An English figured walnut davenport with stunning matched sunburst veneers. The sliding top is fitted with a hinged pen and inkwell drawer raised above four graduated drawers and four dummy panel drawers supported on a shaped plinth base.
- 79cm x 46cm
- **Guide price $13,350**

Piano Front Davenport ▼

- *19th century*

A walnut piano front davenport with a rising stationery compartment, having four drawers, behind a cupboard door, to the right-hand side.

- *91.4cm x 63.5cm x 58.4cm*
- **Guide price $10,410**

Victorian Walnut Davenport ▼

- *1860*

Davenport with green inlayed top and four drawers.

- *height 96cm*
- **Guide price $1,870**

William IV Davenport ▶

- *circa 1835*

William IV satinwood veneered davenport in the Gillows manner with a galleried sliding top and front and rear panelling all standing on lobbed feet with recessed castors.

- *85cm x 57cm x 52cm*
- **Guide price $14,690**

Rosewood Davenport ▲

- *19th century*

A Rosewood davenport having five drawers and decorative carvings

- *1.19m x 30.5cm x 50.8cm*
- **Guide price $5,070**

Mahogany Davenport ▼

- *19th century*

Mahogany davenport desk with brass top columns and old leather top.

- *78.7cm x 53.3cm x 53.3cm*
- **Guide price $4,800**

Expert Tips

The handles of davenport drawers should always be of turned, wooden knobs.

George IV Rosewood Davenport ◀

- *circa 1825*

A rosewood davenport in the manner of Gillows, the sliding top with brass gallery and secret pen drawer and the pedestal with four fluted corner pilasters.

- *90cm x 58cm x 52.5cm*
- **Guide price $15,040**

Desks

Bonheur du Jour ▼
- *circa 1890*
Bonheur du jour with pierced brass rail and two small drawers, flanked by cupboards with circular inlay panels and a gallery single drawer, standing on slender tapering legs.
- *1.04m x 73cm*
- **Guide price $2,050**

Victorian Dressing Table ▼
- *circa 1870*
Fine quality Victorian burr walnut dressing table and mirror supported by scrolled carving.
- *height 1.74m*
- **Guide price $4,980**

George IV Bonheur du Jour ▲
- *circa 1825*
George IV rosewood writing table in solid and veneered rosewood. With pierced gallery drawers and moving writing slide supported by twist columns.
- *height 1.22m*
- **Guide price $13,880**

Sheraton Bonheur du Jour ▲
- *circa 1790*
Fine Sheraton period bonheur du jour, with harewood inlay fold-over tops, enclosing a rising nest of drawers and pigeonholes.
- *89cm x 1.14m*
- **Guide price $40,050**

Victorian Dressing Table ▲
- *circa 1880*
Victorian mahogany dressing table with central mirror and drawer, flanked by eight small drawers.
- *height 1.67m*
- **Guide price $4,180**

Bonheur du Jour ▼
- *circa 1890*
Late Victorian mahogany bonheur du jour with satinwood stringing, a roll top cover, the interior fitted with five pigeonholes and a central small drawer, above a pull-out writing slope and two drawers, the whole on straight legs.
- *1.03m x 72cm*
- **Guide price $2,670**

Chippendale Style Bonheur du Jour ▼
- *circa 19th century*
Chippendale-style bonheur du jour in the style of Angelica Kauffman, decorated with floral designs and classical scenes in the finest satin wood. Shield style bevelled glazed mirror with urn finial, standing on delicate turned legs.
- *1.65m x 1.07m*
- **Guide price $43,610**

Louis XVI Desk ▲

- *circa 1800*

A Louis XVI Swedish Gustavian desk, with long drawer, plain gilt ring handle, raised on slender tapered legs.
- *75cm x 80cm*
- **Guide price $3,470**

Mahogany Partner's Desk ▲

- *circa 1825*

A historically important George IV mahogany partner's desk by Robert Lawson for Gillows of Lancaster. With a central drawer above the kneehole flanked by a bank of four drawers. Each pedestal with vertical reeded pilasters. The pedestals supported on plinth bases with gilded castors, all locks original.
- *79cm x 1.83m*
- **Guide price $169,100**

Louis XV Bureau Plat ▲

- *circa 1900*

Fine French Louis XV style mahogany bureau plat with gilt bronze mounts.
- *80cm x 1.45m x 76cm*
- **Guide price $16,910**

Satinwood Writing Table ▼

- *1870*

Satinwood and ormolu writing table. The top with egg and dart moulded rim, above two side drawers, raised on four reeded legs on original brass castors, by Wright & Mansfield.
- *74cm x 1.1m*
- **Guide price $18,690**

Satinwood Desk ▼

- *circa 1890*

Sheraton revival high quality Victorian inlaid satin wood pedestal desk with two side compartments. The base containing single drawer, stamped "Maple & Co.".
- *1.24m x 1m*
- **Guide price $22,250**

Georgian Mahogany Desk ▶

- *circa 1820s*

Georgian kneehole mahogany desk with leather top, two long and two small drawers, original laurel wreath brass handles.
- *79cm x 1.01m*
- **Guide price $2,400**

George II Partner's Desk ▲

- *circa 1755*

George II ebony-inlaid mahogany partners pedestal desk with a rich, untouched patina. The rectangular leather inset top above three mahogany-lined frieze drawers to each side and two simulated drawers with carrying-handles to each. Raised on a plinth base.
- *80.5cm x 1.4m*
- **Guide price $121,050**

Birchwood Desk ▲

- *circa 1890s*

Swedish free-standing veneered Biedermeier style birchwood desk. The top with leather insert and three drawers, above two pedestals with panelled doors.
- *76cm x 1.43m*
- **Guide price $10,500**

Double-sided Desk

- *19th century*

A rare decorative double-sided Continental pedestal partners desk having pull-out slides to either end with dummy drawers and working cupboards to the rear.
- *1.68m x 91.4cm*
- **Guide price $13,350**

Kidney-shaped Pedestal Desk

- *circa 1840*

Kidney-shaped pedestal desk, by Gillow of Lancaster, finished in mellow English oak, with brown-oak, cross-banded inlays, and mahogany drawer linings.
- *72.5cm x 76cm x 1.36m*
- **Guide price $69,420**

Shoolbred Desk

- *19th century*

A fine oak swivel pedestal desk by J. A. S. Shoolbred.
- *89cm x 71cm x 1.5m*
- **Guide price $12,100**

Golden Oak Desk

- *19th century*

Golden oak panelled kneehole desk with flush fitted brass handles, hide leather top, slides and moulded drawers.
- *1.37m x 86.4cm*
- **Guide price $5,700**

Oak Office Desk

- *20th century*

An all-in-one oak office desk, having seven drawers.
- *1.14m x 68.6cm*
- **Guide price $670**

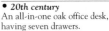

Marquetry Desk

- *19th century*

An exceptional early 19th century double sided pedestal desk having fine inlaid detail to all sides.
- *1.50m x 89cm*
- **Guide price $22,250**

Georgian Slope Top Desk ▶
- *Late 18th – early 17th century*
A fine Georgian slope top writing
desk having tapered legs and a
single cockbeaded drawer with an
early solid brass handle.
- *86.3cm x 45.72cm x 55.88cm*
- **Guide price $1,570**

S-shaped Roll Top Desk ▼
- *19th century*
A 19th century oak S-shaped
roll top desk with well fitted
interior.
- *1.32m x 81.3cm x 1.27m*
- **Guide price $4,450**

Expert Tips

*The best kneehole desks, dating
from the mid-eighteenth
century, have six bracket feet.
Those with only four feet may
have been cut down from
chests of drawers.*

Regency Writing Table ▼
- *1811 – 1830*
A superb quality Regency
mahogany writing table having
three drawers to the front and
three to the rear with original
turned knobs stamped "M
Willson 68 Great Queen Street".
- *1.52m x 96.5cm*
- **Guide price $22,250**

Knee-hole Desk ▼
- *19th century*
A mahogany display serpentine
knee-hole desk with polished lift-
up top and four bracket feet.
- *1.07m x 58.42cm*
- **Guide price $11,570**

Walnut Lady's Desk ▼
- *1870*
Victorian burr walnut lady's desk
with inlay and green leather
insert.
- *80cm x 121cm x 152cm*
- **Guide price $3,470**

Wooten Desk ▼
- *19th century*
A well fitted solid walnut
Wooten desk with rare
provenance.
- *1.52m x 68.6cm x 99cm*
- **Guide price $11,570**

Walnut Cabriole Leg Desk

- **Early 20th century**
Fine walnut leather-topped writing desk raised on cabriole legs, with curved front, the central drawer flanked by two deep drawers.
- *71cm x 61cm x 1.22m*
- **Guide price $3,470**

Walnut Kidney Shaped Pedestal Desk

- *circa 1845*
A pedestal desk with an inset leather writing surface with brass gallery, above three frieze drawers, the right one concealing a mechanism allowing the top to swivel revealing secret recess.
- *78.5cm x 66.5cm x 1.34m*
- **Guide price $119,350**

Mahogany Writing Desk

- *circa 1820*
Early 19th century mahogany writing desk from Gillow model.
- *94cm x 61cm x 56cm*
- **Guide price $22,250**

Mahogany Twin Pedestal Partner's Desk

- *circa 1830*
A partner's desk having a gilt tooled green leather top with each pedestal comprising drawers to one side and a cupboard to the other.
- *76cm x 1.09m x 1.85m*
- **Guide price $42,280**

Carlton House Mahogany Desk

- *circa 1890*
An English George III style kidney-shaped Carlton House mahogany desk with brass gallery and legs terminating in wheels.
- *1.04m x 81cm x 1.39m*
- **Guide price $19,580**

Tambour Front Writing Table

- *circa 1800*
A superb George III mahogany tambour front writing table with roll top. Interior fitted with pigeon holes above a kneehole flanked by nine drawers with brass swan-necked handles.
- *1.01m x 1.37m x 78.7cm*
- **Guide price $22,870**

George III Writing Table ◄
- *circa 1800*

George III mahogany writing table on tapered legs with brass castors, incorporating a raised writing slide.
- *77.5cm x 95.3cm x 64cm*
- **Guide price $8,460**

Walnut Kneehole Desk ▶
- *circa 1715*

George I desk having a quartered top and cross-banded moulded edge. Below is a single drawer supported by three drawers to either side with cock-beaded edges and herringbone decoration and original furniture.
- *73.6cm x 54.6cm x 86.4cm*
- **Guide price $33,820**

Lady's Kneehole Writing Desk ▲
- *1735-40*

A George II lady's kingwood writing desk with a figured surface above a full length drawer. In between sets of three short drawers is a cupboard with moulded panel door and a false drawer with blind fret carving.
- *85cm x 47cm x 83cm*
- **Guide price $51,620**

Pedestal Desk ▲
- *19th century*

A superb pedestal desk having nine drawers to the front and two cupboards to the rear with original turned knobs and a full hide leather top. Formerly owned by Sir Admiral A.H. Markham.
- *1.49m x 83.8cm*
- **Guide price $22,250**

Mahogany Kneehole Desk ◄
- *circa 1910*

A mahogany desk of large size, standing on ogee bracket feet and retaining original handles.
- *width 1.37m*
- **Guide price $3,290**

Mahogany Desk ▲
- *circa 1900*

Early twentieth century kneehole desk with new leather inlay, raised on a plinth base.
- *76cm x 80cm x 1.5m*
- **Guide price $2,630**

Dressers

Oak Dresser Base ▶

- *circa 1780*

George III oak dresser base with central panelled door flanked by two sets of three long drawers with original brass handles, and standing on bracket feet.
- *height 1.1m*
- **Guide price $26,260**

George II Oak Dresser ▲

- *circa 1750*

George II oak dresser with panelled back, two shelves with three small drawers with turned handles and two cupboards below standing on straight square legs.
- *height 2.45m*
- **Guide price $20,920**

Victorian Sideboard ▲

- *circa 1880*

Impressive sideboard with a deep central drawer, centered with a raised ivory classical plaque, flanked by two deep large cupboards, standing on two pedestals with bun feet.
- *90cm x 1.98m*
- **Guide price $8,630**

George III Plate Rack ▲

- *circa 1780*

George III open oak plate rack with pierced rail and architectural side columns.
- *height 1.02m*
- **Guide price $6,680**

Pine Open Dresser ◀

- *circa 1880*

Open back pine dresser with four shelves. The base with three long drawers above three panelled cupboard doors, with alloy handles and fittings.
- *2.75m x 1.7m*
- **Guide price $1,510**

Expert Tips

The earliest English dressers date back to 1680. They were used as serving tables and for storage, and came with or without display racks. Oak was the timber most widely used while yew and fruitwood were more unusual. In France dressers were made from fruitwood, with the earliest raised on turned legs. From around 1730 a popular dressser was one with cabriole legs and a shaped apron.

French Dresser ▼

- *circa 1820*

French provincial fruitwood galleried four shelf dresser with two long drawers and cupboards below.
- *width 1.27m*
- **Guide price $6,850**

Breakfront Sideboard ▲

• *circa 1800*
Mahogany breakfront D-shaped sideboard, one cellaret drawer and a shallow centre drawer over a linen drawer. Raised on four front finely reeded legs and two turned back legs.
• *94.5cm x 1.68m x 66.5cm*
• **Guide price $29,370**

George III Oak Rack ▲

• *circa 1790*
George III oak wall-mounted dresser with moulded and shaped cornice and three shelves flanked either side with additional shelving.
• *height 97cm*
• **Guide price $5,790**

Oak Dresser Base ▲

• *circa 1786*
George III oak dresser base. Carved drawers with geometric designs, with brass drop handles, the whole raised on turned front legs.
• *height 97cm*
• **Guide price $40,050**

Pine Glazed Dresser ▲

• *circa 1840*
Pine dresser with three glazed doors enclosing three shelves, with two long drawers and cupboards below with brass knob handles.
• *2.35m x 1.7m*
• **Guide price $2,850**

Pine Dressers ▶

• *circa 1820*
One of a pair of unusual narrow pine dressers or bookcases with panelled backs and adjustable shelves.
• *width 67cm*
• **Guide price $5,960**

Miniature Dresser ◀

• *circa 1890*
Miniature English oak dresser with moulded gallery, turned supports all above carved panel doors and turned bun feet.
• *height 47cm*
• **Guide price $400**

Oversized Dresser ▲

• *circa 1840*
Large pine dresser painted pea green, with moulded pediment and two central cupboards flanked by four deep long drawers with brass handles, standing on a straight base.
• *height 4.25m*
• **Guide price $6,500**

Dumb Waiters & Whatnots

Mahogany Whatnot
- *circa 1880*
Mahogany whatnot with five graduated serpentine tiers with turned finials and barley twist supports.
- *height 1.25m*
- **Guide price $620**

William IV Dumbwaiter
- *1825*
One of a pair of mahogany dumbwaiters with brass gallery, three well figured shelves, raised on carved supports with bun feet.
- *1.17m x 1.24m*
- **Guide price $29,370**

Brass Cake Stand
- *1890*
Victorian lacquered brass cake-stand with two circular tiers embossed with an organic repeating design, raised on scrolled legs with hoof feet.
- *height 88cm*
- **Guide price $530**

Oriental Cake Stand
- *1880*
Oriental cake stand with three circular tiers carved with six-leaf shaped receptacles, around a central circular design, within a carved frame.
- *height 82cm*
- **Guide price $200**

George II Washstand
- *circa 1750*
George II mahogany two tier washstand with fan carving to the sides, and a small drawer standing on slender legs and pad feet.
- *height 85cm*
- **Guide price $6,850**

Walnut Whatnot
- *1880*
Victorian burr walnut whatnot with pierced gallery and turned finials, three well-figured tiers, with turned supports the lower section with single drawer and wood knob handles, on turned legs with original castors.
- *height 1.22m*
- **Guide price $3,920**

Four Tier Walnut Whatnot ▲

- *circa 1880*

Four tier walnut corner whatnot inlaid with boxwood and burr walnut, with acorn finial and turned supports.
- *height 1.37m*
- Guide price $1,560

Satin Birch Whatnot ▲

- *circa 1840*

An English satin birchwood whatnot with three shelves, the lower section with a single drawer with barley-twist supports, stamped "Mills Cabinetmakers", raised on gadrooned feet with original brass castors.
- *99cm x 53cm x 39.5cm*
- Guide price $7,570

George III Whatnot ◀

- *circa 1790*

Unusual mahogany George III whatnot. The rising with ratcheted bracket and four shelves below. The whole on square section legs and square caped castors.
- *height 1.14m*
- Guide price $11,570

Cake Stand ▲

- *circa 1880*

Mahogany cake stand with satin wood banding, incorporating three graduated circular shelves, within wood frame, open at one side, surmounted by a ball finial, raised on splayed legs.
- *height 93cm*
- Guide price $500

Walnut Whatnot ◀

- *circa 1870*

A Victorian walnut three-tier whatnot with carved scrolled pierced gallery and elaborately turned supports.
- *height 1.32m*
- Guide price $3,470

Mahogany Washstand ▲
- *circa 1860*
Mahogany washstand inset with a circular pink marble top and two shelves, supported by pillared turned legs on a triangular base, raised on shallow bun feet.
- *85cm x 32cm*
- **Guide price $1,750**

Mahogany Plant Stand ▲
- *circa 1870s*
Fine Victorian mahogany plant stand, with a slender baluster column on three curved legs with drop turned finial.
- *90cm x 29cm*
- **Guide price $880**

Walnut Whatnot ▼
- *circa 1870s*
Victorian walnut whatnot, the scrolled gallery with turned finials, above four graduated triangular tiers, with carved apron and turned supports.
- *1.3m x 57cm*
- **Guide price $980**

Teak Whatnot ▼
- *1890*
Victorian corner whatnot made from teak with scrolled gallery, above four graduated tiers, supported by turned Solomonaic columns.
- *height 1.27m*
- **Guide price $800**

Regency Rosewood Whatnot ▲
- *circa 1825*
English Regency rosewood whatnot of small proportions with three well-figured tiers, raised on finely turned supports, the middle tier having a fitted drawer with small brass circular handles.
- *1.02m x 38cm*
- **Guide price $8,280**

French Etagère ▲
- *1890*
French etagère with pierced brass gallery, single narrow drawer with brass handle and two shelves below, on ebonised shaped legs.
- *height 94cm*
- **Guide price $1,200**

Mirrors

Mahogany Dressing Mirror ▶

- *circa 1770*

George III dressing mirror hung between two scratch stock moulded tapered supports with adjustable brass thumb side screws and small brass urn finials. The stepped base is fitted with three oak lined drawers.
- *63cm x 20.5cm x 42.5cm*
- **Guide price $2,670**

Gilt Mirror ▲

- *circa 1880*

Fine Victorian oval mirror with original gilt.
- *1.63m x 1.6m*
- **Guide price $5,790**

Cheval Mirror ▲

- *circa 1815*

Regency mahogany cheval mirror with satinwood inlaid panels, with turned supports and stretchers.
- *1.64m x 58.5cm x 66cm*
- **Guide price $6,230**

Giltwood Convex Mirror ▼

- *circa 1820*

A circular convex mirror with a carved acanthus leaf crest, cornucopia mounted shoulders, and carved scrolling acanthus leaves to the base.
- *1.38m x 82.5cm*
- **Guide price $26,700**

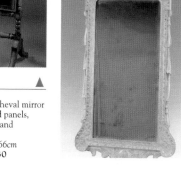

Gilded Wood Pier Mirror ▼

- *circa 1790*

A late eighteenth century Italian carved and gilded wood pier mirror in an English design.
- *1.83m x 86.5cm*
- **Guide price $13,880**

Overmantle Mirror ▼

- *Early 19th century*

Regency overmantle mirror with gilt wood frame and foliate mouldings.
- *1.29m 1.35m*
- **Guide price $2,940**

George II Mirror ◀

- *circa 1730*

A George II mirror with a swan neck pediment, tasselled drapery and a later ho-ho bird. The frame is covered in fine gesso carving with a ring-punched ground typical of the first quarter of the 18th century.
- *1.81m x 87cm*
- **Guide price $45,390**

Giltwood Oval Mirrors ▲

- *circa 1840*
One of a pair of finely carved oval
English mirrors with carved
giltwood vine leaves and grapes
with bead and red moulding, and
original plate glass.
- *1.08m x 90cm*
- Guide price $14,240

French Giltwood Mirror ▲

- *circa 1890s*
Oval French giltwood mirror with
carved roses placed intermittently
on a moulded wood frame.
- *82cm x 51cm*
- Guide price $2,310

Regency Overmantle Mirror ▲

- *circa 1820*
Regency giltwood overmantle
mirror, with architectural designs,
surmounted by a frieze depicting
the procession of Jupiter.
- *length 1.39m*
- Guide price $6,230

Mercury Plate Mirror ▶

- *circa 1800s*
Rectangular Austro-Hungarian
water-gilt looking-glass with a
scrolling floral border and
original plate glass.
- *96.5cm x 81cm*
- £Guide price $9,520

Regency Toilet Mirror ▼

- *circa 1810*
Regency mahogany toilet mirror
with three drawers, cross-banded
in satinwood with boxwood and
ebony stringing.
- *height 68cm*
- Guide price $2,050

French Oval Mirror ▼

- *circa 1850*
Small oval French mirror with
elaborate carved foliate and
acorn border.
- *53.4cm x 46cm*
- Guide price $2,490

Victorian Mirror ▶

- *circa 1870*
Victorian oval gilt framed mirror
with triple candle sconce and
beaded rim, surmounted by a
scrolled finial.
- *height 75cm*
- Guide price $1,220

French Mirror ▲

- *circa 1860*
A fine, imposing French gilt
wood and gesso looking-glass in
the Louis XV manner. The
arched framed headed by a foliate
and shell cresting.
- *1.94m x 1.32m*
- Guide price $3,470

Italian Mirror ▼

- *circa 1780*

An 18th century Italian mirror with egg and leaf design, cavetto and a Rococo shell at the base.
- *1.32m x 86.5cm*
- **Guide price $9,790**

George II Gilt Framed Mirror ▲

- *circa 1740*

A gilt framed mirror with bevelled plate bordered with bead and reel and leaf moulded decoration. The apron decorated with Prince of Wales feathers and rosettes, surmounted by a swan neck pediment.
- *1.35m x 64cm*
- **Guide price $28,120**

Gesso Mirror ▼

- *circa 1890*

An ornately carved French rococo giltwood and gesso mirror.
- *1.24m x 84cm*
- **Guide price $15,130**

Venetian Mosaic and Carved Walnut Mirror ▲

- *circa 1880*

A Venetian mirror depicting day and night, with a walnut maiden with outstretched arms to the left and blossoming foliage and a shooting star that encircles a Venetian scene to the right.
- *1.45m x 1.01m*
- **Guide price $121,050**

Napoleon III Marginal Frame Mirror ▲

- *circa 1850*

One of a pair of French Napoleon III carved and giltwood marginal frame mirrors in the 18th century Regency style.
- *2.76m x 1.73m*
- **Guide price $156,650**

Breman Oval Giltwood Mirror ▲

- *circa 1820*

A German Breman oval mirror, with the plate flanked by guilloched cornucopia issuing flowers and fruit. The cresting is applied with a foliate spray and the apron with eagle heads, flanking a foliate band.
- *87cm x 78cm*
- **Guide price $8,190**

Chinoiserie Overmantle Mirror ◀

- *circa 1815*

Mirror in the "Brighton Pavilion" style carved with umbrellas and a cavetto-moulded cornice with dolphins, with one standing and two seated Chinamen above.
- *1.70m x 1.45m*
- **Guide price $83,660**

Regency Mirror ▲

- *circa 1830*
A small giltwood Regency mirror of rectangular shape.
- *51cm x 1.13m*
- Guide price $3,290

William & Mary Mirror ▲

- *circa 1690*
Fine William & Mary cushion frame mirror, decorated with floral and bird motifs including stained ivory.
- *1.09m x 92cm*
- Guide price $40,050

Giltwood Mirror ▼

- *1870*
French carved giltwood mirror on red bouille, with moulded rim.
- *height 1.17m*
- Guide price $1,160

Victorian Gilt Mirror ▲

- *circa 1860s*
A mid-Victorian circular mirror, verre eglomisé, with swept arch, surmounted by a large carved eagle motif.
- *89cm x 43cm*
- Guide price $3,120

Adam Style Gilt Mirror ◄

- *circa 1880*
English Adam-style gilt mirror surmounted by an urn finial above a strung lyre, flanked by foliate swags. The base with swept berried and bunched laurel bracket carving.
- *1.56m x 71cm*
- Guide price $22,780

Italian Carved Mirror ▲

- *circa 1810*
Giltwood mirror with a carved, scrolled floral border, surmounted by a scallop shell and a head of a young girl at the base.
- *99cm x 68.5cm*
- Guide price $6,410

Regency Convex Mirror ▲

- *circa 1820s*
Fine Regency giltwood convex mirror with ebonised slip and ball-encrusted frame, surmounted by an eagle suspending a ball on a columned finial.
- *99cm x 56cm*
- Guide price $7,030

George II Walnut Mirror ▶

- *circa 1735*

George II walnut and giltwood mirror with fine gilded swan neck pediment culminating in a central golden bird and gilded foliate carved decorations to the sides.

- *1.32m x 3.8cm x 63.5cm*
- **Guide price $12,190**

Walnut and Giltwood Wall Mirror ▲

- *circa 1735*

George II walnut fret-cut mirror with gilded motif and inner slip.

- *1.04m x 46.4cm*
- **Guide price $4,000**

Victorian Wall Mirror ▲

- *circa 1860*

A Victorian gilt composition oval wall mirror with a later glass and fine carved, scrolled floral border.

- *1.6m x 1.02m*
- **Guide price $8,540**

Regency Cheval Mirror ▼

- *circa 1825*

Regency period mahogany cheval mirror with candle arms.

- *1.84m x 61cm x 83cm*
- **Guide price $16,910**

Regency Giltwood Convex Mirror ▼

- *circa 1820*

One of a pair of Regency convex mirrors, fine carved foliate decoration and beading surmounted by an ebonised eagle.

- *1.33m x 6.4cm x 83cm*
- **Guide price $66,750**

Chippendale Mirror ▼

- *circa 1760*

Chippendale carved walnut and giltwood looking glass.

- *71cm x 44.5cm*
- **Guide price $1,690**

Expert Tips

Mirror glass made before the 1780s was small. Large mirrors were made up of several pieces.

Cushion Mirror ◀

- *circa 1710*

Eighteenth century walnut veneered cushion mirror with beaded edges.

- *58.4cm x 54.6cm*
- **Guide price $7,030**

William IV Giltwood Mirror ▲

- *circa 1835*

William IV period giltwood and gesso convex mirror with a carved frame depicting acorns and foliage, surmounted by a crest in the form of a seated deer upon a rocky ground, the mirror fitted with sconces in the form of serpents.
- *1.12m x 76cm*
- **Guide price $13,350**

Irish Mirror ▶

- *circa 1850s*

Irish oval mirror with a blue and gold strip border on the mirror.
- *71cm x 46cm*
- **Guide price $4,450**

Venetian Giltwood Mirror ▲

- *circa 1780*

Venetian giltwood mirror with lion, armorial crest and trophies, with trailing foliate designs to the rim, with original plate glass.
- *84cm x 47cm*
- **Guide price $6,760**

Italian Giltwood Mirror ▼

- *circa 1780*

Italian giltwood swept mirror with carved scrolling, in the form of decoration depicting trailing ivy and small pink roses.
- *49cm x 44cm*
- **Guide price $1,160**

Venetian Mercury Plate Mirror ▼

- *circa 1850s*

Small mid 19th century Venetian blue oval glass mirror, etched with floral sprays, with original mercury plate mirror.
- *56cm x 43cm*
- **Guide price $4,000**

Regency Girandole Mirror ▲

- *circa 1820s*

Regency giltwood convex mirror, with ebonised slip surrounded by a ropework design, surmounted by a giltwood deer and grapevines, at the base stylised leaf designs flanked by two scrolled candle holders of candle holders.
- *1.04m x 56cm*
- **Guide price $7,570**

Victorian Mirror ▲

- *circa 1870s*

One of a pair of rectangular giltwood mirrors with arched top surmounted by a stylised acanthus leaf, flanked by giltwood urn finials, and a carved border with foliate swag decoration.
- *94cm x 53cm*
- **Guide price $5,790**

Gooderson Mirror ▶

- *circa 1730*
Eighteenth century giltwood
mirror in the manner of
Gooderson.
- *1.55m x 90cm*
- **Guide price $27,590**

Victorian Overmantle Mirror ▲

- *circa 1880*
A Victorian gilt composition
overmantle mirror with old glass
and ornate foliate carving.
- *94cm x 1.29m*
- **Guide price $4,180**

Gilt Overmantle Mirror ▲

- *circa 1880*
A fine classical inspired Victorian
gilt composition overmantle
mirror with old glass,
architectural pediment and
scrolled elements to the base.
- *1.70m x 1.57m*
- **Guide price $6,400**

Expert Tips

*Unlike modern glass, mirrors
from the eighteenth century
project a dark and shadowy
image. It will have oxidised
in places and become
non-reflective. Resist the
temptation to restore.*

Victorian Overmantle Mirror ▼

- *circa 1880*
A Victorian gilt composition
overmantle mirror with old glass,
rounded corners, surmounted by
ornate scrolled element.
- *137cm x 122cm*
- **Guide price $4,680**

George III Bird and Leaf Mirror ▼

- *circa 1760*
An early George III mahogany
framed mirror crested with a
gilded ho-ho bird and scrolling
leaf work, attractive carved leaf
drops to either side with gilded
slip holding the original plate.
- *1.18m x 52cm*
- **Guide price $13,530**

Victorian Overmantle Mirror ▼

- *circa 1880*
A Victorian gilt composition
overmantle mirror, with central
gilt scallop shell and foliate
scrolled elements and ornate
gilded columns to the sides.
- *1.27m x 1.63m*
- **Guide price $9,670**

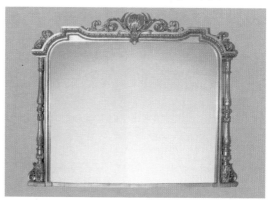

Landscape Wall Mirror ▶
- *circa 1870*
Victorian gilt composition
landscape wall mirror with
original gilding and glass.
- *1.2m x 1.45m*
- Guide price **$11,750**

Glass and Ormolu Wall Bracket ▲
- *circa 1850*
One of a pair of mirrored glass
and ormolu wall brackets with
double candle sconce with ornate
blue and gold scrolled designs.
- *52cm x 23cm*
- Guide price **$6,680**

Victorian Overmantle Mirror ▼
- *circa 1880*
A Victorian gilt composition
overmantle mirror with old glass,
rounded top with carved
pediment, turned and decorated
columns to the sides with vase
finials.
- *1.63m x 1.53m*
- Guide price **$9,080**

"Old French" Giltwood Overmantle Mirror ▲
- *circa 1830*
A carved giltwood overmantle
mirror in the "Old French" or
neo-Rococo style with bold
scrolled acanthus leaf decoration
and reeded columns.
- *2.03m x 1.53m*
- Guide price **$24,030**

Victorial Oval Gilt Mirror ▲
- *circa 1880*
A Victorian gilt composition
overmantle mirror with old glass.
Oval design with beaded edge,
surmounted by ornate scrollwork.
and crest carving.
- *1.24m x 1.12m*
- Guide price **$4,810**

Oval Girandole Mirror ▼
- *circa 1880*
A Victorian gilt composition oval
girandole mirror with a later
glass.
- *1.37m x 71cm*
- Guide price **$6,050**

Miscellaneous

Library Steps ▼
- **1770**
French library steps made from walnut consisting of four steps, with turned and carved decoration.
- **99cm**
- **Guide price $8,630**

Tôle Plant Holder ▲
- **1850**
One of a pair of painted English tôle plant holders decorated with hand painted chrysanthemums and peonies. With pierced gilt foliate rail around the top, flanked by brass lion handles.
- **height 34.5cm**
- **Guide price $2,230**

Chinese Pot Stand ▼
- **18th century**
One of a pair of simple boldly executed pot stands of country craftsman construction, from Southern China.
- **81cm x 50cm**
- **Guide price $5,250**

Music Stand ▼
- **circa 1825**
Regency rosewood music stand with lyre shaped design. The reeded column with turned and gadrooned decoration raised on a tripod base with bun feet.
- **height 1.08m**
- **Guide price $6,410**

Towel Rail ◄
- **circa 1870**
Victorian satin birchwood towel rail with carved and turned decoration.
- **height 90cm**
- **Guide price $390**

Victorian Washstand ▼
- **circa 1870**
Victorian burr-walnut washstand with a grey and white marble top above three drawers and a moulded cupboard, standing on a straight moulded base.
- **85cm x 1.24m**
- **Guide price $1,510**

Knife Cleaner ▲
- **circa 1900**
Circular pine knife sharpener, with the maker's name "Kent's", on cast iron frame support, with a wood and metal handle.
- **1.2m x 75cm**
- **Guide price $850**

Birdcage ▲
- *circa 1850s*
Mid 19th century French birdcage, modelled on Notre Dame cathedral.
- *2.1m x 1.1m*
- **Guide price $12,370**

Cast Iron Trivet ▲
- *circa 1830s*
Early Victorian cast iron trivet with a scrolled design within a lattice border.
- *26cm x 42cm*
- **Guide price $530**

French Plant Holder ▲
- *1880*
Dark green French circular tôle plant holder, standing on gilt paw feet with a laurel wreath design around the lip, and a cartouche of a hand-painted classical scene.
- *height 49cm*
- **Guide price $880**

Georgian Tray ▼
- *circa 1820*
Georgian oval tray, with fruitwood inlay around the rim, brass handles and a central shell design.
- *length 54cm*
- **Guide price $490**

Mahogany Piano Stool ▼
- *circa 1880s*
An ornate Victorian mahogany piano stool with a music compartment under seat with turned and scrolled decoration.
- *56cm x 51cm*
- **Guide price $980**

Luggage Rack ▼
- *circa 1870*
Yew-wood luggage rack, standing on four tapered square legs with shaped apron.
- *45cm x 72cm*
- **Guide price $2,230**

Rosewood Music Stand ▲
- *circa 1820s*
Early 19th century rosewood music stand with candle holders, supported by a turned column on a tripod base with scrolled feet.
- *height 1.5m*
- **Guide price $3,920**

Torchère Stand ▲
- *circa 1890*
A Regency style torchère stand decorated with three female busts, with stylized acanthus leaf designs, surmounted by a black marble top on a tripod base standing with gilt paw feet.
- *height 1.14m*
- **Guide price $800**

Mahogany Gallery Tray ▶

- *circa 1890*
Edwardian mahogany tray with a
fretted gallery surround
incorporating handles.
- *58cm x 41cm*
- **Guide price $850**

Regency Tôle Tray ▲

- *19th century*
Regency tôle tray featuring ducks
bathing. The back is also
decorated in a primitive style
simulating wood.
- *82cm x 59cm*
- **Guide price $5,700**

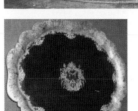

Gilded Tray ▼

- *1865*
Large English papier mâché tray,
gilded with mother-of-pearl inlay.
- *78.8cm x 59.7cm*
- **Guide price $3,320**

Papier Mâché Tray ◀

- *circa 1850*
Shaped Victorian papier mâché
tray, with scalloped decoration.
- *80cm x 67cm*
- **Guide price $1,200**

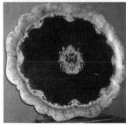

Ironstone Footbath ▲

- *circa 1830*
Ironstone footbath by Hicks
Meigh & Johnson in good
condition.
- *20cm x 32cm x 52cm*
- **Guide price $5,700**

Yew Library Step ▼

- *20th century*
A hand-made solid yew library
step with brass fittings.
- *88.9cm x 38.1cm*
- **Guide price $1,460**

Goats Beneath Trees
Centrepiece ▲

- *circa 1890*
Centrepiece of carved wood
centrepiece of goats beneath an
oak tree with original glassliner.
- *height 37cm*
- **Guide price $6,530**

Mahogany Corner Bar ◀

- *Early 20th century*
Elaborately carved panelled and
canopied corner bar, with
medallion decoration and scrolled
moulding below a moulded
cornice.
- *width 1.52m*
- **Guide price $8,460**

Oak Canopy Bar ▶

- *Early 20th century*
Oak canopy bar with carved panels and galleried and turned designs and etched mirrors. The moulded cornice with leaded glass decorative panels.
- *width 1.22m*
- **Guide price $8,010**

Plate Bucket ▲

- *circa 1780*
A fine 18th century mahogany plate bucket with brass banding and handle.
- *38.1cm x 35.5cm*
- **Guide price $3,470**

Mahogany Library Steps ▲

- *circa 1825*
A set of early 19th century mahogany library steps.
- *77.5cm x 56cm x 40.6cm*
- **Guide price $4,000**

Iron Bound Chest ▼

- *circa 1860*
Nineteenth century Indian teak iron bound chest with brass studs and iron carrying handles.
- *54cm x 62cm x 89cm*
- **Guide price $1,690**

George III Linen Press ▶

- *circa 1800*
A George III mahogany and inlaid linen press in the manner of Gillows of Lancaster still retaining its original brass "bail handles".
- *2.13m x 1.32m*
- **Guide price $18,690**

Papier Mâché Tray ◀

- *circa 1850*
Mid 19th century papier mâché tray on a later stand.
- *71cm x 42cm x 73cm*
- **Guide price $4,000**

Oak Canted Corner Bar ▼

- *Early 20th century*
Highly decorated oak canted corner bar; a hybrid of architectural elements, panelled with scrolled and turned columns and mirrored rear.
- *height 2.2m*
- **Guide price $9,350**

Paris Porcelain and Tulipwood Armoire ◀

- *circa 1850*
Ormolu-mounted parcel armoire surmounted by four finial urns. The breakfront pediment has panels depicting playing putti and the front is centred by a bevelled mirrored cupboard door.
- *2.51m x 63cm x 2.31m*
- **Guide price $409,400**

Expert Tips

Wherever possible, check the thickness of veneer. Eighteenth and early nineteenth century veneers were cut by hand, so anything thinner than 1/16th of an inch thick is later than that.

Screens

Sparrow and Bamboo Screen ▶

- *Edo period 18th–19th century*
A six-fold Japanese paper screen painted in ink and colour on a gold ground with sparrows amongst bamboo. Kano School.
- *94.5cm x 2.9m*
- Guide price $17,440

Waterfall Screen ▲

- *20th century*
A two-fold Japan paper screen painted in ink on a gold ground with a taki (waterfall), signed by Kunsai.
- *1.67m x 1.68m*
- Guide price $17,440

Clothes Rack Screen ▶

- *Meiji Period 19th century*
A four-fold paper screen painted in ink and colour on a gold ground with kimono and obi folded and hanging from the rails of two lacquer clothes racks.
- *54cm x 1.72m*
- Guide price $15,130

Bijin and Sakura Screen ▼

- *Taisho period 20th century*
A two-fold silk screen painted in ink and colour on a buff ground with two young bijin (beauties) beside a palanquin and beneath a flowering sakura (cherry tree). One is making a garland from the fallen blossoms she is collecting whilst the other looks on.
- *1.72m x 1.73m*
- Guide price $14,240

Birds and Cherry Tree Screen ▲

- *Edo period 18th century*
A two-fold paper screen painted in ink and colour on a buff and gold ground with two birds in flight and a hato (dove) perched in a cherry tree in full bloom above a turbulent river.
- *1.59m x 1.89m*
- Guide price $30,080

Weeping Cherry Screen ◀

- *Edo period 17th/18th century*
A paper furosaki screen painted in ink and colour on a gold ground with birds, a snow covered shidare-zakura (weeping cherry) and daffodils in a river landscape in early spring.
- *67cm x 1.58m*
- Guide price $9,790

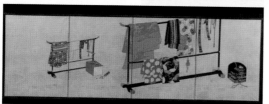

Victorian Screen ◀

- **1870**

A good size painted leather four
fold screen in the 18th century
style, painted with floral
arrangements.
- *1.6m x 1.53m*
- **Guide price $7,480**

Chinese Fire Screen ▲

- *circa 1860*

Chinese fire screen embroidered
with peonies, chrysanthemums,
butterflies and birds, in silk with
gold threads. Supported by a
mahogany stand.
- *78cm x 62cm*
- **Guide price $690**

Victorian Beadwork Screen ▼

- *circa 1840*

One of a pair of excellent
Victorian pole screens in walnut
carved frames containing fine
examples of beadwork of the
period.
- *height 1.4m*
- **Guide price $8,010**

Soolmaker Screen ▲

- **1690**

Dutch six-fold screen by
Soolmaker, with a painted
romantic landscape of an
impression of Italy.
- *1.26m x 2.44m*
- **Guide price $6,760**

Expert Tips

*Original needlepoint or tapestry
must be in good condition and
there should not be any wear or
tears on the picture.*

Regency Rosewood Screen ▲

- *circa 1820*

Regency rosewood pole screen
with floral tapestry panel, on a
turned pedestal and tri-partite
platform base.
- *height 1.43m*
- **Guide price $970**

Settees & Sofas

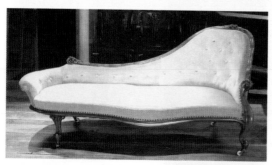

Rosewood Chaise Longue ◄

- *circa 1860*
Mid Victorian rosewood chaise longue, with finely carved rose decoration, scrolled arms, moulded serpentine apron and original porcelain castors.
- *length 1.86m*
- **Guide price $4,980**

Victorian Chaise Longue ▶

- *circa 1860*
Victorian mahogany chaise longue with curved button back and scrolled arm, standing on turned legs with original brass castors.
- *length 1.5m*
- **Guide price $2,450**

Victorian Chaise Longue ▲

- *circa 1870*
Recently upholstered chaise longue dating from the Victorian period. Presented with original marble castors and brass fittings.
- *length 2.13m*
- **Guide price $3,380**

Louis XVI Chaise Longue ▲

- *circa 1890*
Double-ended chaise longue in Louis XVI-style.
- *length 1.7m*
- **Guide price $4,810**

Mahogany Chaise Longue ▲

- *circa 1840*
Victorian mahogany chaise longue with feather padded button back, gold damask upholstery and carved, turned decoration.
- *length 1.89m*
- **Guide price $2,940**

French Chaise Longue ▶

- *circa 1900*
Mahogany walnut Louis XVI-style meridienne.
- *length 84cm*
- **Guide price $2,940**

Double Scroll End Sofa ▶

- *circa 1810*

Regency period rosewood and cut brass inlaid double scroll end sofa, the shaped back inlaid with cut brass quatrefoils and large brass paterae. The frame profusely decorated with foliate brass inlay.
- *85cm x 62cm x 2.03m*
- **Guide price $28,030**

George II Settee ◀

- *circa 1750*

A George II settee of delightfully small proportions, with acanthus and scroll front legs in walnut, the whole on an oak, ash and beech frame. A photograph of the frame is available.
- *94cm x 67.5cm x 1.3m*
- **Guide price $28,920**

Regency Style Canapé ▲

- *circa 1850*

A French canapé surmounted by a carved cresting and flanked to the sides by foliage and mythological beasts, above an arched-shaped padded back. The seat is flanked by arm-rests supported by sphinxes.
- *width 2.7m*
- **Guide price $24,920**

Victorian Sofa ◀

- *19th century*

A fine Victorian sofa with walnut frame, restored and upholstered to the highest quality.
- *length 1.4m*
- **Guide price $6,850**

Walnut Framed Settee ▲

- *circa 1900*

A late Victorian walnut-framed two-seater settee, finely carved with leaf scrolls and flowers, on four cabriole supports, in the French taste.
- *76cm x 68.5cm x 1.23m*
- **Guide price $5,790**

George I Sofa ▲

- *circa 1720*

A George I arched-back sofa with scrolled arms and serpentine front raised on walnut cabriole legs with pad feet to the front and swept walnut legs to the rear, upholstered in 19th century tapestry fabric.
- *91.5cm x 78.5cm x 1.59m*
- **Guide price $40,050**

Expert Tips

Original framework, which should usually be of beech, will show signs of old tack holes.

Carved and Giltwood Chaise Longue ◀

- *circa 1880*

Chaise longue attributed to Fourdinois with floral and ribbon-carved frame, scrolled back, and acanthus-clasped armrest supported by winged putti. The padded back, cushions are covered in floral damask.
- *1.04m x 79cm x 1.83m*
- **Guide price $32,040**

Mahogany Framed Sofa ▲
- *circa 1820*
A Regency period mahogany framed sofa. The scroll ends with fine carved reeded decoration and the two scrolling arms are supported by a swept back with central gadroon carved cresting and brass inlay.
- *91.4cm x 65cm x 2.03m*
- **Guide price $15,670**

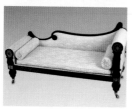

Regency Rosewood and Beechwood Sofa ▲
- *circa 1815*
An English Regency sofa beautifully worked with cut brass inlays and carved decoration, of classical inspiration, very much influenced by the designs of Thomas Hope.
- *width 1.78m*
- **Guide price $17,530**

Lion's Head Settee ▲
- *circa 1880*
English sofa with waisted back and seat set in matching narrow moulded frames with carved lion mask headed cabriole legs terminating in hairy paw feet. The open arms are terminated in eagles' heads.
- *1.07m x 66cm x 1.53m*
- **Guide price $16,910**

Pair of Window Seats ▲
- *circa 1880*
Pair of 19th century decorated window seats with scrolled arms and gilded decoration.
- *70cm x 53.3cm x 1.05m*
- **Guide price $12,190**

Banquette de Croisée ▲
- *circa 1880*
A fine carved gilt wood Louis XV-style banquette de croisée, with armrests and serpentine frieze, decorated with acanthus leaf and flowers.
- *54cm x 49cm x 1.1m*
- **Guide price $9,970**

Scroll End Couch ▲
- *circa 1830*
A fine late Regency mahogany double scroll end couch, with finely carved decorative back.
- *99cm x 61cm x 2.01m*
- **Guide price $9,350**

George IV Window Seat ▼
- *circa 1825*
Window seat in the form of a chaise longue with scroll ends and seat rail decorated with carved acanthus and lotus leaf. The turned, fluted and tapered legs headed with carved anthemion patera.
- *79cm x 79cm x 1.53m*
- **Guide price $29,370**

High Back Settee ▼

- *circa 1880*

A late Victorian mahogany high back settee with scrolled high arched and sides, standing on cabriole legs.

- *1.07m x 88cm*
- **Guide price $5,700**

French Sofa ▲

- *circa 18th century*

French sofa with a high back and curved sides, standing on turned Doric legs on ball feet, with a straight stretcher.

- *height 1.18m*
- **Guide price $15,660**

Gustavian-style Sofa ▲

- *circa 1899*

Swedish Louis XVI and Gustavian-style birchwood sofa, open in form and upholstered in calico with noticeable carved and scrolled armrests and moulded back, the whole resting on carved scrolled feet.

- *1.35m x 1.58m*
- **Guide price $6,050**

High Back Oak Settee ▼

- *circa 1840*

Oak high back four-panelled settee with moulded arms and padded seat, standing on cabriole legs with pad feet.

- *82cm x 1.89m*
- **Guide price $3,340**

Biedermeier Sofa ▲

- *circa 1820*

Biedermeier birchwood sofa with serpentine back and front and carved decoration to the apron, on turned and fluted legs.

- *95cm x 1.99m*
- **Guide price $9,970**

Expert Tips

Always check that the legs are in good condition, especially on a Victorian chaise longue or day bed, where the delicate sabre legs are often broken through heavy wear and tear. Check that the back is secured firmly to the base as often these have been broken and not restored correctly.

High Button-Back Sofa ▲
- *circa 1860*
Victorian rosewood button-back sofa with moulded top rail, sides and arms and four cabriole legs, splayed legs to the rear.
- *length 1.56m*
- **Guide price $4,270**

Regency Sofa ▲
- *circa 1810*
Regency beech wood faux rosewood sofa with double scroll arms and a carved moulded back with scrolling, inlaid with brass decoration.
- *93cm x 1.95m*
- **Guide price $9,350**

Walnut Sofa ▶
- *circa 1890s*
Small late Victorian sofa with arched padded button back and carved walnut frame with small scrolled arms, the whole on slender turned legs.
- *94cm x 1.33m*
- **Guide price $2,140**

Chesterfield Sofa ▼
- *circa 1860*
Victorian Chesterfield sofa upholstered in Venetian damask, with padded moulded back and seat, standing on turned legs.
- *length 1.97m*
- **Guide price $3,470**

French Louis XVIII Sofa ▲
- *circa 1780*
French Louis XVIII sofa with painted and moulded carved wooden frame, curved back and a padded seat and small padded arm rests, by D. Julienne.
- *82cm x 1.91m*
- **Guide price $11,040**

Italian Hallbench ▶
- *circa 1790*
Italian pine hallbench with a straight back swept arms, heavily carved apron and short cabriole legs.
- *82cm x 1.93m*
- **Guide price $8,370**

Stools

Regency X-Frame Stool ▶
- *circa 1820*
Regency mahogany X-frame stool with wooden saddle seat.
- *48cm x 33cm x 51cm*
- **Guide price $3,200**

Victorian Footstools ▲
- *circa 1880*
Pair of Victorian mahogany footstools with rose fabric.
- *15.2cm x 25.4cm x 33cm*
- **Guide price $1,240**

Mahogany Footstool ▲
- *circa 1825*
Early 19th century mahogany foot stool on turned and carved splayed legs.
- *54.6cm x 47cm x 48.3cm*
- **Guide price $1,160**

Expert Tips

Victorians tended to polish mahogany to a red colour, but the natural, rich golden colour is preferred today and is therefore more valuable. It was first imported into England from America in c.1730, quality varies considerably.

Anglo-Indian Stool ▼
- *circa 1850*
Mid 19th century stool with carved and pierced stretcher.
- *45cm x 42.5cm x 80cm*
- **Guide price $2,580**

Oval Footstool ▶
- *circa 1725*
Early 18th century walnut veneered oval footstool featuring three figures on the olive upholstery.
- *45.7cm x 45.7cm x 61cm*
- **Guide price $12,190**

Floral Footstools ▼
- *circa 1880*
Pair of Victorian walnut footstools, recovered with embroidered floral pattern.
- *15.2cm x 30.5cm x 38.1cm*
- **Guide price $1,510**

William IV Ottoman ◀
- *circa 1835*
William IV rosewood upholstered ottoman of waisted form, with hinged lid.
- *47cm x 49.5cm x 49.5cm*
- **Guide price $2,230**

Louis XVI Footstool ▼

- *circa 1780*
Louis XVI giltwood footstool
with carved acanthus moulding
and foliate legs.
- *height 14cm*
- **Guide price $5,160**

Walnut Footstool ▼

- *circa 1880*
Small walnut footstool with
circular re-upholstered padded top
standing on small cabriole legs.
- *width 36cm*
- **Guide price $520**

Rustic Stool ▼

- *circa 1840*
Rustic oak child's stool standing
on four turned legs.
- *20cm x 31cm*
- **Guide price $150**

Tapestry Stool ▶

- *1880*
Fine walnut tapestry Queen
Anne-style stool raised on
cabriole legs carved with
acanthus leaf designs, with claw
and ball feet.
- *48cm x 51cm*
- **Guide price $6,230**

Birchwood Stool ▲

- *1820–1830*
One of a pair of Swedish
Biedermeier birchwood stools
raised on splayed legs.
- *39cm x 35cm*
- **Guide price $6,050**

Mahogany Stool ◀

- *circa 1880*
Mahogany oblong country oak
stool standing on square straight
legs, with scrolls at each corner.
- *56cm x 34cm*
- **Guide price $880**

George I Walnut Stool ◄
- *circa 1720*
George I walnut stool with cabriole legs, carved at each knee with a carved shell.
- *height 54cm*
- **Guide price $40,050**

Mahogany Stool ►
- *circa 1890*
Miniature mahogany stool fashioned as a small table.
- *22cm x 33cm*
- **Guide price $160**

Piano Stool ▲
- *circa 1880*
Walnut revolving piano stool with circular padded seat on cabriole legs with claw feet.
- *height 49cm*
- **Guide price $890**

Piano Stool ▲
- *circa 1830s*
William IV piano stool on adjustable reeded and carved column, on a platform base with scroll end feet and original tapestry seat.
- *height 54cm*
- **Guide price $880**

Ebonised Stool ◄
- *circa 1860*
Ebonised stool with a rush seat, with faux bamboo designs and gilding with curved rails connected by gilded balls.
- *42cm x 40cm*
- **Guide price $390**

Gustavian Bench ▲
- *circa 1800*
Louis XVI Swedish Gustavian pine bench seat painted white with carved arms, raised on turned feet.
- *37cm x 1.09m*
- **Guide price $5,160**

Beechwood Piano Stool ▶

- *circa 1825*

Regency period beechwood revolving piano stool with circular leather padded seat and pierced leaf carved back splat.
- *56cm x 35.5cm*
- **Guide price $5,250**

Carved Walnut Stool ▲

- *circa 1900*

Early 20th century stool on "H" frame stretcher with central finial and carved, turned legs; new upholstery.
- *52cm x 36.8cm x 89cm*
- **Guide price $1,060**

William and Mary Long Stool ▲

- *circa 1920*

A William and Mary style upholstered long stool with early 18th century tapestry covering. On turned legs with pad feet, joined by shaped moulded stretchers with three turned finials.
- *17cm x 18cm x 60cm*
- **Guide price $8,190**

Chippendale Footstool ▼

- *circa 1760*

Chippendale period mahogany footstool with English needlework of the George II period embroidered on canvas with silks and wools.
- *45.7cm x 43cm x 53cm*
- **Guide price $15,750**

Piano Stool in Walnut ▼

- *circa 1900*

Early 19th century walnut piano stool with cabriole legs and carved floral motifs.
- *53.3cm x 40.6cm*
- **Guide price $700**

Saddle Stool ◀

- *circa 1890*

Simple country stool with square legs and well-worn patina.
- *53.3cm x 30.5cm x 45.7cm*
- **Guide price $420**

Expert Tips

Rosewood, predominantly used during the Regency period, can be identified by its black streaks.

Mahogany Stool ◀

- *circa 1850*

Mid 19th century mahogany stool with cabriole legs standing on whirl feet.
- *50.8cm x 53.3cm x 90cm*
- **Guide price $4,580**

Hessian Ottoman ▶

- *circa 1910*
Ottoman covered in cross-stitch hessian with red and blue floral patterns.
- *61cm x 53.3cm x 98cm*
- **Guide price $610**

Rosewood George IV "X" Frame Stool ▲

- *circa 1825*
A rosewood "X" frame stool with acanthus leaf carving, upholstered in leather and terminating on hairy paw feet.
- *36cm x 44cm x 50cm*
- **Guide price $10,320**

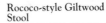

Serpentine Giltwood Single Stool ◀

- *circa 1880*
Stool of serpentine form with cabriole legs crested with satyr's mask ending in scroll feet joined by an scrolling X stretcher. The seat rail is pierced with shells and acanthus foliage.
- *41cm x 43cm x 61cm*
- **Guide price $5,070**

Rococo-style Giltwood Stool ◀

- *circa 1880*
Ornate stool with cabriole legs crested with satyr masks and joined by waved stretchers, ending in scroll feet. The double serpentine seatrail, centred with pierced shells, is surrounded by acanthus foliage.
- *41cm x 41cm x 1.07m*
- **Guide price $9,790**

Pair of Ningbo Stools ▲

- *Late 19th century*
A pair of waisted stools in traditional Ningbo style, using an elm frame with huali (rosewood) floating seat panel and waist. Simple hump back stretchers join legs ending in hoof feet.
- *45cm x 30cm x 55cm*
- **Guide price $450**

Meditation Stool ▲

- *Mid 19th century*
Large fruitwood stool with recessed waist above a simply carved apron with double-mitred braces. Legs end in hoof feet.
- *52cm x 45cm x 90cm*
- **Guide price $570**

Pair of Square Stools ◀

- *Mid 19th century*
A pair of square elm stools with decorative bracing and hump back stretchers above straight base stretchers. Legs end in hoof feet.
- *40cm x 40cm x 40cm*
- **Guide price $490**

Tables

Pier Table ▶

- *circa 1790*

One of a pair of giltwood side table of fluted legs with carved wood frieze of anthemion decoration. The tops are veneered in the finest West Indian satinwood, cross-banded in kingwood with boxwood lines.

- *89cm x 44cm x 1.45m*
- **Guide price $213,600**

Rosewood Sewing Table ▶

- *circa 1840*

Fine rosewood sewing table with drawer, standing on claw feet.

- *76.2cm x 46cm x 61cm*
- **Guide price $6,230**

Irish Mahogany Pie Crust Table ▲

- *circa 1780*

Pie crust table with shaped and moulded two-plank top on a fluted column meeting a tripod base with ball and claw feet.

- *73.7cm x 1.07m*
- **Guide price $29,370**

George III Red Walnut Dish Top Tripod Table ◀

- *circa 1770*

Walnut table with one piece tilt top raised on a ring turned barrel column with a shallow vase design, supported by three tripod legs of traditional design.

- *71cm x 68.5cm*
- **Guide price $4,450**

Rosewood Sutherland Table ▼

- *circa 1850*

Rosewood table with two hinged serpentine leaves, each supported on a single strut, which swing out on a wooden knuckle hinge.

- *73cm x 16.5cm x 1.07m*
- **Guide price $2,670**

Regency Mahogany Coaching Table ▼

- *circa 1820*

English coaching table with a solid mahogany rectangular folding top raised on four shaped legs united at the middle and base by three turned stretchers.

- *73cm x 44cm x 89cm*
- **Guide price $2,670**

Russian Centre Table ▲

- *circa 1790*

A fine Russian oval centre table, the cobalt blue glass top surmounted by a three quarter brass gallery above a brass reeded edge. The frieze fitted with a drawer and decorated with fluted panels alternating with brass-edged square panels and lozenges on fluted turned tapering legs with beaded collars and sabots.
- *81cm x 93cm*
- **Guide price $50,730**

Victorian Occasional Table ▲

- *circa 1860s*

A Victorian rosewood and marquetry inlaid occasional table.
- *64cm x 50cm*
- **Guide price $780**

William IV Table ▼

- *circa 1830s*

William IV mahogany table with brass drop handles and single drawer, raised on turned, tapering, candy twist legs.
- *76cm x 56cm*
- **Guide price $1,340**

Louis XVI Night Table ▼

- *circa 1790*

Louis XVI night table with a pierced brass rail and three small drawers in purple heart and satinwood banding.
- *height 86cm*
- **Guide price $7,570**

Light Oak Side Table ◀

- *circa 1870*

Victorian light oak side table with moulded back and scrolled designs, with side drawers, standing on turned tapering legs.
- *height 1.1m*
- **Guide price $1,690**

Tilt Top Table ▲

- *circa 1890*

Mahogany tilt top table with turned support raised on a tripod base with splayed legs.
- *height 83cm*
- **Guide price $530**

Regency Pembroke Table ▲

- *circa 1810*

Fine quality Regency period mahogany and ebony inlaid Pembroke table. Standing on a twin double "C"- scrolled supports joining out swept legs, with brass caps and castors.
- *73cm x 104cm x 51cm*
- **Guide price $19,490**

Mahogany Writing Table ▲

- *circa 1870s*

Nineteenth century mahogany writing table with tooled leather writing surface and reeded, turned and tapered legs.
- *75cm x 1.1m*
- **Guide price $2,980**

Mahogany Console Table ▼

- *circa 1810*

A console table with a rectangular top with an ebonised moulded edge over a frieze inlaid with repeated brass sunburst motifs on an ebonised background, raised on a pair of columns joined to the panelled back with an arcaded profile. The whole raised on a concave plinth base leading to gilt paw feet, the front two facing forward, the back two to the side.

- *89cm x 95cm*
- **Guide price $17,440**

George III Table ▼

- *circa 1800*

George III small mahogany birdcage table, with well-shaped baluster tripod support on splayed legs.

- *height 79cm*
- **Guide price $4,450**

Victorian Table ▶

- *circa 1870*

Victorian walnut and marquetry table on a pedestal base with carved gadrooned decoration and carved splat legs, by Taylor & Son, Dover St, London.

- *height 1.37m*
- **Guide price $17,440**

Peachwood Centre Table ▲

- *circa 1820*

A rare peachwood centre table with turned legs and bamboo skirting.

- *81cm x 1.75m*
- **Guide price $14,600**

Oval Table ▲

- *circa 1800s*

Small oval table with a George III tray with a scalloped edge on four splayed legs joined by a "X" frame stretcher.

- *height 56cm*
- **Guide price $1,240**

Rosewood Table ▲

- *circa 1835*

William IV rosewood sewing/games table with trestle supports and bun feet.

- *73cm x 61cm*
- **Guide price $4,630**

Victorian Dressing Table ▲

- *circa 1885*

Victorian mahogany dressing table with an oval mirror with heavily carved decoration, above six fitted drawers and turned front legs on bun feet.

- *height 1.3m*
- **Guide price $8,010**

Victorian Games Table ▲

- *circa 1850*

Victorian mahogany inlaid walnut games table with inlaid chessboard and heavily turned column, standing on a tripod base with carved legs.

- *height 82cm*
- **Guide price $1,560**

Expert Tips

During the mid-eighteenth century the tea gardens around London were regarded as vulgar, and it therefore became fashionable to invite friends to drink tea at home. Cabinet makers turned their attention to designing suitable ornamental tables for the occasion.

Victorian Washstand ▼

- *circa 1840*

Victorian mahogany washstand
with two drawers with turned
handles and side table, in
excellent original condition.
- *width 98cm*
- **Guide price $1,060**

Side Table ▼

- *circa 1880*

Mahogany table with moulded
serpentine top supported by two
turned columns, joined by a
turned stretcher above heavily
carved legs with leaf designs.
- *height 89cm*
- **Guide price $1,240**

Mahogany Serving Table ▶

- *circa 1795*

English serving table,of
breakfront "D"-shaped form,
surmounted by the original brass
gallery, the frieze fitted with a
long oak lined drawer, with a
finely flamed mahogany front.
The rounded corner panels and
side panels of the frieze finished
in a similar manner each panel
flanked by finely carved urns
heading the six elegant fluted
tapering legs.
- *82cm x 2.9m*
- **Guide price $49,840**

Sewing Table ▲

- *1870*

Victorian rosewood sewing table
with single drawer standing on a
pedestal base with turned feet.
- *88cm x 84cm*
- **Guide price $3,550**

Mahogany Jardinière ▲

- *1830*

Rare William IV mahogany
occasional table stamped
Freemans on a carved and turned
column raised on a tripod base,
resting on bun feet.
- *76cm x 44cm*
- **Guide price $8,010**

Victorian Tilt Top Table ▼

- *circa 1880*

Victorian mahogany tilt top table
with turned baluster pedestal
base, raised on splayed legs.
- *height 74cm*
- **Guide price $1,030**

Mahogany Side Table ▼

- *circa 1830*

Mahogany side table with square
top single long drawer with brass
handle, standing on four straight
square legs.
- *height 82cm*
- **Guide price $850**

Console Table

- *circa 1825*

One of a pair of George IV mirror backed console tables in rosewood. The marble tops above a rococo carved frieze supported by carved and giltwood acanthus decorated "S" scroll uprights.

- *96cm x 75cm x 36cm*
- **Guide price $33,380**

Cricket Table

- *1790*

Oak cricket table with circular top standing on three splayed legs, joined by a square, panelled sretcher.

- *59cm x 66cm*
- **Guide price $2,270**

Games Table

- *circa 1860*

Victorian mahogany games table with inlaid chess board on a circular top, pedestal column and three splat legs.

- *height 75cm*
- **Guide price $2,140**

Burr Walnut Table

- *circa 1880*

Victorian burr walnut table with a circular top inlaid with boxwood foliate design and carved leaves around the rim, with a turned pedestal standing on a tripod base.

- *height 69cm*
- **Guide price $1,560**

Empire Writing Table

- *1810–1820*

Swedish mahogany Empire writing/console table. The top with fitted drawers and gallery, above a central drawer, raised on four turned columns, with a solid stretcher base.

- *72cm x 74cm*
- **Guide price $6,590**

Console Table

- *circa 1870*

Empire style console figured maple wood table with a pink marble top, central winged brass motif, on a single drawer flanked by ebonised pillars with oriental busts.

- *91cm x 92cm*
- **Guide price $4,270**

Inlaid Mahogany Card Table

- *circa 1900*
Fine inlaid mahogany card table on tapered legs with brass castors.
- *76.2cm x 43cm x 48cm*
- **Guide price $7,030**

Sheraton Lady's Writing Table

- *circa 1795*
Sheraton rosewood lady's writing or work table with rising screen with fine boxwood and satinwood line inlays, the top banded in purpleheart, with pen and ink drawer to the side of the writing drawer.
- *76cm x 47cm x 56cm*
- **Guide price $10,410**

George III Reading Table ◀

- *circa 1770*
A mahogany table, the top fitted with a removable bookrest, rising on a ratcheted adjustable stand, above a line inlaid frieze with a drawer at each end, all raised on a turned column with spiral knop.
- *77.5cm x 47cm x 63cm*
- **Guide price $10,500**

Nested Occasional Tables ◀

- *circa 1890*
A nest of three burr walnut and crossbanded occasional tables with ring turned spindle supports.
- *68.5cm x 27.5cm x 53.5cm*
- **Guide price $4,360**

Walnut Side Table ▼

- *circa 1920*
Walnut drop-leaf side table with drawer on barley twist legs and curved cross stretcher.
- *68.6cm x 35.5cm x 96.5cm*
- **Guide price $3,120**

George IV Console Table ▼

- *circa 1825*
George IV console table, the Verdie Alpie marble top above carved and gilded lions paw and acanthus front supports. The frieze, panelled inset back, and concave fronted plinth all veneered in rosewood.
- *91.5cm x 56cm x 99cm*
- **Guide price $12,820**

Expert Tips

Elegant and plain George II card tables were often "improved" in the early 1900s to enhance their value. Look for carving at the knees and shells and scrolls at the feet.

Walnut Sofa Table ◀

- *circa 1930*
Walnut sofa table with two side extensions, standing on a turned stretcher, drawers and feet with brass fittings.
- *71cm x 56cm x 73.7cm*
- **Guide price $4,900**

Mahogany Night Table ▲
- *1800*

Dutch mahogany night table with tambour front, and small brass round handles and brass handles each side.
- *66cm x 47cm*
- **Guide price $1,770**

Sutherland Table ▲
- *circa 1835*

Walnut Sutherland table with satinwood and boxwood inlay.
- *height 72cm*
- **Guide price $800**

Rosewood Occasional Table ▼

- *circa 1860s*

A good quality Victorian rosewood occasional table with a barley twist column.
- *73cm x 45cm*
- **Guide price $980**

Mahogany Tripod Table ▼
- *circa 1760*

Mahogany tilt-top, birdcage table with turned support raised on splayed legs.
- *height 69.5cm*
- **Guide price $8,540**

Burr-Walnut Card Table ▲
- *circa 1870*

Burr-walnut Victorian card table with marquetry inlay, serpentine basket base and scrolled legs with upturned finial.
- *height 87cm*
- **Guide price $6,680**

Oak Side Bookstand ▲
- *circa 1890s*

Late Victorian oak side table/bookstand with carved scrolled supports.
- *63cm x 57cm*
- **Guide price $1,200**

Irish Side Table ◄
- *circa 1890*

Irish mahogany side table with a gadrooned edge above a plain frieze, the decorative, shaped apron centred by a lion-head mask within a rope twist border, flanked by stylised birds with feathered wings and foliate decoration. Raised on cabriole legs with handsome ball and claw feet decorated at the knees with low relief carved decoration of stylised birds.
- *81cm x 1.58m*
- **Guide price $22,250**

George I Lowboy
- *circa 1720*
A walnut veneered lowboy with
quartered panels surrounded by
herringbone and cross-banded
inlay with a moulded edge. Below
is a single cross-banded drawer all
standing on cabriole legs.
- *71cm x 43cm x 76cm*
- **Guide price $8,540**

Walnut Lamp Table
- *circa 1900*
Square walnut two-tier table on
turned legs.
- *65cm x 42.5cm x 42.5cm*
- **Guide price $290**

Low Elm Table
- *circa 1860*
One of a pair of simple country
style two-tier tables with straight
legs and stretcher.
- *66cm x 28cm x 43.2cm*
- **Guide price $2,040**

Small Carved Table
- *circa 1910*
A pretty two-tier table with scroll
and lotus carved detail and
carved foliate edge.
- *68.6cm x 33cm x 33cm*
- **Guide price $290**

Rosewood and Brass Inlaid Work Table
- *circa 1820*
A continental work table having
a figured top with brass stringing
and a rosewood-lined drawer,
with a cupboard bag underneath.
The piece supported on lyre stiles
on trestle feet, joined by a turned
stretcher.
- *73.7cm x 40cm x 57.8cm*
- **Guide price $15,660**

Regency Pembroke Worktable
- *circa 1820*
A Pembroke worktable with twin
flaps and a single drawer below
with dummy drawer to the
reverse and gadrooned beading.
The workbag supported on
hooped supports, joined by a
turned stretcher.
- *71cm x 43.2cm x 86.4cm*
- **Guide price $12,100**

Tripod Table

- *circa 1860*
Circular table with figured mahogany top, pedestal column standing on three splayed legs.
- *65cm x 52.5cm*
- **Guide price $950**

Regency Table

- *circa 1820*
Adjustable Regency mahogany table, with a central tan hide top, standing on a tall central pedestal and a tripod base.
- *height 1.04m*
- **Guide price $2,480**

Oak Cricket Table

- *circa 1860*
Oak cricket table with circular top, single shelf, standing on three turned pillared legs.
- *70cm x 38cm*
- **Guide price $1,390**

Walnut Table

- *1880*
Small octagonal Victorian walnut table, on a heavily moulded cross-banded stretcher.
- *height 55cm*
- **Guide price $1,060**

Small Tripod Table

- *circa 1780*
Small rustic oak table with inlaid flower in the centre standing on a tripod base.
- *57cm x 40cm*
- **Guide price $700**

Table with Ormolu Mounts

- *1870*
Two tier mahogany table with inlaid shaped top, with ormolu pierced mounts and curved legs.
- *height 88cm*
- **Guide price $2,480**

Portuguese Rosewood Table

- *circa 1700*
A solid rosewood table, the top with a decorative bead moulded edge, the frieze with chevron pattern decoration, raised on spiral-twist legs with discs and bulbous turnings, with similar stretchers, joined at the corners with decorative pegs.
- *79cm x 1.12m*
- **Guide price $12,100**

Expert Tips

The foreruners of the tripod table were the small round topped tables designed to support a lantern or candlestick, which were popular during the second half of the seventeenth century. These tables were an English phenomenon. They were also popular in America, but not on the Continent.

George III Serpentine Lady's Dressing Table ◄

- *circa 1770*

An 18th century rosewood dressing table by John Cobb with a rectangular hinged divided top enclosing an interior with ratcheted sliding mirror, eight lidded compartments and two further compartments.

- *78cm x 54cm x 62cm*
- **Guide price $29,370**

Regency Mahogany Hunt/ Wine Table ▲

- *circa 1810*

Regency mahogany hunt/wine table, the semi-circular top with removable semi-circular inset above a plain frieze on ring turned legs with original brass caps and castors.

- *71cm x 63.5cm x 1.76m*
- **Guide price $12,900**

Calamander Sofa Table ▶

- *circa 1810*

A small calamander veneered sofa table, the top crossbanded with amboyna. Below is a decorative frieze containing two real and two dummy drawers with tulipwood bandings.

- *68.5cm x 61cm x 1.22m*
- **Guide price $40,940**

Japanned and Giltwood Work Table ▶

- *circa 1815*

Regency period japanned and giltwood work table with hinged table top on platform base with carved acanthus leaves on a four scroll legged pedestal.

- *1.03m x 61cm x 96.5cm*
- **Guide price $15,750**

Lacquer Tripod Table ◄

- *circa 1810*

Regency period lacquer tripod table with eight-sided table top on turned candy twist column and with gilt ball feet.

- *76.2cm x 30cm*
- **Guide price $3,120**

Colonial Sutherland Tables ◄

- *circa 1860*

A rare matched pair of Colonial oval Sutherland tables, the tops inlaid with radiating exotic specimen woods with a leaf carved moulded edge, the solid ebony base profusely carved with leaf and scrolls.

- *63cm x 15cm x 61cm*
- **Guide price $26,430**

New Jersey Lowboy ▶

- *circa 1735*
American walnut New Jersey
lowboy with paintbrush feet
topped by wristers mouldings.
- *74cm x 52cm x 86.4cm*
- **Guide price $104,150**

Mahogany Tea Table ◀

- *circa 1815*
Regency mahogany tea table on
turned supports raised on
outswept legs, with brass caps
and castors joined by a solid
inlaid stretcher.
- *47cm x 49cm x 99cm*
- **Guide price $7,030**

Mahogany Games Table ▼

- *circa 1760*
An 18th century mahogany
games table on cabriole legs with
claw feet.
- *71cm x 36.8cm x 66cm*
- **Guide price $7,030**

Penwork Decorated
Work Table ▶

- *circa 1820*
Regency penwork decorated work
table with drop leaf table
standing on trestle supports and
bun feet.
- *77.5cm x 38cm x 52cm*
- **Guide price $6,230**

Mahogany Urn Table ▲

- *circa 1785*
Late 18th century mahogany urn
table with pierced top rail on
square tapered and fluted legs.
- *77.5cm x 28cm x 28cm*
- **Guide price $5,250**

Triple Top Card Table ▶

- *circa 1750*
A George II period mahogany
triple top card table. The shaped
top lifts to reveal a tea table, a
card table, a back-gammon and
chessboard, which opens to
reveal a reading slope with a
compartment below.
- *75cm x 39.4cm x 81.3cm*
- **Guide price $16,910**

Sheraton Writing and Work Table ▼

- *circa 1790*
Sheraton rosewood writing and
work table with sliding pleated
silk needlework compartment,
single drawer with hinged,
leather-topped writing slide on
square tapered legs with original
brass castors.
- *78cm x 47.6cm x 56cm*
- **Guide price $8,460**

George III Centre Table ▶

- *circa 1780*
George III mahogany circular
centre table with good patina on
a turned pedestal with three
splayed legs on a tripod base with
brass caps and castors.
- *73.7cm x 1.13m*
- **Guide price $9,350**

Rosewood Veneered Writing Table ▶

- *circa 1815*
A rosewood veneered writing
table. The surface has green
tooled leather and rosewood
cross-banding. Below are two
drawers with two dummy drawers
to the reverse with original brass
pull handles.
- *71cm x 66cm x 1.17m*
- **Guide price $17,620**

Games and Tea Table ◀

- *circa 1750*
George II solid red walnut triple
top games and tea table.
- *76.2cm x 43.2cm x 83.8cm*
- **Guide price $10,240**

Regency Work and Writing Table ▲

- *circa 1820*
Regency rosewood work and
writing table with hinged writing
slide and inlaid and brass-banded
demi-lune side compartments,
scrolled feet with gilt ormolu
mounts and turned stretcher.
- *71cm x 42cm x 73cm*
- **Guide price $10,410**

Mahogany Kettle Stand with Gallery ▲

- *circa 1750*
Circular mahogany kettle stand
with gallery on a heavily turned
pedestal, standing on a splayed
tripod base.
- *58.4cm x 30.5cm*
- **Guide price $12,190**

Expert Tips

*A good eighteenth century
pedestal table always has a very
substantial support. If the legs
look delicate and short rather
than handsome, then they may
have been redrawn. This is a
difficult alteration to detect –
use your judgement.*

Walnut Writing Table ▶

- *circa 1910*

Writing table with leather inlay, two side drawers on carved cabriole legs.
- *76.2cm x 53.4cm x 89cm*
- **Guide price $1,010**

Three-drawer Side Table ▼

- *Late 18th century*

Mahogany bow fronted three-drawer side table, the drawers with their original brass handles; lovely colour and patination.
- *74cm x 48cm x 84cm*
- **Guide price $6,140**

Victorian Side Table ▼

- *circa 1860*

A Victorian gilt composition side table with original marble.
- *89cm x 58cm x 185cm*
- **Guide price $18,690**

Mahogany Wine Table ▼

- *circa 1840*

Mahogany circular table with good patina on turned pedestal and tripod base.
- *71cm x 39.4cm*
- **Guide price $790**

Regency Rosewood and Brass-inlaid Card Table ▼

- *circa 1820*

Regency card table by John Wellsman. The brass marquetry has been etched and inlaid "contrepartie", and unusually depicts huntsmen inset in a running border of scrolled acanthus leaf with fruiting vines.
- *73.6cm x 45.7cm x 91.4cm*
- **Guide price $15,580**

Regency "Penwork" Games Table ◀

- *circa 1830*

The chequerboard top with its frieze drawer is raised on a tulip pedestal with a quatreform base, ending with bun feet and concealed castors.
- *73.4cm x 58.4cm*
- **Guide price $11,570**

George III Three-part Dining Table ▶

- *circa 1810*

George III period dining table in three parts, made from Cuban mahogany and retaining all original leaves.

- *72.5m x 1.68m x 4.46m*
- **Guide price $133,500**

Regency Twin Pillar Dining Table ▲

- *circa 1810*

A mahogany twin pillar table, the top with a swivel mechanism allowing the two leaves to be supported on a frame. Each leaf with a triple reeded edge and held together with original lacquered brass clips.

- *72cm x 1.27m x 2.54m*
- **Guide price $81,880**

George III Tilt-top Breakfast Table ▶

- *circa 1790*

George III mahogany tilt-top rectangular breakfast table crossbanded with rosewood and satinwood enhanced with ebony stringing. Has rare brass wagon-wheel castors with elongated prongs.

- *76cm x 1.06m x 1.39m*
- **Guide price $32,930**

Drop Leaf Dining Table ▼

- *circa 1750*

George III mahogany drop leaf dining table on shaped cabriole legs terminating in pointed toes, lovely colour and patina.

- *72cm x 1.295m x 1.07m*
- **Guide price $5,960**

William IV Library Table ◀

- *circa 1830*

A late Regency rosewood and brass mounted library table with superb "S" scrolled lyre ends and carved throughout with acanthus leaf, honeysuckle and lotus leaf decoration.

- *73.7cm x 56cm x 1.22m*
- **Guide price $46,280**

Oak Refectory Table ▲

- *circa 1680*

Refectory table with single-plank top over an arcaded frieze with inverted baluster legs ending in block feet.

- *73.7cm x 76.2cm x 2.26m*
- **Guide price $44,410**

Circular Walnut Table ▲

- *circa 1870*

Fine walnut pedestal table supported by three feet.

- *diameter 1.27m*
- **Guide price $8,810**

Regency Mahogany Breakfast Table ▶

- *circa 1820*

A fine breakfast table with rounded corners and inlaid band on a turned pedestal with four splayed legs ending in brass caps and castors.
- *74cm x 1m x 1.32m*
- **Guide price $12,190**

Regency Coromandel Breakfast Table ▼

- *circa 1815*

An unusual table in coromandel wood with rounded corners on a fluted pedestal with four scrolled feet; decorated with fine inlaid brass banding.
- *71cm x 1.12m x 1.51m*
- **Guide price $19,310**

Regency Rosewood Breakfast Table ▲

- *circa 1815*

A Regency period rosewood veneered brass inlaid breakfast or hall table.
- *71.8cm x 1.25m x 1.25m*
- **Guide price $29,370**

Rosewood Circular Table ▶

- *circa 1815*

Rosewood circular table on central pedestal and platform base, with well-figured faded top.
- *74cm x 1.03m*
- **Guide price $11,130**

Rosewood & Marquetry Centre Table ▼

- *circa 1840*

Centre table with circular snap top, centred with a panel of a butterfly amidst exotic flowers within a superb rosewood field. The deep border separated by stringing is decorated with six floral panels.
- *diameter 1.27m*
- **Guide price $46,280**

Regency Extending Dining Table ▲

- *circa 1825*

A mahogany telescopic-action dining table attributed to Gillow of Lancaster. In original condition with four leaves and castors & clips stamped "Copes Patent". Seats up to fourteen comfortably.
- *3.71m x 1.32m*
- **Guide price $45,390**

William IV Dining Table ▼

- *circa 1835*

William IV mahogany circular dining table of large size, standing on a triform base and carved scroll feet.
- *72.4cm x 1.37m*
- **Guide price $8,010**

Expert Tips

Damaged table tops are sometimes replaced. Observe the direction of the grain; on an original top the grain runs across the depth of the table rather than along its width.

Large Wine Table ▶

• *Early 19th century*
Elm wood wine table with
original black lacquer. Round
section recessed legs are joined by
beaded apron and spandrels. The
humpback stretchers back and
front have a simple carved fungus
detail.
• *87cm x 58cm x 1.07m*
• **Guide price $2,670**

Elm Half Table with Carved Apron ▲

• *Mid 19th century*
An elm wood half table in a
waisted design with simple carved
apron, the pieces ending in
stylized dragons' heads.
• *82cm x 48cm x 96cm*
• **Guide price $800**

Regency Mahogany Breakfast Table ▶

• *circa 1820*
A Regency breakfast table with
rosewood crossbanded top, retains
excellent colour and figure.
• *74cm x 76.2cm x 1.37m*
• **Guide price $14,240**

Scholar's Table ▲

• *Early 19th century*
A low fruitwood Regency table
with cloud shaped low-relief
carving to the apron.
• *36cm x 26cm x 1.17m*
• **Guide price $980**

Altar Table ▲

• *Early 19th century*
Northern Chinese table with
everted ends and recessed beaded
legs joined with a pierced carved
panel. The apron and spandrels
are elaborately carved with an
open scrollwork design.
• *96cm x 43cm x 2.1m*
• **Guide price $4,450**

Pair of Tea Tables ◀

• *Early 19th century*
A pair of hardwood tea tables
with drawers and traditional
ridged top. The base stretchers
incorporate an ice crack lattice
framework and the central
shelves are simply panelled.
• *80cm x 39cm x 39cm*
• **Guide price $1,510**

Wardrobes

Architectural Breakfront Wardrobe ▶

- *circa 1850*

One of a pair of ebonised
wardrobes by Anthony Salvin for
Peckforton Castle. Each with
moulded cornice above a central
cupboard, revealing five slides,
with ebonised fascia, over two
short and two long drawers,
flanked by lined hanging
compartments each with brass
rail fixtures. Each door with
decorative panelling, and Arts
and Crafts style brass strap hinges,
engraved with an asymmetric
design, the escutcheons follow
the same design.
- *2.21m x 2.58m*
- **Guide price $49,840**

Georgian Display Cupboard ▲

- *circa 1780*

Georgian cupboard with two
doors enclosing an arched and
pillared interior and two
cupboards below.
- *height 2.4m*
- **Guide price $3,290**

Victorian Wardrobe ▶

- *circa 1880*

Victorian single-door wardrobe
with central mirror, moulded
pediment and one long deep
drawer with turned handles. The
whole standing on a moulded
square base.
- *height 2.07m*
- **Guide price $1,770**

Lacquered Corner Cupboard ◀

- *circa 1770*

Dutch black lacquered corner
cupboard, with a raised gilt
Chinoiserie design of figures,
pagodas and birds, with brass
butterfly hinges.
- *height 1.1m*
- **Guide price $7,030**

Dutch Corner Cupboard ◀

- *circa 1850*

Dutch Chinoiserie painted corner
cupboard with stylised butterflies,
birds and figures, with three green
painted interior shelves, original
brass butterfly hinges and a
moulded base.
- *92cm x 59.5cm x 40cm*
- **Guide price $9,790**

Expert Tips

*Features to look for in
wardrobes and tallboys include:
original handles, feather banding
to drawers, canted corners to
top section, and cross banding
decoration.*

Indian Linen Press

- *circa 1880*

Indian linen press with panelled doors carved with central pleated medallions and corner spandrels, above two long drawers raised on bracket feet.

- *height 1.75m*
- **Guide price $4,450**

French Provincial Cupboard

- *circa 1780*

French painted Provincial cupboard in three parts, with heavily panelled doors on the top cupboard fitted with two serpentine shelves, and elongated hinges.

- *2.23m x 1.72m*
- **Guide price $7,650**

Black Lacquer Cupboard ▶

- *1880*

Small Chinese black lacquer cabinet with fitted interior of one long and seven other drawers. With brass fittings at each corner with curved edges. Flanked by brass carrying handles.

- *37cm x 40cm x 28.5cm*
- **Guide price $4,000**

Mahogany Wardrobe ▲

- *circa 1880*

Fine Victorian figured mahogany moulded two-door wardrobe with scrolled moulding below a moulded pediment. Standing on a straight base.

- *height 2.06m*
- **Guide price $3,290**

George III Commode ▲

- *circa 1790*

George III mahogany tambour-door commode with square tapering legs.

- *79cm x 53cm x 49cm*
- **Guide price $6,140**

Louis XVI Cupboard ▲

- *1800–10*

Swedish Louis XVI Gustavian cupboard in two sections, with architecturally styled pediment and doors to top chest, and the lower chest with two panelled doors, the whole standing on small bracket feet.

- *1.88m x 1.13m*
- **Guide price $4,800**

Mahogany Linen Press ▲

- *circa 1780*

Mahogany linen press with moulded dentil course and two doors with inlaid oval panels concealing original trays. The lower section with two short and two long drawers.

- *2.12m x 1.22m x 58cm*
- **Guide price $19,500**

William IV Linen Press ▲

- *circa 1835*

William IV mahogany linen press retaining its old trays, with two finely figured panelled doors decorated with beading. The lower section with figured drawer fronts and original handles. The whole raised on turned and gadrooned feet.

- *2.14m x 1.2m x 50cm*
- **Guide price $15,580**

Pedestal Cupboard ▲

- *circa 1810*

Swedish Louis XVI Gustavian cream-painted pine pedestal cupboard with two doors and square moulded and painted green base.

- *1.47m x 1.07m*
- **Guide price $5,160**

Flame Mahogany Wardrobe ▶

- *circa 1890*

Flame mahogany Victorian wardrobe with central pediment above bow-fronted doors, with four drawers flanked by long cupboards with oval mirrors.

- *width 2.4m*
- **Guide price $4,720**

Linen Press ▲

- *circa 1800*

Elegant mahogany linen press in original condition, with oval panels of matching veneers and satinwood cross-banded doors.

- *height 2.25m*
- **Guide price $15,930**

Corner Cupboard ▼

- *circa 1790*

George III bow-fronted mahogany corner cupboard, fitted with four shelves and two small drawers, with shell inlay to frieze and Greek key-moulded cornice.

- *height 1.05m*
- **Guide price $4,360**

Mahogany Linen Press ◀

- *circa 1860*

Mahogany linen press, having two arched panelled door enclosing three sliding drawers and two long and two short drawers below.

- *width 1.25m*

Guide price $4,360

Expert Tips

Georgian bookcases were usually made in pine when they were going to be gessoed; gesso is a plaster-like substance applied to carved furniture before gilding. The bookcase would then be painted to complement the decor in the room or library.

Glass

The inherent fragility of glass makes it highly prized, if not widely collected. This fragility also ensures its rarity value.

Notwithstanding the above, glass is still an area where a keen eye is required to eliminate the substantial quantity of items on the market which may deceive the casual collector. Some of these items have undoubtedly been made or altered with the intention to fool buyers and enhance prices. Nevertheless, many more are just honest reproductions.

One difficulty with glass is that it tends to be difficult to date. It is worthwhile visiting museums to view their glass collections as they often house a wide range of examples from different periods, allowing you to familiarise yourself with the styles and distinctive features of glass items through the ages. Collectors' societies are also a valuable source of information and often give you the opportunity to handle the objects. The best source, though, are reputable dealers who, incidentally, by supplying a proper descriptive receipt, bind themselves to their honest opinion and will make amends should they be proved wrong.

Tall Bohemian Blue Vase ▼
- *circa 1880*
Tall slender cobalt blue vase engraved with an interlaced stylised leaf pattern, raised on a domed foot.
- *height 42cm*
- **Guide price $520**

Green Wine Glass ▲
- *1760*
Green wine glass with elegant air twist stem.
- *height 18cm*
- **Guide price $5,340**

Glass Match Striker ▼
- *circa 1890*
Circular glass match container with silver mounts. The body incised with a grooved pattern which functions as a striking surface.
- *height 8cm*
- **Guide price $280**

Expert Tips

Gilding is applied both to the inside and to the surface of glasswares in the form of paint, powder and foil, usually on the surface of plain glass.

401

Wine Glasses ▼
- *1860*

Two green Bristol glass wine glasses.
- *height 12cm*
- **Guide price $80**

Green Wine Glasses ▲
- *1825*

Set of bowl-shaped green wine glasses with raspberry encrustation applied to the stems, raised on circular bases.
- *height 17cm*
- **Guide price $1,070 set of three**

Tall Bohemian Vase ▼
- *circa 1880*

Tall fluted vase with borders of red overlay heavily engraved with gilt scrolled decoration, raised on a domed foot with a shaped edge.
- *height 42cm*
- **Guide price $850**

Bristol Spirit Decanter ▼
- *circa 1825*

Bristol blue spirit decanter inscribed with "Brandy" in gilt lettering, with a lozenge-shaped stopper.
- *height 28cm*
- **Guide price $710**

Toasting Glass ▲
- *circa 1700*

Toastmaster's glass with bell-shaped bowl, large circular knop stem with enclosed tear drop.
- *height 12cm*
- **Guide price $3,200**

Bohemian Decanter with Bowl ▼
- *circa 1880*

Bohemian bottle shaped decanter and dish with jewelled decoration of pink and blue stylised flowers with red beading and gilding.
- *height 28cm*
- **Guide price $1,070**

Cream Skimmer Bowl ▲
- *circa 1800*

Large shallow glass cream skimmer bowl with central boss and moulded rim.
- *diameter 51cm*
- **Guide price $890**

Square Spirit Decanters ▼
- *1900*

Good pair of well-cut square English spirit decanters with original facet ball stoppers.
- *height 22.9cm*
- **Guide price** $450

Opaline Vases ▼
- *1820*

Splendid pair of opaline boulle de Savon urn vases in gilded mounts.
- *height 44.5cm*
- **Guide price** $8,900

Red Glass Dishes ▼
- *1860*

Splendid set of ten red glass dishes, each with cut-shaped rim and base and exceptional gilding.
- *diameter 30cm*
- **Guide price** $500

Green Bowl ▲
- *circa 8th–10th century AD*

A green glass Islamic bowl from Afghanistan with an overall dimple effect.
- *diameter 20cm*
- **Guide price** $530

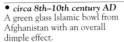

Green Glass Decanters ▲
- *1840*

Three square-cut green glass decanters with gilded labels for Rum, Brandy and Hollands (gin), in silver-plated stand with original stoppers.
- *height 28cm*
- **Guide price** $1,340

Strawberry-Cut Piggin ▲
- *1820*

Large heavily strawberry-cut piggin (cream bowl) and under dish.
- *width 20.3cm*
- **Guide price** $1,600

Cut Glass Cornucopia ▲
- *1830*

A fine pair of French cut glass cornucopia in gilded bronze mounts on marble bases.
- *height 19cm*
- **Guide price** $6,410

Expert Tips

A diamond-shaped mark, with a date and "parcel number" may identify glass made in Britain between 1852 and 1883.

Ogee Bowl ◀
- *1800*

Very large English ogee bowl rummer-shaped punch serving glass on plain stem.
- *height 30cm*
- **Guide price** $1,690

Balustroid Glass ▶
- *1740*

Balustroid wine/ale glass with central ball knop and tall bell bowl.
- *height 20.3cm*
- **Guide price $2,140**

Posy Vase ▲
- *1880*

Charming horn-shaped posy vase in a glass stand on a mirrored base.
- *height 18cm*
- **Guide price $570**

Bristol Blue Decanters ▲
- *1800*

Pair of mallet-shaped Bristol Blue decanters with gilded labels reading "Rum" and "Brandy".
- *height 24cm*
- **Guide price $1,030 for pair**

Gin Glass ▶
- *1740*

Small English inverted baluster stem gin glass with tear inclusion on folded foot.
- *height 12cm*
- **Guide price $2,490**

Ship's Decanter ▼
- *1830*

English ship's decanter with flat slice cutting, four neck rings and target stopper.
- *height 25.4cm*
- **Guide price $2,230**

Green Cup Bowl ▼
- *1880*

English cup bowl of green champagne glass on knop stem.
- *height 10.2cm*
- **Guide price $160**

Cranberry Glass Bowl ▼
- *1880*

Large English cranberry glass bowl, with clear pull up leaf rim on a silver-plated stand.
- *height 28cm*
- **Guide price $2,230**

Georgian Decanter ▼
- *1830*

Half-sized Georgian decanter, with basal flutes, flat cutting and triple neck rings.
- *height 22.9cm*
- **Guide price $280**

Bohemian Glass Bowl ▲

- *circa 1880*
Bohemian amber-coloured glass bowl.
- *height 18cm*
- **Guide price** $360

English Vase ▲

- *circa 1870*
English clear cylindrical glass vase engraved with birds amongst foliage and geometric designs, with a star-cut base.
- *height 38cm*
- **Guide price** $1,210

Red Sweet Dish ▼

- *circa 1890*
Red Bohemian sweet dish painted with alternating panels of portraits and white diamond patterns, within gilt foliage, supported on a white overlay stem with a circular base.
- *height 34cm*
- **Guide price** $2,310

Blue Decanter ▼

- *circa 1880*
Bohemian bottle-shaped glass decanter with blue overlay, painted with red and yellow designs amongst clear glass flowers, made for the Middle Eastern market.
- *height 25cm*
- **Guide price** $660

Bohemian Red Candle Vase ▲

- *circa 1880*
Red Bohemian chalice-shaped vase, with white overlay and a gilt band painted with a floral frieze, above a knopped stem supported on a splayed foot with gilt banding.
- *height 27cm*
- **Guide price** $1,030

Bohemian Style Vase ▲

- *circa 1880*
One of a pair of green Bohemian style English vases of baluster form with an asymmetric rim, decorated with gilding, with a clear glass shield cartouche.
- *height 30.5cm*
- **Guide price** $1,390

Red Bohemian Glass Vase ▼

- *circa 1880*

Red Bohemian glass vase with white panels painted with bull rushes, above a knopped stem raised on a splayed foot decorated with panels of bullrushes within gilt borders.
- *height 31cm*
- **Guide price $680**

Amethyst Cream and Sugar Bowls ▲

- *1800*

Amethyst baluster cream and sugar bowls with gilt writing.
- *height 12cm*
- **Guide price $1,070**

French Opaline Bottle ▼

- *circa 1880*

French opaline bottle and stopper, gilded, with a moulded rim. The body decorated with trailing roses and turquoise foliate designs, raised on a circular base.
- *height 25cm*
- **Guide price $530**

Blue and Gold Bohemian Bottle ▼

- *circa 1890*

Bohemian azure blue glass bottle with gilt floral and leaf designs, surmounted by an oversized lozenge-shaped stopper.
- *height 27cm*
- **Guide price $870**

Bohemian Centrepiece ▲

- *circa 1880*

Bohemian red glass centrepiece, with a circular clear glass dish on a red stem, engraved with a trailing foliate pattern.
- *height 38cm*
- **Guide price $2,490**

Red Glass Candlesticks ▲

- *circa 1880*

Red Bohemian glass candlesticks, each with a scalloped rim, tapered stem on a circular star-cut base with a shaped edge.
- *height 23cm*
- **Guide price $1,160**

Georgian Decanters ▶

- *circa 1800*
Fine pair of English decanters
with geometric cutting design
and knopped stems.
- *height 23cm*
- **Guide price $620**

Spirit Decanter ◀

- *circa 1840*
Fine panel-cut green spirit
decanter with single ring neck
and spire stopper.
- *height 36cm*
- **Guide price $430**

Bowl and Cover ▼

- *circa 1820*
Georgian bowl and cover cut
with combs, steps and panels. Has
a ball-knop stem, star-cut foot
and stepped lid with cut
mushroom knob.
- *height 15cm*
- **Guide price $130**

Magnum Decanters ▲

- *circa 1790*
Pair of Georgian magnum
decanters with panel-cut neck
and shoulders, comb-cut bases
and associated lozenge stoppers.
- *height 32cm*
- **Guide price $2,140**

Two-handled Wine Flask ▶

- *19th century*
Dutch two-handled wine flask,
beautifully trailed, engraved and
"bronzed".
- *height 23.5cm*
- **Guide price $170**

Four-Bottle Tantalus ▼

- *circa 1880*
Unusual and rare four-bottle
tantalus using the Janitor
Chapman's patent, No. 765.
- *height 32.5cm*
- **Guide price $4,100**

Globular Flask ▼

- *19th century*
Trailed globular flask with loop
handles, engraved and gilded
with fruiting vine.
- *height 23cm*
- **Guide price $240**

J. Jacobs Bowl and Dish ▷

- *circa 1810*

Bristol Blue bowl and dish with gilt key pattern design around the rim of the bowl, and a gilt stag in the centre of the plate. Signed on the base of each "J. Jacobs, Bristol", in gilt.
- *height of bowl 9cm*
- **Guide price $1,780**

Amethyst Cream Jug ▲

- *1820*

Pear-shaped amethyst cream jug with "Be canny with the cream" inscribed on the body, trails of gold enamelling, a loop handle, splayed lip and plain base.
- *height 14cm*
- **Guide price $530**

Cordial Glass ▲

- *circa 1720*

A cordial wine glass with flared trumpet bowl, knopped stem and air-folded conical foot.
- *height 17cm*
- **Guide price $1,420**

Newcastle Goblet ▽

- *circa 1750*

Newcastle goblet with a finely engraved foliate design, central air beaded and ball knops to the stem and domed foot.
- *height 19cm*
- **Guide price $3,200**

Jacobite Wine Glasses ▽

- *circa 1750*

Fine pair of Jacobite wine glasses with engraved bowls showing the Jacobite Rose and two buds, on double knopped, multiple spiral air-twist stems and domed bases.
- *height 16cm*
- **Guide price $3,920**

German Liquor Set ▲

- *circa 1890*

German Moser hexagonal decanter and four glasses chased with gilt paisley designs surrounding clear red glass windows, surmounted by a spire-shaped stopper.
- *height decanter 24cm*
- **Guide price $1,030**

Nailsea Glass Cloche ▲

- *circa 1800*

Clear glass bell-shaped garden cloche by Nailsea.
- *height 34cm*
- **Guide price $710**

Green Wine Glass ▲

- *circa 1830*
One of a set of twelve green wine glasses, with conical-shaped bowls, bladed knop stems and a circular base.
- *height 11cm*
- **Guide price $1,600**

Bohemian Vase for Candles ▲

- *circa 1880*
One of a pair of dark green Bohemian candle holders, with white overlay panels painted with pink roses within gilt borders, raised on a conical stem and circular base.
- *height 34cm*
- **Guide price $1,750**

Posset Pot ▼

- *circa 1740*
Posset pot with a trumpet bowl and a carved spout, flanked by two scroll handles, on a plain conical foot.
- *height 7cm*
- **Guide price $1,770**

Nailsea Container ▼

- *circa 1860*
Nailsea double container of clear glass with white pull-up decoration, and emerald green rims.
- *height 21cm*
- **Guide price $280**

Mallet-shaped Decanter ▲

- *circa 1780*
Mallet-shaped decanter engraved with "Port" within an oval cartouche, flanked by trailing vine and grapes.
- *height 31cm*
- **Guide price $1,780**

Amber Glass Cane ▼

- *circa 1810*
Amber glass barley twist cane with knob.
- *length 1m*
- **Guide price $270**

Large Green Goblet ▲

- *circa 1800*
Large dark green goblet with cup-shaped bowl.
- *height 19cm*
- **Guide price** $2,140

Set of Spirit Bottles ▲

- *1840*
A fine set of spirit bottles in amethyst, blue and green glass, with silver foliate bands around the neck and grape finials, resting in a pierced silver stand on three leaf shaped feet.
- *height 36cm*
- **Guide price** $1,750

Bohemian Bottles ▼

- *circa 1880*
Pair of Bohemian bottles with a white bulbous body with pink roses and blue cornflowers, orange flowers painted over red glass, a slender fluted neck, a red lozenge-shaped stopper and gilding.
- *height 22cm*
- **Guide price** $1,390

Bristol Blue Oil Bottle ▼

- *1840*
Bristol Blue bottle inscribed with "Oil" in gilt lettering within a gilt foliate cartouche, with a painted chain around the neck.
- *height 12cm*
- **Guide price** $360

Bohemian Lustre ▲

- *circa 1880*
One of a pair of Bohemian green lustres with white overlay and gilt borders, decorated with clear cut-glass hanging pendants.
- *height 30cm*
- **Guide price** $1,790

William III Glass ▲

- *circa 1780*
Irish wine glass with a cigar-shaped stem and engraved with the figure of King William on horseback with the inscription "The Glorious Memories of William III".
- *height 15.5cm*
- **Guide price** $7,120

Glass Twisted Cane ▼
- *circa 1810*

Turquoise twisted glass walking stick.
- *length 1m*
- **Guide price $270**

Glass Barrel Decanters ▼
- *1820*

Set of three Bristol Blue glass barrel decanters inscribed with "Rum", "Whiskey" and "Brandy" in gilt lettering within gilt banding. Each decanter has a gilt ball stopper.
- *height 20cm*
- **Guide price $2,490**

Bristol Rum Decanter ▼
- *1800*

Rum decanter inscribed with "Rum" in gilt lettering on the body and "R" on the lozenge-shaped stopper.
- *height 28cm*
- **Guide price $500**

Victorian Epergne ▲
- *circa 1890*

One of a pair of Victorian épergnes, with a central flute flanked by matching hanging baskets, suspended on spiral branches.
- *height 48cm*
- **Guide price $3,920**

French Opaline Vase ▲
- *circa 1880*

Opaline pink glass vase with jewelled beading and gilt decoration with an eastern inspiration.
- *height 48cm*
- **Guide price $1,510**

Jacob Sang Wine Glass ▼
- *circa 1759*

Composite air twist stem wine glass, engraved with a scene showing the Customs House in Amsterdam and cargo being unloaded, marked "Jacob Sang 1759", on the foot.
- *height 23.5cm*
- **Guide price $14,240**

Ale Glass ▼
- *circa 1760*

Ale glass with a round funnel bowl engraved with hops and barley and a double series twist stem, standing on a plain foot.
- *height 21cm*
- **Guide price $1,030**

Newcastle Glass Goblet ▼

- *circa 1810*

Large bowl-shaped goblet engraved with a horse and carriage, scrolling foliate and grape design and the words "Newcastle to York", on a domed base.

- *height 24cm*
- **Guide price $1,420**

Baluster Cream Jug ▼

- *circa 1800*

Blue baluster cream jug with pinched lip and barley twist design.

- *height 12cm*
- **Guide price $280**

Bohemian Vases ▲

- *circa 1870*

A pair of Bohemian cranberry glass vases with gilt leaf decoration and central cartouches showing portraits of a lady in a wedding dress and a lady in country dress.

- *height 39.5cm*
- **Guide price $9,790**

Match Holder ▼

- *circa 1890*

Ovoid match holder with a silver rim and etched glass body.

- *height 8cm*
- **Guide price $270**

Blue Decanter ▼

- *circa 1790*

Club-shaped Bristol Blue spirit decanter with a plain lozenge-shaped stopper.

- *height 32cm*
- **Guide price $390**

Green Georgian Wine Glasses ▶

- *early 19th century*
Set of six Georgian green wine glasses with rib-moulded bowls on drawn stems and large feet.
- *height 12cm*
- **Guide price $640**

Ribbed Decanter ▲

- *circa 1875*
Subtly ribbed decanter, the four-sided dimpled body with applied pincer-worked ribs and the neck with milled collar. Original diagonally ribbed stopper with applied pincer-worked edge.
- *height 33.6cm*
- **Guide price $850**

Amethyst Cream Jug ◀

- *circa 1820*
Georgian amethyst cream jug with pincer-worked handle.
- *height 10.2cm*
- **Guide price $530**

Bristol Blue Tankard ▼

- *circa 1820*
Georgian Bristol Blue tankard with waisted body and pincer-worked handle.
- *height 8.9cm*
- **Guide price $330**

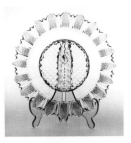

Regency Glass Plate ▲

- *circa 1820*
One of a pair of Regency plates, the centres cut with diamonds, the scalloped rims cut with cross-cut diamonds and prisms.
- *diameter 23cm*
- **Guide price $620**

Irish Canoe Bowl ▶

- *circa 1790*

Irish canoe bowl with trefoil rim above a row of large slice-cut strawberry diamonds on scalloped "lemon squeezer" foot.
- *width 35.6cm*
- **Guide price $4,000**

Kettledrum Bowl ▲

- *circa 1810*

Georgian Irish kettledrum bowl cut with saw tooth rim over a band of large strawberry diamonds on knopped stem and circular foot.
- *height 33cm*
- **Guide price $1,740**

Green Victorian Wine Glasses ▲

- *circa 1890*

Unusual pair of Victorian wine glasses with green conical bowls on clear stems with annular collars, blade knops and clear feet.
- *height 13.3cm*
- **Guide price $240**

Table Lustres ▼

- *circa 1790*

Pair of Georgian table lustres, the sconces cut with diamonds below trefoil rims, the pans also with trefoil rims on cut baluster stems and octagonal feet.
- *height 24cm*
- **Guide price $2,940**

Blue Ice Jug ▼

- *circa 1880*

Unusual Victorian blue "ice glass" baluster shaped ice jug or ewer with ice pocket and rope twist handle.
- *height 29.2cm*
- **Guide price $530**

Georgian Decanters with Neck Rings ◀

- *circa 1820*

Pair of Georgian barrel-shaped decanters with three annular neck rings over cut broad shoulder flutes and a broad band of diamonds above a row of vertical blazes and basal broad flutes.
- *height 35cm*
- **Guide price $1,560**

Georgian Tapered Decanter ▼

- *circa 1780*

Georgian tapered decanter cut with large shoulder and basal zigzags and engraved with stars between two bands of stars, ovals and zigzags. Lozenge stopper.
- *height 30cm*
- **Guide price $880**

Victorian Ice Jug ▼

- *circa 1880*

Unusual Victorian ice glass baluster-shaped ice jug or ewer with ice pocket and rope twist handle.
- *height 29.2cm*
- **Guide price $490**

Small Victorian Wine Glasses ▼

* *circa 1900*
Two of a set of six Victorian small wine glasses with everted rims cut in the Roman style with three rows of small oval lenticles or "printies" over a row of basal circular lenticles, on fluted stems.
* *height 12cm*
* **Guide price $1,060**

Bristol Blue Cream Jug ◀

* *circa 1800*
Georgian Bristol Blue cream jug decorated all over with diamond moulding. Pincer-worked handle.
* *height 10.2cm*
* **Guide price $580**

Green Champagne Glasses ▲

* *circa 1870*
Rare pair of Victorian sea green champagne glasses with double ogee bowls on baluster stems. Designed by T. G. Jackson.
* *height 12cm*
* **Guide price $620**

Ruby Trailing Wine Glasses ▲

* *circa 1880*
Two of a set of six Victorian wine glasses, the cup-shaped bowls decorated with applied ruby trailing on plain stems and feet.
* *height 12cm*
* **Guide price $860**

Ship's Decanter and Coaster ▲

* *circa 1800*
Very rare plain Georgian broad-based ship's decanter with three neck rings and original target stopper on its original turned mahogany coaster resting on three tiny castors with leather rollers.
* *height 23cm*
* **Guide price $2,760**

Expert Tips

The revival of the Venetian glass industry in the 1840s coincided with a demand for honest copies of artefacts from their ancient past. Many items purporting to come from the sixteenth century were in fact made between 1840 and 1880.

Irish Barrel-Shaped Decanter ▶

* *circa 1820*
Georgian Irish barrel-shaped decanter with three annular neck rings over engraved festoons, bows and florets above moulded basal flutes. The decanter is embossed "WATERLOO C CORK".
* *height 27.3cm*
* **Guide price $1,650**

Jewellery

The quality of jewellery is defined more by the quality of design and manufacture than the materials.

For many centuries jewellery-makers would invariably vye with each other to incorporate as many jewels into a piece of precious metal as the item could reasonably hold without becoming cumbersome. This technique was deemed to be an indication of the quality of the jewellery-maker's workmanship as well as a statement of the wealth of the eventual wearer of the piece.

During the early twentieth century, Art Nouveau designers challenged these accepted methods, favouring a more sculptural value and eschewing the intrinsic value of the precious stones. The products of both approaches to jewellery-making have retained their value remarkably well but the latter tends to be less influenced by the fluctuations in the value of precious metals.

Early Victorian Earrings ▼
- *circa 1840*
Early Victorian rock crystal and diamond earrings set in silver and gold.
- *length 3cm*
- **Guide price $5,070**

Etruscan style Earrings ▶
- *circa 1875*
Victorian 15ct gold Etruscan revival-style earrings with an applied globular design.
- *length 2cm*
- **Guide price $1,560**

Salvador Dali Brooch ▼
- *1950*
Eighteen carat gold stylised leaf brooch in the form of a hand with red painted nails, signed "Dali" on the right-hand leaf.
- *length 6.5cm*
- **Guide price $6,680**

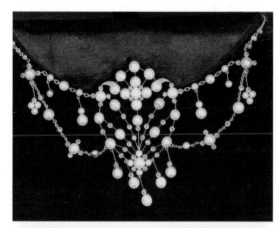

Pearl Necklace ▲

- *circa 1900*
Fifteen carat gold necklace with
half pearls and a second row of
swagged pearls between floral
droplets.
- *length 4cm*
- Guide price $5,260

Art Deco Diamond Clasp ▶

- *1920*
Art Deco jade and diamond clasp
together with a re-strung twisted
cultured pearl necklace.
- *clasp 4cm*
- Guide price $7,030

Pearl and Diamond Necklace ◀

- *circa 1905*
Edwardian pearl and diamond
necklace with droplets and swag
designs.
- *length 6cm*
- Guide price $7,030

Victorian Gold Bracelet ▼

- *circa 1880*
Victorian gold bracelet in the
Etruscan revival style with
architectural designs, set with
pearls.
- *length 8cm*
- Guide price $4,000

Gold Brooch/Pendant ▼

- *circa 1875*
Victorian 15ct gold
brooch/pendant with natural
pearls and floral enamel designs.
- *length 8cm*
- Guide price $2,270

American Gold Bracelet ◀

- *1950*
American heavy-textured gold
link bracelet with geometric
engraving on some of the links.
- *4cm/link size*
- Guide price $5,870

Flower Head Earrings ▶

- *circa 1910*
Sapphire and diamond earrings
set in a flower head design of
platinum and gold.
- *length 3cm*
- **Guide price** $8,630

Diamond Earrings ▲

- *1920*
Pair of diamond earrings with
oval, circular and rectangular
diamonds within gold settings.
- *length 2.5cm*
- **Guide price** $7,830

Gold Victorian Earrings ▲

- *circa 1875*
Victorian Etruscan revival 15ct
gold earrings with a central wheel
motif.
- *width 1cm*
- **Guide price** $1,560

Diamond Leaf Earrings ▼

- *circa 1925*
Mille grain set in platinum
diamond earrings in the form of a
leaf.
- *length 2cm*
- **Guide price** $6,190

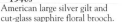

Victorian drop Earrings ▲

- *circa 1880*
Fifteen carat gold articulated
lozenge-shaped earrings.
- *length 5cm*
- **Guide price** $2,300

Expert Tips

*Bear in mind that the majority
of items of jewellery are second
hand and will have been subject
to some wear and tear.*

Silver Gilt Brooch ▼

- *1940s*
American large silver gilt and
cut-glass sapphire floral brooch.
- *7cm x 6cm*
- **Guide price** $170

French Pearl and Diamond Earrings ▼

- *circa 1875*
French enamel, gold and
platinum earrings set with
diamonds and natural pearls.
- *length 3cm*
- **Guide price** $4,720

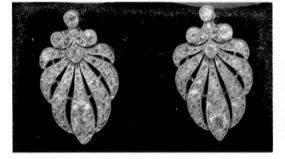

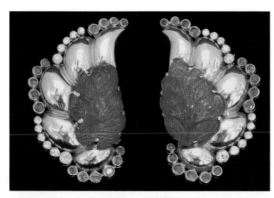

Pair of Ruby Clasps ◀
- *1940*
Pair of ruby and diamond clasps
set in stylised gold leaf.
- *length 5cm*
- Guide price $4,450

Austrian Violet Brooch ▼
- *1950*
Austrian violet brooch with
diamonds and jade leaves, set in
silver.
- *height 6.5cm*
- Guide price $2,940

Edwardian Jade Earrings ▲
- *1910*
Edwardian circular jade earrings
set in plain gold with two bands
of roping.
- *width 1.5cm*
- Guide price $2,140

Glass Italian Necklace ▼
- *circa 1990*
Hand blown glass necklace, made
from blue, gold, red, green and
clear glass squares.
- *length 37cm*
- Guide price $240

Pearl and Diamond Earrings ▼
- *circa 1925*
Pendulous natural pearl and
diamond earrings set in 18ct gold
and platinum.
- *length 3.5cm*
- Guide price $6,740

Emerald Pearl Pendant ▲
- *circa 1890*
French polished emerald set in
18ct gold with floral and swag
designs, with diamonds and a
single pearl.
- *length 8.5cm*
- Guide price $3,520

French Art Deco Bracelet ◀
- *1920*
French Art Deco sapphire and
diamond bracelet by Trabert and
Hoeffer, Mauboussin.
- *length 19cm*
- Guide price $79,210

Zuni Needlepoint ▶

- *circa 1920*
Unusual antique bracelet from Zuni, Arizona. Needlepoint with "Sleeping Beauty" turquoise.
- *width 8cm*
- **Guide price** $1,510

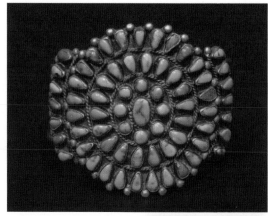

Navajo Bracelet ▲

- *circa 1950*
Antique Navajo American turquoise and coral feather shadow box design with the artist's initials etched into the bracelet "ML Fowler".
- *width 3cm*
- **Guide price** $890

Silver and Turquoise Necklace ▼

- *circa 1920*
Unusual Navajo necklace with five silver and turquoise drops from Arizona.
- *length 44cm*
- **Guide price** $700

Butterfly Belt ▲

- *circa 1920*
Silver Navajo butterfly belt with green turquoise conchos stamped "AJC" on the belt buckle, from Arizona.
- *length 83cm*
- **Guide price** $2,470

Zuni Bow-guard ▶

- *circa 1920*
Pendant or pin and bow-guard, petit point design by Zuni Native American Indians.
- *height 6cm*
- **Guide price** $530

Expert Tips

Replacing missing precious stones substantially enhances the value of antique jewellery items, as long as the replacement stone matches the originals in cut, quality and colour.

Thunderbird Earrings ▲

- *circa 1950*
Zuni Thunderbird earrings with turquoise petit point design.
- *height 7cm*
- **Guide price** $320

Art Deco Feather Pin ◀
- **1920**

Art Deco peacock feather pin encrusted with diamonds on each side.
- *length 8cm*
- **Guide price** $8,010

Zuni Cuff ▼
- **1950**

"Sleeping Beauty" Zuni cuff with 33 turquoise stones set in silver in a traditional design.
- *diameter 9cm*
- **Guide price** $2,140

Zuni Turquoise Pin ▼
- **1920**

Zuni pin flower design with 30 turquoise stones, set on a silver base.
- *diameter 8cm*
- **Guide price** $1,420

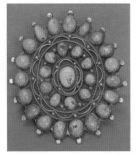

English Silver Brooch ▼
- **1940s**

English silver and enamel brooch modelled as a butterfly.
- *6.5cm x 3cm*
- **Guide price** $220

Sterle Coral Earrings ▲
- **1960**

Coral earrings set in gold with gold balls.
- *height 8cm*
- **Guide price** $11,750

Vic Blister Pearl Heart ▼
- **1920**

Vic Blister heart-shaped pearl pendant set with diamonds.
- *width 2cm*
- **Guide price** $5,250

Gold Linked Bracelet ◀
- **circa 1870**

Gold 15ct linked bracelet with a design of bars with chain link borders.
- *length 15cm*
- **Guide price** $2,630

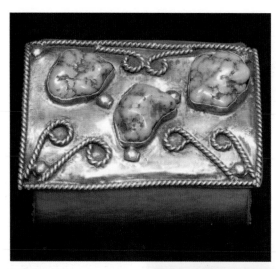

Turquoise Bow-guard ◄

- *circa 1940*

Navajo silver and turquoise bow-guard on its original leather.
- *length 9cm*
- **Guide price $620**

Victorian Choker ▲

- *circa 1880*

Black Victorian jet choker.
- *height 6cm*
- **Guide price $620**

Zuni Bracelet ►

- *circa 1930*

Zuni turquoise bracelet with petal design set on silver. There are arrow heads to each side and a hopi cactus and bird engraving.
- *length 14cm*
- **Guide price $660**

Men's Bracelet ▲

- *circa 1940*

Navajo men's seven stone bracelet with unusual silver setting with a feather one side.
- *diameter 7cm*
- **Guide price $1,420**

Silver Belt ◄

- *circa 1930*

Second-stage concho belt with turquoise stones.
- *length 97cm*
- **Guide price $4,450**

Butterfly Pendant ▲

- *circa 1950*

Navajo silver butterfly pendant with turquoise stone.
- *height 5cm*
- **Guide price $340**

Gold Chainlink Bracelet ◄
- *circa 1940*

Gold 18ct double chainlink bracelet with light and dark gold linkages.
- *length 15cm*
- **Guide price** $2,400

Opal and Ruby Necklace ▼
- *circa 1900*

Opal and ruby necklace with oval opals set in 15ct gold, hanging from a gold chain with ruby linkages.
- *length 47cm*
- **Guide price** $7,090

Peridot Necklace ▼
- *circa 1900*

Peridot and pearl Edwardian necklace set in 15ct gold with lozenge and circular peridots linked by pearls.
- **Guide price** $3,180

Boucheron Diamond Pin ▲
- *1920*

Diamond-encrusted pin in the shape of a tie by Boucheron.
- *length 4cm*
- **Guide price** $20,470

Austrian Bracelet ▼
- *1920*

Austrian Art Deco diamond bracelet set with a large central diamond surrounded by emeralds.
- *length 16cm*
- **Guide price** $26,700

American Earrings ▲
- *1950*

American turquoise glass earrings by Tiffany, modelled as flower petals within gold settings.
- *3.5cm x 3.5cm*
- **Guide price** $150

Amethyst Necklace ▶
- *circa 1890*

Large amethyst necklace with stones of graded size set in 15ct gold, with gold double linkages.
- *length 47cm*
- **Guide price** $6,320

Glass Fruit Necklace ▶

- **20th century**
Venetian glass orange, lemon and
strawberry necklace.
- *length 50cm*
- **Guide price $270**

Silver-wrapped Crystal Beads ▲

- *circa 1900*
Unusually large and long silver-
wrapped crystal beads. The
graduated facetted crystals are
each wrapped in silver ropework
baskets.
- *length 72cm*
- **Guide price $840**

Necklace with Detachable Brooch Pendant ▲

- *circa 1950*
Dramatic white paste necklace
with closed back silver setting,
and detachable pendant with
brooch fittings.
- *length 43cm*
- **Guide price $980**

Victorian Paste Heart ▼

- *circa 1900*
Lovely plump white paste heart
brooch with closed-back silver
setting.
- *6cm x 3.5cm*
- **Guide price $620**

Lanvin Pendant ▼

- *circa 1950*
Large circular black plastic
pendant with red circular disc by
Lanvin.
- *diameter 5cm*
- **Guide price $270**

Expert Tips

*Replacing missing precious
stones substantially enhances the
value of antique jewellery items,
as long as the replacement stone
matches the originals in cut,
quality and colour.*

Victorian Scottish Agate Brooch ▼

- *circa 1860*
Victorian silver brooch set with
multi-coloured Scottish agates.
- *diameter 5.5cm*
- **Guide price $500**

Butterfly Ruby and Diamond Brooch ▶

- *Late 19th century*
A late Victorian ruby and diamond brooch in the form of a butterfly, with the wings set *en tremblant*.
- *5cm x 6cm*
- **Guide price $52,510**

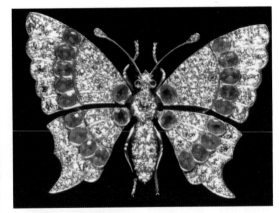

Dragonfly Brooch ▲

- *circa 1900*
A brooch in the form of a dragonfly with enamel and ruby wings set with rose-cut diamonds at the top and tip. The body with a bouton pearl above two diamonds, the tail of shaded enamel, all mounted on yellow gold.
- *6cm x 6.5cm*
- **Guide price $17,360**

Art Deco Diamond Brooch ◀

- *circa 1915*
Diamond brooch with a circular plaque depicting a stylised rising sun over water, the lower section of undulating form with an old brilliant-cut diamond sun above.
- *diameter 4.1cm*
- **Guide price $22,250**

Emerald Brooch ▼

- *circa 1870*
A Victorian brooch with the central emerald set within a border of old-cut diamonds, set against a red enamel border, and 18 principal old-cut diamonds, with green enamel detail and a pearl at each compass point.
- *3.5cm x 3cm*
- **Guide price $52,960**

La Cloche Pendant Watch ◀

- *circa 1930*
A diamond and gemset pendant watch – the rectangular watch back set with brilliant-cut diamonds, suspended by a run of diamonds, and the top and base embellished with carved rubies, sapphires and emeralds.
- *length 11.5cm*
- **Guide price $75,200**

Art Nouveau Flower Pendant ▲

- *circa 1900*
An American Art Nouveau pendant with a shaded blue, white and yellow enamelled flower head with brilliant-cut diamond centre, a fan of enamelled leaves to each side below set with pearls.
- *10cm x 8cm*
- **Guide price $40,050**

Diamond and Garnet Brooch ▼

● **1850**
Large Victorian oval gold filigree pendant with a central ruby surrounded by medium-size and smaller diamonds, three ruby lozenge-shaped droplets and mounted by a diamond-encrusted platinum ribbon.
● *length 9cm*
● **Guide price $28,480**

Snake Brooch ▲

● *circa 1900*
English gilt brooch modelled as a snake with stone settings.
● *6cm x 3cm*
● **Guide price $270**

Venetian Earrings ▲

● *1950s*
Venetian glass earrings modelled as sugared oranges and lemons.
● *2.5cm x 2.5cm*
● **Guide price $80**

Necklace and Bracelet Set ▼

● **1930s**
Rare interlinked diamante necklace and bracelet set by DRGM, Germany.
● *necklace length 36cm bracelet length 18cm*
● **Guide price $620 for the set**

French Gold Necklace ▼

● **1960**
Fine French gold necklace with a graduated design of icicles.
● *length of largest drop 4cm*
● **Guide price $4,270**

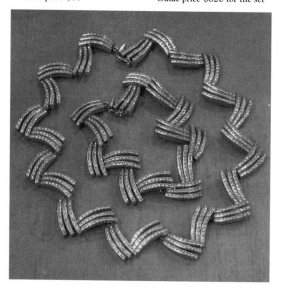

Fly Brooch

- *circa 1850*

A Victorian sapphire, pearl and diamond fly brooch with the body of a sapphire and a pear-shaped natural pearl, the wings set with old brilliant-cut diamonds and the legs with rose-cut diamonds.
- *length 4cm*
- **Guide price** $14,690

Art Nouveau Tiara

- *circa 1900*

An Art Nouveau enamel, diamond and pearl ivy spray tiara. The ivy spray with ten green enamel leaves each with rose-cut diamonds, alternately set with six natural baroque pearls and two natural blister pearls.
- *length 18cm*
- **Guide price** $106,350

Wasp Brooch

- *circa 1890*

A late Victorian enamel and diamond brooch in the form of a wasp, having rose-cut diamond encrusted wings and head, a finely textured yellow gold body and abdomen with black enamel striped markings.
- *length 2cm*
- **Guide price** $4,900

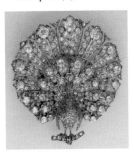

Peacock Diamond Brooch

- *circa 1880*

A Victorian diamond brooch in the form of a peacock, set throughout the body and tail feathers with graduated old-cut and old brilliant-cut diamonds.
- *6.5cm x 6cm*
- **Guide price** $64,080

Gemset Peacock Brooch

- *circa 1890*

An Art Nouveau enamel and gemset peacock brooch, the gold head and body enamelled in shades of blue and green with an emerald set plume above the tail of shaded mauve and a single brilliant-cut diamond suspended below.
- *5.5cm x 6cm*
- **Guide price** $52,950

Floral Cluster Tiara

- *circa 1880*

A Victorian diamond tiara of floral cluster design, the 11 foliate clusters alternately spaced by graduated scroll work motifs, set throughout with old brilliant-cut diamonds. Can be worn as a tiara or necklace.
- *length 42cm*
- **Guide price** $66,750

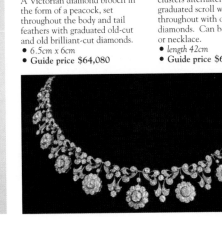

Ruby and Diamond Necklace ▶

- *circa 1880*

A late Victorian ruby and diamond necklace, the locket pendant set with a central ruby and eight pear shaped rubies in petal formation suspended from a graduated necklace of 28 ruby and diamond links.

- *length 40cm*
- **Guide price $84,550**

White Gold Sardonyx Cameo Ring ▲

- *circa 1930*

A man's ring crafted of 14ct white gold and set with a hand-carved sardonyx cameo depicting a Roman god profile. The stone is layered white and ebony and the profile is in distinct relief.

- *1.95cm x 1.55cm*
- **Guide price $480**

Expert Tips

Look out for American jewellery of the 1940s and 1950s. Jewellery manufacturers from France, Belgium and the Netherlands fled from the Nazis, taking a wealth of expertise and materials with them. For the first time America led the world market and the centre of the industry shifted permanently from Europe.

Greek God Cameo Ring ▼

- *1920*

Fourteen carat yellow gold men's ring set with four high quality diamonds in the laurel wreath surrounding the god's head cameo.

- *2.35cm x 2.15cm*
- **Guide price $1,070**

Fabergé Sunray Brooch ▼

- *late 19th century*

A Fabergé brooch, the slightly concave disc with deep blue guilloché enamel of sunray design embellished to one side with a four-leaf clover.

- *length 2.5cm*
- **Guide price $22,250**

Black Pearl and Diamond Brooch ◀

- *circa 1935*

A brooch crafted of yellow and white gold and set with a highly iridescent Tahitian pearl of a rich metallic ebony colour. Surrounding the pearl are 46 round, pear and oval cut diamonds.

- *length 4.5cm*
- **Guide price $1,690**

Gold Oval-Cut Amethyst Ring ◀

- *circa 1920*

A ring crafted of 14ct yellow gold and set with a mixed oval-cut African amethyst, a vibrant violet in colour.

- *2.35cm x 1.9cm*
- **Guide price $640**

Boxer Brooch
- *circa 1900*

French gold "Boxer" dog brooch pendant.
- *length 3cm*
- **Guide price $1,960**

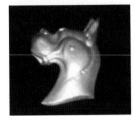

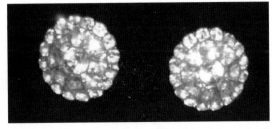

White Paste Buttons ▲
- *circa 1785*

Pair of white paste buttons, close-backed.
- *diameter 3cm*
- **Guide price $1,070 each**

Gold and Coral Suite ▼
- *circa 1860*

Gold and coral suite of brooch and pendant earrings with original case from Naples, Italy.
- *length 10cm*
- **Guide price $5,340**

Gold Floral Bracelet ▲
- *circa 1910*

French carved gold bracelet with flowers in oval panels.
- *length 18cm*
- **Guide price $1,650**

Pearl and Diamond Bracelet ▼
- *circa 1870*

English natural bouton-shaped pearl and diamond cluster bracelet with circles and heart, expandable chain.
- *length 16cm*
- **Guide price $31,150**

Enamel and Paste Clock ▲
- *circa 1770*

English red and white paste clock with blue enamel and white pastes to either side. Possibly by James Cox, the movement by William Ballantine.
- *length 9cm*
- **Guide price $10,680**

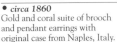

Deco Lapis Bracelet ▶

- *1950*

Art Deco bracelet with circular lapis lazuli discs with gold links and rectangular enamels with dragon designs.
- *length 19cm*
- **Guide price $8,010**

Swiss Balainot Bracelet ◀

- *1960*

Swiss gold bracelet by Balainot from the "Sheet Range".
- *height 6cm*
- **Guide price $7,030**

Snake Bracelet ▼

- *1930*

Gilt bracelet styled as a coiled serpent with a spiralled chainlink, body and scale design to the head and tail.
- *8cm x 8cm*
- **Guide price $150**

Coral and Diamond Earrings ▼

- *circa 1910*

Carved coral ball and lozenge-shaped earrings set in platinum and 18ct gold with a diamond bow linking the upper and lower sections.
- *length 5.5cm*
- **Guide price $4,410**

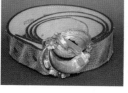

Bear Claw Belt Buckle ▲

- *1950*

Bear claw set in silver foliate design with two flowers of coral and turquoise. Stamped "E. King" and found on an Apache reservation.
- *diameter 7cm*
- **Guide price $1,240**

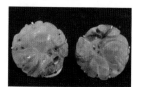

Jade Earrings ▼

- *1930*

Carved flower jade earrings set in 14ct gold.
- *width 2.5cm*
- **Guide price $2,050**

Expert Tips

It is advisable to test all joints in bracelets and necklaces for play, and brooch clasps for security, whilst ring shanks should not be too thin as they can snap.

French Jade Brooch ▶

- *1940*

French jade carved dragon bar brooch set in gold with gold scrolling.
- *length 9cm*
- **Guide price $4,270**

Ruby and Emerald Pendant ▶

- **1950**
French ruby and emerald flower pendant with diamonds and pearls.
- *length 9.5cm*
- **Guide price $34,710**

Santa Domingo Earrings ▲

- **1960**
Pair of oval Santa Domingo turquoise and black earrings from Arizona.
- *length 4cm*
- **Guide price $220**

Navajo Green Bracelet ▲

- **1930**
Navajo silver bracelet with two rosettes each side of a large green stone.
- *length of stone 6cm*
- **Guide price $820**

Metal Enamel Pin ▲

- *circa 1930*
English metal enamel pin by Dismal Desmond, with a seated black dog with a purple bow around its neck.
- *7.5cm x 2.5cm*
- **Guide price $130**

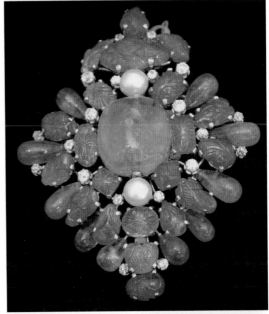

Ruby Heart Locket ▼

- **1850**
Ruby enamelled heart-shaped locket with central gold star of diamonds and a single pearl, surrounded by scrolling set with diamonds and a gold ring clasp on a velvet neck ribbon.
- *width 2.5cm*
- **Guide price $15,930**

Zuni Ceremonial Ring ▲

- **1920**
Lady's Zuni traditional ceremonial ring set with 17 turquoise stones in a flower design.
- *diameter 5cm*
- **Guide price $480**

Expert Tips

Recently, with the return of retro design in both fashion and furniture, jewellery from the 1960s and 1970s has become popular.

Tiger's Head Brooch ▶

- *circa 1875*
Onyx, gold and reverse crystal
tiger's head brooch.
- *diameter 3.5cm*
- **Guide price $4,980**

Indian Diamond Earrings ▲

- *late 19th–early 20th century*
North Indian diamond earrings in
the shape of flowers and leaves on
a vine in gold.
- *10.5cm x 4.5cm*
- **Guide price $20,290**

Diamond Baazuband ▼

- *early 18th century*
An Indian diamond baazuband
(upper arm bracelet) with a
centre section set with five flat
cut diamonds and folding outer
sections to fit on any arm, wrist
or neck.
- *10cm x 3.8cm*
- **Guide price $84,190**

French Tortoiseshell Compact ▼

- *late 1920s*
French celluloid tortoiseshell
lady's head powder compact.
- *diameter 8.4cm*
- **Guide price $210**

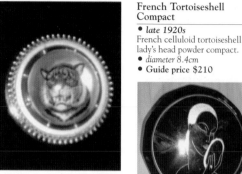

Seven Strand Necklace ▼

- *18th century*
A "satlara" necklace set on seven
strings of natural pearls with
central pendants of rubies and
emeralds in stylised floral motifs
and smaller pendants of yellow
sapphires, rubies and emeralds.
- *length 32cm*
- **Guide price $17,090**

Gold Crescent Brooch ◀

- *circa 1880*
French gold crescent brooch with
diamond-set wisteria and gold
bow within.
- *length 3.5cm*
- **Guide price $5,160**

Stratton Powder Compact ▶

- *1920s*
English Stratton powder compact,
with celluloid lid depicting
stylised lady and two borzois on a
gold-toned engine-turned back
case.
- *diameter 7cm*
- **Guide price $230**

Rectangular Tortoiseshell Compact
▶

- *1920s–30s*
Rectangular tortoiseshell enamel powder compact with trigger-action lid and stylised motif to the front.
- *6cm x 9cm*
- **Guide price** $180

Pink Enamel Compact ◀

- *1920s–30s*
American pink enamelled handbag compact, with silvered link chain, engine-turned back for rouge and powder, stamped with the maker's mark "E.A.M."
- *5cm x 6.5cm*
- **Guide price** $230

Compact with Yacht Decoration ◀

- *circa 1928*
English Gwenda powder compact in pink enamel with celluloid trigger-action lid depicting a yacht in foil finish.
- *4.5cm x 8cm*
- **Guide price** $170

Red and Yellow Enamel Compact ▲

- *1920s–30s*
American red and yellow compact for powder, rouge and lipstick, with fine gilded interior detailing, engine-turned rear case and red and yellow enamelled lid suspended on silvered link chain.
- *5.5cm x 7.5cm*
- **Guide price** $230

Deere Power Compact ▲

- *late 1920s*
American Deere powder book compact with geometric enamelled lid in black, white, gold, red and green with "Deere" written on the spine of the book.
- *5cm x 7cm*
- **Guide price** $210

Federal Building Compact ◀

- *1934*
Green enamel powder compact with metal lid from the World's Fair, Chicago, 1934 depicting the Federal Building.
- *diameter 8cm*
- **Guide price** $210

Combination Compact ▶
- *circa 1926*

Combination compact in green enamel with marbelled lid detail and yellow diagonal band. Sections for powder, cigarettes and money with additional pull-out lipstick holder with attached original tassle.
- *10cm x 5cm*
- **Guide price** $230

Gold Tone Powder Compact ▲
- *circa mid-1920s*

Gold tone powder compact with enamelled lid depicting lady and fan.
- *diameter 5cm*
- **Guide price** $220

Lady Diver Brooch ▲
- *mid-1930s*

Art Deco red enamel and chrome lady diver brooch, made in Czechoslovakia and still on its original card.
- *6cm x 4cm*
- **Guide price** $120

Lady and Mirror Compact Case ▶
- *early 1930s*

French chromed lady and mirror powder compact with engine-turned back case inscribed "MUGUET DE MAI".
- *4.8cm x 4.8cm*
- **Guide price** $230

Organ Grinder and Monkey Brooch ▶
- *circa 1928*

American Art Deco brooch of an organ grinder and monkey linked by a chain with separate pin holders for each.
- *height 5.5cm*
- **Guide price** $120

Aeroplane Brooch ◀
- *mid-1930s*

Celluloid black and white Art Deco aeroplane brooch.
- *5cm x 5cm*
- **Guide price** $150

Lady and Dog Brooch ◀
- *circa 1922*

American Art Deco lady and dog brooch made of white metal.
- *height 6cm*
- **Guide price** $140

Scottie Dog Brooch ▶

- *early 1930s*
Art Deco Scottie dog brooch
made of celluloid on chrome.
- *height 5cm*
- **Guide price $70**

Arrow Brooch ▲

- *early 1920s*
Art Deco sterling silver arrow
brooch by Neja.
- *7cm x 2cm*
- **Guide price $220**

Stylized Art Deco Brooch ▼

- *late 1920s*
French Art Deco celluloid brooch
of a stylized man and woman
leaning against each other.
- *4cm x 9cm*
- **Guide price $150**

Lady Golfer Brooch ◀

- *early 1930s*
American Art Deco gold tone
metal brooch of a stylised lady
golfer.
- *height 6cm*
- **Guide price $40**

Yacht Brooch ▲

- *early 1930s*
Art Deco German celluloid and
chrome yacht brooch.
- *6.5cm x 6cm*
- **Guide price $100**

Vogue Brooch ▼

- *early 1920s*
Art Deco brooch of a flapper with
a dog, given as a gift with a year's
subscription to *Vogue* magazine.
Metal with red detailing.
- *5cm x 7cm*
- **Guide price $100**

Scottie Dog Brooch ▼

- *late 1920s*
Art Deco chrome and red enamel
Scottie Dog brooch.
- *6cm x 5cm*
- **Guide price $70**

Flapper and Dog Brooch ▼

- *early 1920s*
American white metal Art Deco
brooch of a flapper lady with a
dog tugging at the leash.
- *6cm x 5cm*
- **Guide price $120**

Marine Items

Marina antiques provide a rich field of study, dependent on history more than condition.

Marine antiques depend for their value and collectability more on their history than their condition. That is not to say that with two items of equal historical merit the more pristine would not be more valuable, although perhaps its provenance might be more questionable. Bells, blocks, lights, clocks, chronometers, compasses, model ships, bosun's calls, clasp knives and sailor's cap ribbons are just some of the items that fall within this fascinating area, but the sub-divisions are bewildering. There are, for instance, more than 70 different types of bosun's call, ranging in value from £75 to £300.

Collectors of marine items tend to fall into two categories. Those who have an active passion for the sea, and often seek to adorn their yachts with mementoes of the sea, and those who simply appreciate the precision and fine craftsmanship of the instruments.

Model of East Indiaman Ship ▼
- *circa 1860*
A well-made model of an East Indiaman ship.
- *88.9cm x 33cm x 1.17m*
- **Guide price $15,130**

Ship's Saloon Chairs ▼
- *circa 1900*
A pair of English ship's saloon chairs on cast iron stands. The mahogany backs have hand-painted insets depicting a three-masted vessel flanked by mermaids.
- *height 88.9cm*
- **Guide price $2,850**

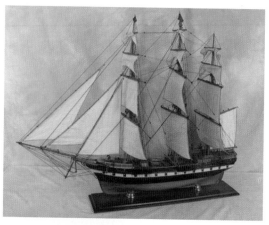

Chronometer by Breguet ▶
- *circa 1865*
A Breguet chronometer No. 885 in mahogany box with brass fittings. The clock has a brass casement with silver face and roman numerals.
- *17.8cm x 16.3cm x 16.3cm*
- **Guide price $8,810**

Napoleonic Model Ship ▶
- *circa 1805*
A handsome Napoleonic prisoner of war model ship made of bone. This third rate ship of the line has carved stern detail.
- *29.2cm x 11.43cm x 34.3cm*
- **Guide price $17,090**

Sextant by Whitbread ▲
- *circa 1850*

Sextant by G. Whitbread, in original oak box with brass fittings.
- *width 27cm*
- Guide price $2,940

Celestial Globe ▲
- *circa 1950*

Celestial globe with brass fittings, and original oak box with carrying handle.
- *height 28cm*
- Guide price $2,280

Octagonal Telescope ▲
- *circa 1780*

Fine octagonal fruitwood telescope with brass single draw and lens housing.
- *length of case 31cm*
- Guide price $1,420

Marine Chronometer ▲
- *circa 1840*

Two-day marine chronometer by Parkinson & Frodsham, Change Alley, London 1705. Housed in a mahogany double-tier case.
- *height 16cm*
- Guide price $12,460

Steam Yacht ▼
- *circa 1910*

Model steam yacht complete with planked hull, working steam engine, brass funnel prop and lights and eight portholes.
- *length 1m*
- Guide price $14,240

Chinese Dish from the Ship "Diana" ▼
- *circa 1817*

Chinese porcelain blue and white dish from the ship "Diana" which sank near Malacca on 4 March, 1817.
- *diameter 28cm*
- Guide price $330

Weichert Chronometer ▼
- *circa 1860*

Two-day chronometer by Weichert, in a coromandel box with brass inlay and handles.
- *height 20cm*
- Guide price $7,650

Tulip Frame Sextant ▶

- *circa 1860*
Tulip frame sextant in original
oak box lined with green base,
brass handle and fittings.
- *width 28cm*
- Guide price $2,230

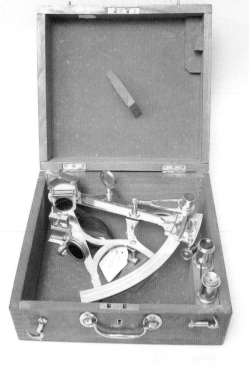

Pond Yacht ▲

- *circa 1900*
Pine pond yacht with three sails
and brass fittings modelled as a
pilot cutter.
- *width 1.64m*
- Guide price $2,670

Bone Beaker Aberdeen Schooner ▲

- *circa 1880*
Bone beaker with the inscription;
"Succefs to the Aberdeen
Schoone Proto", below an
engraved schooner in full sail.
- *height 9.5cm*
- Guide price $570

Dry Land Compass ▼

- *circa 1800*
Gimballed dry land compass in
brass case.
- *diameter 11.5cm*
- Guide price $2,050

Georgian Coconut Cup ▲

- *circa 1810*
Georgian coconut cup with silver
mounts raised on splayed legs
with paw feet.
- *height 13.5cm*
- Guide price $1,230

Half-Boat ◀

- *circa 1900*
Half-boat racing yacht, made
from fruitwood for use as a boat-
builder's model.
- *width 87cm*
- Guide price $2,850

Small Brass Barometer ▶

- *circa 1800*
Barometer H. M. S. Britannia
Prize, by Coomes Devenport in
original leather box.
- *diameter 5.5cm*
- **Guide price $1,510**

Model of S.S. "Rallus" ▲

- *circa 1900s*
A builder's scale model of the
S.S. "Rallus", which was built for
the Cork Steam Ship Co Ltd,
Cork, Ireland by Swan Hunter &
Wigham Richardson Ltd. Masts,
derricks and rigging with scale
ivorine and nickel plated blocks,
deck details including anchor
winches, fairleads, bollards,
ventilators, deck rails, hatches,
and deck winches. The
superstructure with lifeboats.
- *67cm x 2.34m*
- **Guide price $16,910**

Nelson's Last Signal ◀

- *circa 1910*
Nelson's last signal, "England
expects that every man shall do
his duty."
- *38cm x 57cm*
- **Guide price $770**

Parallel Brass Rule ▲

- *circa 1920*
Brass parallel rule.
- *length 46cm*
- **Guide price $210**

Model of the Queen Mary ◀

- *circa 1940*
Model of the Queen Mary by
Bassett-Lowke, with display case.
- *width 32cm*
- **Guide price $710**

Musical Instruments

Some musical instruments are now purely decorative. Those that are still musical are to be preferred.

The development of musical instruments is inextricably linked to the development of music. As new contexts for music-making arose, so new instruments were devised in response. Some instruments became obsolete altogether, while others evolved to accommodate the developments. Music was then written specifically for the new instruments. The cycle continues to the present day.

Musical instruments have also evolved because of extraneous factors – by the beginning of the nineteenth century,

for instance, the violin had acquired a longer neck and fingerboard, a larger bass bar and a thicker soundpost. This type of development was due, at least in part, to the need for louder noises that could be heard easily in larger rooms.

Every musical instrument is unique, but expensive mistakes can be made by collectors who are ignorant about what makes a musical instrument collectable. For example, pianos and grand pianos can vary wildly in price, depending on their maker and date of construction.

Single Action Square Piano ◄
- *1783*
A square piano by John Broadwood. Five octaves, single action, with brass underdampers. Mahogany case with string inlay, raised on trestle support.
- *1.63m x 57.2cm*
- **Guide price $12,820**

Dolmetsch Spinet ▼
- *1915*
Five-octave Arnold Dolmetsch spinet in red, gold and black decorated by the Omega Workshop.
- *1.17m x 78cm*
- **Guide price $12,460**

Grecian Harp ▼
- *circa 1821*
Forty-three string S & P Erard Grecian harp in black and gold.
- *1.7m x 80cm*
- **Guide price $17,040**

Schwieso and Erard Harp ◄
- *circa 1820*
A double-action harp in full playing order. The black lacquer body with gilt line decoration, the fluted column surmounted by gilt gesso Grecian terms. Eight pedals and with louvres intact.
- *height 1.73m*
- **Guide price $16,910**

Gretsch Guitar ▼
- *1957*
Gretsch guitar. Model 6120, with original white cowboy case. S/N:22080
- *height 1.05m*
- **Guide price $9,870**

Gibson Guitar ▼
- *1953*
Gibson Model SJ200. Sunburst finish. S/N A17263.
- *height 1.05m*
- **Guide price $10,410**

Gibson Guitar ▲
- *1960*
Gibson. Model Les Paul Special. Finish TV Yellow. S/N O 1432.
- *height 1m*
- **Guide price $6,850**

Gibson Guitar ▲
- *1960*
Gibson. Model: ES330. Sunburst finish. Dot neck. Factory order No. R29523.
- *height 99cm*
- **Guide price $5,070**

Fender Guitar ▼
- *1959*
Fender. Model: Esquire. Blond finish. S/N 40511.
- *height 95cm*
- **Guide price $9,790**

Fender Guitar ▼
- *1959*
Fender. Model: Jazzmaster. Sunburst finish. Original tweed case. S/N 31596.
- *height 1.04m*
- **Guide price $3,730**

Fender Guitar
● *1952*
Fender. Model: Esquire with original thermometer case.
S/N 4047.
● *height 98cm*
● **Guide price $13,350**

Gibson Guitar
● *1949*
Gibson. Model: SJ200. Maple back and sides stained and a new scratch guard added by Gibson in the mid-1960's. S/N A3487.
● *height 1.05m*
● **Guide price $8,810**

Epiphone Guitar ▼
● *1958*
Epiphone. Model: Coronet.
Refinished in black.
● *height 96cm*
● **Guide price $3,370**

Martin Guitar ▼
● *1965*
Martin. Model: D28. Brazilian rosewood. Replaced fingerboard.
S/N 201923.
● *height 1.03m*
● **Guide price $4,090**

Martin Guitar ▲
● *1965*
Martin. Model: O18. S/N: 208 916.
● *height 99cm*
● **Guide price $3,370**

Epiphone Guitar ▲
● *1967*
Epiphone. Model: casino. Long scale model. Near mint condition. Original card case.
● *height 1.08m*
● **Guide price $4,450**

Broadwood Six Octave Piano

- **1827**
Square piano by Broadwood in fine mahogany case with turned reeded legs, the instrument has six octaves and is fully restored.
- *1.73m x 63.5cm*
- **Guide price $13,710**

Broadwood Square Piano ▲

- **1802**
A restored square piano by Broadwood with five and a half octaves, single action, and brass underdampers. Mahogany case raised on square tapered legs.
- *1.63m x 60cm*
- **Guide price $10,410**

Longman and Broderip ▲

- *circa 1795*
A restored square Longman and Broderip piano. Five octaves with double action. Mahogany case raised on square tapered legs, the nameboard with floral swags to the enamel nameplate.
- *1.58m x 53.3cm*
- **Guide price $13,350**

Stodart Square Piano ▼

- *circa 1823*
A square piano by Stodart. A fine double-action instrument in mahogany case with rosewood crossbanding and brass trim, two music drawers and supported on six turned reeded legs.
- *1.7m x 62cm*
- **Guide price $13,350**

Adam Beyer Piano ▲

- **1788**
A fully restored square piano by Adam Beyer. Five octaves with single action, in a mahogany case supported on a trestle stand with pedal to operate the swell mechanism.
- *1.58m x 56cm*
- **Guide price $14,690**

Expert Tips

Wooden-framed pianos of the late nineteenth century are pretty but impossible to tune.

Glass Bugle ▶

- *late 18th–early 19th century*
Georgian wrythen bugle made from glass with a double-loop to the tube.
- *length 28cm*
- **Guide price $160**

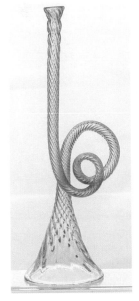

Concert Grand Piano ▶
• *1935*
Model D concert grand in a very
unusual mahogany high gloss
polish (most concert grands are
black). Fully rebuilt by Steinway
and Sons.
• *length 2.7m*
• **Guide price $104,150**

Mahogany Cased Organ ▲
• *1805*
Rare organ by Broderip &
Wilkinson, London, in full
working order, complete with six
barrels each with up to eight
different tunes.
• *height 2.26m*
• **Guide price $43,610**

Rickenbacker Guitar ▲
• *1967*
Rickenbacker. Model: 365.
Fireglow finish. S/N GC1415.
• *height 98cm*
• **Guide price $3,370**

Fender Guitar ▼
• *1969*
Fender. Model: Jazzbase. Sunburst
finish. Original case. S/N 283918.
• *height 1.15m*
• **Guide price $4,000**

Gretsch Guitar ▲
• *1962*
Gretsch. Model: 6120. Original
case. S/N 67410.
• *height 1.09m*
• **Guide price $4,450**

Tomkinson Square Piano ▶

- *circa 1815*

Square double-action piano by
Tomkinson. The case of rosewood
with satinwood crossbanding and
satinwood legs, with three music
drawers.
- *1.68m x 61cm*
- **Guide price $22,250**

Broadwood Grand Piano ◀

- *circa 1868*

John Broadwood and Sons of
London grand piano with
rosewood case and carved legs.
- *length 1.75m*
- **Guide price $8,580**

Erard Paris Gothic Harp ▲

- *1896*

Forty-six string Erard Paris gothic
harp made of rosewood and gold.
- *1.7m x 90cm*
- **Guide price $27,770**

Harp Lute ▼

- *circa 1810*

Light harp lute with painted
black case decorated with gold
work and raised detailing on the
pillar.
- *height 83.5cm*
- **Guide price $4,500**

Erard Gothic Harp ▲

- *circa 1859*

Forty-six string Erard gothic harp
made in Paris of maple and gold
with decorated pillar.
- *length 2.16m*
- **Guide price $26,700**

Rosewood Gothic Harp ◀

- *circa 1896*

Erard Paris gothic harp with 46
strings made of rosewood and
gold.
- *1.76m x 94cm*
- **Guide price $27,770**

Expert Tips

*The provenance of a musical
instrument is often of more
consideration than its manufacture.
Jimi Hendrix's Woodstock guitar
is worth about 300 times more than
a similar Fender Stratocaster.*

Silver & Pewter

**Antique silver seems to be out of fashion right now –
but it won't be for ever.**

Silver prices have fallen to an all time low at the moment, which means that for collectors this really should be a good time to buy before prices start to rise again.

On the whole, decorative silver has remained in its original form since the time of manufacture, so it is important to beware of reproductions. Fortunately, fake silver items are not common simply because the workmanship involved in making fine silver pieces makes it uneconomical. Fake hallmarks have been known to appear on the market from time to time, though, so always make sure that you take a dealer's receipt when buying items. Utilitarian pieces, however, have often evolved, so look out for jugs that may have started out as saucepans or mugs.

Child's Whistle ▶
- *early 18th century*
Very unusual child's silver whistle with pierced engraving of tulips circling the mouthpiece.
- *length 10cm*
- **Guide price $1,770**

Dressing Set ◀
- *circa 1875*
A first quality French silver dressing set made by Aucoc et Cie in Paris. The set has perfume bottles, powder jars and a soap box sitting in a fitted wooden case.
- *height 15cm*
- **Guide price $22,250**

Heart-shaped Mirror ▲
- *1896*
This unusual heart-shaped mirror was made in London by William Comyn. The mirror has decorations of flowers and cherubim for ornamentation, and an easel back, while the glass itself swivels to suit the person using it.
- *47cm x 37cm*
- **Guide price $4,000**

Silver Wall Sconce ▶
- *1912*
This silver wall sconce was made by L A Crichton in London in a style that would have been popular during the reign of Charles II. The decoration shows two cherubim amid flowers and birds with the two candleholders having gadroon borders.
- *30cm x 20cm*
- **Guide price $3,200**

Archibald Knox Candlestick ◀

- *circa* 1900
One of a pair of pewter candlesticks by Archibald Knox for Liberty, with a tulip design, on a large circular base.
- *height 19cm*
- **Guide price $5,340**

Silver Cruet Set ▲

- *circa* 1880
Silver cruet set with salt, mustard and pepper pot with lobed lower bodies and gadrooned borders.
- *height 11cm*
- **Guide price $340**

French Liquor Set ▼

- 1880
French liquor set of 12 silver cups with foliate scrolling and matching tray, engraved with the initials "J. C."
- *height of cup 5cm*
- **Guide price $1,020**

Loving Cup ▲

- *circa* 1900
Tudric pewter loving cup with double handles with "honesty flower" design and a cartouche with the inscription "For Old Times Sake", by Veysey for Liberty.
- *height 20cm*
- **Guide price $1,160**

Silver Centrepiece ▲

- 1865
A silver centrepiece with finely chased figures of "romantic" children by The Barnards. Fully hallmarked.
- *height 33cm*
- **Guide price $10,240**

Silver Salts ▶

- *circa* 1760
Pair of Georgian silver salts with beaded decoration and blue glass liners.
- *height 7cm*
- **Guide price $1,200**

Basket Centrepiece ▶

- *1918*

A silver three-basket centrepiece made by Sharman Dermott Neill in Chester. The centre bowl would have been used for fruit or flowers while the side baskets, which are detachable, would contain nuts, fruit or sweets.
- *30cm x 22cm*
- **Guide price $5,340**

Victorian Decanter Set ▲

- *1880*

A Victorian silver-plated and gold-plated barrel decanter set made in Sheffield. This piece would have generally been used for whisky and brandy and is still in very good working order.
- *29cm x 27cm*
- **Guide price $4,250**

Victorian Coffee Pot ▲

- *1840*

Victorian silver coffee pot made by EE & JW Barnard of London. This pot is finely chased with floral designs, an insulated handle, and a chrysanthemum finial.
- *height 30cm*
- **Guide price $3,330**

Victorian Cake Basket ▼

- *1843*

Victorian silver cake basket with hand-chased floral decorations and a scroll border, made by William Brown in London.
- *21cm x 26.5cm*
- **Guide price $3,470**

Victorian Inkstand ▼

- *1867*

A Victorian silver inkstand made in London by D & C Hands. The stand has a leaf and floral design and a removable inkwell with hinged cover.
- *8cm x 17cm*
- **Guide price $1,400**

Pair of Silver Candlesticks ▶

- *1911*

Pretty pair of silver candlesticks of George II design, made in Sheffield.
- *height 16cm*
- **Guide price $1,560**

Edwardian Photo Frame ▼

- *1903*

A beautiful Edwardian pierced and embossed photo frame, decorated with lion mask, cherubs, birds, foliage and wild beasts. The frame was made by WJ Myatt & Co. in Birmingham and has a dark blue velvet backing.
- *13cm x 9cm*
- **Guide price $1,040**

Georgian Candle Snuffer and Tray ▼

- *1806*

A Georgian silver candle snuffer and tray made in London – the snuffer by William Barratt in 1806 and the tray by Tim Renou in 1792. It is not unusual for items of this type to be of separate dates and makers and subsequently put together over the years.
- *24cm x 9cm*
- **Guide price $2,580**

Victorian Silver Cruet ◄

- **1867**

A fine solid silver cruet comprising ten items, with pierced scrolled sides and scrolled central handle, by G Angel, London.
- *25cm x 30cm*
- **Guide price $6,680**

Art Nouveau Frame ▲

- *circa 1900*

Silver and enamel Art Nouveau picture frame by William Connell.
- *height 23cm*
- **Guide price $4,990**

Silver Teapot with Bee ►

- *circa 1900*

Silver teapot with unusual foliate and insect design with a bee finial and stylised bamboo spout and handle.
- *height 16cm*
- **Guide price $2,670**

Continental Pewter Plate ▼

- *circa 1790s*

Continental pewter plate with a rifle stamp on the border and a single reeded rim.
- *diameter 25.5cm*
- **Guide price $120**

Liberty Biscuit Tin ▲

- *circa 1900*

Pewter tudric box by Archibald Knox with floral design.
- *height 12.5cm*
- **Guide price $2,140**

Tudric Jug ▲

- *circa 1900*

Tudric Liberty pewter "fish and the sea" jug with brass handle, and the inscription "U. C. C."
- *height 19cm*
- **Guide price $1,210**

Expert Tips

On most coasters one must look out for a hallmark on the lower rim, which overlaps the wooden base.

Asprey Square Waiter
- *1927*

A small square salver/waiter with serpentine corners to the raised border, on four hoof feet. Made in London by Asprey & Co.
- *17.5cm x 17.5cm*
- **Guide price $530**

Hester Bateman Sugar Tongs
- *1776*

A fine pair of George III brightcut sugar tongs, made in London by Hester Bateman.
- *length 13.5cm*
- **Guide price $400**

Pair of Scottish Toast Racks
- *1937*

A pair of Scottish five piece toast racks of rectangular form with celtic knot lug handles. Made in Edinburgh by Hamilton & Inches.
- *length 10cm*
- **Guide price $490**

Bettridge Vinaigrette
- *1833*

Lightly gilded vinaigrette with engine turned decoration to base and lid, enclosed within a foliate border. Gilded interior, with hinged pierced floral grille. Made in Birmingham by Joseph Bettridge.
- *3.4cm x 2.4cm*
- **Guide price $570**

Sovereign Case with Sovereign
- *1900*

A fine sovereign case cum Vesta/match safe; initialled "CE" and well decorated. The case was made in Birmingham by Constantine & Floyd and holds a 1914 gold sovereign.
- *length 7.6cm*
- **Guide price $440**

Smith Vinaigrette
- *1843*

A vinaigrette engraved and initialed "AR". Silver hinged grill and gilded interior base and cover. Made in Birmingham by Edward Smith.
- *3.5cm x 2.4cm*
- **Guide price $580**

Irish Lighthouse Sugar Castor
- *1896*

Victorian Irish lighthouse-shaped sugar duster or castor, with embossed floral designs on lid and body, standing on a circular pedestal foot. Made in Dublin by Charles Lambe.
- *height 10.5cm*
- **Guide price $490**

Victorian Sovereign Case
- *1898*

A fine engine-turned sovereign case, initialled "HR" within a gartered cartouche which includes an 1887 half sovereign. Made in Birmingham by Deakin & Francis.
- *diameter 3.5cm*
- **Guide price $400**

Art Nouveau Sauceboat ▶

- *circa 1900*
German Art Nouveau pewter
sauceboat with fixed base
designed by Orovit.
- *height 12cm*
- **Guide price $530**

Salts with Shell Feet ▲

- *1913*
Pair of silver circular salts with
a serpentine scalloped rim,
standing on three scalloped
feet.
- *diameter 7.5cm*
- **Guide price $700**

Scrolled Silver Box ▼

- *1840*
Oblong silver box with embossed
scrolling and floral designs and a
cartouche inscribed with the
name "Hilda".
- *length 13cm*
- **Guide price $310**

Silver Pepper Castor ▲

- *circa 1860*
Silver pepper castor of baluster
form with a pierced and engraved
cover surmounted by a finial lid.
- *height 19cm*
- **Guide price $580**

Silver Milk Jug ▶

- *circa 1940*
Silver milk jug with a lobed body,
engraved and embossed
decoration and a reeded handle.
- *height 11cm*
- **Guide price $530**

Silver Tea Set ◀

- *circa 1851*
Three-piece silver tea set with
large scrolled handle standing on
small paw feet.
- *height/teapot 17cm*
- **Guide price $960**

Pair of Victorian Salt Cellars ▶

- **1866**

Pair of Victorian salt cellars of compressed circular form, each with beaded rim, embossed foliate design and three hoof feet. Made in London by Robert Hennell III.
- *diameter 5cm*
- **Guide price $290**

Pair of Pierced Napkin Rings ▲

- **1879**

Pair of elegant pierced napkin rings with raised beaded rims and vacant cartouches. Made in Birmingham by Frederick Elkington.
- *3cm x 4cm*
- **Guide price $260**

George III Child's Mug ▲

- **1819**

George III child's mug of tapering cylindrical form, with beaded rim and foot and reeded bands. Made in London by William Eaton.
- *diameter 5.5cm.*
- **Guide price $530**

Pepper Castor ▼

- **1765**

A George III pepper castor of plain baluster form on spreading foot, with beaded rims and spiral knop finial. Made in London by John Delmester.
- *height 12cm*
- **Guide price $760**

Edinburgh Fish Slice ◀

- **1820**

A George IV fish slice with fiddle pattern and a pierced blade and scroll border, initialled "GMæ". Features two maker's marks: Charles Robb and D McL. Made in Edinburgh.
- *length 32cm*
- **Guide price $490**

Chick Pepperette ▼

- **1908**

A finely modelled chick pepperette, sitting on a flat base with pierced removable head. Import marks for Chester; imported by Berthold Muller.
- *4cm x 4cm*
- **Guide price $350**

Cherub Place Name Holders ▼

- *circa 1880*

A set of four silver place name holders depicting cherubs holding a plate of fruit aloft. Probably made in Germany.
- *9cm x 6cm*
- **Guide price $580**

Grape Scissors ▼

- *circa 1880*

A fine pair of plated grape scissors or shears with decorated stems.
- *length 16.5cm*
- **Guide price $170**

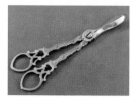

Edwardian Porringer Christening Cup ▲

- **1906**

An Edward VII porringer christening cup, circular with everted rim, embossed with gadroons and flutes, with reeded strap handles. Inscribed "Pamela Ann Sutherland, 1906". Made by C J Vander Ltd.

- *7.5cm x 14.5cm*
- **Guide price $650**

Aeroplane Cruet Stand ▼

- *circa 1930*

A rare and fine early 20th century silver-plated cruet stand in the form of an aeroplane, with four bottles, salt container and toothpick holder.

- *25.5cm x 38cm x 35.5cm*
- **Guide price $9,970**

Horse's Hoof Cigar Lighter ▼

- *circa 1908*

A rare and unusual cigar lighter in the shape of a horse's hoof, in tortoiseshell and silver. The hunting horn unscrews to reveal a reservoir. A small wick would go up through the horn to light cigars.

- *height 10cm*
- **Guide price $2,580**

Afternoon Tea Pot ▲

- **1782**

A George III afternoon teapot of slightly compressed bullet form, later embossed with roses and trailing foliage, with wooden "mushroom" finial, scrolled fruitwood handle and curved spout.

- *10cm x 21cm*
- **Guide price $880**

William and Mary Silver Clothes Whisk ▲

- **1693**

William and Mary sterling silver clothes whisk of conical shape. A family coat of arms is engraved just above the hallmark and is currently being researched.

- *height 16.7cm*
- **Guide price $7,830**

Aeroplane Desk Set ▲

- *circa 1930*

Exceptionally fine early twentieth century silver-plated desk set in the form of an aeroplane.

- *16.5cm x 36cm x 37cm*
- **Guide price $8,540**

Silver Book Mark ▲

- *circa 1899*

Unusual boxed silver book mark with ship anchor and motto "Here I cast".

- *length 10cm*
- **Guide price $1,750**

Expert Tips

Pierced silver often has a leather backing, making it hard to clean without staining the leather or damaging the delicate silver. Once you have cleaned it, use a preservative spray.

Dutch Urn ▼
- *circa 1800*

A Dutch urn and cover with an embossed floral leaf design and a wood knob finial.
- *13cm x 10cm*
- **Guide price $120**

Pewter Ladle ▼
- *circa 1780*

English pewter soup ladle with shallow bowl and plain thumb piece.
- *length 32cm*
- **Guide price $90**

Butter Dish ▲
- *circa 1900*

German pewter Art Nouveau butter dish on raised feet, with foliate and tulip designs, by Kayserzinn.
- *height 13cm*
- **Guide price $530**

Silver Salt and Pepper Pot ▲
- *circa 1923*

Matching silver salt and pepper pot, of octagonal baluster form with finial lid, from E. Johnson & Son Ltd., Derby.
- *height 9cm*
- **Guide price $430**

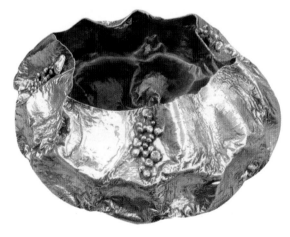

Continental Pewter Bowl ▼
- *18th century*

Continental pewter deep dish, with floral engraving to the centre, and a single reeded rim.
- *diameter 23cm*
- **Guide price $120**

Cigarette Case ▼
- *circa 1920*

Silver cigarette case with meshed effect and lines of gold inlay.
- *length 12cm*
- **Guide price $120**

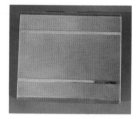

Pewter Continental Bowl ▼
- *circa 1900s*

Continental pewter bowl with a wide border and moulded rim.
- *diameter 30cm*
- **Guide price $210**

Silver Bowl ◄
- *1930*

Silver "Crumpled Paper" bowl with fruit decoration.
- *height 16cm*
- **Guide price $1,960**

French Silver Bowl ◀

- *circa 1890*

Silver punch bowl/wine cooler
with elaborate chasing and foliate
designs, four scrolled handles,
acanthus leaf swags and
ribboning.
- *height 47cm*
- **Guide price $57,850**

Silver and Glass Jar ▶

- **1945**

Glass cosmetic container with a
silver cover and a bone moon
shaped thumbpiece, made in
London.
- *height 9cm*
- **Guide price $270**

Silver Bon-Bon Dish ▼

- **1901**

Liberty & Co. cymric silver bon-
bon dish designed by Oliver
Baker. Hallmarked "Birmingham
1901".
- *9cm x 10.5cm*
- **Guide price $2,670**

Art Nouveau Mirror ▲

- *circa 1930*

Art Nouveau silver mirror with
elaborate scrolling and a young
lady holding a light in the shape
of a lily.
- *height 59cm*
- **Guide price $8,010**

Condiment Set ▲

- **1911**

Condiment set comprising two
glass bottles with faceted
stoppers, on a silver stand with
extended ring handle, supported
on silver ball feet.
- *height 21cm*
- **Guide price $430**

Hunt & Roskell Butter Shells ▶

- **1889**
A pair of Victorian sterling silver butter shells by Hunt & Roskell made in the shape of clam shells and supported by three feet in the shape of snail or cockle shells.
- *10.4cm x 10.7cm*
- **Guide price $1,210**

Justis Brandy Warmer ◀

- **1761**
George III brandy warmer by William Justis with a bowl-shaped body that flares outwards at the rim. The handle is partly silver but continues as a plain, turned wooden handle to facilitate a cool grip of the pan.
- *6.1cm x 19.3cm*
- **Guide price $4,270**

Silver Wax-jack ▲

- *circa 1769*
Silver wax-jack, or taper stand by John Carter II. Consists of a six-sided pierced base with a gadroon border. A silver vertical pillar rises from the centre of the base and ends in a detachable flame finial.
- *15.2cm x 10.67cm*
- **Guide price $4,450**

Hester Bateman Silver Sugar Basket ▼

- **1789**
Unusual George III sterling silver sugar basket by Hester Bateman made without a handle. The boat-shaped body is plain and the rim of the body has an applied reeded moulding.
- *9.9cm x 16.26cm x 10.67cm*
- **Guide price $3,470**

George III Silver Shoe Horn ▲

- **1817**
George III sterling silver shoe horn with a simple backward curving shape. The plain cast handle is joined to the body of the shoe horn with a clearly visible seam.
- *17.5cm x 4.7cm*
- **Guide price $2,220**

Victorian Silver Owl Pepper Pot ▲

- **1854**
Victorian novelty pepper pot in the shape of a seated owl. The head pulls off so that the body can be filled with pepper and the top of the head is pierced with scroll-shaped holes.
- *8.9cm x 3.1cm*
- **Guide price $2,670**

Pewter Teapot ▼

- *mid-19th century*
Pewter squat teapot with mother-of-pearl knob.
- *height 10.8cm*
- **Guide price $130**

Pair of Electroplate Double Salt Cellars ▲

- *circa 1850*
A pair of Victorian salt cellars in the form of two open cowrie shells. The inside of the shells is silver gilt and the shells are mounted on branches of coral supported on the back of a dolphin.
- *7.6cm x 14.5cm x 9.4cm*
- **Guide price $5,120**

George II Sugar Nips ▶

- *circa 1740*

One of a pair of George II silver gilt cast rococo sugar nips. The nips have shell-like decoration on the bowls and on the central pin and leaf decoration on the arms and the finger grips.

- *length 12.7cm*
- **Guide price $560**

Victorian Sweetmeat Dish ▼

- *1841*

Victorian sweetmeat dish in the shape of an open oyster shell by William Moulson. Apart from around the edges, the silver is smooth both on the front and on the back.

- *9.1cm x 7.9cm*
- **Guide price $1,190**

George III Sauceboat ▼

- *1811*

Irish George III sauceboat by James Le Bas. The plain body is oval and has a strong band of reeding while the body is supported by three cast shell and hoof feet and also has a cast flying scroll handle.

- *10.7cm x 17cm x 8.6cm*
- **Guide price $3,120**

Victorian Table Cigar Lighter ▲

- *1871*

Victorian table cigar lighter with oval curved body rising to a domed centre. At both ends of the lighter's body are cast ram's heads which hold a detachable torch with flame finial and circular cage terminal.

- *12.2cm x 12.2cm x 8.9cm*
- **Guide price $2,490**

Half-gill Tankard ▲

- *late 19th century*

English pewter half-gill measure tankard.

- *height 6.4cm*
- **Guide price $70**

Pewter Half-pint Measure ▲

- *19th century*

Half-pint pewter measure stamped "VR" with slight nick to rim.

- *height 8.9cm*
- **Guide price $90**

Gill Tankard ▼

- *18th century*

English pewter one-gill measure tankard with hallmarks on the rim of a stamp, a crown, and the letters "C", "V" and "R".

- *7.5cm x 6.3cm*
- **Guide price $60**

Pewter Vases ▼

- *circa 1890*

Pair of nineteenth-century hammered pewter vases on square bases by T.W. & S.

- *height 21cm*
- **Guide price $110**

Pewter Half-pint Tankard

- *19th century*

English half-pint tankard with small hole to base by Yates & Birch, Isle of Man.
- *height 9cm*
- **Guide price $70**

Large Pewter Charger

- *18th century*

A charger of simple proportions, flat-rimmed and undecorated.
- *diameter 51.5cm*
- **Guide price $530**

English Half-pint Tankard

- *18th century*

Pewter tankard with hallmarks on the rim: James Yates, Castle Stamp, Letters No. 6, Crown over Letters V R over Numbers 154, Number 36.
- *9.3cm x 7.5cm*
- **Guide price $60**

Pewter Charger

- *18th century*

English pewter charger initialled "E.H." on reverse.
- *diameter 37.5cm*
- **Guide price $320**

Pewter Pint Tankard

- *early 19th century*

English pewter pint tankard by James Yates.
- *height 11.4cm*
- **Guide price $90**

Pewter Plate

- *18th century*

Plain pewter flat-rimmed plate, the only decoration being a single incised band to the interior.
- *diameter 22.9cm*
- **Guide price $130**

George I Silver Etui

- *circa 1725*

Silver étui case containing a variety of implements including a knife, fork, spoon, scissors, a ruler, a pair of dividers, tweezers, a pencil and ivory tablets.
- *height 9.5cm*
- **Guide price $11,040**

Expert Tips

Unless it is polished very regularly pewter soon develops a thin oxide patina which is hard for a faker to replicate – particularly since there are no fakes earlier than 1920.

Silver Soup Tureen

- *late 17th century*

An exceptional Baltic parcel-gilt soup tureen, possibly from Estonia, cornucopia-shaped handles, stylised fruit ball feet and moulded garland decoration centred with classical heads.
- *22.8cm x 40.6cm*
- **Guide price $258,100**

Silver Goblets

- *1970*
Set of four silver goblets with silver gilt interiors with rusticated stems on circular bases, by Christopher Lawrence.
- *height 15cm*
- **Guide price $1,780**

French Measures

- *circa 1850*
Set of French pewter jug measures from demi-litre to demi-decilitre.
- *17cm x 12cm*
- **Guide price $360**

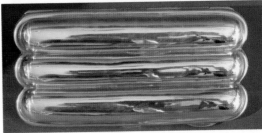

Pewter Coffee Pot

- *circa 1860*
Coffee pot by James Dickson of Sheffield of baluster form with scroll handle and acorn leaf finial.
- *23cm x 23cm*
- **Guide price $130**

Continental Pewter Plate ▲

- *circa 1780s*
Continental pewter plate with single reeded rim.
- *diameter 25cm*
- **Guide price $130**

Cigar Case ▲

- *circa 1920*
Silver cigar case with three compartments allowing for half coronas.
- *length 12cm*
- **Guide price $280**

English Quart Tankard ▼

- *circa 1860*
Pewter quart tankard with strap handle and banded decoration.
- *18cm x 13cm*
- **Guide price $180**

Georgian Silver Basket ◀

- *circa 1799*
Oval Georgian sweetmeat basket, with a swing handle, pierced foliate designs and apron support.
- *11cm x 38cm*
- **Guide price $7,120**

Adam Style Teapot ◄

- *circa 1860*
English Adam style pewter teapot
with floral and swag decoration,
surmounted by ivory finial.
- *16cm x 25cm*
- Guide price $120

Silver Perfume Spray ▼

- *circa 1910*
Silver perfume spray on a faceted
glass circular bottle.
- *height 17cm*
- Guide price $310

Glass Sugar Shaker ▼

- *circa 1906*
Glass sugar castor of baluster
form, with a pierced silver cover,
engraved floral designs and ball
finial.
- *height 16.5cm*
- Guide price $400

English Pewter Ladle ▼

- *circa 1820*
English pewter ladle with a wide
circular bowl.
- *length 33cm*
- Guide price $90

Pepper Castor ▲

- *circa 1800*
English pewter pepper castor of
baluster form with acorn finial.
- *height 12cm*
- Guide price $50

Georgian Silver Candlesticks ◄

- *1782*
A superb set of four Georgian
silver candlesticks, fully
hallmarked by John Parsons,
Sheffield, England.
- *height 34cm*
- Guide price $19,140

Regency Silver Coasters ▶

• **1823**
A set of four coasters, finely
chased with flowers and shells.
Made in Sheffield by T & J
Settle.
• *width 17.5cm*
• **Guide price $10,240**

Dutch Nautilus Cup ▼

• *circa 1875*
A rare Dutch nautilus cup in the
seventeenth century style. The
shell is finely engraved with
classical scenes.
• *height 25cm*
• **Guide price $9,350**

Teak Cigarette Box ▶

• **1903**
Teak cigarette box within a silver
frame with "Cigarettes" in silver
on the lid.
• *width 13cm*
• **Guide price $460**

Cigarette Box ▼

• *circa 1900*
Sheffield silver cigarette box with
a diamond pattern lid and plain
panel, the interior containing two
compartments.
• *width 17cm*
• **Guide price $320**

"Neff" Model Ship ▶

• *circa 1875*
A German solid silver model of a
mythical vessel.
• *height 28cm*
• **Guide price $4,900**

Parcel-gilt Beaker

- *circa 1570*

An early and rare French beaker by Steffan Vesuch, the base engraved with initials "I.H. 6 1/2 lot", divided into two main registers, the top decorated with intricate arabesque design and the lower half with beaten and incised roundel motifs.
- *height 7.6cm*
- **Guide price $60,520**

Set of Four Victorian Salts ▲

- *1874–5*

Victorian silver salts by Charles Favell & Co with spoons by J. A. Rhodes.
- *height 9.2cm*
- **Guide price $3,920**

German Silver Snuff Box ▼

- *1717–18*

Circular snuff box by Philip Stengelin, Augsburg, the lid depicting a seascape set in a cartouche and scrolling arabesque decoration.
- *diameter 7cm*
- **Guide price $12,460**

Victorian Sugar Bowl ▼

- *1880–1*

Highly unusual silver sugar bowl by R. Martin and E. Hall with hand-hammered or martelé finish.
- *height 10.8cm*
- **Guide price $7,030**

George II Cream Jug ◄

- *1747–8*

Silver cream jug by Edward Wakelin, London, with scrolling feet and moulded foliate decoration.
- *height 14cm*
- **Guide price $21,360**

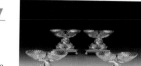

Odiot Parcel-gilt Salts ▲

- *circa 1820*

Set of four salts by Odiot, Paris in the form of dolphins with intertwined tails supporting shells, stamped "ODIOT" under base.
- *height 10.16cm*
- **Guide price $62,300**

Régence Snuffer Tray ▲

- *1718*

French Regency snuffer tray by Toussaint Bingeant, profuse beading decoration to the rim on four claw feet.
- *length 22.2cm*
- **Guide price $16,380**

Pair of Charles II Covered Vases ▲

- *circa 1670*

Silver-gilt covered vases or ginger jars decorated with putti amongst scrolling acanthus foliage and arabesques.
- *height 40.3cm*
- **Guide price $240,300**

Silver Cruet Set ◀

- *circa 1930*

Silver Art Deco cruet set consisting of mustard, salt and pepper in the style of tankards.
- *height 5cm*
- **Guide price** $640

English Charger ▼

- *circa 1740*

Georgian English pewter charger, of plain design with a single reeded rim.
- *diameter 46cm*
- **Guide price** $620

Silver Vesta Box ▲

- *circa 1880*

Small silver vesta box with floral engraving and a ring at the side.
- *length 3.5cm*
- **Guide price** $130

Silver Vesta Box ▲

- *circa 1880*

Ladies' silver vesta box with floral engraving and a plain shield panel, ring to the side.
- *length 5cm*
- **Guide price** $130

Vesta Box ▲

- *circa 1880*

Plain silver vesta box with hinged lid and striker on the base.
- *length 5.5cm*
- **Guide price** $130

Four-section Cigar Case ▲

- *circa 1930*

Four-section silver plate cigar case.
- *length 13cm*
- **Guide price** $90

Georgian Silver Tureen ▶

- *circa 1825*

Georgian oval entrée dish of plain design with banded decoration, surmounted by a handle in the form of a coiled snake.
- *length 28cm*
- **Guide price** $1,590

George II Chocolate Pot ▼
- *1753–4*

Chocolate pot in silver and fruitwood incorporating a chinoiserie plaque and maker's mark of Thomas Heming.
- *height 29.2cm*
- **Guide price $39,160**

Fiddle Soup Ladle ▼
- *1800*

George III sterling silver fiddle pattern soup ladle, hallmarked in London by Eley & Fearn.
- *length 33cm*
- **Guide price $580**

Victorian Tea Set ▲
- *1879–80*

Three-piece tea set by Richard Martin and Ebenezer Hall in silver and parcel gilt. A very rare British essay into the hand-finished or martelé silver that was being produced in America at this time.
- *height 14.6cm*
- **Guide price $25,810**

George III Tea Caddy ▲
- *1780*

George III sterling silver tea caddy with original crest and bead detail, hallmarked in London.
- *height 10cm*
- **Guide price $5,830**

Silver Pheasant ▲
- *1966*

Hand chased sterling silver pheasant, hallmarked "London".
- *length 19cm*
- **Guide price $1,740**

George II Tea Urn ▼
- *1729–30*

George II Scottish tea urn by Hugh Gordon, Edinburgh, with maker's marks and slightly later Baring arms.
- *height 33.6cm*
- **Guide price $92,560**

Harris Silver Salver ▼
- *1892*

Victorian sterling silver salver with bead detail, hallmarked in London by Charles Stuart Harris.
- *diameter 15cm*
- **Guide price $490**

George II Sauceboat ▼
- *1748*

George II sterling silver sauceboat with fine scroll decoration and standing on three shell feet.
- *height 11cm*
- **Guide price $1,740**

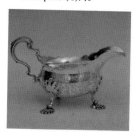

Silver Ashtray ▶

● *1900*
Silver ashtray made in London
with five recesses within the
border.
● *width 8cm*
● **Guide price $3,380**

Silver Art Nouveau Vase ▼

● *1850*
Silver Art Nouveau vase with
green glass lining and profuse
pierced decoration.
● *height 34cm*
● **Guide price $3,290**

Silver Soap Box ▲

● *circa 1888*
Victorian silver soap box of plain
design with curved corners.
● *width 8cm*
● **Guide price $400**

Four Silver Salts ▼

● *circa 1808*
Set of four urn-shaped silver salts
with gadrooned and fluted
decoration, made in London.
● *height 6cm*
● **Guide price $850**

Claret Jug ▲

● *circa 1880*
Victorian claret jug with silver
spout and collar with scrolled
decoration, made in London.
● *height 21cm*
● **Guide price $2,400**

Georgian Silver Salt ▲
- *circa 1794*

Elegant silver Georgian salt with a fluted body and scrolled handles, on a square base.
- *height 8cm*
- **Guide price $370**

Set of Four Salts ▶
- *1883*

Set of four silver salts embossed with bird and floral designs and four silver spoons with gilt bowls in original box finished in velvet and silk.
- *width of box 21cm*
- **Guide price $1,200**

Art Nouveau Creamer ▼
- *circa 1936*

Art Nouveau silver cream jug, with moulded lip, strap handle and raised on a square moulded base.
- *height 8.5cm*
- **Guide price $280**

Continental Pewter Dish ▼
- *circa 1790*

Continental dish with single reeded rim and the owner's initials "I.F.B." on the front and rear.
- *diameter 35cm*
- **Guide price $360**

Stamp and Cigarette Case ▼
- *circa 1910*

Silver stamp and cigarette case with blue enamel lid.
- *width 9cm*
- **Guide price $490**

Silver Cocktail Shaker ◀
- *circa 1910*

Art Deco silver cocktail shaker with plain sides and banded decoration.
- *height 22cm*
- **Guide price $1,020**

George III Teapot ▶

- 1784
George III sterling silver teapot decorated with fine bright-cut engraving, hallmarked in London by Samuel White.
- *height 13cm*
- Guide price $2,840

George III Sugar Basket ◀

- 1796
George III sterling silver sugar basket, bright-cut, engraved and hallmarked by Urquart & Hart.
- *height 16cm*
- Guide price $1,740

Silver Toast Rack ▼

- 1895
Victorian unusual sterling silver toast rack, hallmarked in London.
- *height 10cm*
- Guide price $830

Silver-chased Bowl ▲

- 1845
Victorian sterling silver-chased bowl, hallmarked in London by Angel & Savory.
- *diameter 15cm*
- Guide price $970

Hancock Silver Bowl ▲

- 1911
Sterling silver bowl with cut card decoration, hallmarked in London by George Hancock.
- *diameter 12cm*
- Guide price $650

Sheffield Pierced Dish ▼

- 1919
Sterling silver pierced dish, hallmarked in Sheffield by William Hutton.
- *width 26cm*
- Guide price $1,770

Silver Coffee Pot ▲

- 1774
Silver coffee pot made in London by William Collings, with replacement handle.
- *height 31cm*
- Guide price $4,720

Edwardian Candlesticks ▲

- 1905
Edwardian pair of sterling silver square based candlesticks, hallmarked.
- *height 22cm*
- Guide price $2,540

Vignelli Carafe ▶

- **1970**

Christofle and Venini silver carafe and six shots, designed by Vignelli. Stamped "Christofle, Italy".
- *height of carafe 22.5cm*
- **Guide price $3,560**

Silver Photograph Frame ▲

- **1935**

Silver photograph frame with a concave design.
- *height 26cm*
- **Guide price $620**

Pair of Decanters ▶

- **1910**

Pair of glass decanters with silver mounts and handle, made by Walker and Hall.
- *height 23cm*
- **Guide price $6,940**

Twenties Toastrack ▼

- *circa 1929*

Silver Art Deco toastrack with six bays, canted corners and a pierced apron.
- *height 6cm*
- **Guide price $340**

Archibald Knox Barrel ◀

- **1902**

Tudric pewter biscuit barrel designed by Archibald Knox, with blue and green enamelling.
- *15cm x 13cm*
- **Guide price $2,670**

Embossed Mustard Pot and Spoon ▼

- *1826*
Embossed silver mustard pot, made in London by Thomas Ballam. The whole is ornately decorated with cartouches and scrolling foliate designs.
- *height 7.5cm*
- **Guide price $1,590**

Lion's Head Salt Cellar ▼

- *1895*
Silver salt cellar with lion head decoration and paw feet. Made in London by John Bodman Carrington.
- *height 5.5cm*
- **Guide price $1,240**

Leaf Dish ▼

- *1900*
Silver leaf-shaped dish with curled rim and vein pattern. Made in Birmingham by Joseph Gloster.
- *length 17.5cm*
- **Guide price $220**

Silver Mustard Pot ▲

- *1864*
Made in Birmingham by Hirons, Plante & Co, the body is of a pierced lattice design and the lid flips open with the aid of a scalloped shell motif.
- *height 7cm*
- **Guide price $620**

Silver Salt Cellar ▲

- *1824*
One of a pair of salt cellars made in London by Charles Fox of a stylised acanthus leaf form on a pedestal base.
- *height 5cm*
- **Guide price $1,740**

Pair of Sauceboats ▼

- *1888*
Late Victorian sauceboats, made in London by John Marshall Spink with scalloped decoration.
- *height 10cm*
- **Guide price $1,160**

Oval Mustard Pot ▼

- *1804*
Oval silver mustard pot made in London by Peter, Ann & William Bateman. The round bowl condiment spoon has matching marks.
- *height 7cm*
- **Guide price $1,240**

Expert Tips

Long-term cleaners or foaming preparations which can be applied by sponge are best for cleaning your silver. When cleaning, always protect the hallmark with your thumb and use a cloth especially kept for the purpose. Any proprietary cleaner is bound to remove a little of the surface silver, so use it sparingly and infrequently.

Whisky Measure ◄

- *1876*
Silver whisky measure in the shape of a thimble with the motto "Just a thimbleful" along the rim. Made in Birmingham in by Hilliard & Thomason.
- *height 5.5cm*
- **Guide price $490**

Liberty & Co. Tea Set ◀

- **1903**

Pewter tudric tea set with turquoise enamel mount, and tray designed by Archibald Knox for Liberty & Co.
- *length 42cm*
- **Guide price $8,010**

Silver Pierced Dish ▼

- **1950**

Silver dish with pierced border, supported on a pedestal base with banded decoration.
- *height 15cm*
- **Guide price $310**

Silver Gilt Heron Cigarette Box ▲

- *circa 1909*

Silver gilt heron standing on a silver box, the mechanism opens the cover for the heron to bend and pick out a cigarette. Made by W. H. Sparrow of Birmingham.
- *height 30cm*
- **Guide price $7,570**

Set of Salts ▶

- **1880**

Set of six silver gilt salts with individual spoons with original presentation box.
- *width 24cm*
- **Guide price $1,960**

Polar Bear Inkwell ◀

- *circa 1900*

Continental silver polar bear inkwell and tray, with a pair of silver candlesticks, together with silver letter opener.
- *18cm x 29cm*
- **Guide price $4,000**

Pair of Match Strikers ◀

- *1897*

Pair of glass match strikers with silver rims, made in Birmingham.
- *height 10.5cm*
- **Guide price $1,340**

Victorian Pewter Cup ▼

- *circa 1870*

Victorian engraved pewter cup with floral engraving, scrolled handle and banded decoration, inscribed with the name "Maude".
- *7.5cm x 10cm*
- **Guide price $90**

Silver Tea Strainer ▼

- *circa 1920*

Silver tea strainer made in Sheffield, England, with pierced and engraved decoration and lattice handle.
- *length 13cm*
- **Guide price $280**

Sheffield Silver Dish ▼

- *1937*

Octagonal silver dish with double handles of ivory, made in Sheffield, England.
- *diameter 30cm*
- **Guide price $320**

Expert Tips

Regular cleaning of antique silver produces a patina quite different from that of new silver, and one which cannot be accelerated or reproduced artificially.

Silver and Glass Bowl ▶

- *1920*

Ladies' melon-shaped glass bowl with a silver banded collar and tortoiseshell insert.
- *diameter 15cm*
- **Guide price $500**

Caddy Spoon ▼

- *1847*

Made in Sheffield by Aaron Hadfield, this caddy spoon is of an irregular scallop-shaped form with elaborate scrolled handle.

- *length 15cm*
- **Guide price $760**

Lily Pattern Flatware ▼

- *1865*

Set of lily pattern flatware by George Adams, London, including large and small ladles, three types of spoon and two types of fork.

- *length 15cm*
- **Guide price $14,240**

Pair of Silver Wine Coasters ▶

- *1820*

Silver wine coasters by Charles Fox, London, with wooden bases and scrolling acanthus leaf decoration.

- *diameter 15cm*
- **Guide price $6,230**

Castletop Vinaigrette ◀

- *1837*

Silver vinaigrette with decorated lid of a castletop mansion. Made by Taylor & Perry, Birmingham.

- *3.5cm x 2.2cm*
- **Guide price $1,340**

Irish Dish Ring ▲

- *1916*

Irish silver dish ring decorated with foliage, flowers, birds and animals by Weir of Dublin.

- *8cm x 19cm*
- **Guide price $4,810**

Silver Horse Figurine ▲

- *1903*

Silver figure of a horse in motion with mouth open and flowing mane and tail, by Nereisheimer in Chester.

- *17cm x 23cm*
- **Guide price $4,450**

Expert Tips

Photograph and catalogue your silver, and keep valuations up to date. Insurance companies prefer accurate descriptions.

Silver Tureen and Stand ▼

- *1788*

Silver soup tureen with two large side handles and lid on a gently curving stand, by Fogelberg & Gilbert.

- *37cm x 55cm*
- **Guide price $53,400**

Four Scofield Candlesticks ▲

- *1783*

A set of four silver candlesticks supported on circular patterned bases by John Scofield, London.

- *height 30cm*
- **Guide price $33,820**

Venison Dish ▼

- *1845*

Large silver venison dish supported on four feet with two handles and a large domed lid, by Hamilton & Co.

- *35cm x 65cm x 47cm*
- **Guide price $48,060**

Storr Silver Salts ▲

- *1814*

Set of four silver salts with out-turned embossed rims raised on four ornate feet by Paul Storr, London.

- *6cm x 8.5cm x 7cm*
- **Guide price $21,360**

Storr Fish Slice ▲

- *1820*

Silver fish slice with decorated handle by Paul Storr, London.

- *length 24cm*
- **Guide price $4,090**

Vinaigrette with Flowers ▲

- *1819*

Silver vinaigrette by Betteridge with an outer raised floral border surrounding an inner rectangular pattern of stylised flowers.

- *2.7cm x 1.8cm*
- **Guide price $1,070**

Horse Hooves Ink Well ▶

- *circa 1900*

Silver writing set made of two
horse hooves, set in silver with
two ink wells with silver covers,
standing on a silver base on ball
feet.
- *width 46cm*
- **Guide price $1,600**

Small Silver Teapot ▼

- *circa 1904*

Edwardian silver teapot of small
proportions with bone handle
and finial lid.
- *height 15cm*
- **Guide price $430**

William Commings Frame ▼

- *1899*

Silver William Commings
hourglass frame decorated with
cherubs and foliage.
- *height 22cm*
- **Guide price $800**

Letter Rack ▲

- *1937*

Silver letter rack, with a double
circle design, mounted on a
mahogany base.
- *height 17cm*
- **Guide price $620**

Victorian Sauceboat ◀

- *circa 1891*

Victorian silver sauceboat with
vacant panel within embossed
decoration raised on a splayed
foot.
- *height 9.5cm*
- **Guide price $430**

Sporting Items

Collecting sporting memorabilia is irresistible, but it pays to keep an eye on the future before spending lavishly.

So much of sporting memorabilia is desperately ephemeral. At the time of writing, Jonny Wilkinson's right boot, with which he kicked the drop goal that won the 2003 Rugby World Cup for England, must be virtually priceless. Geoff Hurst's 1966 Football World Cup winner may not be quite as financially glossy as it once was – who knows? What will happen if we win several more Rugby World Cups? Or when the memory of

Wilkinson is known only to the students of arcanity, when rugby has long been outlawed as too dangerous?

The safest investments in sport are probably ones that do not feature as the most romantic at the moment. For example, a well-made fishing reel or rare tennis racquet may stand the financial test of time better than the boots of any Golden Boy of sort. What price now for one of Henry Cooper's Lonsdale Belts? Henry who?

General

Child's Football Boots ▶

- **1930**
Child's leather football boots in original condition.
- *length 18cm*
- **Guide price $220**

Bowling Balls ▼

- **circa 1900**
Pair of lignum bowling balls with ivory central plaques, on a stand.
- *diameter 12cm*
- **Guide price $200**

Riding Crop ▲

- **circa 1930**
Bamboo riding crop with 13 crosses on the bone handle, above a silver collar, engraved with the letters "H. S."
- *length 61cm*
- **Guide price $120**

Trophy Cap ▲

- **1923–4**
Black velvet cap with gold braiding and tassel with the letters "S. S. O. B." in gold.
- *medium*
- **Guide price $80**

Snow Shoes ▲

- *circa 1900*
Canadian snow shoes made from wood with leather mesh base and fasteners.
- *length 1.03m*
- **Guide price $170**

Bamboo Shooting Stick ▶

- *circa 1920*
Bamboo shooting stick with a folding rattan seat, with metal spike and brass fittings.
- *length 75cm*
- **Guide price $350**

Leather Football Boots ▼

- *1930*
Leather football boots in excellent condition appointed by Stanley Matthews.
- *length 30cm*
- **Guide price $220**

Goggles ▲

- *1940*
Goggles with brass and metal rim on a leather backing with adjustable rubber straps.
- *width 18cm*
- **Guide price $50**

Leather-cased Thermos ▼

- *circa 1900*
Brass thermos with original leather case with the inscription "B. R." and a long leather carrying handle with leather buckle.
- *height 38cm*
- **Guide price $220**

Billiard Scorer ◀

- *circa 1910*
Wall-mounted mahogany billiard scorer, with brass numerals and sliding markers.
- *92cm x 35cm*
- **Guide price $500**

Leather Riding Boots ▼

- **1930**
Pair of gentleman's brown leather polo boots with laces, three straps with brass buckles and wood shoe trees.
- *height 61cm*
- **Guide price $300**

Leather Gaiters ▲

- *circa 1920*
Pair of leather gaiters with leather straps and metal buckles.
- *length 29cm*
- **Guide price $50**

Football Trophy ▼

- **1956**
Football trophy presented to Mr. and Mrs. Clarke of Berkhampstead Football Club 1956.
- *height 17cm*
- **Guide price $80**

Leather Football ▼

- *circa 1940*
Novelty miniature leather football.
- *miniature*
- **Guide price $35**

Saddle Bags ▲

- *circa 1930*
Brown leather saddle bags in fine condition with leather straps and brass buckles.
- *length 18cm*
- **Guide price $280**

Leather Gaming Bag ▼

- *circa 1900*
Leather gaming bag in original condition with brass clasp and leather carrying strap.
- *width 30cm*
- **Guide price $220**

Child's Riding Seat ▶

- **1880**
A child's saddle made from wicker, with curved base and leather fasteners, to fit on a pony.
- *height 57cm*
- **Guide price $490**

Expert Tips

Hesitate before buying an over-polished sporting item such as a saddle bag or football, as this can decrease the value of the condition item.

Travelling Primus Stove ▲

- *circa 1890*

Travelling primus in a circular leather case with leather strap.
- *diameter 13cm*
- **Guide price $280**

French Boules ▼

- *circa 1900*

Pair of French boules with original leather carrying strap.
- *diameter 20cm*
- **Guide price $60**

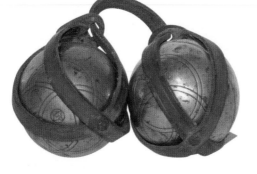

Riding Whip ▶

- *circa 1900*

Leather riding whip, with silver collar.
- *length 1.70m*
- **Guide price $250**

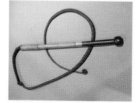

Travelling Sandwich Tin ▲

- *circa 1890*

Travelling leather case, the interior enclosing a sandwich tin and flask.
- *15cm x 15cm*
- **Guide price $280**

Child's Skis ▼

- *1920s*

Child's wooden skis with matching poles and bindings.
- *1.05m x 8cm*
- **Guide price $210**

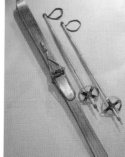

B C F C Cap ▼

- *1933*

B C F C velvet blue and maroon football cap with silver braiding and tassel. On the inside "English manufactured Christys, London, Horton Stephens, Ltd., The Shops Brighton College and Ward 1933–45".
- *diameter 20cm*
- **Guide price $80**

Cribbage Board ▼

- *circa 1900*

Marchline tartanware cribbage board box.
- *26cm x 10cm*
- **Guide price $550**

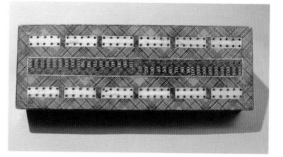

Fishing

Brass Gaff
- 1880

A Hardy telescopic brass gaff with lignum handle.
- *length 35cm*
- **Guide price** $270

Trout Priest
- 1910

An unusual trout priest in staghorn, carved in the form of an eagle with a dragonfly motif.
- *length 30cm*
- **Guide price** $450

Perfect Fly Reel
- *1920–1*

Rare Hardy "Perfect" duplicated MK-2 salmon fly reel with smooth alloy foot held with two screws, ivorine handle, nickel silver line guide and duplicated check.
- *diameter 10.8cm*
- **Guide price** $280

Expert Tips

Fishing reels proliferate but usually only the good ones have survived. If in doubt, at least make sure it works.

Uniqua Fly Reel
- *circa 1923*

Hardy "Uniqua" duplicated MK-2 trout fly reel with horseshoe latch, ivorine handle, smooth brass foot and retaining most of the black lead finish.
- *diameter 7.3cm*
- **Guide price** $250

Allcocks Reel
- *circa 1920–40*

Wood fishing reel by Allcocks with brass fittings and ebonised handles.
- *diameter 9cm*
- **Guide price** $90

Fishing Flies
- 1920

A case of 45 fishing flies.
- *15cm x 10cm*
- **Guide price** $270

Cased Flies
- 1920

A case of 70 fishing flies.
- *15cm x 10cm*
- **Guide price** $270

Fly Rod ◄
- *circa 1880*
Green heart trout rod of three sections, with brass reel and ivory handle.
- *length 2.8m*
- **Guide price** $340

Fly Box ▼
- *circa 1915*
Leather lined box with 12 glass and alloy containers for flies, with original tweezers and pocket.
- *13cm x 10cm*
- **Guide price** $160

Small Fishing Reel ◄
- *circa 1920–40*
Small wood fishing reel with a brass plate and turned decoration.
- *diameter 7cm*
- **Guide price** $45

Fishing Reel ▼
- *circa 1920–40*
Wood fishing reel with brass handles and plate with turned decoration.
- *diameter 10cm*
- **Guide price** $80

Leather Fly Wallet ▼
- *circa 1920–40*
Leather fly wallet with eight compartments.
- *width 16cm*
- **Guide price** $50

Wood Fishing Reel ▼
- *circa 1920–40*
Wood fishing reel with banded decoration, brass fittings and ebonised double handles.
- *diameter 8cm*
- **Guide price** $60

Hardy Fly Box ◄
- *circa 1920*
Hardy alloy fly box, includes collection of trout flies.
- *13cm x 10cm*
- **Guide price** $200

Nottingham Walnut Reel ▶

- *1912*

Rare Hardy Nottingham reel made of seasoned walnut, with patent lever "Silex" action, fitted with twin cow horn handles on elliptical brass seats and Bickerdyke line guide.
- *diameter 10.2cm*
- **Guide price $270**

Bernard & Sons Reel ▲

- *circa 1928*

J. Bernard & Sons salmon fly and trolling or harling reel with a fixed calliper check, strap over rim mounted tension adjuster and unventilated drum with ivorine handle.
- *diameter 12.7cm*
- **Guide price $160**

Wide Drum Perfect Reel ▼

- *circa 1955*

Hardy wide drum salmon "Perfect" fly reel fitted with revolving nickel silver line guide, and duplicated check and ridged brass foot reel.
- *diameter 9.5cm*
- **Guide price $250**

Nottingham Fly and Trolling Reel ▶

- *circa 1900*

Hardy Nottingham fly and trolling reel with twin horn handles on elliptical brass seats, Bickerdyke line guide and early spring steel calliper.
- *diameter 12.7cm*
- **Guide price $220**

Hercules Fly Reel ▲

- *early 20th century*

Hardy "Hercules" raised-face brass fly reel with ivoreen handle, wasted and ventilated foot, and oval logo.
- *diameter 10.2cm*
- **Guide price $270**

St George Fly Reel ▲

- *1935*

Hardy "St George" fly reel with ridged brass foot, three screw drum release, grey agate line and ebonite handle.
- *diameter 8.6cm*
- **Guide price $210**

Sea Fishing Reel ▶

- *Early 20th century*

A Nottingham sea fishing reel made of walnut with twin bulbous handles on elliptical brass seats, brass cross on the back with sliding on/off check button and fitted with a brass Bickerdyke line guide.
- *diameter 14cm*
- **Guide price $80**

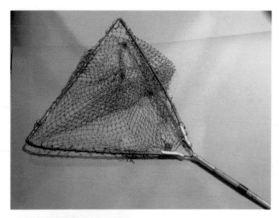

Hardy Landing Net ◄
- *circa 1890*

Hardy's triangular folding landing net with brass fittings.
- *1.15m x 48cm*
- **Guide price** $410

Starback Fishing Reel ▲
- *circa 1920–40*

Starback wood fishing reel with turned decoration and brass fittings.
- *diameter 12cm*
- **Guide price** $100

Willow Creel ▼
- *circa 1900*

Small willow fishing creel with leather strap handle.
- *25cm x 19cm*
- **Guide price** $160

Starback Reel ▲
- *circa 1920–40*

Starback wooden fishing reel with brass fittings and double handles.
- *diameter 9cm*
- **Guide price** $100

Hardy Fishing Reel ▲
- *circa 1930*

Hardy platewind fishing reel. Silex no 2.
- *diameter 10cm*
- **Guide price** $500

Dry Fly Tin ◄
- *1900*

A Hardy black japanned dry fly tin with lift lid and ivorine pencil inside lid.
- *15cm x 10cm*
- **Guide price** $270

Brass Reels ▲
- *circa 1910*

Three brass fly fishing reels.
- *7cm/left; 5.5cm/centre; 5cm/right*
- **Guide price** $80

Wood Reels ►
- *circa 1920*

Two wooden fly fishing reels with brass cross backs.
- *9cm/left; 9cm/right*
- **Guide price** $130

Shooting

Leather Gun Case ▼
- *circa 1890*
Leather leg of mutton gun case
with leather shoulder strap and
carrying handle.
- *length 79cm*
- **Guide price $220**

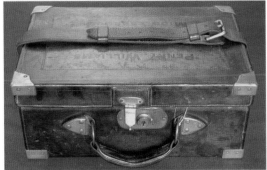

Holland & Holland Rifle ▼
- *2001*
Holland & Holland 375 H&H.
New bolt-action magazine rifle.
- *length 1.19m*
- **Guide price $27,800**

Magazine Case ▲
- *circa 1920*
Ammunition case with brass
fittings and leather straps by
Penry Williams, Middlesbrough.
- *41cm x 16cm*
- **Guide price $1,690**

Cartridge Case ▲
- *circa 1890*
Gannochy loader canvas
cartridge case with holders for
30 rounds of ammunition.
- *26cm x 13cm*
- **Guide price $2,670**

Magazine Box ▲
- *circa 1890*
Leather magazine box with strap,
buckle and a lock, by James
MacNaughton, Gun and Rifle
Maker, Edinburgh.
- *23cm x 24cm*
- **Guide price $1,160**

Brass Powder Flask ▲
- *circa 1875*
Brass black powder flask with
embossed decoration.
- *10cm x 19cm*
- **Guide price $90**

Four-Bore Shotgun ▲
- *1928*
Holland and Holland four-bore
shotgun with black powder only.
- *length 1.5m*
- Guide price $9,790

Gun Case ▼
- *circa 1890*
Leather gun case with brass
reinforced corners and leather
carrying handle.
- *30cm x 82cm*
- Guide price $680

Twenty-Bore Shotgun ▶
- *2001*
Holland & Holland sporting over
and under 20-bore single-trigger
shotgun.
- *length 1.15m*
- Guide price $44,500

Expert Tips

*When purchasing firearms it is
important to ensure that they
come with a proofing certificate
of fireworthiness.*

Bullet Mould ▼
- *circa 1895*
Sixteen-bore brass bullet mould.
Paradox stock.
- *27cm x 8cm*
- Guide price $980

Royal Rifle ◀
- *1945*
Holland & Holland Royal model
300 back-action double rifle, with
sights.
- *length 1.14m*
- Guide price $56,960

Cartridge Case ▲
- *circa 1890*
Gannochy loader leather
cartridge case with canvas
shoulder strap, made by
McArthur and Prain.
- *25cm x 9cm*
- Guide price $2,140

Flintlock Pistol ▲
- *circa 1840*
Flintlock percussion double-
barrel pistol with back-action
locks, engraved lockplates and
trigger guards.
- *25cm x 10cm*
- Guide price $770

Taxidermy

Photographers often use stuffed animals for advertisements because of their lifelike and naturalistic poses.

The art of taxidermy as a technique for keeping animals, birds, insects and fish in a preserved state is of great importance to both the scientist, academic researcher and sportsmen alike. Taxidermy has always been a popular and desirable way of preserving a trophy, especially at the turn of the century when big game was hunted in Africa and India.

Nowadays however, it is more usual to find a smaller stuffed animal, such as your Aunt Betty's favourite dog, than to find a large stuffed lion in someone's house. These wilder and more exotic animals can now be found decorating a film set or photo shoot, where they are being used more and more, not only because they don't move, but also because it is a lot safer and cheaper than working with the real thing.

In the past, before the advent of photography and television, the majority of people would not have known what a polar bear, tiger or chameleon looked like, except from drawings or paintings.

Albino Cobra ▼
- *20th century*
Albino cobra shown in an aggressive pose.
- *60cm x 28cm*
- **Guide price $350**

Mallards ▲
- *20th century*
Two male mallards, one shown standing and the other recumbent.
- *40cm x 64cm*
- **Guide price $530**

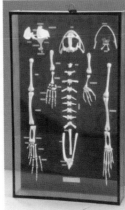

Hooded Crow ▼
- *20th century*
Hooded crow shown perched on a branch and mounted on a plinth base.
- *57cm x 28cm*
- **Guide price $220**

Bullfrog Skeletons ◄
- *20th century*
Bullfrog skeleton in sections with documentation.
- *30cm x 40cm*
- **Guide price $250**

Tawny Owl ▼

- **20th century**
Tawny owl naturalistically posed and mounted on a circular base, with original glass dome.
- *55cm x 27cm*
- **Guide price $700**

Eagle Owl ▼

- **20th century**
Eagle owl in fine condition with a good expression mounted on a circular base.
- *65cm x 35cm*
- **Guide price $980**

Sparrowhawk ▼

- **20th century**
Sparrowhawk with wings pinned back.
- *27cm x 35cm*
- **Guide price $190**

Yorkshire Terrier ▲

- **20th century**
Yorkshire terrier seated with a curious expression and a red ribbon.
- *30cm x 20cm*
- **Guide price $440**

Tropical Birds ▲

- **circa 1880**
Victorian glass dome containing various tropical birds.
- *54cm x 36cm*
- **Guide price $1,160**

Roach ▼

- **1996**
Roach in a bow-fronted case with natural grasses and weeds, with gilt lettering documenting the catch.
- *32cm x 50cm*
- **Guide price $690**

Barn Owl ▼

- **20th century**
Barn owl with wings outstretched at the point of take off, mounted on a branch.
- *70cm x 70cm*
- **Guide price $490**

Red Fox ▼

- **20th century**
Red fox vixen shown recumbent with head slightly raised.
- *35cm x 57cm*
- **Guide price $360**

Textiles

A fascinating area of collection and study, where the original artists may have been amateur, but accurately reflect the tastes and skills of their time.

London is particularly rich in museums exhibiting textiles and costumes throughout the ages, but there are very good museums across the country with experts who will help you in this fascinating area of antique study and collection. Textiles are of particular interest to the historian because they so accurately reflect the social and industrial history of their time. Every textile, with the exception of felt, is produced by weaving – the interlinking of the "warp" and "weft" thread on a loom. However, the richer the society the more that textiles are patterned during this process, or are decorated afterwards, either by a needle, as in embroidery, or by painting or printing. Although early tapestries and sixteenth and seventeenth century needlework command prices of thousands of pounds, nineteenth century samplers can be obtained for only a few hundred.

Chinese Evening Coat ▶
- **1918**
Chinese black ladies' coat embroidered with pink yellow and blue floral design and lined with white rabbit.
- *full length*
- **Guide price $3,560**

Cloche Hat ▶
- **1920**
Brown silk cloche hat with velvet brim and a large gold silk flower and leaf.
- *height 23cm*
- **Guide price $350**

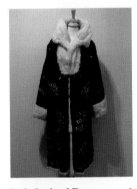

Pink Cocktail Dress ◀
- *circa 1950*
Short pink satin cocktail dress.
- *length 1.06m*
- **Guide price $400**

Art Deco Evening Dress ▼
- **1920**
Black Art Deco silk chiffon evening dress with silver beading.
- *full length*
- **Guide price $1,600**

Blue Evening Dress ▼

- *circa 1930*
Royal blue net evening dress.
- *full length*
- **Guide price** $310

Short Velvet Jacket ▲

- *circa 1920*
Pale pink velvet short evening jacket.
- *length 44cm*
- **Guide price** $220

Pink Chiffon Dress ▼

- *circa 1960*
Pale pink chiffon layered evening dress with large pink satin ribbon.
- *full length*
- **Guide price** $310

Silk Cape ▼

- *circa 1910*
Silk cape decorated with red chrysanthemums within a trailing foliate design.
- *length 96cm*
- **Guide price** $470

Silk Day Dress ▲

- *circa 1940*
Silk day dress with lace design background and stripes of pink, yellow and green with matching bow.
- *full length*
- **Guide price** $240

Silver Lurex Dress ▼

- *circa 1965*
Silver lurex hand-crocheted dress.
- *mid-length*
- **Guide price** $220

Patchwork Quilt ▼
- *circa 1840–70*
Victorian patchwork quilt made up of predominantly pink and white hexagonal patches dating from the mid nineteenth century.
- *2.5m sq*
- **Guide price $1,590**

Patchwork Quilt ▼
- *circa 1950*
Patchwork quilt with a bold, multi-coloured and patterned geometric design.
- *1.6m x 1.56m*
- **Guide price $350**

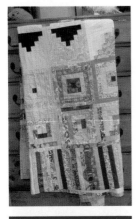

Silk Smoking Hat ▲
- *circa 1870*
Brown silk smoking hat with trailing foliate embroidery of small white flowers.
- *size 6*
- **Guide price $220**

Tartan Umbrella ▲
- *circa 1930*
Tartan umbrella with a handle in the shape of a swan with glass eyes.
- *length 67cm*
- **Guide price $120**

Cream Child's Dress ▶
- *circa 1880*
Cream cotton child's dress with lace trim and navy blue ribboning on the hips and collar.
- *small*
- **Guide price $470**

Victorian Cushion Cover ▼
- *circa 1880*
Cut pile cushion cover with a red and black diamond geometric design.
- *40cm x 45cm*
- **Guide price $170**

Gentleman's Slipper Cut Out ▼
- *circa 1880*
Gentleman's unused embroidered slipper "cut out" with a diamond design of cream, beige and variegated reds within black borders.
- *size 9*
- **Guide price $170**

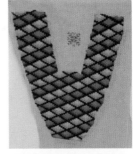

Welsh Patchwork Quilt ▲
- *circa 1880*
Welsh patchwork quilt with a white and lilac diamond design centered with lilac floral sprays.
- *80cm x 80cm*
- Guide price $1,160

Smoking Hat ▲
- *circa 1880*
Black velvet smoking hat with white embroidered floral design, a central yellow silk button, pink gold and white tassel, with original box in good original condition.
- *size 7*
- Guide price $290

Cut Pile Cushion Cover ▼
- *circa 1880*
Cut pile Victorian cushion cover with a red, green and pink geometric design.
- *42cm x 30cm*
- Guide price $170

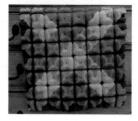

Ivory Fan ▼
- *circa 1904*
Cream silk fan with a trailing design of pink and yellow apple blossom mounted on carved ivory spines.
- *length 35cm*
- Guide price $220

Slipper Pattern ▼
- *circa 1850*
Fine continental unused beaded slipper "cut out" pattern, with a turquoise background, pink and yellow flowers and two deer by a river.
- *length 22cm*
- Guide price $400

Purple Silk Kimono ▲
- *circa 1900*
Purple silk kimono with trailing pink apple blossom design.
- *medium*
- Guide price $530

Gentleman's Smoking Hat ▲
- *circa 1880*
Black velvet gentleman's smoking hat with trailing foliate designs of pink and blue flowers, surmounted by a red satin-covered button on the top with a trailing green, white and red tassel.
- *size 6*
- Guide price $200

Beaded Pelmet ◄
- *circa 1880*
Beaded cream pelmet with red tassel design below a gold and red diamond design.
- *length 3.2m*
- Guide price $880

Gold Cocktail Dress ▶

- *circa 1960*
Hand-beaded gold cocktail dress
with gold beading and topaz
stones.
- *mini*
- **Guide price** $230

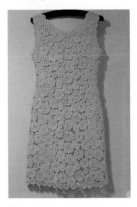

Rafia Cocktail Dress ▲

- *circa 1960*
Pink hand-crocheted raffia
sleeveless shift dress.
- *short*
- **Guide price** $230

Navy Blue Cocktail Dress ▲

- *circa 1960*
Navy blue strapless cocktail dress
with white frill.
- *mid-length*
- **Guide price** $180

Strapless Cocktail Dress ▼

- *circa 1950*
Yellow and white cotton strapless
cocktail dress by Frank Usher
with swathed bodice detail and
gathered skirt.
- *mid-length*
- **Guide price** $180

Nylon Flower Dress ▼

- *circa 1960*
Nylon flower power print dress
with smock detail on the hips and
interesting orange belt.
- *long dress*
- **Guide price** $130

Silk Floral Hat ▼

- *circa 1950*
A summer hat lavishly decorated
with silk faux flowers and leaves
intertwined with fine veiling.
- *length 22cm*
- **Guide price** $90

Lilac Petal Hat ▶

- *circa 1950*

Faux lilac petals and lilac wire and mesh "leaves" arranged to form a decorative summer headpiece.
- *diameter 22cm*
- **Guide price $40**

Military Breeches ▲

- *circa 1910*

Gentleman's war-issue military tweed breeches.
- *medium*
- **Guide price $170**

Black Mortarboard ▲

- *1940*

Black mortarboard by Ede & Ravenscroft, by appointment to the King and Queen, 93 & 94 Chancery Lane, London.
- *circumference 17cm*
- **Guide price $50**

Pink Mini Dress ▼

- *circa 1960*

Pink floral silk mini dress with chiffon sleeves and a matching hat.
- *mid-length*
- **Guide price $270**

Straw Boater Hat ▶

- *1930*

Gentleman's straw boater with black band, by Falcon.
- *circumference 32cm*
- **Guide price $50**

Silk Top Hat ▲

- *1910*

Black silk top hat by Battersby, Northumbland Av, Trafalgar Square, London.
- *circumference 17cm*
- **Guide price $130**

Mother-of-Pearl Fan ▲
- *circa 1910*
Cream silk lace fan covered with cream floral lace and a mother-of-pearl handle.
- *length 29cm*
- **Guide price $490**

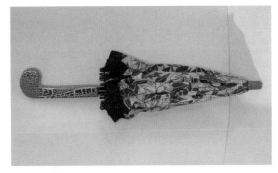

Lady's Red Hat ▲
- *circa 1920*
Lady's red soft silk mesh hat by Pauline Louy's, decorated with red felt flowers.
- *medium*
- **Guide price $260**

Russian-Style Cape and Hat ▲
- *circa 1950*
Dramatic red Russian-style cape with black embroidery and white fur lining, with matching hat.
- *medium*
- **Guide price $1,240**

Lace Fan ▼
- *circa 1905*
Cream lace fan with silk backing and cream ivory handle with a cartouche of a raised lily.
- *length 32cm*
- **Guide price $670**

Lady's Parasol ▲
- *circa 1920*
Lady's parasol with a black floral design and a handle with a black and beige geometric pattern.
- *length 53cm*
- **Guide price $170**

Child's Shoes ◀
- *1870*
Child's leather shoes with black studs and metal fittings.
- *length 13cm*
- **Guide price $120**

Italian Allegorical Panel ▼
- *1763*
Rare set of Italian silk-work allegorical panels signed "Gaetano Pati, Rome". Part of a set of eight panels composed of fine silk threads, arranged and pressed into wax. The facial and body detailing is hand painted onto finely woven silk. The tonal detailing and intricacy is very fine.
- *34cm x 27cm*
- **Guide price $56,960**

Panama Hat ▶

- *1940*
Gentleman's Panama hat with
black band.
- *circumference 21cm*
- **Guide price $60**

Miriam Hunt Sampler ▲

- *1722*
Sampler worked by Miriam Hunt
with polychrome silk threads on
linen which features the Lord's
Prayer surrounded by a border of
flowers and berries.
- *22cm x 32cm*
- **Guide price $5,070**

Jean Smith Sampler ▲

- *1807*
Polychrome silk threads on
tammy sampler by Jean Smith
featuring a house guarded by a
black man in a folly, surmounted
by a band of flowers and Adam
and Eve below.
- *44cm x 52cm*
- **Guide price $13,970**

Ann Chapman Sampler ▼

- *1839*
Pictorial sampler by Ann
Chapman depicting a country
house and garden with people,
surmounted by a verse and
various motifs. Polychrome silk
threads on tammy.
- *44cm x 32cm*
- **Guide price $14,150**

Elenor Dickenson Sampler ▶

- *1749*
Sampler signed "This is The
Work of Elenor Dickinson in The
11th Year Of Her Age 1749"
depicting alphabets, numerals,
verses, flowers and foliage
surrounded by an intricately
worked border.
- *22cm x 32cm*
- **Guide price $8,010**

Expert Tips

*Early samplers were in long
narrow strips and dates, names
and ages all add value.*

Isabella Blacklin Sampler ▼

- *late 18th century*
Sampler by Isabella Blacklin with
a naive interpretation of a goat
surrounded by a man sitting
beneath a tree, a rural cottage
scene and bordered by stylised
flowers.
- *28cm x 41cm*
- **Guide price $4,450**

Blue Silk Kesi ▼

- *late 18th–early 19th century*
A Japanese blue silk ground Kesi (priest's robe) with gold Kinran cloud designs.
- *2.18m x 1.2m*
- **Guide price $8,540**

Chinese Court Robe ▶

- *circa 1870*
An embroidered silk court robe worked in couched gold thread in multi coloured satin stitch. The upper half with dragons and Buddhist emblems, the attached apron with 12 dragon roundels.
- *medium*
- **Guide price $16,020**

Silk Kesi ▲

- *19th century*
A fine Japanese silk Kesi (priest's robe) cleverly constructed using an eighteenth century Chinese blue and gold brocade dragon robe on a gold brocade ground.
- *2.28m x 1.14m*
- **Guide price $8,010**

Chiné Woven Silk Polonaise ◀

- *circa 1780*
Silk polonaise with a cream silk ground woven with a satin stripe with pink roses and green leaves. The square necked bodice and elbow sleeves trimmed with wide pleated ruffle.
- *depth 23cm*
- **Guide price $4,450**

Shibori Kimono Designs ▼

- *circa 1920*
A bold set of nine Japanese blue and white designs for kimono decorated in Shibori, stylised from traditional designs. Framed and glazed.
- *48cm x 79cm*
- **Guide price $4,980**

Manchu Woman's Fuschia Jacket ▼

- *1875–99*
Jacket with satin ground applied with jui shapes around and embroidered with flowers. Lined with light blue silk, the piece has golden engraved buttons.
- *small*
- **Guide price $1,340**

Crewel Wool Work Hanging

- *mid-17th century*

Hanging with fine twill weave ground (wool and linen) embroidered in shades of mid-green, blue, forest and dark green wools with thick stems from which acanthus-style leaves hang.
- *1.93m x 54.6cm*
- **Guide price $4,450**

Silkwork Picture ▲

- *circa 1800*

Silkwork picture of a young woman gazing at a rose, worked in a variety of stitches in shades of soft yellow through green with black highlighting. Her face and the sky are painted.
- *28cm x 21.6cm*
- **Guide price $890**

Brussels Wedding Veil ▲

- *19th century*

A wedding veil of Brussels lace.
- *1.36m x 1.2m*
- **Guide price $850**

Lace Lawn Shawl ▼

- *19th century*

Lawn shawl with a lace border and applied lace motifs throughout.
- *2.3m x 1.2m*
- **Guide price $490**

Scarlet Crinoline Frame ▼

- *1865–68*

Thomson's Empress crinoline frame for a young girl, with shaped red cotton waistband with central oval and wide red patterned attached to 11 steel hoops.
- *waist 56cm*
- **Guide price $1,070**

Expert Tips

Honiton Lace from Devon: look for designs which include a rose, shamrock and thistles and with crosshatched centres to flowers.

Maltese Lace Handkerchief ▼

- *19th century*

Handkerchief in silk with a Maltese lace surround.
- *28cm x 28cm*
- **Guide price $30**

Bobbin Lace ▼
- **19th century**
A flounce of Duchesse applied bobbin lace.
- **3m x 62cm**
- **Guide price $450**

Milanese Lace ▲
- **17th or 18th century**
Fine piece of Milanese lace displaying very interesting fillings and designs.
- **3.2m x 32cm**
- **Guide price $1,030**

Olive Green Parasol ▲
- **1920**
Olive green silk parasol with black netting overlay, gold thread roses and an ivory handle. Black engraved with an eagle and tiger's eye.
- **height 75cm**
- **Guide price $320**

Edwardian Parasol ▲
- **1880**
Black Edwardian parasol with bone handle and gilt scrolled band with shield.
- **height 87cm**
- **Guide price $150**

Evening Waistcoat ▲
- **1820**
Gentleman's evening waistcoat, pink silk with leaf pattern of gold thread.
- **medium**
- **Guide price $700**

Paisley Silk Dressing Gown ▲
- **circa 1930**
Gentleman's black and gold paisley design silk dressing gown.
- **full length**
- **Guide price $220**

Chinese Silk Jacket ◄
- **circa 1960**
Cream cotton Chinese design jacket with wide burgundy silk lapels and belt.
- **full length**
- **Guide price $110**

Orange Silk Dressing Gown ►
- **circa 1980**
Orange silk dressing gown with design, by Georgina Von Ernodof.
- **full length**
- **Guide price $350**

Gleneagles Coat ▲

- *circa 1980*

Gentleman's single-breasted three-quarter length cream light wool coat.

- *three-quarter length*
- **Guide price** $210

Burgundy Scarf ▲

- *circa 1940*

Burgundy paisley silk gentleman's scarf with gold and burgundy tassels.

- *length 1.1m*
- **Guide price** $50

Tweed Suit ▶

- **20th century**

Gentleman's Harris tweed suit with matching waistcoat.

- *medium*
- **Guide price** $270

Velvet Waistcoat ▼

- *circa 1970*

Velvet waistcoat with broad paisley pattern and wide lapels.

- *length 60cm*
- **Guide price** $170

Silk Evening Scarf ▲

- *circa 1920*

Cream silk evening scarf with black and white wool tassels.

- *length 1.3m*
- **Guide price** $50

Corduroy Breeches ▲

- *circa 1920*

Olive green corduroy breeches with side lacing below the knee and cotton with buttoning. Two large angled pockets and one smaller.

- *length 1m*
- **Guide price** $180

Animal Print Scarf ▲

- *circa 1950*

Burgundy wool gentleman's scarf with ethnic print of figures, animals and flowers.

- *length 70cm*
- **Guide price** $50

Toys, Games & Dolls

Until the 1940s the largest producers of toys were based in Germany, where they also created special versions of toys for export.

Toy collecting has grown in stature over recent years with many collectors tucking away new toys in pristine boxes in the hope of a good profit – dream on! Old toys are valuable because they were used and very rarely survived in good condition. It wasn't until the eighteenth century that parents realised that their children could learn through play. When William Hamley opened his doors in 1760 the trend started. The industrial revolution created inexpensive production techniques and the new middle classes the demand. Now any pre-war toy in good condition will fetch high prices and examples from the eighteenth century are very rare. Most collectors collect specific categories and become expert in identification, price and the difference condition can make to value. Collectors can tell the difference between signs of love and signs of abuse, and love is a market winner.

Gold Cadillac ▲
- *circa 1950*
American gold cadillac with red interior and chromed fittings, made by Bandiai, Japan.
- *length 29cm*
- **Guide price $270**

Fred Flintstone ▼
- *1960*
Tin plate "Fred Flintstone" sitting astride his dinosaur "Dino", made by Louis Marks in Japan.
- *length 2cm*
- **Guide price $470**

Smiley of the Seven Dwarfs ▲
- *circa 1930*
Padded soft toy of "Smiley", one of the dwarfs from the children's story, "Snow White and the Seven Dwarfs".
- *height 27cm*
- **Guide price $290**

Huntley & Palmers Van ◄
- *circa 1920*
Brown toy van with a hinged lid to store biscuits and the gilt inscription, "Huntley & Palmers Ltd, Reading Biscuits" and a Royal Crest above.
- *19cm x 25cm*
- **Guide price $1,560**

Bru Walker Doll ▲

• *circa 1880*
Bru "Kiss throwing walker doll" with long auburn hair and brown glass eyes, wearing a cream cotton and lace dress, a bonnet with lilac bows and brown leather shoes.
• *height 62cm*
• **Guide price $6,680**

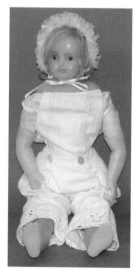

Wax Doll ▲

• *circa 1900*
Wax girl doll with blonde hair, blue eyes and a painted face, wearing a linen top and pantaloons with lace embroidery, and a lace cap.
• *height 48cm*
• **Guide price $850**

Tin Plate Racing Car ▼

• *circa 1930*
English tin plate cream racing car, with a red radiator grill and red line decoration, bonnet straps, and the number five on the side and on the tail back.
• *length 38cm*
• **Guide price $470**

Noddy ▼

• *1980*
Noddy wearing a red shirt, yellow spotted scarf and blue hat with a yellow pom-pom, in his yellow rubber car with red fenders.
• *19cm x 27cm*
• **Guide price $50**

Japanese Motor Launch ▼

• *circa 1950*
Japanese red, yellow, orange and blue motor launch with driver in a helmet, and hand crank.
• *length 21cm*
• **Guide price $130**

Drummer Boy ▲

• *1930*
Drummer boy with a tin plate body, legs and arms, and a celluloid head, with the makers name "Fecuda", Japan.
• *24cm*
• **Guide price $490**

Red Double Decker Bus ▲

• *1960*
Red bus with "Mobilgas" and "Double Decker Bus" decals on the side, in fine condition.
• *height 22cm*
• **Guide price $260**

Spanish Racing Car ▼

• *circa 1920*
Blue and yellow racing car with driver and passenger, and the number seven on the side. Manufactured by Paya in Spain.
• *length 27cm*
• **Guide price $400**

Mickey Mouse ▼

- *circa 1930*
Velvet padded Mickey Mouse
with a large smiling expression.
- *height 33cm*
- **Guide price** $200

Ferrari Pedal Car ▲

- **1970**
Red Ferrari pedal car with the
number three on the side.
- *length 1.17m*
- **Guide price** $450

Heubach Boy Doll ▼

- *circa 1890*
Heubach jointed porcelain boy
doll with a painted face, wearing
a matching beige and cream
outfit with hat.
- *height 25cm*
- **Guide price** $700

Steiff Owl ▲

- *circa 1950*
Steiff owl with large glass eyes
and a menacing expression.
- *height 14cm*
- **Guide price** $90

Tri-ang Red Racing Car ▼

- **1950**
Red Tri-ang Mimic racing car
with driver, the car bearing the
number three.
- *length 15cm*
- **Guide price** $80

Dream Baby ▲

- *circa 1920*
Porcelain jointed black "Dream
Baby", in perfect condition.
- *height 28cm*
- **Guide price** $700

Expert Tips

*Any toys associated with
popular books or films today,
for example the Harry Potter
series, are worth investing in
now for the future.*

Petrol Tanker ▶

- **1930**
Red lead petrol tanker by Taylor and Barrett.
- *length 10cm*
- **Guide price $150**

Alfa Romeo ▼

- *circa 1960*
Red Alfa Romeo 1900 "Super Sprint", made by Dinky, no. 85, with original box.
- *length 10cm*
- **Guide price $110**

Oriental Baby Doll ▼

- *circa 1930*
Small oriental porcelain jointed baby doll with brown glass eyes and a painted face.
- *height 18cm*
- **Guide price $530**

Austin Seven ▲

- *circa 1940*
Cornflower-blue Austin Seven, 35 series with pneumatic tyres.
- *height 3cm*
- **Guide price $70**

Horse and Milk Float ▲

- **1950**
Matchbox horse-drawn red milk float with driver.
- *height 3cm*
- **Guide price $30**

Kestner Doll ▼

- *circa 1900*
Porcelain jointed doll by Kestner with blue glass eyes and long auburn hair, wearing linen and lace dress and brown leather shoes.
- *height 38cm*
- **Guide price $1,060**

Chad Valley Teddy ▼

- **1950**
Chad Valley padded teddy with glass eyes and a pleasant expression.
- *height 44cm*
- **Guide price $450**

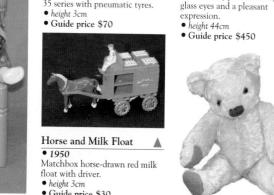

Mickey Mouse ▲
- *1950*
Mickey Mouse puppet carved
from wood with yellow
composition feet, by Pelham.
- *height 29cm*
- **Guide price** $130

Tri-ang Blue Van ▶
- *1950*
Tri-ang Mimic navy-blue London
and North Eastern Railway van.
- *length 18cm*
- **Guide price** $400

German Fire Engine ◀
- *1950*
Red German fire engine with
fireman, manufactured by
Gamma.
- *length 43cm*
- **Guide price** $200

Mummy Bear ▼
- *circa 1930*
Padded jointed bear with glass
eyes and cloth paws.
- *height 39cm*
- **Guide price** $150

XK Yellow Jaguar ▲
- *circa 1950*
XK yellow Jaguar with a bottle
green top, and chromed bumper,
made by Hoku.
- *length 25cm*
- **Guide price** $400

Ovaltine Van ▶
- *circa 1950*
Blue Dinky Bedford 10cwt
Ovaltine van, inscribed "Ovaltine"
and "Ovaltine Biscuits" on the
side, with original box.
- *length 8cm*
- **Guide price** $120

Terrafish ◀
- **1960**

Green Terrafish with yellow spots and large white eyes, from the Gerry Anderson TV show, by Lakeside Toys, Japan.
- *length 23cm*
- **Guide price $490**

Shoe-Shine Panda ▼
- *circa 1960*

Shoe-shine soft panda, battery-operated, sitting with a pipe in its mouth and a brush in each paw, wearing red dungarees.
- *height 25cm*
- **Guide price $140**

American Racing Car ▲
- **1930**

Red and silver racing car and driver, made from an interesting combination of metals, die cast and cast iron, probably by Hubbly American. No. 22 on the side.
- *length 25cm*
- **Guide price $120**

Bobby Bear ▶
- **1950**

Padded "Bobby Bear" made by Pedigree, in good overall condition.
- *height 44cm*
- **Guide price $160**

Yellow Milk Float ▼
- *circa 1960*

Rare yellow Dinky promotional milk float, with "Jobs Dairy" inscribed on the front and rear, with red interior and hubs.
- *length 7cm*
- **Guide price $260**

Orober Fire Engine ◀
- **1920**

Fire engine set of two vehicles with a driver on a pumper, and three figures on the fire engine carrier, complete with red garage, made by Orober in Germany.
- *19cm x 33cm*
- **Guide price $1,160**

Playing Card Box ▲
• *circa 1875*
Late Victorian mother-of-pearl playing card and games box containing two sets of original playing cards and a cribbage board.
• *length 22cm*
• **Guide price $3,470**

Dutch Silk Plush Bear ▲
• *1950s*
Dutch brown art silk plush bear in superb original condition with bulging cheeks, black and white plastic eyes, brown plastic nose, black stitched mouth, white plush pad, and excelsior filling.
• *height 43.2cm*
• **Guide price $120**

Expert Tips

Only teddy bears which can be traced to their maker and are in a good condition achieve top prices. Look for the small STEIFF button in the left ear.

Backgammon and Chess Board ▲
• *circa 1860*
Mid-nineteenth century mahogany folding backgammon and chessboard with backgammon counters, dice and shakers.
• *52cm x 36cm*
• **Guide price $1,770**

Golden Blonde Mohair Bear ▲
• *circa 1910*
Early American golden blonde mohair bear, probably by Harman. Brown glass eyes, black fabric nose, black stitched mouth and claws, peach felt pads, excelsior filling, humped back and front final seam.
• *height 49.5cm*
• **Guide price $1,220**

Blonde Mohair Bear ▶
• *circa 1920*
English blonde mohair bear with glass eyes, black stitched nose and mouth, original linen pads (extensively darned), inoperative tilt growler, excelsior filling and pronounced humped back.
• *height 50.8cm*
• **Guide price $580**

Gold Mohair Bear ▲
• *circa 1918*
A dark gold German short bristle mohair bear with black boot button eyes, black stitched nose and mouth, replaced tan felt pad, and excelsior filling.
• *height 36cm*
• **Guide price $510**

Telstar Kaleidoscope ▼
- *1960*

Telstar kaleidoscope with a rocket, stars and satellite and a blue background, made by Green Monk of England.
- *height 17cm*
- **Guide price $35**

Nestlé's Austin Van ▲
- *circa 1950*

Red Austin van inscribed with "Nestlé's" in gold letters on the side, made by Dinky, no. 471.
- *length 9cm*
- **Guide price $220**

Baby Doll ▼
- *circa 1900*

Porcelain jointed baby doll with blue eyes, blonde hair and painted face, wearing a matching hat and outfit.
- *height 26cm*
- **Guide price $530**

Daimler Ambulance ▲
- *circa 1950*

Primrose-yellow Dinky Daimler ambulance, no. 253, with a red cross on the side, red hub plates and original box.
- *height 4cm*
- **Guide price $80**

Matchbox Fire Engine ▲
- *1950*

Red Matchbox fire engine with driver.
- *height 3cm*
- **Guide price $40**

Expert Tips

Look out for finely made jointed porcelain dolls by French makers such as G Vichy, or ballet dancers by Lambert, as these are very rare and highly collectable items.

MG Midget TD ▼
- *1950*
Matchbox yellow MG Midget TD with red interior, driver, grey wheels and a wheel on the boot.
- *height 2cm*
- Guide price $40

Scalextric Green BRM ▼
- *1960*
Scalextric tin plate green BRM with racing driver. No. Three on the side.
- *length 15cm*
- Guide price $170

Vespa and Driver ▲
- *1960*
Green Vespa with a driver wearing red, made in England by Benbros.
- *height 5cm*
- Guide price $40

Velam Bubble Car ◄
- *1960*
French cream Velam bubble car with grey roof, made by Quiralu, with original box.
- *height 4cm*
- Guide price $140

Pintel & Godchaux Doll ▲
- *circa 1900*
French porcelain jointed doll with blonde hair, blue eyes and painted face, wearing a lace dress, with a pink satin bow and lace socks, made by Pintel and Godchaux.
- *height 43cm*
- Guide price $1,060

Cottage Doll ▲
- *circa 1950*
Small padded "Cottage Doll" made by Glenda O'Connor, with blonde plaits, blue eyes and a pleasant expression, wearing a pink gingham dress, green hat, top and shoes.
- *height 21cm*
- Guide price $100

Folding Games Board ▶

- *circa 1675*
Rare ivory inlaid, ebony and
ebonised, south German folding
games board, the interior having
a backgammon board and two
panels of hunting scenes. One
side of the exterior having a
chessboard, the other with Nine
Men's Morris board.
- *16cm x 99cm x 56cm*
- **Guide price $31,150**

Silver King Locomotive ▼

- *1953–54*
Hornby Dublo EDL11 Silver
King locomotive.
- *length 28cm*
- **Guide price $120**

Tri-ang Hornby Tank Loco ▲

- *1967–70*
Triang Hornby R754 0-4-4 Class
M7 Tank Locomotive. Complete
with instructions, service sheet
and crew.
- *length 15cm*
- **Guide price $120**

Hornby Dublo Signal Home ▲

- *1950s*
Rare Hornby Dublo 5065 Single
Arm Signal Home, an electrically
operated signal.
- *length 8cm*
- **Guide price $80**

Tri-ang Tank Locomotive ▶

- *1961–67*
Tri-ang TT Railways T99 2-6-2
Class 4MT Tank Loco in
excellent boxed condition with
internal packing and oil bottle.
- *length 14cm*
- **Guide price $130**

Tri-ang Hornby Train Station ▲

- *1965–71*
Tri-ang Hornby R459 train station set, part of their range of accessories and rolling stock with "Picture Boxes".
- *32cm x 19cm*
- **Guide price $170**

Wrenn Locomotive ▲

- *1976–89*
Wrenn W2221 Cardiff Castle locomotive in excellent condition with box.
- *length 25cm*
- **Guide price $180**

Hornby Duplo Train ▶

- *1962–64*
Hornby Dublo 2234 Deltic Diesel Electric 2 Rail train in excellent condition with box.
- *length 25cm*
- **Guide price $270**

Minic Red Steam Lorry ▼

- *1966–68*
Minic Motorway M1564 Red Steam Lorry to compliment and run with Tri-ang OO scale railways.
- *length 7cm*
- **Guide price $310**

Topsy-Turvy Doll ◀

- *1930s*
A British Topsy-Turvy doll which changes from black to white when turned upside down. The heads are composition with painted features.
- *height 30cm*
- **Guide price $270**

Tri-ang Accessories ▲

- *1960s*
Tri-ang TTRailways T27 signal box.
- *length 9cm*
- **Guide price $70**

Staunton Chess Set

- *early 20th century*
Early twentieth century ivory
tournament size Staunton chess
set, with leather folding board.
- *height 6cm*
- Guide price $5,520

Tinplate Fire Engine

- *circa 1960*
Tinplate clockwork fire engine
with three-piece extending
ladder. Made in Japan and
marked with "K" trademark.
- *length 33cm*
- Guide price $260

Twin Rotor Helicopter

- *circa 1960*
ALPS Japanese tinplate battery-
driven twin rotor helicopter with
plastic rotors.
- *length 35cm*
- Guide price $320

Coal Truck

- *1931–36*
Hornby "O" gauge Meccano coal
truck.
- *length 17cm*
- Guide price $160

Tinplate Crane

- *circa 1950*
Tinplate tower three function
crane N.B.L., made in Western
Germany.
- *height 42cm*
- Guide price $150

LNER 504 Locomotive

- *circa 1930*
Bing for Bassett Lowke 4-4-0
George V LNER Locomotive
504, with clockwork, "O" gauge.
- *length 42cm*
- Guide price $670

CN Budd Dummy Railcar

- *1965–71*
Rare r352cn CN Budd Dummy
unpowered locomotive.
- *length 25cm*
- Guide price $70

Expert Tips

*Pre-war Dinky toys have no
model names or numbers, white
tyres and plain metal hubs.*

Treen

The most mundane item was not beneath the notice of imaginative craftsmen, and the ordinary in their hands quickly became a work of art.

Treen applies to those items which are carved from wood, and encompasses a wide range of items, from the simple napkin ring to the highly decorative and heavily carved oak plaque. The word treen actually means "made from trees" and therefore the beauty of collecting treen lies in the variety of artefacts that are available. Occasionally objects dating back to the seventeenth century arrive on the market, with the workaday items, such as cups and other vessels being fashioned from hardwoods such as sycamore and holly, while the more important were carved from lignum vitae, which had to be imported into England.

If you are about to embark on your first journey to collect treen it is worth noting that boxes and love tokens are amongst the most desirable types of treen. Look out for burr walnut or rosewood snuff boxes, which attract the collector with their sleek lines and simple design.

As a new collector treen is a good place to start as some of the items are still relatively inexpensive.

Rosewood Box ▼
- *circa 1825*
Small rosewood box with a silver plaque with the letters "E. M."
- *4cm x 7cm*
- **Guide price $400**

Pressed Wood Box ▼
- *circa 1840*
Pressed circular wood box with a carving of a boy and sword beside a dog jumping.
- *diameter 6cm*
- **Guide price $980**

Fruitwood Box ▲
- **1830**
Small fruitwood box with gold foliate banding between bands of gold leaves on a black background.
- *2cm x 8cm*
- **Guide price $490**

Tunbridge Ware Box ▲
- *circa 1850*
Tunbridge Ware box by Burrows. From Tunbridge Wells.
- *8cm square*
- **Guide price $250**

Carved Deer Heads ▼
- *circa 1860*
One of a pair of continental carved reindeer with red paint and genuine horns.
- *height 64cm*
- **Guide price $3,200**

Four Egg Cups ▲
- *circa 1840*
A set of four turned mahogany egg cups.
- *height 9cm*
- Guide price $670

Yew Wood Coaster ▲
- *circa 1840*
Yew wood coaster with a raised diamond flower in the centre and a linked border, with maker's name, M. Scott.
- *diameter 17cm*
- Guide price $1,160

Austrian Stamp Box ▲
- *1860*
Small Austrian stamp box with carved relief of oak leaves.
- *1.5cm x 5cm*
- Guide price $60

Rosewood Snuff Box ▲
- *circa 1780*
Circular snuff box with the inscription "A. C. B. to J. G. B. 1821".
- *diameter 9cm*
- Guide price $680

Burr-Walnut Snuff Box ▲
- *circa 1770*
Burr-walnut snuff box with a vacant silver plaque on the lid.
- *length 8.5cm*
- Guide price $680

French Carved Stand ▼
- *1780*
One of a pair of French carved stands, with scrolled foliate designs and seven giltwood flowers on a moulded serpentine base.
- *height 93cm*
- Guide price $2,580

Pipe Taper with Royal Charter ▼
- *circa 1780*
Pipe taper with a "Royal Charter" label on the base.
- *length 7.5cm*
- Guide price $620

Tribal Art

Even the creators of these works of art didn't choose to share their houses with them; today people are making money doing just that.

Tribal art is often considered to be something of a macabre field of collection. It is surrounded by fetish and the worship of ancestor gods, extending from the fetish figures, through chieftain's stools carved in the shape of a kneeling figure, to dance masks that were often truly horrific.

The god figures, which were often carved from ironwood and polished with sand, would usually be kept in dark huts or caves. It was only on festive occasions, religious rituals or, perhaps, prior to a war, that these items would be brought out and put on view. They would be sprinkled with blood while descendant tribesmen would dance themselves into a frenzy, some going into trances in order to speak to their distant ancestor gods.

All this might seem to be deep, dark stuff, but tribal art is markedly appreciating in value. Collectors should be wary of modern copies, though, which are proliferating in response to growing tourism.

Zuni Fetish Frog ▼
- 1930
Large Zuni fetish circular silver pendant with a central turquoise styled frog flanked by silver leaves.
- *length 4.5cm*
- **Guide price $110**

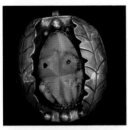

Kple Kple Mask ▲
- *circa 1920*
Kple Kple junior mask of the Golidance, one of the most abstracted masks of Africa, from a collection in France.
- *height 43cm*
- **Guide price $8,900**

Nigerian Delta Region ◀
- *circa 1910*
Spirit mask from the Nigerian Delta region, the head crowned by four men and a boat, with classical red pigmentation. The figures, originally white, have been overpainted black.
- *height 53cm*
- **Guide price $1,960**

Suku Fetish ▼
- *circa 1900*
Suku finely carved figure used as a fetish with additional fibre, beads and feathers, from Northern Zaire.
- *height 43cm*
- **Guide price $1,690**

Buffalo Helmet Mask ◄

- *circa 1920*
Kanos buffalo carved wood mask from the Ivory coast of Africa.
- *height 38cm*
- Guide price $2,490

M'Bun Currency ▼

- *unknown*
M'Bun status currency in throwing knife form.
- *48cm x 39cm*
- Guide price $1,280

Guardian of the Spirits ▼

- *circa 1820*
West Nepalese bronze figure of a village guardian of the spirits.
- *height 22cm*
- Guide price $1,280

Pulley Guro Bete ▲

- *circa 1890*
Figure of a pulley Guro Bete.
- *height 19cm*
- Guide price $870

Man Betu Gabon ▼

- *circa 1890*
A cephalomorphic ceramic from the Man Betu, Gabon, used only in court art.
- *height 42cm*
- Guide price $1,120

Igbo Tribe Figure ▲

- *circa 1910*
One of a pair of figures from the Igbo tribe. A terracotta seated ancestorial couple, with typical central crested headdress and multiple anklets, bracelets and necklaces symbolising wealth.
- *height 54cm*
- Guide price $11,570

Bhutan Nepal Mask ◄

- *circa 1700*
Early mask of dynamic primitive form relying on simplicity, from Bhutan on the Nepalese border. Very rare and in excellent condition.
- *height 33cm*
- Guide price $2,460

Dan-Karan Mask ▲
- *circa 1900*
Fine heavily patinated Dan-Karan mask, a powerful and abstracted mask from the Ivory Coast. From a collection in France.
- *height 25cm*
- **Guide price $6,410**

Himalayan Tribal Mask ▲
- *unknown*
Himalayan tribal mask with heavy patination on the inside, the exterior has been constantly painted with red, black and cream paint. Origin unknown.
- *height 28cm*
- **Guide price $1,100**

Apache Smoking Pouch ▼
- *1950*
Apache Indian smoking pouch with a red, white and black butterfly, and an orange background made from glass beads sewn on leather.
- *12cm x 7cm*
- **Guide price $280**

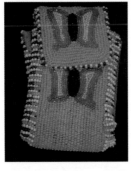

Mask with Cowrie Shells ▼
- *circa 1910*
Mask with applied cowrie shells on the nose and cheeks, iron rings through the nose and ears, and erect hair.
- *height 36cm*
- **Guide price $5,700**

Yonba Maternity Figure ▲
- *circa 1910*
Yonba carved wood maternity figure of a seated woman with a child at her breast.
- *height 59cm*
- **Guide price $3,030**

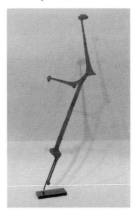

Kul Status Currency ▲
- *unknown*
Kul status currency in abstract human form, from West Africa.
- *height 51cm*
- **Guide price $570**

Tshokwe-Mbuna ◀
- *circa 1910*
Striking Tshokwe-Mbuna mask with natural patination and fibre additions.
- *height 37cm*
- **Guide price $710**

Twentieth-Century Design

The designers Charles Eames and Eero Saarinen were the first to experiment with moulded plywood, fibreglass and plastic.

From the 1900s the design of furniture and ceramics took on an exciting futuristic vibrancy, with designers experimenting with moulded plywood, fibreglass, plastic and leather. The famous Eames chair, successfully manufactured from the 1950s by the Herman Miller Company, with its moulded rosewood veneer and steel base, exemplifies this. These new materials completely changed the way furniture design was viewed, and the moulded organic shape became popular, with the innovators Eames and Saarinen winning prizes for their prototype chairs at the Organic Design in Home Furnishings Exhibition held at the Museum of Modern Art in New York in 1940. This exhibition was to have a profound effect on post war ceramic design.

Roy Midwinter designed two startling ranges of ceramics known as "Stylecraft" and "Fashion" in the new curving shapes, and commissioned innovative new ranges of patterns from the resident designers Jessie Tait and Terence Conran.

Ceramics

Italian Fishbone Vase ▲
- 1970
Grey Italian flask-shaped vase with a raised grey fishbone design on a burnt orange ground.
- *height 33cm*
- Guide price $170

Owl by Goldscheider ▼
- 1890
Owl by Goldscheider, with menacing glass eyes, standing on two books.
- *height 32cm*
- Guide price $1,250

Totem ▶
- *circa 2000*
"Giogold" by E. Sottsass, a vase of cylindrical form with dark blue and gold banding above a blue circular base.
- *height 38cm*
- Guide price $680

Goldscheider Wall Mask ▶
- *circa 1930*
An Italian Art Deco wall mask, executed in the Goldscheider style, of a young woman with stylized turquoise ringlets.
- *height 27cm*
- **Guide price $670**

Royal Dux Centrepiece ▲
- *circa 1910*
An Art Nouveau Royal Dux centrepiece of two nude maidens intertwined amongst the waves.
- *20cm x 40cm*
- **Guide price $1,060**

Beswick Wall Mask ▲
- *circa 1930*
An English Art Deco wall mask by Beswick depicting a young lady in profile.
- *height 27cm*
- **Guide price $700**

Expert Tips

As with everything else in Art Deco, it is still possible to pick up quality ceramics at reasonable prices if one is prepared to look for the lesser-known names, notably from the French Robj factory and Shelley of Staffordshire.

Art Deco Wall Mask ▼
- *circa 1930*
An Art Deco terracotta coloured wall mask of a woman with black hair and turquoise collar. Marked "Kunstkeramik Adolf Prischl Wien".
- *height 25cm*
- **Guide price $260**

Goldscheider Figure ▼
- *circa 1930*
An Art Deco figure by Goldscheider, designed by Claire Herezy, of a young lady in a blue dress profusely decorated with flowers.
- *height 35cm*
- **Guide price $1,420**

Katzhutte Figure ▼
- *circa 1930*
An Art Deco figure by Katzhutte of a woman in a pink floral dress.
- *height 26cm*
- **Guide price $790**

Doulton Art Nouveau Jug ◀
- *circa 1905*
Doulton jug with pink and green Art Nouveau design with brown edging.
- *height 19cm*
- **Guide price $400**

Torso by Zaccagnini ▼
- *circa 1940*

Ceramic torso of a nude lady by
Zaccagnini.
- *height 61cm*
- **Guide price $1,870**

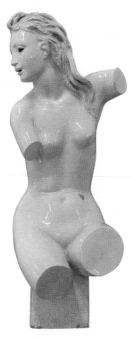

Tissue and Cotton Jars ▼
- *circa 1950*

Italian jars by Fornasetti for
cotton and tissues with mermaids,
scallop shells and gilt banding.
- *height 23cm*
- **Guide price $450**

Taurus ▶
- *1950*

Blue stylised bull "Taurus"
standing on all fours with head
bowed and tail up by Gambone.
- *height 25cm*
- **Guide price $3,560**

Retino ▲
- *circa 2000*

"Retino" by E. Sottsass, container
of conical form, with a design of
turquoise and gold banding above
a gilded circular base.
- *height 16cm*
- **Guide price $450**

French Grey Vase ▲
- *1950*

Small French vase of conical form
with a textured finish and a black
geometric design with a large red
dot.
- *height 16cm*
- **Guide price $100**

Valaurido Plate by Capron ▼
- *1970*

Plate by Roger Capron for
Valaurido with a red and orange
design within borders of matt
grey.
- *diameter 22cm*
- **Guide price $150**

Basket Pattern ▼
- *1956–7*

Basket pattern Poole pot designed
by Anne Read.
- *height 19cm*
- **Guide price $390**

Cheese Dish ▲

- *circa 1940*
Cream-coloured cheese dish and cover with a floral design and moulded rim.
- *14cm x 20cm*
- **Guide price $50**

Poole Pottery Vase ▲

- *circa 1930*
Poole pottery bulbous vase with stylised yellow lilac flowers and green foliage.
- *height 13cm*
- **Guide price $130**

Lambeth Vase ▼

- **1900**
Lambeth vase with green foliate design and pale blue flowers on a dark grey background, by Francis Pope.
- *height 30cm*
- **Guide price $3,380**

Poole Vase ▼

- *circa 1930*
Poole vase of ovoid form with yellow, blue and green design.
- *height 26cm*
- **Guide price $700**

Rosenthal Pottery ◄

- *circa 1950*
Peynet vase of conical form designed by Rosenthal Pottery entitled "The Marriage".
- *height 29cm*
- **Guide price $530**

Poole Floral Vase ▲

- *circa 1930*
Poole pottery vase with stylised yellow and purple flowers and a purple, green and lilac design around the rim.
- *height 20cm*
- **Guide price $360**

Peynet Design Plate ▲

- *circa 1950*
Rosenthal Germany pottery plate, showing spring with a couple on a bridge.
- *height 30cm*
- **Guide price $360**

Expert Tips

An important influence in Italian postwar design was surrealism, which can be clearly seen in the prolific designs of Piero Fornasetti in the 1950s.

Gouda Vase ▶

- *circa 1900*

A Dutch Gouda vase profusely decorated with stylised flowers.
- *height 16.5cm*
- **Guide price $210**

Katzhutte Figure ▲

- *circa 1930*

An Art Deco figure by Katzhutte, posing in a pink dress, with Katzhutte marks.
- *height 26cm*
- **Guide price $970**

Terracotta Wall Mask ▼

- *1930s*

An Art Deco terracotta wall mask, in the German/Austrian style, of a woman with black glazed hair, a mottle glazed face, and orange lips.
- *height 27cm*
- **Guide price $280**

Goldscheider Art Deco Figure ▶

- *circa 1930*

An Art Deco figure by Goldscheider of a young girl posing tending to a small fawn.
- *height 15cm*
- **Guide price $700**

Katzhutte Art Deco Figure ▼

- *circa 1930*

A German Katzhutte Art Deco figure of a stylish woman dancing in a multi-coloured dress.
- *height 29cm*
- **Guide price $850**

Ernst Wahliss Dish ▼

- *circa 1900*

An Art Nouveau dish by Ernst Wahliss with a young woman emerging from under three waterlilies.
- *width 33cm*
- **Guide price $1,770**

Lorenzl Art Deco Figure ▼

- *circa 1930*

An Art Deco figured designed by Lorenzl of a stylish young woman posing in a grey lace effect dress.
- *height 30cm*
- **Guide price $1,060**

Butter Container ▼
- *circa 1940*

Cream ceramic butter dish with a lattice and apple blossom design in relief.
- *12cm x 18cm*
- **Guide price** $50

De Morgan Plate ▼
- *circa 1900*

William de Morgan designed pottery, decorated with a yellow bird with a trailing cornflower design on a turquoise border, painted by Charles Passenger.
- *diameter 20cm*
- **Guide price** $360

Ovoid Vase ▲
- *circa 1920*

Italian bottle-shaped vase with yellow, green and brown abstract design.
- *height 29cm*
- **Guide price** $450

English Cup and Saucer ▲
- *circa 1920*

English cup, saucer and plate with a cartouche of a painted bird within gilt borders, surrounded by pink roses and cornflowers.
- *height 7.5cm*
- **Guide price** $70

Cigarette Holder ▼
- *1950*

Circular cigarette holder with push-action lid to extinguish the cigarettes.
- *height 21cm*
- **Guide price** $70

Janice Tchlenko Vase ▼
- *circa 1999*

Poole pottery vase of baluster form with a vibrant candy strip design by Janice Tchlenko.
- *height 37cm*
- **Guide price** $360

Dutch Jar ◀
- *circa 1923*

Dutch jar with cover by Corona Gouda, designed by W. P. Harispring.
- *height 11cm*
- **Guide price** $500

Shelley Tea Plate ▲
- *1927*

Shelley tea plate with orange border, black trees and green woodland border.
- *diameter 16cm*
- **Guide price $35**

Vase Tulip Pattern ▲
- *1934*

Vase of baluster form, hand-painted by Clarice Cliff with a "tulip" pattern and green and red banding on a blue ground.
- *height 12cm*
- **Guide price $1,160**

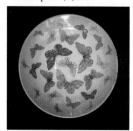

Butterfly Charger ▲
- *2001*

Charger with painted butterflies by Tania Pike for Dennis China Works.
- *diameter 37cm*
- **Guide price $790**

Highland Stoneware Vase ▼
- *circa 2000*

Highland stoneware vase of baluster form with a narrow neck and splayed lip painted with trout underwater.
- *height 31cm*
- **Guide price $260**

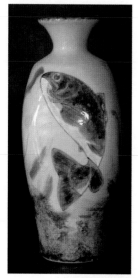

Alan Caiger Smith Goblet ▼
- *circa 1963*

Lustre glaze goblet by Alan Caiger Smith, the bowl with swirled designs above a knopped stem, raised on a circular base.
- *height 14cm*
- **Guide price $180**

Ocelot Vase ▼
- *2000*

Catherine Mellor vase with a design of a leopard in blue on a leopard spot ground.
- *height 24cm*
- **Guide price $730**

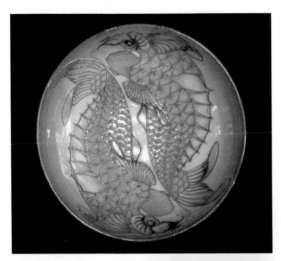

Carp Charger ▲
• *circa 2000*
Pottery charger with a design of
two carp on a green background,
by Dennis China Works.
• *diameter 36cm*
• **Guide price $960**

Ocelot Design Vase ▶
• **2000**
Dennis China Works pottery vase
of a leopard on a leopard spot
background, painted by
Catherine Mellor.
• *height 24cm*
• **Guide price $730**

Shelley Bon-Bon Dish ▼
• **1927**
Bon-bon dish with a serpentine
rim, orange centre and four black
trees.
• *diameter 11cm*
• **Guide price $120**

Shelley Cake Plate ▼
• **1927**
Shelley cake plate with a
scalloped border and bold black
trees within an orange border.
• *diameter 24cm*
• **Guide price $120**

Bulb Vase ▼
• **1936**
Clarice Cliff bulb vase with metal
rim from the "Citrus Delicier"
collection.
• *diameter 20cm*
• **Guide price $620**

Nuage by Clarice Cliff ◀
• **1935**
"Nuage" bowl by Clarice Cliff,
with hand painted flowers and
leaves with an orange centre on a
green ground.
• *diameter 19cm*
• **Guide price $1,690**

Keramik Wall Mask ▶

- *1930s*

A terracotta Gmundner Keramik
wall mask made in Austria and
printed with flowerpot mark.
- *height 20cm*
- **Guide price $290**

Leather Texture Bowl ▼

- *1960s*

Oval stoneware bowl by
Rorstrand with dark brown
leather-textured glaze, with
incised parallel lines.
- *19cm x 16cm*
- **Guide price $140**

Gunnar Nylund Vase ▼

- *1950s*

A vase by Gunnar Nylund for
Rorstrand, incised "R" and three
crowns. Stoneware with a brown
and black glaze.
- *height 17cm*
- **Guide price $200**

Poole Vase ▼

- *early 1950s*

Poole carafe designed by Alfred
Read made of hand-thrown white
earthenware with a pattern of
purple stripes and the rim in red.
- *height 30cm*
- **Guide price $600**

Hand Painted Wall Plaque ▶

- *1930s*

A quality china wall plaque hand
painted in pastel colours and
unsigned, but most likely a
Beswick piece.
- *27.9cm x 20.3cm*
- **Guide price $500**

Poole Butterfly Pattern Vase ▼

- *1956–7*

Poole vase designed by Alfred
Read and decorated by Gwen
Haskins. Hand-thrown white
earthenware decorated with
purple and red butterflies.
- *height 21cm*
- **Guide price $360**

Rorstrand Miniature Vase ▼

- *1950s*

Miniature stoneware vase by
Gunnar Nylund for Rorstrand
with a matte white glaze with
stripes of brown.
- *height 8cm*
- **Guide price $200**

Expert Tips

*Ceramics valuers hate damage,
however slight. The true collector
will buy genuine but damaged
items and seek to trade up.*

Furniture

Red Leather Chair ▲
- *circa 1960*
One of a pair of Italian chairs, one red and the other black leather, with teak legs and back rest.
- *height 98cm*
- **Guide price $1,420**

Wine Table ▲
- *1900–15*
Edwardian wine table with a circular top, satinwood banding and a central flower, the whole standing on a turned column with a tripod base.
- *47cm x 26cm*
- **Guide price $300**

English Hall Cupboard ▼
- *circa 1900*
English hall cupboard in medium oak with marquetry panel of a Dutch genre scene. With copper strapwork, hinges and escutcheons.
- *83cm x 62cm*
- **Guide price $2,670**

Reclining Armchair ▼
- *circa 1900*
One of a pair of oak reclining armchairs of solid design with slated side panels, raised on square tapered legs.
- *90cm x 70cm*
- **Guide price $1,600**

Arts and Crafts Chair ▲
- *circa 1905*
One of three Arts and Crafts single chairs with moulded top rail and curved splat with fruitwood inlay standing on straight square legs.
- *88cm x 44cm*
- **Guide price $4,010**

Dieter Rams Armchairs ▼
- *1962*
Armchairs by Dieter Rams, for Vitsoe, made from green leather on a white fibreglass base.
- *69cm x 86cm*
- **Guide price $5,160**

SP4B Armchair ▼

- *circa 1931*

An SP4B armchair by Oliver Bernard for PEL, the seat fully upholstered in green rexine and supported on a canterlevered chrome frame.
- *height 71cm*
- **Guide price $350**

Teak Chair ▼

- *circa 1960*

One of a set of four Danish teak chairs with black vinyl seats.
- *height 80cm*
- **Guide price $280**

Ercol Occasional Table ▲

- **20th century**

An Ercol occasional table, the elm top supported on a beech frame.
- *49.5cm x 84cm*
- **Guide price $220**

Teak and Glass Coffee Table ▼

- *1950s*

A teak and glass coffee table, the boomerang-shaped legs and cross stretchers supporting a circular glass top.
- *40.5cm x 73.5cm*
- **Guide price $120**

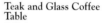

Supporto Office Chair ▼

- *circa 1979*

A Supporto office chair, by Fred Scott for Hille, with grey enamel finish and black cloth upholstery.
- *height 1.24m*
- **Guide price $490**

Cleopatra Sofa ▼

- *1970s*

"Cleopatra" sofa designed by Geoffrey Harcourt, produced by Artifort. Has a Urethane-padded metal frame on castors, with original black stretch fabric.
- *68cm x 1.80m*
- **Guide price $1,690**

Italian Lounge Chair ▶

- *1960s*

"Lady" lounge chair designed by Marco Zanuso, made by Arflex. Wood and fibreglass frame, on tubular brass legs with black ferrules, fully upholstered in yellow fabric.
- *78cm x 78cm x 78cm*
- **Guide price $1,160**

"Reigate" Rocker ◀

- *1965*

William Plunkett rocker and footstool with coated steel frame, aluminium seat and arms, rubber webbing and cushions upholstered in original orange tweed fabric.
- *92cm x 56cm x 84cm*
- **Guide price $1,250**

Hans Wegner Daybed ▲

- *1960s*

Danish daybed designed by Hans Wegner and upholstered in oatmeal tweed. Has a dark oak frame and the back lifts up to reveal storage and a canvas roll-out cover to protect sofa whilst sleeping.
- *1.95m x 86cm x 76cm*
- **Guide price $1,420**

Jason Stacking Chairs ▲

- *1950*

A set of five "Jason" stacking chairs designed by Carl Jacobs for Kandya. Formed plywood seat section over a turned beech base.
- *74cm x 52cm x 38cm*
- **Guide price $1,250 for set**

Expert Tips

Chairs are for sitting on more than looking at. Always try them for comfort as well as inspecting their design.

Swedish Desk ▶

- **1920–30**
Gustavian-style Swedish free-standing desk.
- ● *76cm x 1.44m*
- ● **Guide price $5,160**

Edwardian Three-Tier Stand ▲

- **circa 1905**
An unusual wrought iron and copper Edwardian three-tier stand with scrolled decoration.
- ● *95cm x 25cm*
- ● **Guide price $240**

Oak Hallstand ▲

- **circa 1880**
A very good quality Arts and Crafts hallstand and two matching hall chairs by "Minton Hollins and Co. Patent Tile Works, Stoke-on-Trent".
- ● *2.08m x 1.28m*
- ● **Guide price $3,290**

Arts and Crafts Table ▼

- **circa 1910**
Arts and Crafts oak table of solid construction with straight supports and circular stretcher.
- ● *52cm x 69cm*
- ● **Guide price $500**

Art Nouveau Bureau ▼

- **circa 1905**
Art Nouveau oak bureau with folding writing slope above a single drawer with organically designed copper metalwork.
- ● *1.2m x 90cm*
- ● **Guide price $1,010**

Nursery Chest ▲

- **circa 1930**
Heal's oak nursery chest with double and single panelled doors, three short drawers and two long drawers.
- ● *1.5m x 1.15m*
- ● **Guide price $3,290**

Arts and Crafts Lamp Table ▲

- **circa 1905**
Arts and Crafts mahogany occasional table with three supports and carved and pierced decoration.
- ● *69cm x 43cm*
- ● **Guide price $390**

Art Deco Occasional Table ▲

- *1930s*

Art Deco occasional circular table with a quartered veneered top in an attractive warm "golden" burr walnut and a quartered sectioned base in differing heights.
- *60cm x 58.5cm*
- **Guide price $700**

Plywood Coffee Table ▲

- *1930s*

A circular two-tiered coffee table made by "Gerald Summers, Makers of Simple Furniture". Made of birch plywood, formed and stained.
- *41cm x 68cm*
- **Guide price $980**

Magistretti Coffee Table ◄

- *1964*

Low coffee table by Vico Magistretti in ebonised wood with end drawers, drop flap sides, a central storage well and brass top.
- *1.28m x 96cm*
- **Guide price $890**

French Bedside Cabinet ►

- *1930s*

Art Deco French bedside cabinet with heavily figured walnut veneers and almost organic shape.
- *58.5cm x 60cm x 32cm*
- **Guide price $450**

Italian Leather Chair ▲

- *1930s*

Very rare large Italian Art Deco leather chair. In excellent condition with little sign of wear.
- *78cm x 1.16m x 92cm*
- **Guide price $510**

French Chinese-style Chair ▼

- *circa 1920*

One of a pair of French oak chairs with a strong Chinese influence and a distressed paint effect, standing on straight square legs.
- *height 74cm*
- **Guide price $2,230**

Art Deco Cabinet ▼

- *circa 1930*

Art Deco figured mahogany walnut cocktail cabinet of circular design with pull-out mixing surface.
- *1.61m x 85cm*
- **Guide price $1,770**

Art Deco Three-Piece Suite ▶

- *circa 1930*

A very rare and unusual Art Deco upholstered leather three-piece suite.
- *86cm x 95cm*
- **Guide price $9,480**

Red Stereophonic Chair ▼

- *circa 1960s*

Red moulded fibreglass egg chair on a circular metal base, with grey and white wool-padded upholstery and leather-padded seat cover and back rest, with fitted stereo and matching ottoman, designed by the Lee Co. of California for a commission.
- *1.29m x 86cm*
- **Guide price $7,480**

Dressing Table ◀

- *circa 1950*

Modernist oak dressing table with two columns of graduated drawers and single drawer above knee hole.
- *1.65m x 1.22m*
- **Guide price $400**

Leather Armchair ▲

- *1970s*

Danish leather armchair with formed beech frames and upholstered in grey leather with buttoned back and seat.
- *76cm x 57cm x 60cm*
- **Guide price $360**

Walnut Bureau ▲

- *circa 1940*

A very good early twentieth century figured walnut bureau in the George II style.
- *1.04m x 84cm*
- **Guide price $3,370**

French Leather Chairs ▼
● **1977**
Pair of chairs by Michel Cadestin and George Laurent for the Library of the Centre Pompidou Beaubourg, made from wire with leather seat and back. Illus: Les Années 70, by Anne Bony.
- *height 74.5cm*
- **Guide price $2,140**

Arts and Crafts Dining Chair ▼
● *circa 1905*
One of a pair of oak Arts and Crafts carvers with scrolled arms and turned supports.
- *1.05m x 58cm*
- **Guide price $980**

Japanese Chest ▲
● *circa 1920s*
Special Japanese Isho Dansu (storage chest) for fabrics. The wood has not been sealed or lacquered first.
- *1.02m x 54cm*
- **Guide price $4,720**

Chrome Dining Chair ▲
● **1975**
One of a set of four dining chairs with grey leather and chrome, by Prebenfabricus & Dorgen Kastholm for Alfred Kill.
- *height 70cm*
- **Guide price $3,920**

Mahogany Dining Chair ▼
● *circa 1950s*
One of a set of six mahogany dining chairs with pierced backsplat, drop-in seat cushion and cabriole legs.
- *1m x 48cm*
- **Guide price $2,230**

Stool by Verner Panton ▼
● *circa 1960*
Wire stool with original circular suede padded cover, by Verner Panton Danish.
- *height 43cm*
- **Guide price $1,330**

Harlow Chairs ◄
● **1971**
Set of four "Harlow" chairs with red wool-padded seats and backs, standing on aluminium bases and stands, by Ettore Sottsass for Poltronova.
- *height 82cm*
- **Guide price $6,230**

Modernist Chest of Drawers ▶

- **1930s**

Art Deco modernist style chest of drawers. The underwood is mahogany which has been grained in a blonde colour, surrounding the front edging is walnut feather banding. There are six graduated drawers.

- *96cm x 38cm x 50cm*
- **Guide price $1,040**

Cocktail Cabinet ▲

- **1930s**

Art Deco cocktail cabinet in figured walnut, shaped like a half drum. The top part of the cocktail cabinet has an all-mirrored interior and internal light. The doors to the top and base storage areas roll open and shut.

- *1.38m x 1.14m x 35cm*
- **Guide price $1,960**

Bird's Eye Circular Coffee Table ▲

- **1930s**

Art Deco pale blonde bird's eye maple circular coffee table. This rare table features grained maple veneers and a classic Deco circular base with walnut feather banded decoration.

- *56cm x 73cm*
- **Guide price $970**

Burr Walnut Table ▼

- **1930s**

Art Deco burr walnut table featuring a beautifully grained walnut veneered top, with a second tier underneath and four tapering ebonised legs.

- *59cm x 80cm x 52cm*
- **Guide price $400**

Savoy Trolley ▼

- **1930s**

English Art Deco circular "Savoy" hostess trolley with three walnut shelves, frame and castors.

- *78cm x 70cm x 43cm*
- **Guide price $610**

Cocktail Table ▼

- **1930s**

Art Deco walnut cocktail table featuring a central compartment in the top, accessed by sliding open two covers. Octagonal in shape, this piece also has two shelves and a ribbed pattern on the side panels.

- *62cm x 60cm*
- **Guide price $670**

Expert Tips

Fashionable in the 1930s, large pieces of Art Deco furniture, veneered pale to be less overpowering, were expensive at the time but are good value today.

U-Base Table ◀

- **1930s**

Original Art Deco U-base occasional table in a figured burr walnut with two walnut columns and glass top for protection.

- *62cm x 70cm x 70cm*
- **Guide price $850**

Eames Armchair ▲
- *circa 1975*
One of a pair of Eames padded brown armchairs with aluminium arms and base.
- *height 1.01m*
- **Guide price $2,580**

Leather Rotating Chair ▲
- *1970*
Tan leather rotating and adjustable desk chair with padded seat and back, and metal legs on wheels.
- *height 74cm*
- **Guide price $880**

Walnut Buffet ▶
- *1930*
Art Deco breakfront walnut buffet with solid supports and moulded decoration.
- *84cm x 1.06m*
- **Guide price $1,160**

Black Leather Armchair ▼
- *circa 1960*
Black leather armchair with padded seat and back, with metal and leather arms, standing on a rotating star-shaped metal base.
- *height 89cm*
- **Guide price $1,340**

Edwardian Chest of Drawers ▼
- *circa 1905*
Edwardian chest of two small and two long drawers, with metal foliate handles standing on straight legs.
- *82cm x 1.08m*
- **Guide price $420**

Butterfly Chair ▲
- *circa 1950*
One of a pair of plastic mock snakeskin butterfly chairs on a early tubular frame, manufactured by Knoll.
- *height 1m*
- **Guide price $980**

White Folding Bench ▲
- *circa 1920*
Continental pine folding bench, painted white, on metal legs and arms.
- *90cm x 1.25m*
- **Guide price $390**

Glass

Cameo Glass Vase ▶

- *circa 1905*

A large Art Nouveau cameo glass vase by Richard, the body carved and etched with a landscape.
- *height 33cm*
- **Guide price $1,560**

Kosta Paperweight ▲

- *1955–63*

A Kosta paperweight, the teardrop shape consisting of internal cranberry pink glass surrounded by a controlled pattern of bubbles encased in clear glass.
- *height 8cm*
- **Guide price $130**

Lalique Bowl ▼

- *1920s*

An opalescent Lalique bowl in the "Poisson" pattern, marked "R.LALIQUE FRANCE".
- *diameter 24cm*
- **Guide price $980**

Orrefors "Ariel" Vase ▼

- *1972*

A strikingly beautiful Orrefors "Ariel" vase designed by Ingeborg Lundin. A thick slightly flaring vase with a continuous design, the inner in olive green glass, the whole cased in clear glass.
- *height 18cm*
- **Guide price $2,760**

Art Deco Decanter ◀

- *circa 1930*

Art Deco conical ruby cased decanter cut to clear with horizontal bands of broad flutes. Original clear conical stopper cut with broad flutes.
- *height 23cm*
- **Guide price $760**

Expert Tips

René Lalique (1860–1945) mass-produced glass. Although it is avidly collected and expensive, it is not especially hard to find.

Abstract Glass Structure ▲

- *circa 1990*
Orange and black abstract glass vase of cylindrical form with gold flaked inclusions, by Nichetti for Murano.
- *height 27cm*
- **Guide price $680**

Mosaic Vase by Ferro ▲

- *1998*
Mosaic Murano glass vase by Ferro, for the Venice Biennale 1998.
- *height 29cm*
- **Guide price $2,140**

Tiffany Centrepiece ▶

- *circa 1930*
L. Tiffany's gold iridescent centrepiece with organic designs.
- *diameter 25cm*
- **Guide price $7,120**

Glass Paperweight Abstract Sculpture ▼

- *circa 1960*
Italian orange, red, black and white abstract glass sculpture.
- *height 16cm*
- **Guide price $220**

Murano Paperweight ▼

- *circa 1960*
Murano paperweight of compressed globular form with an abstract pattern of blue, white, lime green, pink and gold.
- *diameter 23cm*
- **Guide price $580**

Blue Cactus Vase ▼

- *circa 1950*
Blue glass "Cactus" vase by Recardo Licata for Murano.
- *height 44cm*
- **Guide price $2,140**

Lalique Box Lid ◄

- *1920s*

An opalescent Lalique box lid, marked "R.LALIQUE". This lid was used on a presentation set by Houbigant 1928–1930.

- *diameter 14cm*
- **Guide price $260**

Cordonato d'Oro Vase ▲

- *1950s*

"Cordonato d'Oro" vase of red glass in a tapering ribbed shape above a bulbous body, with gold leaf.

- *height 26.5cm*
- **Guide price $530**

Expert Tips

Modern vases showcase the influence of contemporary trends in their form and decoration.

Red and Yellow Murano Vase ▼

- *1950s*

Murano sommerso vase, red and yellow cased in clear glass, with original label.

- *height 11cm*
- **Guide price $120**

Toso Glass Vase ▲

- *contemporary*

Heavy clear glass vase by Stefano Toso of Murano with swirls of orange and blue.

- *height 22cm*

Guide price $620

Large Murano Glass Vase ▲

- *contemporary*

A large glass vase designed by Stefano Toso of Murano with dominant colours of green, yellow and red.

- *height 38cm*
- **Guide price $800**

Green and Yellow Murano Vase ▶
- *1950s*
Murano sommerso vase, emerald green and lemon yellow cased in heavily facetted clear glass.
- *height 7.5cm*
- **Guide price $120**

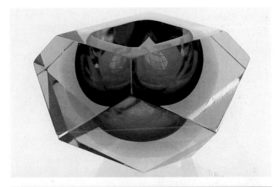

Art Deco Lemonade Set ▲
- *circa 1930*
Art Deco "lemonade" set consisting of a tall jug with an amber handle and six matching glasses with amber stems and feet, all engraved with vertical lines.
- *height 24cm*
- **Guide price $350**

Cameo Glass Vase ▲
- *circa 1920*
Le Verre Français cameo glass vase, acid-etched, with an orange and green design on a yellow ground, applied with the Millifiori cane mark.
- *height 30cm*
- **Guide price $1,420**

Set of Conical Goblets ▼
- *circa 1930*
Two of a set of six Art Deco conical goblets decorated in intaglio with stylised zigzag pattern on conical uranium green feet.
- *height 20.3cm*
- **Guide price $880**

Gilded Glass Bowls ▲
- *early 20th century*
Three of a set of ten dimple-ribbed bowls and stands gilded with rural scenes.
- *diameter 15cm*
- **Guide price $530**

Art Deco Candelabra ▼
- *circa 1935*
Pair of American Art Deco candelabra with ribbed arms and icicle drops suspended on rectangular bases cut underneath with diamonds.
- *height 19.7cm*
- **Guide price $1,240**

Mosaic Murrina Vase ▼

- *1998*

Mosaic vase of baluster form, with blue and yellow organic design by "Murrina".
- *height 29cm*
- **Guide price $2,670**

Amber Bowl ▼

- *circa 1970*

Amber glass bowl on a clear stand by Cevedex.
- *height 23cm*
- **Guide price $890**

Fish in Glass by Cenedese ▲

- *1950*

Glass object with a seascape design including a tropical fish with underwater plants, by Cenedese for Murano.
- *width 14cm*
- **Guide price $400**

Green Vase with Cactus ▲

- *circa 1950s*

Green "Cactus" vase by Recardo Licata for Murano.
- *height 44cm*
- **Guide price $2,140**

Hutton Vase ▼

- *circa 1920*

Clear glass vase by Oroffords and etched by John Hetton.
- *height 33cm*
- **Guide price $1,780**

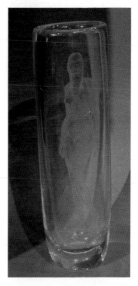

Italian Glass Fish ▼

- *1960*

Italian glass object fashioned as a stylised coiled fish.
- *height 24cm*
- **Guide price $510**

Small Daum Jug ◄

- *circa 1900*

Small Daum variegated amber to pink jug with "Bleeding Heart" floral overlay.
- *6cm x 12cm*
- **Guide price $3,920**

Cranberry Glass Vases ▲
- *circa 1900*

A pair of Bohemian cranberry glass vases with engraved decoration depicting castles and a forest setting with a leaping deer, on a faceted and moulded base.
- *height 44cm*
- **Guide price $7,480**

Vase by Baxter ▲
- *circa 1969*

Whitefriars kingfisher-blue vase by Baxter with an abstract design and textured finish.
- *height 29cm*
- **Guide price $420**

Martini Jug by Baxter ▼
- *circa 1962*

Whitefriars kingfisher-blue Martini jug with a clear handle. A "Whitefriars Studio" range by Peter Wheeler.
- *height 36cm*
- **Guide price $170**

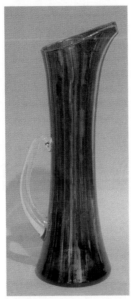

Silvio Vigliaturo Sculpture ▼
- *1999*

Glass "Ikomos" series sculpture by Silvio Vigliaturo, signed and dated.
- *height 40cm*
- **Guide price $2,140**

Tall Italian Vase ▲
- *1982*

Italian tall glass vase with a moulded lip, cerulean blue variegated to paler blue with moulded banding within the glass.
- *height 63cm*
- **Guide price $1,780**

Red Bubble Ashtray ▲
- *1958*

Ruby red lobed bubble ashtray with an organic moulded design by Harry Dyer.
- *diameter 13cm*
- **Guide price $45**

Whitefriars Vase ▶

- *circa 1969*
Rare Whitefriars ovoid brown
and orange vase. "Studio Range"
by Peter Wheeler.
- *height 22.5cm*
- Guide price $440

Glass Vase by Laura Diaz ▼

- *1990–1*
"Incalmo" ink-blue glass vase,
with a cane pattern neck and
white glass wheel carved bulbous
base by Laura Diaz, Ref: *il vetro a
venezia* by Marino Baronier.
- *height 30cm*
- Guide price $3,200

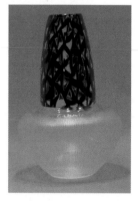

Swedish Translucent Vase ▼

- *1955–6*
Swedish translucent tall glass
vase with white trailing lines and
one red line made for Kosta.
- *height 38cm*
- Guide price $3,920

Tangerine Vase ▶

- *1969*
Tangerine vase with concentric
circular design and a textured
finish by Baxter.
- *height 18cm x 17cm*
- Guide price $250

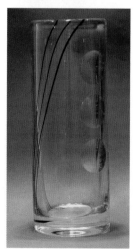

Glass Vase ▲

- *1973*
Glass vase with circular design by
Olle Alerius. Orrefors Co. 1973,
Expo A 248, signed and
illustrated by Lilane.
- *height 20cm*
- Guide price $3,920

Guitar Mirror ▼

- *1950*
Guitar-shaped metal mirror.
- *length 83cm*
- Guide price $210

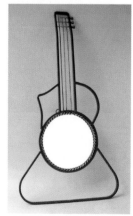

Lighting

French Desk Lamp ▶
- *1955–65*
French chromed steel desk lamp with light green painted shade and base.
- *height 35cm*
- **Guide price $110**

Art Deco Lady Lamp ▲
- *1930s*
Art Deco figural lamp featuring a semi-naked female holding a white glass globe shade. The figure is white metal and has been gilded on top in copper and gold tones. She rests on an oval alabaster base.
- *40cm x 22cm x 12cm*
- **Guide price $930**

Sepia Chrome Lamp ▲
- *1930s*
Art Deco chrome lamp with an all chrome base and a rare sepia coloured segmented shade with slivered detailing.
- *38cm x 12.5cm*
- **Guide price $510**

Chrome Table Lamp ▼
- *1930s*
Art Deco original chrome table lamp with square-sided marbled cream and brown glass shade which gives off a warm sepia toned glow. Fully rewired.
- *42cm x 12.5cm*
- **Guide price $290**

Desk Lamp ▼
- *1950–60*
A steel blue metal desk lamp by "Elekthermax" with chrome stem and finial.
- *42cm x 42cm*
- **Guide price $450**

Skyscraper Lamp ▼
- *1930s*
Art Deco chrome lamp featuring a skyscraper frosted glass shade in a wonderful sepia colour.
- *height 45cm*
- **Guide price $450**

Pink and Brown Marbled Lamp ▶

- *1930s*

Art Deco original chrome table lamp with glass shade marbled dusty pink and brown. Fully rewired and in excellent condition.

- *40cm x 12cm*
- **Guide price $420**

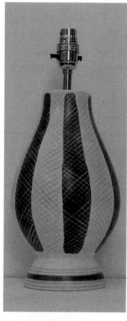

Blue-stripe Freeform Lamp ▲

- *1954–7*

Poole pottery lamp with a cross-hatched abstract design.

- *height 24cm*
- **Guide price $490**

Patterned Freeform Lamp ▲

- *1954–7*

Poole lamp with brown and black abstract design, a brown band to the upper and lower edges.

- *height 12cm*
- **Guide price $220**

Poole Vine Lamp ▼

- *1954–7*

Poole pottery lamp base, the body of bulbous form decorated with a leaf ribboned pattern.

- *height 24cm*
- **Guide price $490**

Aeroplane Lamp ▼

- *1930s*

French Art Deco figural lamp featuring a classic brass aeroplane sitting on a soft brown veined marble base.

- *16cm x 23cm x 10cm*
- **Guide price $240**

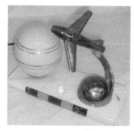

Solid Freeform Lamp ▼

- *1954–7*

Poole lamp with attractive ice green glaze.

- *height 24cm*
- **Guide price $170**

Tubular Lamp ▲
- *1950*
Italian chrome graduated tubular lamp with coiled decoration.
- *height 44cm*
- **Guide price $450**

Italian Gold Mesh Lamp ▲
- *circa 1940*
Table lamp with mesh lampshade supported on a black and white marble base.
- *height 49cm*
- **Guide price $1,600**

Expert Tips
Italian designers were at the forefront of early postwar lighting producing stylish, sophisticated lamps in organic shapes.

Art Deco Verdigris Lantern ▼
- *circa 1930*
Art Deco bronze lantern of tapered form, each side centred by a moulded oval motif below a stepped fan cresting, fitted with replaced glass, the sides at the base of the lantern centred by scrolls issuing palmettes, with s-scroll brackets leading to a lower suspended bracket.
- *94cm x 41.5cm sq*
- **Guide price $11,570**

Yellow Sunhat Lamp ▼
- *circa 1960*
Large yellow Italian sunhat lamp with a green ribbon and assorted floral design.
- *diameter 44cm*
- **Guide price $520**

Murano Glass Lamps ▲
- *circa 1960*
Murano Italian glass lamp with yellow and orange ribbed body. The metal covers are ashtrays.
- *height 32cm*
- **Guide price $800**

Pan-pipes Lamp ▲
- *circa 1970*
Italian pan-pipes table lamp with chrome and perspex columns surmounted by lights.
- *height 85cm*
- **Guide price $1,780**

Poole Atlantis Lamp ◀
- *1972–7*

Poole pottery lamp with a brown and beige glaze.
- *height 36cm*
- **Guide price $350**

Rye Sphere Lamp ▼
- *1950–60*

Spherical Poole pottery lamp with yellow glaze, very minimal in style.
- *height 15cm*
- **Guide price $100**

Candy Stripe Lamp ▲
- *1950–60*

A red and white glaze striped Rye lamp.
- *height 16.5cm*
- **Guide price $100**

Slim Bottle Lamp ▲
- *1954–7*

Poole freeform lamp with negative leaf design on striped-coloured ground.
- *height 26.5cm*
- **Guide price $350**

Stylised Clown Lamp ▲
- *1930s*

French mood lamp of spelter with two stylised clowns who have fallen asleep on top of the original crackle-glaze shade, mounted on a pink marble base tall.
- *29.2cm x 30.5cm*
- **Guide price $1,690**

Peanut Lamp ▲
- *1954–7*

Poole freeform lamp with negative leaf design on striped background of green, mauve and brown.
- *height 27cm*
- **Guide price $380**

Poole Helios Lamp

- *circa 1964*
Poole pottery square-shaped lamp
of an abstract geometric design
with moss green glaze.
- *12cm x 10cm*
- **Guide price $70**

Patterned Poole Helios Lamp

- *circa 1964*
A bluish grey/white glaze
decorated Poole lamp of grid-style
design.
- *height 12cm*
- **Guide price $90**

Celtic Lamp ▼

- *circa 1960*
Pottery lamp decorated with a
yellow and black stylised dragon
pattern, swirls and black banding
to the upper and lower registers.
- *height 35cm*
- **Guide price $170**

Small Carafe Lamp ▲

- *1957*
Sky blue glazed lamp by Poole in
a carafe shape.
- *height 27cm*
- **Guide price $170**

Spelter Lady Lamp ▲

- *early 1920s*
A spelter Egyptian-themed
French lady lamp, possibly by
Voliente although very Chiparus
in detail. This lamp is with a
crackle-glass shade and is
mounted on an ovular red marble
base with pebbled detail.
- *35.5cm x 29.2cm*
- **Guide price $1,320**

Conical Lamp ▶

- *1930s*
Large French metal ceiling lamp
in conical form with green
patinated ring detailing and
chrome outer ring.
- *45.7cm x 61cm*
- **Guide price $1,060**

Perspex Lamp ▼

• *1970*
Italian U-shaped perspex lamp on a metal base by Stilnovo.
• *38cm x 32cm*
• **Guide price $2,140**

Brancusi Standing Light ▼

• *1990*
Brancusi standing light made from Japanese paper with a metal base, by Tom Dixon.
• *height 2.8m*
• **Guide price $2,850**

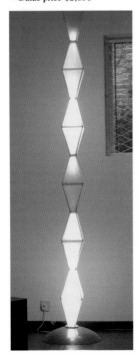

Art Deco Lamp ▲

• *circa 1930*
Art deco lamp with a twisted metal stand and a white glass lampshade with a grey geometric pattern.
• *height 47cm*
• **Guide price $130**

Italian Light ▲

• *circa 1950*
Italian light with a white conical shade supported on a black circular base.
• *height 40cm*
• **Guide price $500**

Wall Light by Vemini ▼

• *circa 1950*
One of a pair of abstract Italian glass wall lights with a design of assorted squares with amber, tobacco and clear glass, by Vemini.
• *31cm square*
• **Guide price $2,280**

Cube Floor Light ▼

• *1970*
Free-standing floor light made from three white and yellow glass cubes, connected by metal bands with a circular metal top and handle.
• *height 1.15m*
• **Guide price $1,960**

Large Classical Lady Lamp

- *1920s–30s*

Large lamp made of green patinated spelter featuring a woman standing bare breasted and wearing a short brown skirt, on a black marble top-hat base.

- *height 69cm*
- **Guide price $2,130**

"Vers l'Oasis" Lamp

- *late 1920s*

"Vers l' Oasis", a signed spelter lamp by Fayral of a woman holding a yellow glass urn mounted on a Portorro base.

- *height 47cm*
- **Guide price $2,480**

Expert Tips

Spelter is zinc treated to look like bronze and was widely used as an inexpensive substitute in Art Deco figures. It should be lightly dusted with a dry cloth.

Arctic Scene Lamp

- *mid-1930s*

An enormous spelter polar bear and a pair of penguins sitting either side of an iceberg lamp on a base of cream and pale green onyx.

- *33cm x 81cm x 22.9cm*
- **Guide price $3,020**

Lady Pastille Burner Lamp

- *1925*

A spelter lamp with two ladies on stepped tapering columns sitting on either side of a globe. Both women hold a container with removable lids which appear to be pastille burners.

- *25.4cm x 36.8cm*
- **Guide price $2,290**

Lorenzl Spelter Lady Lamp

- *mid-1920s*

Spelter lamp of a woman in her under-clothes with a silvered enamel patina and peach coloured hightlights. Mounted on a Portorro Extra marble base, unsigned by Lorenzl.

- *28cm x 15.3cm*
- **Guide price $1,160**

Alabaster and Spelter Lamp

- *circa 1925*

Gold patinated lady-lamp with base of cream onyx, nude woman figure of spelter, and steps and urn shade – which glows when lit – of alabaster.

- *18cm x 25.4cm*
- **Guide price $880**

Italian Globe Lamp ▼

- *circa 1960*

One of a pair of clear and ripple effect globe table lamps with a white band running through the body.

- *height 54cm*
- **Guide price** $530

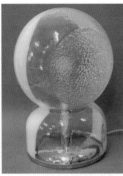

Kodak Lampshade ▲

- *1970*

Plastic lampshade with the lettering "Kodak" in red on a deep yellow background.

- *height 25cm*
- **Guide price** $270

Art Deco Lamp ◄

- *1930*

French Art Deco chrome table lamp with a domed shade, curved stand and circular base.

- *height 32cm*
- **Guide price** $450

Italian Wall Light ▼

- *circa 1970*

Italian wall light by Marlotta, with a perspex background with metal tubes projecting from it in a variety of sizes, the whole on a square metal frame.

- *60cm x 60cm*
- **Guide price** $2,850

Italian Table Lamp ▼

- *1950*

Black Italian table lamp of baluster form with blue, yellow and red dots, within a white graffiti-patterned border.

- *height 15cm*
- **Guide price** $90

Baccarat-Style Chandelier ◄

- *20th century*

One of a pair of Baccarat-style cranberry glass chandeliers with scrolled moulded decoration and numerous crystal glass droplets, with 36 arms.

- *height 2.08m*
- **Guide price** $35,600

Raised Band Lamp ▼

- *circa 1950*
Pink Poole pottery lamp of
pleasing proportions.
- *height 16cm*
- **Guide price $100**

Seal Lamp ▼

- *mid-1920s*
French Art Deco spelter seal
lamp by Carvin mounted on a
marble base.
- *27cm x 31cm*
- **Guide price $530**

Art Deco Gymnast Lamp ▼

- *1923*
French Art Deco spelter lamp
featuring a woman doing the
splits supporting a globe, signed
by Balleste.
- *28cm x 36cm*
- **Guide price $1,350**

Art Deco Lady Lamp ▲

- *early 1930s*
French Art Deco spelter lamp of
a woman supporting a globe,
mounted on a Portorro marble
and onyx base.
- *height 45.7cm*
- **Guide price $880**

Spelter and Alabaster Lamp ▲

- *early 1930s*
English Art Deco lamp of a
woman supporting a globe with
one hand. Made of gold patinated
spelter and mounted on an
alabaster triangular base.
- *height 40cm*
- **Guide price $780**

Silvered Bronze Lamp ▼

- *1923*
Art Deco silvered bronze lady
lamp mounted on a Verdigris
marble base, made by the French
artist Janle and signed on the
bottom of the figure.
- *40cm x 30cm*
- **Guide price $2,840**

Crouching Woman Lamp ▼

- *late 1920s*
Art Deco lamp of a woman in a
crouched position supporting the
fixture. Made of spelter with a
gold enamelled patina.
- *height 38cm*
- **Guide price $880**

Bronze Art Deco Lamp ▼

- *early 20th century*
French Art Deco bronze lamp by
Molins-Balleste. The lamp shade
is made of hand-made glass fruit
and flowers sitting in an alabaster
basket.
- *45cm x 50cm*
- **Guide price $5,240**

Metalware

Art Deco Lady ▼
- *circa 1930*

Bronze and ivory figure of a lady in theatrical costume. Excellent colour and detail, signed "Josef Lorenzi".
- *height 26cm*
- **Guide price $4,980**

Young Girl in Bronze and Ivory ▼
- *circa 1925*

Highly detailed gilt bronze and ivory figure of a young girl, signed and inscribed "Etling, Demetre Chiparus, Romania".
- *height 19cm*
- **Guide price $5,870**

Robin Hood Figure ▲
- *1934*

French spelter and ivorine figure of a male archer modelled on Robin Hood.
- *height 68cm*
- **Guide price $1,770**

Dancing Maiden Figure ▲
- *circa 1930*

Bronze figure of a young lady dancing in striking pose, signed "Georges Angerle", raised on an onyx base.
- *height 24cm*
- **Guide price $1,690**

Paul Philippe Bronze ▼
- *circa 1920*

Striking bronze figure of a young lady with arms outstretched with a golden patination standing on a circular marble plinth, signed by Paul Philippe.
- *height 46cm*
- **Guide price $7,030**

Bronze Flute Player ▼
- *circa 1920*

Bronze figure of a young girl in a seductive dancing pose with golden patination, signed "Claire Colinet".
- *height 48cm*
- **Guide price $8,540**

Bronze Vase ▼
- *circa 1900*

Two-colour patinated gilt bronze
with cats' heads around the rim
and field mice, wheat and poppies
encircling the body, signed by
Leopold Savine, L. Colin and
Cie. With Paris founder's mark.
- *height 27cm*
- **Guide price $11,570**

Italian Seal ▼
- *1950*

Italian silver torpedo-shaped seal
stamp with base by Murini.
- *height 18cm*
- **Guide price $210**

Fugare Spelter Figure ▲
- *circa 1893*

Gilded spelter figure of winged
Mercury engraved "A.
Recompense by Fugare" and
exhibited in Paris in 1893.
- *height 34cm*
- **Guide price $770**

Bronze Lady ▲
- *1911*

Gilt bronze figure of a lady with a
parasol by H. Varenne.
- *height 20cm*
- **Guide price $4,450**

Letter Rack ▼
- *circa 1950*

Black wire cat letter rack, the
body in the form of a spring with
plastic eyes and rotating eye balls.
- *height 14cm*
- **Guide price $80**

Italian Chrome Teapot ▼
- *circa 1950*

Round chrome teapot with cork
stopper for the spout.
- *height 19cm*
- **Guide price $120**

Chrome Coffee Pot ▼
- *circa 1950*

Italian circular chrome coffee pot.
- *height 24cm*
- **Guide price $90**

Draped Bronze Dancer ▼

- *circa 1925*
Fine bronze and ivory figure of a beautiful young lady in dancing pose, stamped and signed "Paul Philippe".
- *height 24cm*
- **Guide price $8,810**

Etling Bronze ▲

- *circa 1925*
Detailed gilt bronze and ivory figure of a young girl, signed and inscribed "Etling".
- *height 19cm*
- **Guide price $5,870**

Josef Lorenzi Bronze ▼

- *circa 1930*
Austrian bronze figure of a dancer with carved ivory head, raised onyx base and signed "Josef Lorenzi".
- *height 24cm*
- **Guide price $3,470**

Pantalon Dancer Bronze ▼

- *circa 1935*
Bronze cold-painted figure of a young lady dancing in a stylised pose by Josef Lorenzi.
- *height 24cm*
- **Guide price $2,580**

Exotic Dancer Figure ▲

- *circa 1920*
A bronze figure of a young woman in exotic dress with rich green patina on cream marble base by Samuel Lypchytz.
- *height 33cm*
- **Guide price $3,190**

Uriano Rock-man Figure ▲

- *late 1920s*
Large green and bronze patinated spelter male figure with base of black and Portorro Extra marbles. In excellent condition with original partina, by Uriano, unsigned.
- *38.1cm x 73.6cm*
- **Guide price $1,350**

Scarf Dancer Bronze ▼

- *circa 1930*
Cold-painted gilt and brown Austrian bronze figure of a young lady dancing with a scarf, signed "Joseph Lorenzij".
- *height 28cm*
- **Guide price $3,290**

La Liseuse Figure

- *circa 1920*

Figure of a lady in medieval dress seated on a chair with a book in one hand, signed on the skirt "Dominique Alon".

- *height 26cm*
- **Guide price** $6,500

Bird Brass Charger

- *20th century*

One of a pair of brass chargers of aesthetic movement design, this one depicting a bird on a branch.

- *diameter 31cm*
- **Guide price** $1,070

Le Gauyard Wallplaque

- *circa 1900*

A French Le Gauyard metal wallplaque depicting a reclining nude maiden.

- *length 39cm*
- **Guide price** $420

WMF Centrepiece and Liner

- *circa 1900*

An Art Nouveau WMF centrepiece and liner with an Art Nouveau maiden's face in profile and typical whiplash handles.

- *length 31cm*
- **Guide price** $530

Fish Brass Charger

- *20th century*

One of a pair of brass chargers of aesthetic movement design, this one depicting a leaping fish with water lilies.

- *diameter 31cm*
- **Guide price** $1,070

WMF Fruit-knife Stand

- *circa 1905*

WMF fruit-knife stand with an Art Nouveau maiden in profile, containing 12 knives.

- *height 30cm*
- **Guide price** $530

Alphonse Saladin Bronze

- *circa 1910*

Gilt bronze figure of a young naked woman holding a posy of flowers, signed and raised on a plinth.

- *height 31cm*
- **Guide price** $4,000

Pop Art Metal Tray

- *circa 1970*

A pop art metal tray decorated in typical 1970s colours and design. Made in Great Britain and marked "Worcester Ware".

- *diameter 38cm*
- **Guide price** $80

Expert Tips

Art Deco is avidly collected for its innovation and craftsmanship, but also because of the exciting jazz and Hollywood era which it evokes. Whether the same will be true of the 1950s and 1960s remains to be seen. You shouldn't spend on personal nostalgia and expect to make a profit.

Liberty Bombvase ▼

- *circa 1905*
A Liberty bombvase by Knox in polished pewter with a open-work tendril design
- *height 17cm*
- **Guide price $1,250**

Silvered Bronze Dancer ▼

- *early 20th century*
A silvered bronze lady dancer by J.D. Guirande sitting on a wooden stepped base.
- *53cm x 57.2cm*
- **Guide price $6,480**

Dianne Figure ▶

- *1928*
Large French "Dianne" figure in spelter by De Marco of the quality and weight of a bronze, and mounted on a Portorro Extra wedge-shaped marble base.
- *73.6cm x 32.5cm x 11.4cm*
- **Guide price $1,950**

Chromed Dancer Figure ▲

- *late 1930s*
Tall Art Deco figure of a stylish lady, based on a 1920s dancer. Chromed on top.
- *height 40cm*
- **Guide price $280**

Lady on a Bridge Figure ▼

- *1928*
A signed figure of a lady and a deer on a metal slabbed bridge over a stream of green onyx with ribbed waterfall detail and a black marble river bank to either side.
- *36.8cm x 78.7cm*
- **Guide price $2,640**

Lady and Deer Figures ▼

- *early 20th century*
"The Gift" by D.H. Chiparus, a spelter figure of a lady and deer group.
- *24cm x 49.5cm x 11.3cm*
- **Guide price $1,710**

Nude Spelter Figure ▼

- *early 1930s*
Green patinated pointing figure of spelter, "Look'", by Joe De Roncourt, mounted on a Belgian black marble base and signed on the right-hand end.
- *48.3cm x 53.3cm*
- **Guide price $970**

French Bon-bon Dish ◀

- *circa 1900*
French gilt bronze bon-bon dish with a young girl on the lid, by A. Charpentiers.
- *16cm x 29cm*
- **Guide price $6,230**

Circular Electric Fan ▲

- *circa 1960*
Salmon-pink circular metal electric fan standing on metal legs.
- *diameter 65cm*
- **Guide price $210**

La Musicienne ▼

- *1912*
French gilt bronze of a lady with a Sistrum, by Muller.
- *height 18.5cm*
- **Guide price $4,450**

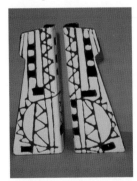

World War I Frame ▲

- *circa 1914*
Iron sculpture of a winged angel of Mercury and a soldier with a lion, fashioned as a picture frame.
- *height 47cm*
- **Guide price $500**

Metal Door Handles ▲

- *1950*
Metal door handles with ceramic and enamel yellow and brown geometric design.
- *26cm x 10cm*
- **Guide price $280**

Benson Tea Set ▶

- *circa 1900*
Copper and brass tea set designed and made by W.A.S Benson. Stamped "Benson".
- *42cm x 18cm*
- **Guide price $1,590**

"Puppet Dancer" Bronze ▼

- *1927*

A bronze by Ignacio Gallo of a
nude dancer holding a jester
puppet in her hand. She has a
silvered finish with golden hair
and a signed base made of
Portorro Extra and Sienna
marbles.
- *44.5cm x 12.7cm*
- **Guide price $3,550**

Spelter Mother and Child ▲

- *late 1920s–mid 1930s*

An unusual French spelter and
ivoreen mother and child group
by Menneville. The lady has an
ivorine face and hands and is
mounted on a signed ovular
Portorro marble and onyx base.
- *28cm x 66cm*
- **Guide price $1,500**

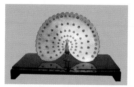

Japanese Bronze Peacock ▲

- *circa 1930*

A Japanese Showa period hakudo
bronze peacock on original black
lacquer stand decorated with
inlaid abalone shell and the
signature of the artist, Kano
Seiun, on the reverse.
- *35.5cm x 53.3cm*
- **Guide price $3,380**

Spelter Archer ▲

- *mid 1920s*

French green patinated male
archer figure, signed by the artist
Mellani, with original bow and
mounted on a black and white
marble base.
- *45.7cm x 61cm*
- **Guide price $1,240**

Rivière Nude Bronze ▶

- *1920s*

"Balance", a silvered bronze nude
athletic woman balancing on a
brown marble ball by Guiraud
Rivière Beautiful. Her toes are
spread for balance and she has a
very stylised bobbed Deco hair
detailing, all on a tapered base.
- *49.5cm x 10.2cm x 10.2cm*
- **Guide price $7,290**

Toga Dancer Figure ▲

- *1927*

A signed, green patinated spelter
toga dancer figure by Carlier set
on a pyramid marble base.
- *height 39.4cm*
- **Guide price $1,020**

Bronze and Marble Figure ▶

- *mid-1920s*

French silvered bronze and chrome figure on a base of figured verdigris and black marbles with lovely verdigris columns.
- *30.5cm x 45.7cm x 25.4cm*
- **Guide price $7,800**

Diana the Huntress Figure ◀

- *1928*

French spelter figure of Diana the Huntress with brown skin tone and a bronzed scarf wrapped around her. Signed on the right-hand end of the marble base by Dauvergne.
- *length 83.8cm*
- **Guide price $1,560**

Reclining Maiden Bronze ▲

- *circa 1920*

Bronze Art Deco figure of a naked young woman reclining, signed "Amadeus Generalli".
- *height 24cm*
- **Guide price $5,250**

Uriano Spelter Pair ▶

- *1930*

A spelter figure of a woman and a dog, unsigned but by Uriano. The woman has a natural skin patina and a blue and gold dress. The walled base is made of black marble, Portorro Extra and onyx sections.
- *43.2cm x 45.7cm*
- **Guide price $1,320**

Hunter and Leopard Figures ▼

- *early 1930s*

A French spelter man and leopard group mounted on a base of Portorro and brown marble and onyx, with a ziggurat back wall in brown marble and onyx. The man wearing enamel shirt and trousers, and holding a shield and chrome spear.
- *43cm x 63.5cm*
- **Guide price $2,040**

Spelter Woman and Peacock ▲

- *early 1930s*

Large French spelter figure of a woman feeding a peacock with berries, the base of green onyx and black and brown marble.
- *30.5cm x 78.7cm*
- **Guide price $1,360**

Circus Figure ▲

- *1926*

A large figure of a woman in circus costume juggling hoops. The base brown marble and cream onyx with circles and semi-circles of green onyx and brown marble.
- *55.8cm x 55.8cm*
- **Guide price $2,100**

Life-size Bronze Torso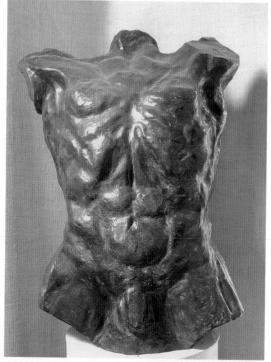
- *circa 1930*

Emotive life-size bronze torso by
Hubert Yenge from the foundry of
Alexis Rudier, Paris founder to
Rodin.
- *71cm x 55cm*
- **Guide price $15,580**

Figure by H. Varenne
- *1912*

Figure of a lady with a large hat
by H. Varenne, founder's mark
Susse Frères.
- *height 19cm*
- **Guide price $4,450**

Chrome Egg Cups ▶
- *circa 1950*

Pair of Italian chrome egg cups
with covers.
- *height 11cm*
- **Guide price $90**

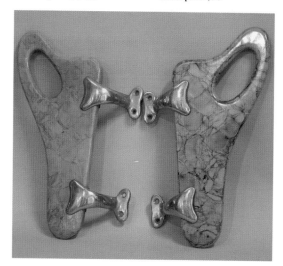

Expert Tips

*Women were the most popular
subjects for bronzes; not the
pre-First World War seductress,
but the newly independent self
possessed female.*

Turquoise Door Handles ◀
- *circa 1960*

Italian stylised pallette-shaped
metal door handles with
turquoise marbled enamel overlay
and large brass mounts.
- *length 33cm*
- **Guide price $570**

"The Lesson" Spelter Figure ▼

• *1928*

"The Lesson" by Limousin, a huge French figural group of a black patinated spelter man giving his son a lesson in how to shoot an arrow. The base is of black marble with white striations, and is signed by the artist.

• *71cm x 76.2cm*
• **Guide price $1,770**

Spelter Male Hunter Figure ▲

• *late 1920s*

A male hunter figure made of spelter and signed by the artist Joe De Roncourt, sitting on a canted edged brown marble base.

• *38.1cm x 55.8cm x 17.8cm*
• **Guide price $1,420**

"Group Atlante" Spelter Figure ▼

• *1920s–30s*

"Group Atlante", a spelter figure of Diane hunting a leaping gazelle on a granite stone base by De Marco.

• *76.2cm x 96.5cm*
• **Guide price $3,020**

Mother and Child Spelter Group ▲

• *late 1920s–early 30s*

A signed figural group by Menneville, made in France of spelter and ivorine on a black Belgian marble and onyx base.

• *33cm x 58.4cm*
• **Guide price $2,030**

Painted Silver Art Deco Bronze ▲

• *circa 1930*

Art Deco cold-painted silver bronze figure of a sensuous naked young lady.

• *height 35cm*
• **Guide price $1,690**

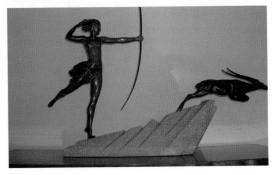

Wine-related Items

The ultimate antiques for daily use where collections can be started for a few pounds.

When the daily newspapers are regularly running stories about the amount of money that city traders are happy to spend on wine in restaurants and when the nation's taste for fine wines seems to be developing across the board, it is no surprise to find that wine-related silver is sitting at the top table of the market at the moment. Coasters, labels, corkscrews and funnels are all performing well and attracting good prices. Equally, at the other end of the scale, wine coolers are in great demand.

One area that does not seem to have benefited from the interaction of the wine merchants and the money-makers is that of the Victorian decanter and claret jug. Surprisingly, it is still possible to pick up a cut-glass decanter made by a reputable manufacturer for less than £300 while a silver and glass claret jug can usually be obtained for no more than twice that price. For collectors, this certainly looks like a good area of the wine-related market to consider investing in at the moment.

Champagne Corkscrew ▼
- *circa 1900*
Rare and unusual boxwood champagne corkscrew made by McBindes.
- *length 11cm*
- **Guide price $530**

Wine Funnel ▲
- *circa 1820*
Clear glass wine funnel.
- *diameter 10cm*
- **Guide price $130**

Brass Cocktail Shaker ▼
- *circa 1930*
Brass cocktail shaker with screw lid.
- *height 20cm*
- **Guide price $90**

Victorian Claret Jug ▼
- *1888*

A rare claret jug, the body cut with an unusual design, The Barnards, London.
- *height 40cm*
- **Guide price $8,460**

Magnum Claret Jug ▼
- *1872*

An extremely rare Victorian magnum claret jug, with beautiful engraving, the cast silver mount with dragon handle, by Stephen Smith, London.
- *height 40cm*
- **Guide price $15,580**

Queen Anne Shilling Ladle ▲
- *circa 1777*

Eighteenth century punch ladle with whalebone handle and a Queen Anne shilling incorporated in the base of the bowl.
- *length 33cm*
- **Guide price $270**

Rosewood Corkscrew ▲
- *circa 1850–80*

Rosewood corkscrew with grip shank and brush.
- *length 13cm*
- **Guide price $210**

Rosewood Corkscrew ▼
- *circa 1850*

Rosewood gripshank corkscrew.
- *length 13cm*
- **Guide price $320**

Small Silver Coaster ▼
- *circa 1820*

Old Sheffield silver-plated wine coaster with lattice work decoration.
- *diameter 12cm*
- **Guide price $170**

Staghorn Corkscrew ▼
- *circa 1890*

Staghorn corkscrew with brush.
- *length 15cm*
- **Guide price $210**

William IV Mahogany Wine Cooler ▶

- *circa 1835*
A fine mahogany wine cooler on a pedestal base with four elaborately carved paw feet.
- 88.9cm x 48.3cm x 53.3cm
- **Guide price $12,900**

Wine Cooler ▲

- *early 19th century*
Regency period mahogany open brass bound wine cooler with original lead lining; important lion mask ring handles.
- 39cm x 48cm x 74cm
- **Guide price $8,630**

Sheffield Plated Wine Coolers ▼

- *circa 1820*
A pair of campana (bell) shaped plated wine coolers with shell and gadroon borders with removable capes at the top.
- 23cm x 27cm
- **Guide price $6,500**

Scottish Wine Label ▼

- *circa 1845*
An unusual wine label in the form of a cut out letter "S" with foliate chasing. Made in Edinburgh by Alexander Wigful.
- *height 3.5cm*
- **Guide price $440**

Regency Period Oval Wine Cooler ▼

- *circa 1825*
A very rare oval mahogany wine cooler, exquisitely decorated with inlaid marquetry garland design, carved and moulded paw feet and gadrooned edging.
- 62cm x 63.5cm x 93cm
- **Guide price $70,310**

Silver Campana ▼

- *1838*
An early Victorian silver campana-shaped presentation wine goblet with a fine inscription and gilded bowl. Made by Benjamin Smith.
- 23.5cm x 14.5cm
- **Guide price $1,240**

Thistle-shaped Cup ◀

- *1880*
An unusual thistle-shaped dram cup with gilded bowl on a curved stem with a well decorated foot inscribed "DINNA FORGET". Made in Edinburgh.
- *height 9cm*
- **Guide price $700**

Expert Tips

Wine coolers are generally oval in shape with short legs. Octagonal and hexagonal, lead-lined, static wine containers with longer legs are, correctly, "cellarets."

Wine Strainer ▲
- *circa 1820*
Silver-plated wine strainer.
- *height 14cm*
- **Guide price** $390

Claret Jug ▲
- *1890*
English claret jug with floral engraving and a silver handle and lid.
- *height 30cm*
- **Guide price** $1,100

Oak Handle Corkscrew ▼
- *circa 1880*
Oak handle corkscrew with a metal screw and brush.
- *length 13cm*
- **Guide price** $170

Rum Label ▼
- *1830*
Silver rum label, made in London.
- *length 5cm*
- **Guide price** $120

Spirit Labels ▼
- *1910*
Spirit labels on chains. Port, Shrub, and Madeira.
- *length 5cm*
- **Guide price** $80

Victorian Port Decanter ▲
- *circa 1890*
Victorian circular port decanter with faceted design on the body.
- *height 30cm*
- **Guide price** $100

Ice Bucket ▲
- *circa 1930*
Silver-plate ice bucket with plain moulded handles to the sides.
- *height 21cm*
- **Guide price** $330

Pair of George III Goblets ▼

George III silver-gilt goblets by Richard Morson and Benjamin Stephenson, decorated with crest and rampant lions.
- *height 17cm*
- **Guide price $15,130**

George IV Wine Cooler ▼

- *1828–9*

Set of four wine coolers by Robert Garrard, London, highly decorated with scrolling foliate motifs, centred cartouches, cornucopias and acanthus leaves.
- *height 25.4cm*
- **Guide price $445,000**

Double-action Corkscrew ▶

- *19th century*

An English Thomason type double-action corkscrew with turned bone handle, ringed brass barrel with patent tablet marked "PATENT" between lion and unicorn supporters. Helix worm.
- *19.7cm x 8.5cm*
- **Guide price $700**

George IV Sherry Label ▼

- *1824*

A George IV sherry label with its original chain. Made in Birmingham by Joseph Willmore.
- *4cm x 2.5cm*
- **Guide price $200**

Italian Lever Corkscrew ◀

- *20th century*

All brass Italian lever corkscrew making use of the cog and ratchet principle. Rosati's patent. Archimedian worm, crown cork opener in handle and marked "ITALY" below.
- *17.5cm x 7cm*
- **Guide price $230**

George III Corkscrew ▲

- *circa 1790*

A corkscrew in the finest condition initialled "ML" on the cap of the screw sheath, along with the maker's mark. Made in Birmingham by Samuel Pemberton.
- *length 9.5cm*
- **Guide price $1,560**

George III Scottish Silver Wine Goblet ▲

- *1807*

Made in Edinburgh by John McKay, the vase-shaped body is mainly plain and stands on a circular foot with applied reeded rim and curved stem. The top of the bowl has a band of engraved bright-cut decoration of grapes and vine leaves.
- *17.3cm x 9.7cm*
- **Guide price $3,380**

Farrow and Jackson Corkscrew ▼

- *19th century*
A fine brass Farrow and Jackson corkscrew (unmarked) with helix worm.
- *17.8cm x 7.4cm*
- **Guide price $670**

Heeley King's Screw ▼

- *19th century*
An English narrow rack King's Screw with turned bone handle (no brush and hairline cracks), shaped steel side handle, ringed bronze barrel with unusual gilt tablet marked "HEELEY & SONS". Helix worm.
- *20.5cm x 10.5cm*
- **Guide price $1,020**

King's Screw with Bell Collar ▲

- *19th century*
A fine English four-pillar narrow rack King's Screw with shaped bone handle, bell collar, turned steel side handle and helix worm.
- *21.7cm x 11cm*
- **Guide price $1,110**

Victorian Claret Jug ▲

- *1878*
Victorian sterling silver claret jug, with Bacchus detailed mount, hallmarked in London by Charles Boynton.
- *height 28cm*
- **Guide price $4,530**

King's Screw ▼

- *19th century*
An English narrow rack King's Screw with shaped bone handle, shaped steel side handle, ringed bronze barrel with tablet marked "PATENT" between a lion and unicorn supporters. Helix worm.
- *20.5cm x 11.5cm*
- **Guide price $890**

Archimedian Screw Corkscrew ▼

- *19th century*
A three-fingered simple one-piece metal corkscrew with Archimedian screw.
- *14cm x 7.5cm*
- **Guide price $30**

Silver Beer Mugs ◀

- *circa 1940*

Silver beer mugs with glass bottoms and bamboo decoration.
- *height 13cm*
- Guide price $230 the pair

Cocktail Shaker ▼

- *1920*

Silver-plated cocktail shaker.
- *height 20cm*
- Guide price $120

Claret Jug ▼

- *circa 1880*

Continental elegant claret jug with fine engraving around the body and a silver geometric band around the neck, standing on a plain silver circular base.
- *height 29cm*
- Guide price $600

Pair of Glass Decanters ▲

- *circa 1890*

Pair of glass decanters with diamond pattern on the body and stopper.
- *height 27cm*
- Guide price $270

Spirit Barrels ▼

- *circa 1880*

Three oak spirit barrels with silver banding and taps, on an oak stand with silver banding.
- *36cm x 37cm*
- Guide price $1,920

Oak Water Jug ▶

- *circa 1880*

Oak cordial jug with silver lid and ball finial, spout with a shield below standing on three ball feet.
- *height 29cm*
- Guide price $590

Fluted Wine Funnel ▲
- *circa 1820*
Clear fluted glass wine funnel.
- *diameter 10cm*
- **Guide price $150**

Silver Wine Taster ▲
- *1939*
Silver wine taster engraved
"Souvenir of Schroder and
Schyler & Co. Bordeaux
1739–1939".
- *diameter 8cm*
- **Guide price $260**

Claret Jug ▲
- *1880*
Victorian claret jug with diamond
faceted body and silver handle
and lid.
- *height 21cm*
- **Guide price $480**

Spirit Decanter ▼
- *1890*
Spirit decanter with moulded
body and fluted silver neck and
four spouts, known as a Kluk
Kluk.
- *height 27cm*
- **Guide price $750**

Beehive Spirit Decanter ▼
- *1880*
Beehive spirit decanter with
spout.
- *height 24cm*
- **Guide price $290**

Spirit Decanter ▲
- *1840*
One of a pair of fine oblong spirit
decanters with faceted shoulders
and lid.
- *height 28cm*
- **Guide price $980**

Henley Corkscrew ▲
- *circa 1890*
Steel corkscrew made by Henley.
- *height 16cm*
- **Guide price $320**

George III Goblet ▼
- **1795**

George III sterling silver panelled goblet, hallmarked in London by Peter Podio.
- *height 17cm*
- **Guide price $1,720**

George III Wine Coasters ▲
- **1797**

Pair of George III sterling silver engraved wine engraved coasters, hallmarked in London by Richard Crossley.
- *diameter 12cm*
- **Guide price $5,150**

Baluster-shaped Wine Ewer ▼
- *circa 1850*

Baluster-shaped wine ewer decorated with finely engraved vertical bands of flowers and foliage separated by frosted vertical bands cut with polished lines and mitre cuts.
- *height 27.3cm*
- **Guide price $760**

Victorian Wine Ewer with Ivy ▶
- *circa 1860*

Victorian amphora-shaped wine ewer finely engraved with bands of ivy. The foot is also engraved with ivy. Rope twist handle.
- *height 30.5cm*
- **Guide price $1,240**

Victorian Claret Jug ▼
- *circa 1890*

Victorian amphora-shaped "rock crystal" engraved claret jug finely decorated all round in intaglio with birds with foliage, flowers and blackberries, on domed and star-cut foot. Original matching hollow blown stopper.
- *32cm*
- **Guide price $1,650**

Helmet-shaped Wine Ewer ◀
- *circa 1870*

Rare Victorian helmet-shaped wine ewer beautifully acid etched with a scene composed of figures preparing for a sacrifice.
- *height 35.5cm*
- **Guide price $1,650**

Spirit Decanter

- *1930*

Spirit decanter with moulded body and lozenge-shaped stopper with foliate and bird engraving.
- *height 27cm*
- **Guide price** $570

Horn Corkscrew

- *circa 1910*

Corkscrew with a horn handle and metal screw.
- *length 12cm*
- **Guide price** $80

Silver Coaster ▶

- *circa 1920*

Silver-plated circular coaster, one of a pair, with scrolled rim and a teak base.
- *diameter 17cm*
- **Guide price** $280

Claret Jug ▼

- *1850*

Deeply faceted claret jug, electroplated lip and cover, twisted rope handle and an acorn finial.
- *height 20cm*
- **Guide price** $780

Lion-handled Coaster ▼

- *circa 1900*

Silver circular coaster with scrolling to the rim and lion ring handles to the side.
- *height 16cm*
- **Guide price** $130

Bone Handle Corkscrew ▲

- *circa 1900*

Bone handle corkscrew with brass end and metal screw.
- *length 14cm*
- **Guide price** $130

Wine Coaster ▲

- *circa 1900*

Silver-plate wine coaster with scrolled handles and pierced floral and geometric design.
- *height 57cm*
- **Guide price** $130

Key-patterned Wine Ewer ▼

- *circa 1860*

Victorian amphora-shaped wine ewer engraved with anthemion, the Greek key pattern and pennants.

- *height 30.5cm*
- **Guide price $1,240**

Engraved Claret Jug ▼

- *circa 1870*

Victorian claret jug, the silver-plated mount finely engraved with festoons, bows and tassels, the lid surmounted with a rope twist bow, the plaited rope-twist handle terminating with a bow and tassels.

- *height 30.5cm*
- **Guide price $1,160**

Wine Ewer with Cartouches ▲

- *circa 1870*

Tall Victorian wine or champagne ewer engraved with latticework surrounding a cartouche on each side, one containing a bird perched over a pool, the other with a butterfly and an insect.

- *height 28cm*
- **Guide price $860**

Silver Wine Coaster ▶

- *1774*

Silver pierced wine coaster made in London by Robert Hennell.

- *height 3.2cm*
- **Guide price $2,230**

Victorian Wine Ewer with Teared Handle ▼

- *circa 1880*

Victorian amphora-shaped claret jug engraved with a band of Greek key pattern to the neck and another to the shoulder below etched scroll border and above engraved vertical lines. Engraved foot and "teared" handle.

- *height 33cm*
- **Guide price $650**

Silver Madeira Label ◀

- *1852*

Silver leaf-shaped Madeira wine label on a chain. Made in London by Charles Rawlings & Wm. Summers.

- *width 8cm*
- **Guide price $220**

Expert Tips

Hand-made decanters are marked on the rim and stopper with a scratched number. These are sometimes hard to discern, but it is worth taking the time to find them and ensure that they are the same.

Works of Art & Sculpture

The Japanese were more prolific than the Chinese in their carving, particularly in the second half of the nineteenth century.

This area of the market is a fascinating one, yet it tends to be fraught with problems for the collector. The most immediate and obvious of these hindrances is that there is no way of knowing what quantities of artefacts were made and have been preserved. This means that inevitabaly some fake items have been allowed to enter the market. Although it is possible to have a piece thermo-luminescence tested to establish its age to within 300 years or so, it is not impossible for the determined criminal to circumvent this process. Then there is exportation and importation and the documentation required for both. All antiques and woks of art can be imported into the United Kingdom, as long as the correct paperwork is completed, but it is not necessarily as easy to export from a country of origin. Of course, all these problems become exacerbated in direct ratio to the value of the artefact purchased, and great pleasure can be derived with little red-tape and risk if your requirements are modest.

Asian/Oriental

Stone Vishnu ▲
- *6th–7th century*
Khmer Phnom Du stone standing Vishnu.
- *height 55cm*
- **Guide price $80,100**

Versali Bronze ▲
- *10th century*
Burmese Versali bronze seated figure.
- *height 3cm*
- **Guide price $890**

Bronze Geese ▲
- *1868–1912*
A cast pair of Japanese silvered bronze geese from the Meiji period, signed "Masatsune".
- *22.5cm x 25cm*
- **Guide price $8,540**

Indian Elephants Vase ▲
- *1868–1912*
A bronze Japanese vase of the Meiji period, cast as three standing Indian elephants, with well-modelled heads and carefully rendered hides. Signed "Seiya".
- *height 35cm*
- **Guide price $7,480**

Malachite Axe Head ▼

- *1600–1000 BC*

Bronze axe head encrusted with malachite from the Shang Dynasty.

- *length 20cm*
- **Guide price $1,340**

Incense Burner ▼

- *Han Dynasty 206 BC–220 AD*

Incense burner in the shape of a mountain (representing the Isles of the Blessed, the abode of the mortals). The incense burner rests on a tall tray with a solid foot hollowed out beneath the stem.

- *height 21cm*
- **Guide price $530**

Arite Blue and White Vase ▼

- *early 19th century*

A Japanese Arita blue and white bottle vase with decoration of peonies and butterflies potted in the late seventeenth century style.

- *height 38.1cm*
- **Guide price $1,160**

Machang-type Jar ▲

- *late 3rd or early 2nd millennium BC*

Machang-type jar of painted pottery, Gansu or Qinghai province, with an unusual circular design and geometric pattern.

- *height 32cm*
- **Guide price $1,160**

Bronze Belt Hook ▲

- *3rd–4th century BC*

Bronze belt hook.

- *length 15cm*
- **Guide price $270**

Han Dynasty Vase ▲

- *206 BC–220 AD*

Unusual garlic-headed bottle-shaped vase with original pigment of pink, white and crimson with a geometric design around the neck.

- *height 34cm*
- **Guide price $1,340**

Stick Figure ▼

- *206 BC–220 AD*

Stick figure of a man standing, from the Han Dynasty.

- *height 60cm*
- **Guide price $2,140**

Shaman Beads ▼

- *206 BC–220 AD*

Cream jade beads that once belonged to a Shaman, from the Han Dynasty.

- *length 2cm*
- **Guide price $3,560**

Zodiac Animals ▼

- *7th–9th century AD*

Rare group of pottery Zodiac animals from the China Tang Dynasty.

- *height 28cm*
- **Guide price $980**

Kwannon Incense Burner ▲

- *pre-1900*

A Japanese late Edo/early Meiji period koro depicting the goddess Kwannon seated on a Shi Shi. The figure of Kwannon lifts off to allow access to the incense container in the body of the Shi Shi.

- *33cm x 33cm*
- **Guide price** $3,170

Sung Dynasty Lidded Jar ▲

- *1128–1279 AD*

Lidded jar from the Southern Sung dynasty with soft greenish black patina.

- *height 23cm*
- **Guide price** $1,580

Ming Dynasty Vase ▲

- *circa 1450–1500*

A Chinese ironwork vase from the early Ming Dynasty. Hexagonal with individual figures of immortals placed on each surface.

- *height 26.7cm*
- **Guide price** $1,480

Tanuki Censer ▲

- *circa 1890*

A small signed Japanese bronze censer from the Meiji period, modelled as a Tanuki with a woven silver lid, silver rings and gold inlaid eyes.

- *length 17.8cm*
- **Guide price** $1,690

Witch Doctor ▲

- **Han Dynasty 206 BC–220 AD**

Chinese Han Dynasty witch doctor with large ears and a ferocious face holding a snake.

- *height 1.1m*
- **Guide price** $4,980

Bronze Chicken ▶

- *late 17th century*

A Japanese cast bronze censer depicting a standing chicken, unusually ornamented with cloud designs. Featuring a lovely soft and glossy chestnut brown patina overlaid with black incense deposits.

- *26.7cm x 24cm*
- **Guide price** $2,230

Double Gourd Vase ▲

- *circa 1900*

A lovely Japanese polychrome patinated double gourd vase, with unusual mottled green, ochre and red patina, signed on the base by the artist.

- *height 26cm*
- **Guide price** $1,850

Terracotta Horse ▲
- **206 BC–220 AD**
Horse and groom standing with
hand extended, from the Han
Dynasty.
- *height of horse 29cm, height of groom 26cm*
- **Guide price $2,140**

Lacquer Figure ▲
- **206 BC–220 AD**
Wooden figure of a lady with
arms folded, wearing a dress with
red and black lacquer details,
from the Han Dynasty.
- *height 51cm*
- **Guide price $2,140**

Reclining Lion ▲
- *circa 17th century*
Grey selegon jade lion shown in a
reclining position. Ming Dynasty.
- *height 8cm*
- **Guide price $1,510**

Burmese Table ▼
- *circa 1900*
Carved wood circular table top
with carved legs in the style of an
elephant's head and trunk.
- *70cm x 1m*
- **Guide price $2,140**

Bronze Buddha Sakyamuni ▼
- *circa 1800 or earlier*
A large bronze of the Buddha
Sakyamuni, with gently smiling
features. The mandorla is cast
separately, and slots into a lug
cast on the back of the piece.
- *63.5cm x 43cm*
- **Guide price $3,660**

Banshan Pottery Jug ▼
- *mid-3rd millennium BC*
Banshan-type painted pottery jug
from the Gansu or Qinghai
province of Majiayao culture.
- *height 35cm*
- **Guide price $2,230**

Standing Soldier ▲
- **206 BC–220 AD**
One of five soldiers standing,
from the Han Dynasty.
- *height 47cm*
- **Guide price $1,340**

Dinosaur Egg ▲
- **60–70 million years old**
Dinosaur egg from outer
Mongolia.
- *height 13cm*
- **Guide price $530**

Expert Tips

*Ivories from the Ming dynasty
are usually distinguishable by
extensive surface cracking
caused by oils within the ivory
evaporating over time.*

Marble Buddha Head ▼

- *18th century*
Burmese Shan marble Buddha
head with downcast expression
and traces of pigment.
- *height 35cm*
- **Guide price $5,340**

Giltwood Dancer ▼

- *19th century*
Burmese Mandalay gilt wood
animated dancing figure in
superbly detailed traditional
costume.
- *height 72cm*
- **Guide price $4,450**

Buddhist Painting ▲

- *18th–19th century*
Tibetan thangka (painting) of
Buddha with lohans and
guardians and textile border.
- *77cm x 59cm*
- **Guide price $8,900**

Horse Procession Fragment ▲

- *11th century*
Khmer Baphuon–style tympanum
fragment of procession with
horse.
- *43cm x 90cm*
- **Guide price $13,350**

Bronze Okimono ▲

- *pre-1920*
Japanese bronze okimono as a
laughing seated Tanuki holding a
ruyi sceptre, symbol of power and
authority.
- *25.4cm x 25.4cm*
- **Guide price $2,220**

Kneeling Disciple Statues ▲

- *19th century*
Pair of Burmese Mandalay gilt
wood kneeling disciples.
- *height 36cm*
- **Guide price $3,560**

Wooden Devi Statue ▲

- *19th century*
Burmese carved wood Devi
goddess figure holding a lotus,
traces of green and red pigment.
- *height 92cm*
- **Guide price $2,230**

Bronze Ikebana Vase ▶

- *17th century*

Rare Japanese engraved and polychrome lacquered bronze ikebana vase decorated with panels depicting Fukurukuju and his deer on one side, and Kwannon riding a Kylin on the reverse.

- *height 23cm*
- **Guide price $1,480**

Meiji Ikebana Vase ▲

- *circa 1880*

A Japanese carved bamboo lotus form ikebana vase from the Meiji period in perfect condition, with a beautiful warm patina.

- *height 38cm*
- **Guide price $1,000**

Vietnamese Animal Container ▼

- *18th century or earlier*

A rare Vietnamese bronze food container fashioned in the shape of an elephant-like animal, cast in two pieces, with the legs attached.

- *length 33cm*
- **Guide price $2,310**

Shi Shi Bronze ◀

- *circa 1870*

Large Meiji period Japanese bronze of a seated Shi Shi, the traditional Oriental temple guardian, on original hardwood base with glossy chestnut colour patina.

- *40.6cm x 45.7cm x 28cm*
- **Guide price $3,030**

Chinese Burial Object ▲

- *206 BC–220 AD*

Burial object of a well-modelled horse's head, with strong traces of pigment, highlighting a red bridle, from the Han Dynasty.

- *height 15cm*
- **Guide price $530**

Japanese Cloisonné Vase ▲

- *late 19th century*

A Japanese cloisonné vase, crafted with silver and gold wirework and silver rims depicting birds flying amongst chrysanthemum flowers and leaves.

- *height 30.5cm*
- **Guide price $2,850**

Nagasaki Watercolours ▲

- *1868–1912*

One of three rare Nagasaki school watercolours on paper from the early Meiji period in Japan. Featuring Dutch and Russian families and traders in flamboyant traditional dress.

- *1.24m x 1.24m*
- **Guide price $24,030**

Terracotta Buddha Head ▲

- *11th century*

Burmese Pagan terracotta head of Buddha, smiling and with downcast eyes.

- *height 22cm*
- **Guide price $7,120**

Votive Plaques ▲

- *9th–13th century*

Three Pagan terracotta votive plaques with figures of the seated Buddha with hands placed in various mudra.

- *length 18cm*
- **Guide price $13,350**

Guan Yin Head ▲

- *19th century*

Chinese wooden Guan Yin head with traces of pigment.

- *height 53cm*
- **Guide price $1,690**

Thai Monk Statues ◄

- *18th century*

Pair of Thai gilded bronze Rattanakosin Monks standing on lotus bases in devout pose.

- *height 1.05m*
- **Guide price $21,360**

Khmer Buddha Head ▲

- *15th century*

Khmer post-Bayon period bronze Buddha head with fine features, downcast gaze and exceptional "smile".

- *height 26cm*
- **Guide price $44,500**

Stone Warrior Head ▲

- *12th century*

Jin Chinese stone guardian warrior head; the carved headdress mirrors the features of the fiercely expressive head.

- *height 42cm*
- **Guide price $9,790**

Islamic

Cylindrical Flask
- *7th century BC*
Islamic cylindrical flask with
brown, cream and blue marbling.
- *height 13cm*
- **Guide price $2,140**

Syrian Table
- *circa 1920*
Hexagonal mother-of-pearl and
bone inlay table with pierced
masharabi panels on turned legs.
- *49cm x 35cm*
- **Guide price $360**

Vase Bowl and Saucer
- *circa 1910*
Matching blue and turquoise
floral pattern vase bowl and
saucer.
- *height 37cm*
- **Guide price $530**

Syrian Tea Table
- *circa 1910*
A tea table from Damascus with a
brass circular top.
- *47cm x 59cm*
- **Guide price $270**

Persian Copper Vase
- *circa 1950*
A Persian copper and brass vase.
- *height 75cm*
- **Guide price $450**

Islamic Chess Pieces
- *9th century BC*
Islamic wooden chess pieces.
- *height 5cm*
- **Guide price $5,340**

Buddha Water Jug

- *12th century*
Small bronze Islamic water jug
with stylized handle and face of
Buddha on the base.
- *height 20cm*
- **Guide price $2,670**

Algerian Brass Teapot ▼

- *circa 1930*
Brass inlay teapot on a tall brass
stand with circular base.
- *length 1.72m*
- **Guide price $1,160**

Mother-of-Pearl Chair ▲

- *circa 1930*
Mother-of-pearl and bone inlay
chair, with carved top rail and
scrolled arms.
- *93cm x 64cm*
- **Guide price $890**

Mother-of-Pearl Table ▲

- *circa 1920*
Mother-of-pearl and bone inlay
in geometric patterns with
architecturally carved legs.
- *64cm x 44cm*
- **Guide price $710**

Crystal Chess Piece ◄

- *8th–7th century BC*
Clear lozenge-shaped crystal
chess piece.
- *height 4cm*
- **Guide price $1,780**

Bronze Gazelle Figure ▶

- *11th century AD*
A green patinated bronze figure
of a gazelle leaping.
- *9cm x 14cm*
- **Guide price** $2,140

Islamic Floor Tile ▲

- *circa 1900*
Islamic glazed mosaic floor tile
with incised geometric design
- *14cm x 14cm*
- **Guide price** $140

Cat Water Vessel ▼

- *10th century AD*
A ceramic water vessel styled
with the face of a cat.
- *height 28cm*
- **Guide price** $1,250

Small Turquoise Bowl ▼

- *12th century*
Ceramic turquoise glazed bowl
from Afghanistan with scroll
design.
- *height 15cm*
- **Guide price** $1,070

"Saluk" Jug ▲

- *12th century*
Saluk turquoise water jug with
Islamic script.
- *height 20cm*
- **Guide price** $890

Expert Tips

*If you cannot find a long
provenance on any Islamic
work of art of significant
value, then it should be
accompanied by a certificate
of authentication from a
museum in its country of
origin and a customs release
document.*

Turkish Table ▲
- *circa 1920*
Turkish table with mother-of-pearl and bone inlay on architecturally carved legs.
- *64cm x 44cm*
- **Guide price $710**

Damascus Table ▲
- *circa 1920*
Side table from Damascus with mother-of-pearl and bone inlay, single small drawer with brass handle, standing on cabriole legs.
- *43cm x 36cm*
- **Guide price $270**

Persian Charger ▲
- *circa 1940*
Persian oval brass charger or tray.
- *diameter 75cm*
- **Guide price $360**

Mirror and Stand ▲
- *circa 1900*
Elaborate mother-of-pearl and ivory oblong inlay mirror with scrolled carving, and chest with one long drawer and two smaller, with carved moulded top, and feet, from Damascus.
- *height 2.1m*
- **Guide price $10,680**

Architectural Table ▶
- *circa 1910*
Mother-of-pearl hexagonal table with geometric patterns and architectural legs.
- *55cm x 43cm*
- **Guide price $360**

Tiger Bowl ◄

- **12th century**
Islamic ceramic bowl with brilliant turquoise glaze and tigers.
- *height 18cm*
- **Guide price $3,560**

Terracotta House Plaque ▶

- **13th century**
Terracotta Islamic plaque with blue raised Islamic writing and a symbol of a house.
- *25cm x 24cm*
- **Guide price $19,580**

Persian Vases ◄

- **circa 1930**
A pair of fluted Persian blue and turquoise floral pattern vases with two handles on circular bases.
- *height 56cm*
- **Guide price $360**

Bronze Incense Burner ▲

- **12th century**
Bronze Islamic incense burner on three moulded feet inscribed with Islamic writing and surmounted by a bird.
- *height 20cm*
- **Guide price $2,140**

Terracotta Cow Figures ◄

- **12th century**
A pair of terracotta cows of rudimentary form with faint traces of decorative pigment.
- *8cm x 12cm*
- **Guide price $8,010**

Russian

Russian Gilt Enamel Spoon ▶
- *circa 1900*
Silver gilt spoon with pink, blue, red and yellow foliate design.
- *length 18cm*
- **Guide price $1,780**

Moscow Yacht Tankard ▼
- *circa 1871*
Miniature silver tankard with arms of the Moscow Yacht Club.
- *height 6cm*
- **Guide price $1,340**

Fabergé Hand Mirror ▲
- *1910*
Silver hand mirror by Fabergé, with raised engraved crest.
- *length 21cm*
- **Guide price $2,490**

Fabergé Kovsh ▲
- *1910*
Fabergé ceramic and silver kovsh with set cut amethysts.
Provenance: Princess of Baden, from the Baden collection.
- *height 15cm*
- **Guide price $8,900**

Soviet Pen Tray ▼
- *circa 1930*
Soviet pottery pen tray with a reclining Uzbek reading *Pravda* after Natalia Danko.
- *width 19cm*
- **Guide price $1,160**

Enamel Blotter ▼
- *circa 1900*
Enamel blue and pink floral design blotter with gold borders by Semonova.
- *length 14cm*
- **Guide price $1,600**

Miniature Tankard ▲
- *circa 1787*
Miniature "Charka", or silver tankard, engraved with two eagles above two flowers connected by a ribbon.
- *height 4cm*
- **Guide price $1,110**

Enamelled Spoon ◀
- *circa 1900*
Silver spoon enamelled with a dark blue, green and pink foliate design on a cream background.
- *length 15cm*
- **Guide price $2,310**

Silver Gilt and Enamel Spoon ▼

- *circa 1900*

Silver gilt spoon with turquoise, white, green and dark blue, foliate design with an emerald-green border.
- *length 11cm*
- **Guide price $710**

Russian Frame ▶

- *circa 1920*

Russian rosewood picture frame with brass borders and bearing the crest of two eagles with a portrait of Tsar Nicholas II of Russia.
- *28cm x 21cm*
- **Guide price $2,310**

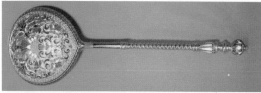

Silver Gilt and Enamel Beaker ▼

- *circa 1885*

Silver gilt beaker with blue scrolling and white flowers.
- *height 11.5cm*
- **Guide price $3,290**

Small Fabergé Mirror ▲

- *1910*

Small Fabergé silver mirror with raised engraved crest.
- *length 17.5cm*
- **Guide price $2,490**

Fabergé Spoon ▼

- *circa 1900*

Silver spoon with gilt bowl, by Fabergé.
- *length 16cm*
- **Guide price $760**

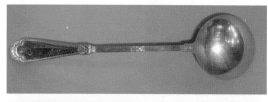

Musicians by Yakovlevich ◀

- *circa 1910*

Pair of terracotta musicians by Golovin Alexander Yakovlevich.
- *height 28cm*
- **Guide price $9,790 the pair**

Expert Tips

Any works of art by Fabergé are usually extremely valuable due to the intricate nature of the workmanship involved, their historical importance and their beauty.

Russian Kovsh ▶

- *circa 1900*

Russian enamel kovsh, highly
decorated with blue turquoise
foliate design by Lubwin.
- *length 19cm*
- Guide price $2,140

Soviet Tea Holder ▼

- *1967*

Soviet silver propaganda tea glass
holder with a scene showing a
man in the foreground with a
harvest and a rocket flying into
space and the sun in the
background.
- *height 10cm*
- Guide price $140

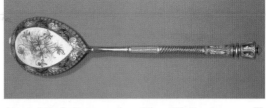

Arts and Crafts Spoon ▲

- *circa 1900*

Arts and Crafts silver spoon by
Knox, with a handle fashioned as
a peacock and the bowl as a leaf.
- *length 16cm*
- Guide price $1,420

Silver Gilt Spoon ▼

- *circa 1900*

Silver gilt spoon with blue flowers
on a cream background with a
green and orange foliate design.
- *length 17cm*
- Guide price $1,340

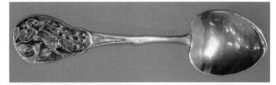

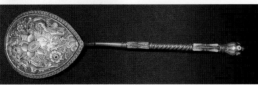

Enamel Russian Spoon ▲

- *circa 1900*

Russian silver spoon enamelled
with blue and pink floral design
on gold with a turquoise circular
border design.
- *length 20cm*
- Guide price $1,070

Silver Gilt Tea Set ▼

- *circa 1875*

Silver gilt tea pot, water jug and
milk jug, with foliate scrolling
and a central cartouche of a
palace, by Ovchinnikov.
- *height 15cm*
- Guide price $4,450

Silver Gilt Engraved Goblet ▲

- *1839*

Silver fluted gilt goblet from
Moscow with foliate design.
- *height 20cm*
- Guide price $2,140

Set of Salts ▼
- *circa 1877*

Set of six circular silver salts on three ball feet with silver spoons by Gachen in original oak box.
- *diameter 18cm*
- **Guide price $1,340**

Opaline Glass Sweet Jars ▲
- *circa 1905*

Opaline glass sweet jars modelled as busts of the Tsar and Tsarina Nicholas and Alexandra, made for the Imperial visit to France.
- *height 35cm*
- **Guide price $890 the pair**

Baboushka ▲
- *circa 1930*

Soviet white glazed porcelain figure of a baboushka with impressed hammer and sickle mark and initials of Boris Kustodiev (1878–1927) from the Lomonosov factory.
- *height 27cm*
- **Guide price $2,230**

Lenin Inkwell ▼
- *circa 1924*

The Lenin inkwell, with facsimile signatures and inscription "Proletariat of the World unite" and anniversary inscription on the cover. By Natalia Danko (1892–1942) from the Lomonosov factory.
- *height 17cm*
- **Guide price $2,230**

Stalin ▼
- *circa 1920*

Soviet white glazed porcelain figure of Stalin shown in his youthful revolutionary "Hero" style. Signed.
- *height 36cm*
- **Guide price $4,360**

Soviet Inkwell ▶
- *circa 1929*

Soviet pottery inkwell, surmounted by a young lady with a red headscarf reading a book, the lid modelled as books and pamphlets. After Danko.
- *height 16cm*
- **Guide price $2,230**

Puss in Boots ▲
- *circa 1930*

A brightly coloured Soviet figure of Puss in Boots, unmarked, probably by Boris Kustodiev.
- *height 23cm*
- **Guide price $800**

Lenin ▼

- *circa 1920*
Rare plaster figure of Lenin by
Mauetta.
- *height 34cm*
- **Guide price $4,360**

Grey Horses with Riders ▲

- *circa 1930*
Pair of grey horses with riders,
one pointing, on a foliate square
base.
- *26cm x 18cm*
- **Guide price $4,720**

Soviet Porcelain Plate ▲

- *circa 1920*
Russian, Soviet porcelain plate
with floral design and stylised
"CCCP" by Natalya Girshfeld.
- *diameter 23cm*
- **Guide price $2,940**

Constructivist Plate ◄

- *1928*
Constructivist plate painted with
female skiers in linear form with
strong colours. Signed and dated
1928.
- *diameter 24cm*
- **Guide price $2,940**

Accordion Player ▼

- *circa 1930*
Soviet white glazed figure of an
accordion player by Boris
Kustodiev.
- *height 23cm*
- **Guide price $870**

Soviet Bowl ▼

- *circa 1921*
Soviet bowl painted with strong
brush-strokes in vibrant colours
by Rudolf Vilde (1868–1942).
- *diameter 26cm*
- **Guide price $3,920**

Arctic Rescue Tea Set ◄

- *circa 1925*
Tea set commemorating an
Arctic rescue of the Swedish
Arctic Expedition, led by Nobel,
by the Soviet icebreaker "Krasin".
- *diameter of plate 24cm*
- **Guide price $4,450**

Tea Caddy Spoon ▶

- *circa 1900*
Silver gilt tea caddy spoon
showing an Imperial Russian
scene and a foliate design.
- *length 8cm*
- **Guide price $330**

Commemorative Tea Holder ▼

- *1970*
Soviet silver tea holder with a
central cartouche showing
Lenin's head, an industrial scene
and the dates "1920–1970",
surrounded by a foliate design.
- *height 10cm*
- **Guide price $140**

Fabergé Picture Frame ◀

- *circa 1890*
Fabergé satinwood picture frame
with silver beading, the gold
initial "A", and four silver roses at
each corner. The photo shows
Tsarina Alexandra.
- *14cm x 11cm*
- **Guide price $8,010**

Silver Tankard ▲

- *circa 1900*
A Russian silver tankard made for
political propaganda, with
engraved cartouches showing a
bountiful harvest.
- *height 8cm*
- **Guide price $3,380**

Reclining Man Reading Newspaper ◀

- *circa 1930*
Reclining figure of a man reading
a newspaper dressed in white with
a black and white hat.
- *length 21cm*
- **Guide price $1,030**

Writing Equipment

The Art Deco period produced some beautifully designed ink pots and pens which are now highly sought after.

The vast range of collectable writing equipment is overwhelmingly Victorian. The Victorians were fervent writers, and as a result an abundance of writing-related items were created in this period. Victorian ink trays were often inlaid with mother-of-pearl and were highly decorative. Some were made of enamel and decorated in a chinoiserie style, which was a very fashionable decorative effect at the time.

If you are a first-time collector, the field of writing equipment is a great place to start with as there is huge scope for the collector and the items can be very affordable, and are also usuable. They can make a bold and striking statement on any desk or in a study as they are not only decorative, but are also a great talking point.

Pens are always collectable with the leading brands such as Parker, Mont Blanc and Waterman continuing to attract the highest prices because of their timeless workmanship and superior quality.

Quill Box ▶

- 1920
Quill box made from ebonised wood and quills.
- 5cm x 16cm
- **Guide price $80**

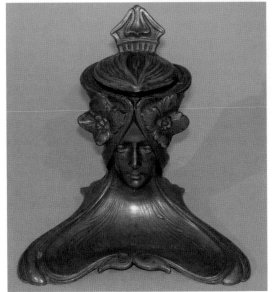

Salter Letter Balance ▼

- **1930**
Small metal letter balance with a brass dial, with the manufacturer's mark "Salter-and-made in England" on the dial.
- *height 22cm*
- **Guide price $90**

French Inkwell ◀

- *circa 1900*
French Art Nouveau inkwell of a lady reclining on large flowers with a lid concealed in the top of her long hair.
- *height 16cm*
- **Guide price $2,140**

Dog Inkwells ▶

- *circa 1890*
Carved wooden dog with a shaggy coat and an interior concealing two cut-out glass inkwells.
- *height 13cm*
- **Guide price** $3,920

Shell Inkwells ▲

- *circa 1800*
Regency mythological dolphins holding shell inkwells with original patina.
- *height 14cm*
- **Guide price** $9,260

Monkey Inkwell ▼

- *circa 1880*
Austrian bronze monkey inkwell. The tree stump contains the inkwell.
- *height 15cm*
- **Guide price** $2,400

Bulldog Inkwell ▼

- *circa 1880*
Austrian bronze bulldog head inkwell with cast insert removable to accommodate a glass reservoir. Locket on the collar has engraved opening doors and recess for a small picture.
- *17cm x 14cm*
- **Guide price** $3,920

Waterwheel Inkwell ◀

- *circa 1880*
Excellent French silvered bronze and ormolu model of an inkwell disguised as a waterwheel. The waterwheel rotates.
- *13cm x 14cm*
- **Guide price** $1,160

Bear Inkstand ▶

- *circa 1890*
Carved wood inkstand with mother bear holding her cub.
- *height 13cm*
- **Guide price** $1,160

Expert Tips

Inkwells of mahogany, walnut, maple, oak or pine were popular in the mid-nineteenth century.

Rhinoceros Inkwell ◀

- *circa 1880*
Unusual inkwell in the form of a standing rhinoceros, the reservoir concealed by the natural armour of the beast's back. On an oval base with pen stand resting behind.
- *19cm x 29cm*
- **Guide price $1,960**

Crocodile Inkwells ▲

- *circa 1880*
Well cast bronze crocodile double inkwell with original liners.
- *length 26cm*
- **Guide price $1,390**

Dog Stamp Box ▼

- *circa 1880*
Delightful and rare bronze stamp box modelled as a dog, with a gilded interior.
- *height 2cm*
- **Guide price $1,300**

Fox Head Inkwell ▼

- *circa 1900*
Fox mask with tail saucer concealed inkwell with original paint.
- *height 9cm*
- **Guide price $2,140**

Ostrich Inkpot ▼

- *circa 1880*
Bronze ostrich inkwell on a gilt brass oval stand.
- *height 20cm*
- **Guide price $840**

Napoleon Bonaparte ▲

- *circa 1850*
An unusual French inkwell featuring Napoleon Bonaparte standing upon a highly decorated plinth with Imperial eagles at each corner. Napoleon folds down by means of a hinge to reveal the inkwell, set on a black marble base.
- *height 23cm*
- **Guide price $1,740**

Double Glass Inkwell ▶

- *circa 1910*

Double glass inkwell with silver rims around the lids, in a square oblong container.
- *width 11cm*
- **Guide price $170**

Swirl Glass Inkpot ▼

- *1890*

Swirl glass inkpot with silver-plated hinged lid with floral design.
- *height 16cm*
- **Guide price $1,140**

Ebony Ink Tray ▼

- *circa 1820*

Ebony ink tray with two square inkwells with brass lids, and central stamp compartment.
- *width 34cm*
- **Guide price $350**

Ball Inkwell ▼

- *1914*

Brass inkwell consisting of four brass balls resting on each other, one of which contains the ink, with a metal and wood base.
- *diameter 17cm*
- **Guide price $140**

Parker Propelling Pencil ▲

- *circa 1930–5*

Mottled green Parker propelling pencil.
- *length 13cm*
- **Guide price $390**

Circular Glass Inkwell ◀

- *circa 1890*

Circular inkwell with a brass hinged lid.
- *height 9cm*
- **Guide price $480**

Marquetry Stationery Box ▶

- *circa 1860*

Dutch mahogany case inlaid with floral marquetry within rectangular panels of boxwood stringing. Cedarwood lined interior with pen tray and original glass inkpot with a brass screw top.

- *32.5cm x 16.5cm x 23.5cm*
- Guide price $2,670

Bronze Paper Clip ▲

- *circa 1900*

Vienna bronze dog's head paper clip with original paintwork.

- *7.6cm x 14cm x 12.7cm*
- Guide price $1,690

Pineapple Inkstand ▲

- *circa 1880*

French gilded and patinated green bronze pineapple inkstand.

- *19cm x 19cm x 19cm*
- Guide price $980

Letter Scale ▶

- *1870–80*

English cast brass letter scale.

- *31cm x 11.4cm x 16.5cm*
- Guide price $1,340

Expert Tips

Early inkwells would often be added to a candleholder by candleholder specialists.

Rosewood Writing Slope ▼

- *circa 1820*

Regency rosewood writing slope with rectangular lid which opens to reveal two glass inkpots, a wafer slide, and a dipped removable pen tray. The writing surface is lined in maroon hide with a gilded border.

- *14cm x 22cm x 35cm*
- Guide price $890

Armadillo Inkstand ▼

- *circa 1860*

Cast brass armadillo inkstand with two wells inside.

- *9cm x 7cm x 17.8cm*
- Guide price $700

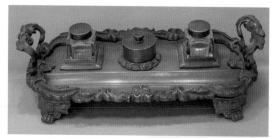

Glass Inkwell ▶
- *circa 1901*
Glass inkwell with faceted base
and silver hinged lid.
- *height 9cm*
- Guide price $520

Green Malachite Blotter ▼
- *circa 1860*
Green malachite blotter with
knob handle.
- *length 19cm*
- Guide price $290

Victorian Writing Tray ◀
- *circa 1870*
Victorian double-handled brass
writing tray with two inkwells
and a central sander, decorated
with C-scrolling and raised on
four paw feet.
- *width 27cm*
- Guide price $310

Glass Square Inkpot ▲
- *circa 1860*
Square glass inkpot with faceted
stopper and moulded shoulders.
- *height 9cm*
- Guide price $150

Paperweight Inkpot ▼
- *1890*
Victorian circular paperweight
inkwell with brass lid.
- *diameter 11cm*
- Guide price $90

Butterfly Letter Rack ◀
- *circa 189*
Brass butterfly letter rack
standing on a rustic base.
- *height 10cm*
- Guide price $420

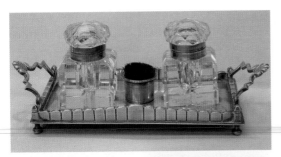

Brass Inkstand ◀
- **1830**

Double-handled brass inkstand with scalloped design, holding two glass inkpots with faceted lids and brass rims, and a brush in a brass container.
- *length 21cm*
- **Guide price $610**

Cut-Glass Inkwell ▼
- *circa 1900*

Cut-glass inkwell with a hinged silver cover.
- *height 10cm*
- **Guide price $460**

Silver Inkwell ▲
- **1930**

Small silver circular inkwell with hinged lid.
- *diameter 9cm*
- **Guide price $100**

Non-Spill Inkpot ▲
- *circa 1900*

Non-spill vaseline glass ink pot of ovoid form with a central teardrop reservoir.
- *height 6cm*
- **Guide price $40**

Satin Glass Inkpot ▲
- *circa 1870*

Satin glass turquoise inkpot with a white flower and hinged lid.
- *height 11cm*
- **Guide price $390**

Wood Blotter ▲
- *circa 1860*

Wood ink blotter with brass inlay.
- *length 19cm*
- **Guide price $280**

Old Sheffield Inkstand ▶
- *circa 1840*

Old Sheffield silver inkstand with serpentine border decorated with floral and leaf design, two faceted glass inkwells and a central silver sander.
- *width 27cm*
- **Guide price $530**

Ivory Boat Blotter ▶

- *circa 1890*
Ivory boat blotter with knob handle.
- *length 11cm*
- **Guide price** $310

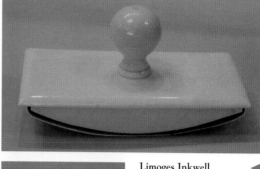

Victorian Inkpot ▼

- *circa 1830*
Victorian inkpot of ovoid form with ball stopper.
- *height 7cm*
- **Guide price** $150

Limoges Inkwell ◀

- *1930*
Limoges enamel inkwell with red flowers on a white ground and brass banding.
- *height 5.5cm*
- **Guide price** $200

Glass Inkpot ▼

- *circa 1830*
Faceted clear glass inkpot with star-cut stopper.
- *height 9cm*
- **Guide price** $150

Gutta-percha Writing Set ◀

- *circa 1860*
Ink tray made from gutta-percha with two inkwells set on a scrolled base.
- *width 27cm*
- **Guide price** $220

Slide Action Dip Pen ◀

- *1890*
Edward pod slide action travelling dip pen in "Gothic design" with rolled gold nib.
- *length 14cm*
- **Guide price** $220

Main Chinese Periods

SHANG DYNASTY	c. 1523 – 1027 BC
CHOW DYNASTY	1027 – 221 BC
WARRING STATES PERIOD	481 – 221 BC
CH'IN DYNASTY	221 – 206 BC
HAN DYNASTY	206 BC – 220 AD
THREE KINGDOMS	220 – 280
SIX DYNASTIES	280 – 589
NORTHERN WEI	385 – 535
EASTERN WEI	535 – 550
WESTERN WEI	535 – 557
NORTHERN CH'I	550 – 577
NORTHERN CHOW	557 – 581
LIU SUNG (SOUTH)	420 – 478
SOUTHERN CH'I	479 – 501
LIANG	502 – 557
CH'EN	557 – 588
SUI DYNASTY	589 – 618
T'ANG	618 – 906
FIVE DYNASTIES	907 – 959
SUNG DYNASTIES	960 – 1280
YUAN DYNASTIES	1280 – 1368
MING DYNASTIES	1368 – 1643
CH'ING DYNASTIES	1644 – 1912

Ming Period

HUNG WY	1368 – 1398
CHIEN WIEN	1399 – 1402
YUNG LO	1403 – 1424
HUNG HSI	1425 – 1425
HSUAN TE	1426 – 1435
CHENG T'UNG	1436 – 1449
CHING T'AI	1450 – 1457
T'IEN SHUN	1457 – 1464
CH'ENG HUA	1465 – 1487
HUNG–CHIH	1488 – 1505
CHENG TE	1506 – 1521
CHIA CHING	1522 – 1566
LUNG CH'ING	1567 – 1572
WAN LI	1573 – 1619

Ch'ing Period

SHUNG CHIH	1644 – 1661
K'ANG HSI	1662 – 1722
YUNG CHENG	1723 – 1735
CH'IENG LUNG	1736 – 1795
CHIA CH'ING	1796 – 1820
TAO KUANG	1821 – 1850
HSIEN FENG	1851 – 1861
T'UNG CHIH	1862 – 1873
KUANG HSU	1874 – 1908
HSUAN T'UNG	1909 – 1912

Korean Periods

LO LANG	106 BC – 313 AD
PAEKCHE	18 BC – 663 AD
KOGURYO	37 BC – 668 AD
SILLA	57 BC – 668 AD
GREAT SILLA	668 – 936
KORYO	918 – 1392
YI	1392 – 1910

Japanese Periods

JOMON PERIOD	1000 BC – 200 BC
YAYOI PERIOD	200 BC – 500 AD
TUMULUS PERIOD	300 – 700
ASUKA PERIOD	552 – 645
EARLY NARA PERIOD	645 – 710
NARA PERIOD	710 – 794
EARLY HEIAN PERIOD	794 – 897
HEIAN OR FUJIWARA PERIOD	897 – 1185
KAMAKURA PERIOD	1185 – 1392
ASHIKAGA PERIOD	1392 – 1573
MOMOYAMA PERIOD	1573 – 1615
TOKUGAWA PERIOD	1615 – 1868

French General Periods

FRANÇOIS-PREMIER	1515 – 1547	Reign of Francis I
HENRI-DEUX	1547 – 1559	Reign of Henri II
	1559 – 1560	Reign of Francis II
	1560 – 1574	Reign of Charles IX
	1574 – 1589	Reign of Henri III
HENRI-QUATRE	1589 – 1610	Reign of Henri IV
LOUIS-TREIZE	1610 – 1643	Reign of Louis XIII
LOUIS-QUATORZE	1643 – 1715	Reign of Louis XIV
LOUIS-QUINZE	1715 – 1774	Reign of Louis XV
LOUIS-SEIZE	1774 – 1793	Reign of Louis XVI
EMPIRE	1799 – 1814	Reign of Napoleon

English General Periods

TUDOR	1485 – 1558	Reigns of Henry VII Henry VIII Edward VI Mary
ELIZABETHAN	1558 – 1603	Reign of Elizabeth I
JACOBEAN	1603 – 1649	Reigns of James I Charles I
COMMONWEALTH	1649 – 1660	Protectorship of Cromwell
CAROLEAN / LATE STUART	1660 – 1689	Reigns of Charles II James II
WILLIAM AND MARY	1689 – 1702	Reign of William and Mary
QUEEN ANNE	1702 – 1727	Reigns of Anne George I
GEORGIAN	1727 – 1820	Reigns of George II George III
REGENCY	1800 – 1830	Reigns of George III George IV
WILLIAM IV	1830 – 1837	Reign of William IV
VICTORIAN	1837 – 1901	Reign of Victoria
EDWARDIAN	1901 – 1910	Reign of Edward VII

English Monarchs since 1066

WILLIAM I	1066 – 1087
WILLIAM II	1087 – 1100
HENRY I	1100 – 1135
STEPHEN	1135 – 1154
HENRY II	1154 – 1189
RICHARD I	1189 – 1199
JOHN	1199 – 1216
HENRY III	1216 – 1272
EDWARD I	1272 – 1307
EDWARD II	1307 – 1327
EDWARD III	1327 – 1377
RICHARD II	1377 – 1399
HENRY IV	1399 – 1413
HENRY V	1413 – 1422
HENRY VI	1422 – 1461
EDWARD IV	1461 – 1470
HENRY VI	1470 – 1471
EDWARD IV	1471 – 1483
EDWARD V	1483 – 1483
RICHARD III	1484 – 1485
HENRY VII	1485 – 1509
HENRY VIII	1509 – 1547
EDWARD VI	1547 – 1553
MARY	1553 – 1558
ELIZABETH	1558 – 1603
JAMES I	1603 – 1625
CHARLES I	1625 – 1649
COMMONWEALTH	1649 – 1660
CHARLES II	1660 – 1685
JAMES II	1685 – 1688
WILLIAM AND MARY	1688 – 1694
WILLIAM III	1694 – 1702
ANNE	1702 – 1714
GEORGE I	1714 – 1727
GEORGE II	1727 – 1760
GEORGE III	1760 – 1820
GEORGE IV	1820 – 1830
WILLIAM IV	1830 – 1837
VICTORIA	1837 – 1901
EDWARD VII	1901 – 1910
GEORGE V	1910 – 1936
EDWARD VIII	1936 – 1936
GEORGE VI	1936 – 1952
ELIZABETH II	1952 –

Not all of the terms that follow appear in this volume, but they may all prove useful in the future.

abadeh Highly-coloured Persian rug.

acacia Dull yellow hardwood with darker markings used for inlay and bandings towards the end of the eighteenth century.

acanthus A leaf motif used in carved and inlaid decoration.

Act of Parliament clock Eighteenth-century English clock, wall mounted and driven by weights, with a large, unglazed dial and a trunk for weights. These clocks often hung in taverns and public places and were relied on by the populace after the Act of Parliament of 1797, which introduced taxation on timepieces.

air-beaded Glass with air bubbles resembling beads.

air-twist Spiral pattern enclosed in a glass stem with air bubbles.

albarello Waisted ceramic drug jar.

alder Wood used for country-style furniture in the eighteenth century.

ale glass Eighteenth-century glass drinking vessel with long stem and tall, thin bowl.

amboyna West Indian wood used for veneers, marquetry and inlays. Light brown with speckled grain.

anchor escapement Late seventeenth-century English invented clock movement, named after the anchor shape of the linkage which moves the escape wheel.

angle barometer Also known as signpost barometers. Barometers where the movement of mercury is shown almost on the horizontal.

andiron Iron support for burning logs.

annulated Ringed (of glass).

apostle spoon Spoon with the figure of an apostle as the finial.

applied Attached or added, rather than modelled or carved as part of the body.

apron The decorative panel of wood between the front legs of a chair or cabinet.

arbor The axle on which the wheel of a clock's mechanism is mounted.

arch (clockmaking) The arch above the dial of a post-1700 longcase clock.

argyle Double-skinned metal pouring jugs and tea and coffee pots.

armoire French wardrobe, linen press or large cupboard.

ash Hardwood used for making country furniture and for its white veneer.

astragal Small semi-circular moulding, particularly used as glazing bar in furniture.

automaton clock A clock where the strike is performed by mechanically operated figures.

backboard The unseen back of wall furniture.

backplate The rear plate supporting the movement of a clock, often the repository of engraved information relating to its manufacture.

baff Knot in rug-making.

balance Device counteracting the force of the mainspring in a clock's movement.

balloon-back chair Popular, rounded-backed Victorian dining or salon chair.

baluster (adj.) Having a dominant convex swell at the base, culminating in a smaller, concave one at the neck. (noun) One of a set of upright posts supporting a balustrade.

banjo barometer Wheel barometer dating from circa 1775-1900, with shape resembling a banjo.

barley-sugar twist Spiral-turned legs and rails popular in the seventeenth century. Colloquial.

bat printed Transfer printed (of ceramics).

beech Hardwood used in the manufacture of country furniture and, when stained, as a substitute for mahogany.

bellarmine Stoneware flagon made in Germany from the sixteenth century.

bergère French for an armchair, used in English to describe a chair with caned back and sides.

bevel Decorative, shaved edge of glass, particularly mirror.

bezel The metal rim of a glass cover or jewel.

bird-cage Support mechanism at the top of the pedestal of some eighteenth-century tilt-top tables.

birch Hardwood used principally for carcassing; occasionally for low-quality veneer.

bird's eye maple Wood of the sugar maple with distinctive figure caused by aborted buds. Used in veneering.

biscuit (bisque) Ceramics fired but unglazed, originating in France in the eighteenth century.

blind fretwork Fretwork carving on a solid background.

block front Front shaped from thick boards allowing for a recessed centre section.

blue-dash Blue dabs around the rim of a delftware plate.

bob The weight at the bottom of a pendulum.

bobbin Turned furniture element, resembling a row of connected spheres.

bocage Foliage, bushes and shrubs supporting, surrounding or standing behind porcelain or pottery figures.

bombé Having an outswelling front.

bone china Clay with bone ash in the formula, almost entirely porcelanous. First produced at the end of the eighteenth century.

bonheur du jour Small, lady's writing desk with a cabinet and drawers above. Originally French, from the mid eighteenth century.

bottle glass Low quality coloured glass for bottles, jars etc.

boulle An eighteenth-century marquetry style employing brass and tortoiseshell.

boxlock Flintlock gun with the mechanism enclosed in the breach.

boxwood Pale yellow, close-grained hardwood used for carving and turning and for inlay and pattern veneers.

bow front Convex curve on the front of chests of drawers.

bracket clock Domestic clock so called because of the necessity of standing it on a bracket to allow its weights to hang down, the term later applied to domestic clocks of the eighteenth and nineteenth centuries regardless of their motive force.

bracket foot Plain foot carved into the rail or stretcher to form an ornamental bracket.

brandy saucepan Miniature, bulbous or baluster shaped saucepan with long handle at right angles to the spout.

breakfront Describing a piece of furniture with a central section which projects forward.

breech Rear end of the barrel of a gun.

breech-loading Gun loaded through an opening in the breech.

bright cut Late eighteenth-century silver engraving technique, making the design brilliant in relief.

Bristol glass Eighteenth century coloured (often blue) glass produced in Bristol.

Britannia metal Form of refined pewter used as a silver substitute in the early nineteenth century.

British plate Silver substitute from the nineteenth century, immediately preceding the introduction of EPNS.

broken arch Arch above the dial of a long-case clock which is less than a semi-circle, indicating an early Georgian date.

broken pediment Pediment with a symmetrical break in the centre, often accommodating an urn or some such motif.

bun foot Flattened spherical foot often found on later seventeenth-century furniture.

bureau Desk with a fall front enclosing a fitted interior, with drawers below.

bureau bookcase Bureau with glazed bookcase above.

burr Veneer used in furniture making, with a decorative pattern caused by some abnormality of growth or knotting in the tree. Usually taken from the base of the tree.

cabriole leg Leg of a piece of furniture that curves out at the foot and in at the top.

Introduced in the seventeenth century.

caddy Tea caddy.

caddy spoon Short-handled, large bowled spoon for extracting tea from the caddy.

calendar / date aperture Window in the dial of a clock displaying day, month or date.

canted corner Decoratively angled corner.

canterbury An eighteenth-century container for sheet music.

carcase/carcass The inner frame of a piece of furniture, usually made of inferior wood for veneering.

card case Case for visiting cards, usually silver, nineteenth century.

carriage clock Portable timepiece, invented in nineteenth-century France, with handle above.

cartel clock Eighteenth-century French wall clock with profusely decorated case.

case furniture Furniture intended as a receptical, e.g. chest of drawers.

caster / castor 1. Sprinkling vessel for e.g. sugar. 2. Pivoted wheel attached to foot.

Castleford ware Shiny white stoneware made in Castleford and elsewhere from circa 1790.

caudle cup Covered cup, often in silver.

cellaret A wine cooler or container, usually eighteenth century.

centrepiece Ornament designed to sit in the centre of a dining table. Often in silver.

chafing dish Serving dish, often in silver, with stand incorporating a spirit lamp to retain heat.

chain fusée The fusée of a clock from which a chain unwinds on to the barrel of the mainspring.

chamfer A flattened angle; a corner that has been bevelled or planed.

chapter ring The ring on a clock dial on which the numbers of the hours are inscribed.

Chesterfield Deep-buttoned, upholstered settee from the nineteenth century.

chest on chest Tallboy having two chests fitting together, the lower with bracket feet, the upper with pediment. From the seventeenth and eighteenth centuries.

chest on stand Known as a tallboy or highboy, a chest of drawers on a stand.

cheval mirror Tall mirror supported by two uprights on swivels.

chiffonnier Side cupboard, originally, in the eighteenth century, with solid doors, but latterly with latticed or glazed doors.

chinoiserie Oriental-style decoration on lacquered furniture or artefacts.

chronometer Precision timepiece, often for navigation.

circular movement Clock movement of circular plates.

cistern Chamber containing mercury at the base of the tube of a barometer.

claw-and-ball foot Foot modelled as a ball clutched in a claw, frequently used to terminate a cabriole leg.

clock garniture Mantelpiece ornamentation with a clock as centrepiece.

close helmet Helmet covering the whole head and neck.

coaster Small, circular tray, often in silver, for holding a bottle.

cockbeading Bead moulding applied to the edges of drawers.

cock bracket Bracket supporting a watch mainspring.

coin glass Early eighteenth-century English drinking glass with a coin moulded into the knop of the stem.

commode High quality, highly decorated chest of drawers or cabinet, with applied mounts.

compensated pendulum Pendulum with mercury reservoir, the mercury rising and falling to compensate for the effects on the pendulum of changes of temperature.

composition Putty-like substance for moulding and applying to e.g. mirror frames, for gilding.

console table Often semi-circular table intended to stand against a wall on the pier between two windows (hence also pier table). Usually with matching mirror above.

cordial glass Glass originating in the seventeenth century, with a small bowl for strong drinks.

corner chair Chair with back splats on two sides and a bowed top rail, designed to fit into a corner.

cornice Horizontal top part of a piece of furniture; a decorative band of metal or wood used to conceal curtain fixtures

coromandel Wood from India's Coromandel coast, used for banding and inlay.

counter-well The small oval wooden dishes inset into early Georgian card tables for holding chips or cash, hence also guinea-well.

country furniture Functional furniture made outside the principal cities. Also provincial furniture.

countwheel strike Clock mechanism determining the number of strikes per hour.

cow creamer Silver or china cream jug modelled as a cow.

crazing Fine cracks in glaze.

creamware Earthenware glazed in a cream colour giving a porcelain effect, in a widely used technique originally devised by Wedgwood in the 1760s.

credence table Late seventeenth-century oak or walnut table with folding top.

credenza Long Victorian side cabinet with glazed or solid doors.

crenellated Crinkly, wavy.

crested china Ware decorated with heraldic crests; originally by Goss, but subsequently by many Staffordshire and German potteries.

crinoline stretcher Crescent-shaped stretcher supporting the legs of some Windsor chairs.

cross-banding Decorative edging with cross-grained veneer.

cruet Frame for holding condiment containers.

crutch The arm connecting a clock's pendulum to the pallet arbor.

cuirass Breastplate (of armour).

cup and cover Round turning with a distinctly separate top, common on legs until circa 1650.

damascene Inlay of precious metal onto a body of other metal for decorative purposes.

davenport Small English desk, reputedly originally produced by Gillow for a Captain Davenport in 1834. A day-bed or sofa in the USA.

deadbeat escapement Version of the anchor escapement that eliminates recoil and improves accuracy.

deal Sawn pine wood.

delftware Seventeenth- and eighteenth-century tin-glazed earthenware, often decorated in the style of Chinese blue and white porcelain or after Dutch seventeenth-century painting, after the style pioneered by the Delft pottery.

Delft ware Items of delftware which actually emanate from Delft.

dentil Small, block-shaped moulding found under a furniture cornice.

dialplate Frontplate of a clock.

diamond cut (of glass) Cut in diamond shape.

dinanderie Fifteenth-century brass artefact from the factories of Dinant, Belgium.

dished table top Hollowed-out, solid top, particularly of a pie-crust, tripod table.

distressed Artificially aged.

dovetails Interlocking joints used in drawers.

double-action A gun which may be cocked or self-cocking.

douter Scissor-like implement for extinguishing a candle.

dowel Peg holding together wooden joint.

dram glass Small, short-stemmed glass with rounded bowl.

drop-in seat Framed, upholstered seat which sits in the framework of a chair.

drop handle Pear-shaped brass furniture handle of the late seventeenth and early eighteenth centuries.

drop-leaf table Table with a fixed central section and hinged flaps.

drum table Circular writing table on a central pedestal with frieze drawers.

dry-edge With unglazed edges.

dummy drawer False drawer with handle.

Dutch strike Clock chime which strikes the next hour on the half hour.

ebonise To stain a wood to the dark colour of ebony.

ebony Much imitated exotic black hardwood, used as veneer in Europe from the seventeenth century, generally for very high quality pieces.

écuelle Two-handled French soup bowl with cover and stand, often Sèvres.

electroplate The technique of covering one metal with the thin layer of another.

elm Hardwood used in the manufacture of chair seats, country furniture and coffins.

embossing Relief decoration.

enamel Second, coloured glaze fired over first glaze.

endstone In a clock mechanism, jewel on which an arbor pivots.

English dial Nineteenth-century English wall clock with large painted dial, previously a fixture in railway stations.

Engshalskrüge Large German tin-glaze jug with cylindrical neck.

épergne Centrepiece of one central bowl surrounded by smaller ones.

escritoire Cabinet with a fall-front which forms a writing surface. With a fitted interior.

escutcheon Brass plate surrounding the edges of a keyhole.

étuis Small, metal oddments box.

everted Outward turned, flaring (e.g. of a lip).

facet-cut (of glass) Cut criss-cross into straight-edged planes.

faience Tin-glazed earthenware.

fairings Porcelain figures, especially German, made in the nineteenth and twentieth centuries in the mould. Usually comical and carrying descriptive captions.

fall front Flap of a bureau or secretaire that pulls out to provide a writing surface.

famille rose Predominantly pink-coloured Oriental porcelain.

famille verte Predominantly green-coloured Oriental porcelain.

fauteuil Open-sided, upholstered armchair with padded elbows.

feather banding Two bands of veneer laid at opposite diagonals.

field Area of a carpet within its decorated borders.

fielded panel Raised panel with chamfered edge fitting into a framework.

figure Natural pattern created by the grain through the wood.

finial Decorative, turned knob.

flamed veneer Veneer cut at an angle to enhance the figuring.

flatware Plates, knives and forks.

flintlock Gun mechanism whereby the priming in the pan is ignited by a spark created by a flint.

flute glass Glass with tall, slender bowl.

fluting Decorative parallel grooving.

foliate carving Carved flower and leaf motifs.

foliot Primitive form of balance for clock mechanisms.

fretwork Fine pierced decoration.

frieze Long ornamental strip.

frit The flux from which glass is made. An ingredient of soft-paste porcelain.

frizzen The metal which a flint strikes to create a spark in a flintlock mechanism.

fruitwood Generally the wood of apple, cherry and pear trees, used for ebonising and gilding, commonly in picture frames.

fusee The conical, grooved spool from which a line or chain unwinds as it is pulled by the mainspring of a clock movement.

gadroon Carved edge or moulded decoration consisting of a series of grooves, ending in a curved lip, with ridges between them.

Gainsborough chair Deep, upholstered armchair with padded, open arms and carved decoration.

galleried Having a wood or metal border around the top edge.

garniture Set of ornamental pieces of porcelain.

gateleg Leg that pivots to support a drop leaf.

gesso Plaster-like substance applied to carved furniture before gilding or moulded and applied as a substitute for carving.

gilt-tooled decoration Gold leaf impressed into the edges of leather on desk-tops.

gimbal Mounting which keeps a ship's barometer level at all times.

girandole Wall-mounted candle holder with a mirrored back.

gorget Item of armour for protecting the throat.

Goss china Range of porcelain, particularly heraldic, produced in Stoke-on-Trent from 1858.

greave Armour protecting lower leg.

Greek key Ancient key-shaped decoration often repeated in fretwork on furniture.

gridiron pendulum Clock pendulum consisting of rods of a mix of metals positioned in such a way that the dynamics of their behaviour when subjected to heat or cold keep the pendulum swing uniform.

halberd Double-headed axe weapon with projecting spike.

half hunter Watch with an opening front cover with glass to the centre and a chapter ring, giving protection to the glass over the dial.

hallmark The mark by which silver can be identified by standard, place of assay and date.

hard-paste porcelain Porcelain made with kaolin and petuntse in the Chinese fashion, pioneered in Europe at Meissen in the early eighteenth century.

hunter Watch with a hinged, opening front cover in solid metal.

husk Formalised leaf motif.

ice glass Glass with uneven, rippling surface.

Imari Japanese porcelain made in and around Arita from the early eighteenth century and shipped to Europe from the port of Imari. Blue, red and gold coloured.

improved A pejorative term implying that a piece has been altered in order dishonestly to enhance its value.

inlay The decorative setting of one material into a contrasting one.

intaglio Incised design.

ironstone Stoneware patented by Mason in 1813, in which slag from iron furnaces was mixed with the clay to toughen the ware.

istoriato Of some Italian majolica, meaning 'with a story on it'.

japanned Painted and varnished in imitation of Oriental style lacquer work.

jardinière An ornamental pot or vase for plants.

jasper ware Variety of coloured stoneware developed by the Wedgwood factory.

joined Manufactured with the use of mortice and tenon joints and dowels, but without glue.

kabuto Japanese Samurai helmet.

kingwood Exotic, purplish hardwood used in veneer.

kneehole desk Desk with a recessed cupboard beneath the frieze drawer.

knop Rounded projection or bulge in the stem of a glass.

lacquer Resinous substance which, when coloured, provides a ground for chinoiserie and gilding.

ladder-back Chair with a series of horizontal back rails.

lantern clock Clocks made in England from the sixteenth century, driven entirely by weights and marking only the hours. Similar in appearance to a lantern.

lappit Carved flap at the top of a leg with a pad foot.

latten Archaic term for brass.

lead crystal Particularly clear, brilliant glass including lead in the process.

lead-glazed the earliest glaze for Western pottery, derived from glass making.

lever escapement Modification of the anchor escapement for carriage clocks and, particularly, watches.

lion's paw foot Foot carved as a lion's paw. Commonly eighteenth century and Regency.

lock Firing mechanism of a gun.

lockplate Base holding firing mechanism on a gun barrel.

loo table Large Victorian card or games table.

longcase clock The 'grandfather' clock, housed in a tall wooden case containing the weights and pendulum.

loper Pull-out arm that supports the hinged fall of a bureau.

lowboy Small side table with cabriole legs, from the seventeenth century.

lustre ware Ceramic ware decorated with a metallic coating which changes colour when fired.

mahogany The hardwood most used in the production of furniture in England in the eighteenth and nineteenth centuries. Used as a solid wood until the nineteenth century, when its rarity led to its being used for veneer.

majolica Originally tin-glazed earthenware produced in Renaissance Italy, subsequently all nineteenth century wares using the same technique.

mantel clock Clock with feet designed to stand on a mantelpiece.

maple North American hardwood used for its variety of veneers.

marine chronometer Precision clock for use in navigation at sea.

marquetry The use of wooden and other inlays to form decorative patterns.

married Pejorative term applied to a piece of furniture which is made up of more than one piece of the same period.

matchlock Firing mechanism of a gun achieved by lowering a slow match into the priming pan.

mazarine Metal strainer fitting over a dish.

mercury twist Air-twist in glass of a silver colour.

millefiori Multi-coloured or mosaic glass.

moonwork Clock mechanism which computes and displays the phases of the moon.

moquette Heavy imitation velvet used for upholstery.

morion Helmet with upturned front peak.

mortice Slot element of a mortice and tenon joint.

moulding decorative, shaped band around an object or a panel.

mount Invariably metal mounting fitted to a piece of furniture.

mule chest Coffer with a single row of drawers to the base.

musical clock Clock with a cylinder which strikes bells to play a tune.

Nailsea Late eighteenth-century, boldly coloured, opaque glass from Nailsea, near Bristol.

nest of tables Set of three or four occasional tables which slot into each other when not in use.

oak Hardwood which darkens with age, predominant in English furniture manufacture until the middle of the seventeenth century.

obverse The front side of a coin or medal.

ogee An S-shaped curve.

ogee arch Two S-shaped curves coming together to form an arch.

oignon Onion-shaped French watch of the eighteenth century.

ormolu From French *dorure d'or moulu*: 'gilding with gold paste', gold-coloured alloy of copper, zinc, and sometimes tin, in various proportions but usually containing at least 50% copper. Ormolu is used in mounts (ornaments on borders, edges, and as angle guards) for furniture, especially eighteenth-century furniture.

orrery Astronomical clock which shows the position of heavenly bodies. Named after Charles Boyle, fourth Earl of Orrery.

overglaze See **enamel**.

overmantel mirror Mirror designed to hang over a mantelpiece.

ovolo A rounded, convex moulding, making an outward curve across a right angle.

oyster veneer Veneer resembling an open oyster shell, an effect achieved by slanting the cut across the grain of a branch.

pad foot Rounded foot on a circular base, used as termination for cabriole legs.

pair-case A double case for a watch, the inner for protection of the movement, the outer for decoration.

pallet Lever that engages in a clock's escapement wheel in orderb to arrest it.

papier mâché Moulded and lacquered pulped paper used to make small items of furniture and other artefacts.

parian Typically uncoloured, biscuit-style porcelain developed in the nineteenth century by Copeland and named after Parian white marble.

parquetry Veneered pattern using small pieces of veneer, often from different woods, in a geometrical design.

patera Circular ornament made of wood, metal or composition.

patina The layers of polish, dirt, grease and general handling marks that build up on a wooden piece of furniture over the years and give it its individual signs of age, varying from wood to wood.

pearlware White, shiny earthenware, often print decorated.

pedestal desk A flat desk with a leathered top standing on two banks of drawers.

pediment Architectural, triangular gable crowning a piece of furniture or a classical building.

pegged furniture Early furniture constructed with the use of mortice and tenon joints and pegged together with dowels.

pembroke table Small, two-flapped table standing on four legs or a pedestal.

pepperette Vessel, often in silver, for sprinkling pepper.

petuntse Chinese name for the feldspathic rock, an essential element of porcelain, which produces a glaze.

pewter Alloy of tin, lead and often various other metals.

pie-crust Expression used to describe the decorative edge of a dished-top tripod table.

pier glass Tall mirror for hanging on a pier between windows.

pietra dura Composition of semi-precious stones applied to panels of – usually Italian – furniture.

pillar (watchmaking) A rod connecting the dial-plate and backplate of a movement.

pillar rug Chinese rug made to be arranged around a pillar.

pine Softwood used for carcassing furniture.

platform base Flat base supporting a central pedestal and table-top above and standing on three or four scrolled or paw feet.

plinth base Solid base not raised on feet.

pole screen Adjustable fire screen.

pommel Knob at the end of the handle of a dagger.

pontil mark Mark made by the pontil, or blowpipe, on the base of hand-blown glass.

porcellanous Having most of the ingredients or characteristics of porcelain.

porringer Large, two-handled cup with cover.

potboard Bottom shelf of a dresser, often just above the floor.

pounce box A sprinkler for pounce, a powder for drying ink.

Prattware Staffordshire earthenware of the late eighteenth and early nineteenth centuries, decorated in distinctive colours on a buff ground.

print decoration Mass-produced decoration. Not hand painting.

provincial furniture See **country furniture**.

punch bowl Large bowl for the retention and dispensation of punch.

quartered top Flat surface covered with four pieces of matching veneer.

quartetto tables Nest of four occasional tables.

quillon Cross-piece of a sword.

rail A horizontal member running between the outer uprights of a piece of furniture.

rating nut Nut under the bob of a clock's pendulum by which the rate of swing may be adjusted.

redware Primitive eighteenth-century American ware made from a clay which turns red when fired.

reeding Parallel strips of convex fluting.

re-entrant corner Shaped indentation at each corner of a table.

register plate Plate on a barometer with inscriptions to be read against the level of mercury.

regulator Precision timepiece of the eighteenth century.

relief Proud of the surface.

repeating work Mechanism by which the pull of a cord or the press of a button operates the striking mechanism of a clock or watch to the last hour.

repoussé An embossed design which has been refined by chasing.

rosewood Named after its smell when newly cut, rather than its flower or colour, a dark-brown hardwood with an attractive stripe or ripple, used for veneering.

rule joint Hinge on furniture which fits so well that, when open, no join can be detected between two hinged parts.

runners Strips of wood, fitted to furniture, on which drawers slide.

sabre leg Chair leg in the shape of a sabre, typical of the Regency period.

saltglaze Stoneware in which salt is added to the recipe creating a porcellanous, glassy surface. Dates back to the early eighteenth century.

salver A large metal dish or tray for transporting smaller dishes.

satinwood A light golden-coloured, close-grained hardwood used for veneer, panelling and turning from the mid-eighteenth century onwards.

scagiola Composite material resembling marble.

scalloped Having a series of circular edges in the shape of a scallop shell.

scalloped leaf Serpentine flap on some pembroke tables.

sconce 1. Cup-shaped candle holder. 2. Metal plate fixed to the wall, supporting candle holder or light.

scratch blue Eighteenth-century saltglaze decoration where the body is incised and the incisions painted blue.

scroll, scrolling Carving or moulding of a curled design.

seat rail Horizontal framework below the chair seat uniting the legs.

secretaire Writing desk with false drawer front which lets down to reveal a writing surface and fitted interior.

secretaire bookcase Secretaire with bookcase fitted above.

serpent The arm holding the match or flint by which the priming of a gun was ignited.

serpentine Of undulating shape.

settee Upholstered settle.

settle Hard bench seat with back. The earliest form of seating for two or more people.

Sheffield plate Rolled sheet silver placed either side of a layer of copper and fused. Recognised by the Sheffield assay office in 1784, but made elsewhere, notably Birmingham, as well.

shoe piece Projection on the back rail of a chair into which the splat fits.

side chair Chair without arms designed to stand against the wall.

side table Any table designed to stand against the wall.

skeleton clock Clock with the workings exposed.

slipware Earthenware to which mixed clay and water has been added as decoration.

sofa Well-upholstered chair providing seating for two or more people.

sofa table Rectangular table with hinged flaps designed to stand behind a sofa.

soft-paste porcelain Porcelain using frit or soapstone instead of the petuntse of hard-paste porcelain. English, from the eighteenth century.

spade foot Square, tapered foot.

spandrel Pierced, decorative corner bracket found at the tops of legs.

sparrow-beak jug Jug with a triangular spout.

spill vase Container for lighting-tapers.

spindle Thoroughly turned piece of wood. The upright bars of a spindle-back chair.

splat The central upright of a chair back.

sprig Applied or relief ornamentation of any kind on a ceramic artefact.

squab Detachable cushion or upholstered seat of a chair or bench.

standish Inkstand, often in silver.

stick barometer Barometer with a straight, vertical register plate running alongside the mercury tube.

stiles Archaic term for the vertical parts of the framework of a piece of furniture.

stoneware Earthenware that is not porous after firing.

stretcher Rail joining the legs of a table or chair.

strike / silent ring Dial to disengage or re-engage the striking of a clock.

stringing Fine inlaid lines around a piece of furniture.

stirrup cup Cup used for alcoholic refreshment prior to hunting, usually shaped in the head of a fox or, less usually, a hound.

stuff-over seat Chair that is upholstered over the seat rail.

subsidiary dial Small dial, usually showing seconds, within the main dial of a clock or watch. Hence **subsidiary seconds**.

swagged With applied strips formed in a mould (of metal).

swan-neck pediment Pediment with two broken curves.

swan-neck handle Curved handle typical of the eighteenth century.

sycamore Hardwood of the maple family, light yellow in colour, used for veneering.

tang The end of the blade of a sword, covered by the hilt.

tankard Large beer-mug with a hinged lid and thumb-piece.

tazza Italian plate, cup, basin or wide-bowled glass.

teapoy Small piece of furniture designed for holding tea leaves. Usually Anglo-Indian.

tenons The tongues in mortice and tenon joints.

thumb moulding Decorative concave moulding.

thumb-piece Projection attached to a hinged lid which will open the lid when pressure is applied by the thumb.

tine Prong of a fork.

tin-glazed Lead-glazed earthenware to which tin is added, e.g. majolica.

toilet mirror Small dressing mirror with a box base and drawers.

touch mark Individual mark of the maker of a piece of early English pewter.

transfer Ceramic print decoration using colours held in oil.

trefid spoon A seventeenth-century spoon with the handle terminating in the shape of a bud, usually cleft or grooved into two lobes.

trefoil Having three lobes.

trembleuse Cup-stand with feet.

tripod table Small, round-topped table on three-legged base.

tulipwood Pinkish, naturally patterned hardwood used in veneer.

turnery Any wood turned on a lathe.

tureen Large bowl in porcelain or metal, usually with a lid and two handles.

turret clock Clock of any size driven by a weight suspended by a rope wrapped round a drum.

underglaze Colour or design painted below the glaze of a ceramic artefact.

uniface Medal or coin with modelling on one side only.

urn table Eighteenth-century table designed to hold an urn.

veneer A thin sheet of wood laid across a cheaper carcase or used as inlay decoration.

verge escapement Mechanism for regulating a clock movement before the anchor escapement.

Vesta case Match box for Vesta matches, often in silver, from circa 1850.

vinaigrette Small, eighteenth-century box, often silver, to hold a sponge soaked in vinegar to ward off germs and the unpleasant odours of the day.

wainscot chair Joined chair with open arms and a panelled back.

walnut The hardwood used in England for the manufacture of furniture from the Restoration, originally in solid form but mostly as veneer, particularly burr walnut, after the beginning of the eighteenth century.

well Interior of a plate or bowl.

Wemyss ware Late nineteenth-century lead-glazed earthenware originally from Fife, Scotland.

whatnot Mobile stand with open shelves.

wheel-back chair Originally late eighteenth-century chair with circular back with radiating spokes.

windsor chair Wooden chair with spindle back.

yew Tough, close-grained hardwood used for turning, particularly in chair legs, and in veneer.

MEASUREMENT CONVERSION CHART

This chart provides a scale of measurements converted from centimetres and metres to feet and inches.

1cm	$\frac{2}{5}$in
2cm	$\frac{4}{5}$in
3cm	$1\frac{1}{10}$in
4cm	$1\frac{3}{5}$in
5cm	2in
10cm	$3\frac{7}{8}$in
15cm	$5\frac{9}{10}$in
20cm	$7\frac{3}{4}$in
25cm	$9\frac{4}{5}$in
30cm	$11\frac{4}{5}$in
40cm	1ft $3\frac{3}{4}$in
50cm	1ft $7\frac{2}{3}$in
75cm	2ft $5\frac{1}{2}$in
1 m	3ft $3\frac{1}{3}$in
1.25m	4ft $1\frac{1}{5}$in
1.5m	4ft 11in
1.75m	5ft $8\frac{9}{10}$in
2m	6ft $6\frac{3}{4}$in
2.25m	7ft $4\frac{3}{5}$in
2.5m	8ft $2\frac{2}{5}$in
3m	9ft $10\frac{1}{10}$in